Karl Rudolf Hagenbach, Evelina Moore

History of the reformation in Germany and Switzerland chiefly

Vol. 1

Karl Rudolf Hagenbach, Evelina Moore

History of the reformation in Germany and Switzerland chiefly
Vol. 1

ISBN/EAN: 9783337198053

Printed in Europe, USA, Canada, Australia, Japan

Cover: Foto ©ninafisch / pixelio.de

More available books at **www.hansebooks.com**

CLARK'S

FOREIGN

THEOLOGICAL LIBRARY.

NEW SERIES.

VOL. LIX.

Hagenbach's History of the Reformation in Germany and Switzerland chiefly.

VOL. I.

EDINBURGH:
T. & T. CLARK, 38 GEORGE STREET.
1878.

PRINTED BY MURRAY AND GIBB,

FOR

T. & T. CLARK, EDINBURGH.

LONDON, .	HAMILTON, ADAMS, AND CO.
DUBLIN, . . .	ROBERTSON AND CO.
NEW YORK, . .	SCRIBNER AND WELFORD.

HISTORY

OF

THE REFORMATION

IN

GERMANY AND SWITZERLAND CHIEFLY.

BY

DR. K. R. HAGENBACH,

LATE PROFESSOR-IN ORDINARY OF THEOLOGY AT BASEL.

Translated from the Fourth Revised Edition of the German

BY

EVELINA MOORE.

VOL. I.

EDINBURGH:
T. & T. CLARK, 38 GEORGE STREET.
1878.

AUTHOR'S PREFACE.

THE *History of the Reformation in Germany and Switzerland,* with which, thirty-six years ago, I commenced my public lectures at Basel, here appears in its fourth edition, and constitutes, according to chronological order, the third volume of my entire *History of the Church.* The present volume required a complete remodelling, such as was not necessary in the case of its two predecessors, and such, also, as will probably not be requisite in the volumes which are to follow. As the first seven lectures of the earlier editions presented portions of Church History—relating to the Primitive and Middle Ages—which are now treated of in the first and second volumes of the entire work, it was requisite, in order to avoid unnecessary repetitions, to strike out those seven lectures—or rather, to reduce them to one chapter, which should briefly recapitulate the points already enlarged upon, and introduce the topics which were about to be discussed. Ample compensation for the loss of such expunged matter was furnished, however, by a far more detailed presentation of the History of the Reformation, as will appear upon a comparison of the book in its present form with the earlier editions of the work. I may say, indeed, that of the original structure not one stone has been left upon another; and when it has been possible to make use of one of these old stones, it has seldom been fitted into its appropriate place without some alteration. Still, I have endeavoured as much as possible to preserve in these lectures the character borne by those that were actually delivered. While I have rejected all such references as were called for by the local and temporary circumstances of thirty-six years ago, but which would fail to interest the present generation, I have continued to present, side by side with my history of the Reformation in Germany, a more extended account of the *Swiss* Reformation than is usually to be met with. Nor could I make up my mind to omit those rather more detailed sections which refer to the Reformation of *Basel*, and which, when the lectures were originally delivered, were, for my purpose, among the most important portions of the whole work. Should any of my readers find the parts to which I have reference too lengthy, they may pass them by. Other readers there are—and those not of a superficial class —who take pleasure in such specialties, who like to have presented to them, in the minuteness of detail of a comparatively small historical picture, the particulars of some of those events whose progress they have watched as a whole. At this time, as before, I have confined myself to a history of the Reformation of *Germany* and *Switzerland*, with the exception only that I have devoted a few pages to a consideration of the Reformation in other countries, by way of preliminary to a more circumstantial treatment of it in connection with the *History of Protestantism* (in vol. iv. of my *Church History*).

The quotations which I have inserted will probably be too numerous for some of my readers, and too few for others. So far as the majority of educated people (including ladies) are concerned, these quotations might have been entirely omitted; yet it did not appear to me to be wholly superfluous to refer even the ordinary class of readers, now and then, to a good book, from which they might gain some additional information. And, moreover, I thought that, although the book is not intended for learned men, there might be among my readers one and another belonging to the class of theologically-educated teachers to whom a reference to documents and a citation of passages in the original languages might be welcome. The furnishing of complete references to the sources from which I have compiled the present volume would have occupied too much space, and converted the book into a *compend* of Church History, which it does not profess to be. I was also frequently unable to furnish such references, the documents not being accessible at the time. I can assure my readers, however, that it has been my effort, as far as possible, to communicate nothing which is not, in some way or other, vouched for by good authority. If, nevertheless, I should be convicted of any erroneous statements, I can only be grateful for the correction, as for every morsel of information.

If God give me health and strength, I hope soon to lay before the circle of my readers a revision of my *History of Protestantism* (in its antithesis to Catholicism) as developed in the second half of the sixteenth and in the seventeenth century, and also a revised edition of my *History of the Church in Modern Times*, which will complete my entire *Church History*.

HAGENBACH.

CONTENTS.

VOLUME I.

PAGE

CHAPTER I.

The Reformation : Its Tasks and its History— Retrospect,   1

CHAPTER II.

Plan of the Present History—Chronological Limits and Periods of the History of the Reformation—General Condition of the World and of Religious Feeling, ...   22

CHAPTER III.

Reuchlin and the Humanists—Hutten, Erasmus, Wimpheling, .   45

CHAPTER IV.

The Dumb Comedy—Luther : his History down to the Posting of his Theses and the Commencement of the Reformation,   .   .   77

CHAPTER V.

Controversy concerning the Theses—Luther at Augsburg before Cajetan, Miltitz, Karlstadt, Melanchthon—Disputation of Leipsic, .   .   100

CHAPTER VI.

Results of the Leipsic Disputation—The German Nobility and Luther's Relation to it—His Writings entitled, "To the Christian Nobles of the German Nation ;" "Concerning the Babylonish Captivity ;" and "Concerning the Liberty of a Christian"—The Romish Bull—Diet of Worms—Life in the Wartburg—Translation of the Bible,   .   123

CHAPTER VII.

Examination of Luther's Translation of the Bible continued—His Ideas in regard to the Bible generally—Melanchthon's *Loci communes*—Luther's further Literary Labours at the Wartburg, and the Continuation thence of the Conflict,   .   .   .   151

CHAPTER VIII.

Progress of the Gospel—Proceedings at Wittenberg—Karlstadt and the Prophets of Zwickau—Luther leaves the Wartburg—(His Interview with two young Switzers at Jena)—He subdues the Storm—His Strife with Henry VIII.—Adrian VI.—Diet of Nuremberg (1523) —Clement VII., ... 170

CHAPTER IX.

View of the Extension of the Reformation within and outside of Germany —The First Martyrs—Public Feeling and the Press, . . 195

CHAPTER X.

The Reformation in Switzerland—Ulrich Zwingle—History of his Youth —His Life at Glarus and Einsiedeln—Call to Zurich—His Mode of Preaching—His Relation to Luther, ... 231

CHAPTER XI.

General Glance at the Condition of Switzerland—Cardinal Schinner— Bernardin Samson—First Beginnings of the Reformation in other parts of Switzerland—Bern—John Haller—Religious Condition of the City of Bern—The Jetzer Affair—Francis Kolb, Berthold Haller, and Sebastian Meyer—Nicholas Manuel—Basel—Its Political Condition—Bishop Christopher von Utenheim—First Reformers: Wolfgang Capito, William Röublin, Wolfgang Wyssenburger, ... 246

CHAPTER XII.

John Œcolampadius—Relation of Erasmus to the Reformation and to Luther—Ulrich von Hutten at Basel and Mühlhausen—His Quarrel with Erasmus—His Death—Relation of Erasmus to Zwingle —History of the Swiss Reformation continued—Occurrences at Zurich—First Religious Conference and its Results—Iconoclasm— Second Disputation (Konrad Schmid, Commander of Küssnacht), . 275

CHAPTER XIII.

Immediate Consequences of the Second Disputation of Zurich— Banishment and Martyrdom of Hottinger—His Last Struggles— Third Disputation—Abolishment of the Mass and of Images—A Eucharistic Controversy previous to Luther's (Joachim am Grüt)— Zwingle's Celebration of the Sacrament; and his Liturgy—Zwingle's Sermons (on the Clearness and Certainty of the Divine Word; and The Shepherd), ... 306

CHAPTER XIV.

Review of the Reformation of Zurich—Zwingle's Co-labourers, Leo Juda, Oswald Myconius, and Megander—Synoptical View of the Beginnings of the Reformation in other portions of Switzerland: Bern, Basel, Mühlhausen, Biel, Soleure, Schaffhausen, Thurgau, St. Gall, Appenzell, and the Grisons—Interior Switzerland, . 324

CHAPTER XV.

The Eucharistic Controversy—Import of the Lord's Supper—Parallel between Luther and Zwingle—Karlstadt—Zwingle- Œcolampadius—Erasmus—Brenz and the Swabian Syngramma—Words of Peace from Œcolampadius, ... 350

CHAPTER XVI.

Import of the Eucharistic Controversy—The Peasant War—Münzer and the Twelve Articles—Views of the Reformers (Brenz, Melanchthon, Luther) in regard to the same—Insurrections of the Peasants in Switzerland (Zurich and Basel)—Marriage of Zwingle and Luther—Domestic Life of the Reformers, and Luther's Circle of Friends, . 373

HISTORY OF THE REFORMATION.

CHAPTER I.

THE REFORMATION: ITS TASKS AND ITS HISTORY—RETROSPECT.

THE *History of the Reformation* forms the transition from mediæval to modern church history. It constitutes, at the same time, the dividing line between those two forms of the development of Christianity, of which *one* espoused the principles of the Reformers, as set forth in the great and world-historic conflict which we are about to examine, rearing its structure, on the basis of the Confessions which embodied those principles, in the EVANGELICAL PROTESTANT CHURCH; whilst the *other*, though it did not deny the necessity for a reform which should accord with the needs of the times, yet contended that such a reform was attainable only in connection with the heretofore dominant Romish Church and her traditions, and hence, in opposition to the advance of Protestantism, continued its pretensions to the character of the only true, *i.e.* the CATHOLIC APOSTOLIC, CHURCH. It is self-evident that the delineation of this conflict must vary with the position occupied by its portrayer, as belonging to the one or to the other of these two churches, and sharing the views, the convictions, and the hopes of the side on which he has ranged himself. From a teacher of Protestant theology no more can be expected than a *History of the* REFORMATION —in good sooth, such a one only as must necessarily be given from the standpoint of evangelical Protestantism; at the same time, however, we will be credited with so much historical impartiality as consists in an honest endeavour to be as just as possible to that church which calls itself *the Catholic*, to the exclusion of all other churches, and which, in a certain degree, is the continuation, though not a pure continuation, of the Church of the Middle Ages.

But again, even from the Protestant standpoint, there are various, if not mutually contradictory conceptions of the *nature* of the Reformation. Whilst some perceive in it merely a *return* to biblical Christianity, to the simple and pure doctrine of the gospel, divested of all which they regard as a later addition, as the "ordinance of men," and as a disfigurement of the primitive apostolic type of religion (the holders of this view deny that there is any such thing as historical development, or a further unfolding of what has once been positively given), others behold in the Reformation of the sixteenth century only the first impulse to a movement which, supported by the acquired privilege of free investigation, is pressing resistlessly forward, thrusting aside everything, of divine or human origin, which lays claim to authority, and, consequently, regarding the systems of belief drawn up by the Reformers as barriers to further progress, the utter destruction of which is reserved for modern times. Whilst it is the chief concern of the one class to establish the connection of the Reformation, as to its principles, with biblico-apostolic Christianity—whilst they hold that the task of Protestantism consists in the maintenance of this very connection, the other class believe that the work of the Reformation will be accomplished only when even this connection shall be dissolved—when mankind, in its onward march, shall be conducted *beyond* the standpoint of that faith which the Reformers held fast as something that had not yet been superseded, and for which, as every page of their history shows, they were ready to forfeit their possessions and their lives. In a word, these two tendencies bear toward each other the relation of affirmation and negation: the representatives of the one tendency behold in the Reformation the restoration to primitive perfection of that which had become degenerated and distorted; the representatives of the other tendency hail the Reformation as the dawn of an entirely new period—a time which is rupturing all the bonds which connect it with the past, and pressing onward toward a goal scarcely dreamed of by the Reformers.

What shall we say to all this? Which of the two views is the right one? Which do we purpose to adopt in our picture of the Reformation? We can yet give only a precursory answer to these questions. We hope in the following chapters to prove that the germs of these opposite views of the Reformation are contained in its very essence and history. It is the inevitable attribute of an abstract view of history—and by this we mean such a contemplation of it as is averted from real life, and is under the dominion of a system of preconceived ideas and opinions—one-sidedly to perceive and follow to the extreme this or that factor of historical turning-points as well as of individual events, whilst an unprejudiced and sober observation of facts will, as of necessity, be led to pursue through many intricacies the tangled strands of that knot which abstraction cuts with its sword; and even where such an observation does not succeed in unravelling the tangles, it at least, by dint of patient scrutiny, brings the difficult task of their solution nearer to a successful termination. Without wearying the reader, therefore, with what are usually denominated the *principles* of the Reformation, we shall endeavour to let facts, so far as they are attainable, speak for themselves; and only when this labour is completed shall we essay to group the varied and manifold phenomena under general points of view, and thus, in comprehensive features, exhibit the *essence* of the Reformation as deducible from its *history*. Our main effort in this course of procedure will be to preserve our mental vision unobstructed on all sides, in order to the perception of the positive as well as the negative pole of the movement, of the religious as well as the scientific and humanistic impulses that were at work, of that yearning after salvation which was manifesting itself in the depth of men's consciences, as well as of those ideas of political freedom and scientific progress which were stirring in awakened brains and preparing to make themselves a way in the world. In watching the sparks, showering far into futurity, of mental freedom struggling to separate itself from the authority of the Church, we shall not fail to observe the flame of religious enthusiasm, fed by the central fire of the sanctuary; in viewing the bubbling of the must, in its ofttimes wanton fermentation, we shall not leave out of consideration the earnest and lasting workings of repentance, and of that moral regeneration which is accomplished in the stillness and silence of the soul. We shall not neglect that which is edifying for those humanly gladdening and entertaining items in which the history of the Reformation is so rich; in view of the times, we shall be as ready to excuse that boldness and defiantness which are inherent in every opposition, as, on the other hand, to pardon the severity of a discipline which bowed under the law of God—to pardon even in cases when it erected its barriers against a justifiable impulse of liberty. We shall not be dissuaded from honouring, after the fashion of our fathers, the men through whom God hath done such great things,—from honouring them as His instruments, and as "men of God,"—even while, with men of our own time, we are ready to regard the Reformers as, in other respects, children of *their* time, and men who, after the manner of men, erred and sinned. We shall see that, in the case of different men who were equally honest thinkers and strivers, it was possible for some to fail to reach the mark; whilst others overshot it, and, actuated solely by their zeal for purification, together with the evil rejected the good. We shall also refrain from harshly judging those who, when the waves of the conflict rose too high for them, were not able to follow the bold course of the times, and preferred to accommodate themselves to the old order of things until God should indicate such a way out of the difficulty as should appear clear to themselves. Only in striving thus to act shall we continue upon that eminence to which historical science, in connection with Protestantism, has attained. Whilst our forefathers, who were still standing upon the glowing lava of the volcano which had burst into action in the Reformation, had words of indignation and condemnation only for that ancient Church in which they beheld "apostate Babylon;" whilst the pope, as a matter of course, was by them entitled "Antichrist;" whilst they regarded the "pure word of God" as contained only in the preaching of the "blessed Reformers;" and whilst, again, at a later period in the eighteenth century, enlightened minds—although no longer acquiescing in this tone, yet maintaining that the essence of Protestantism consisted in nought save protesting—rejected as a relic of mediæval barbarism everything that related to the Church, whether passing under the name of Catholic or Protestant, and spoke of the Bible and of Christianity in a way that would have horrified Luther, Zwingle, and Calvin in their inmost souls, it is now an understood principle that every time must be apprehended by its own light and measured by its own standard; and obstinate though the grapple of opposing parties may be in the present, violent as may be the "onset of mind against mind," all parties, in so far as they lay claim to scientific recognition on the part of their contemporaries, strive after as all-sided, and hence as just, an appreciation as possible of the different items of which history is composed. This is an advance over which all may equally rejoice, and for which we cannot sufficiently thank God. And thus, though every one may view history from his own standpoint, survey its sources with his own eyes and read them through his own spectacles, contemplate and connect events after his own method,—though every one may present general outlines and individual details in accordance with the bent of his own mind, and stamp upon that which is presented the impress of his own peculiar personality,—if all this is but done in uprightness of heart and with understanding, the cause of truth will still be advanced.

It is not that colourlessness of presentation which sinks into the pallor of the corpse; it is not that cold unsympathizing statement of facts which is lacking in throb of pulse or heart; it is not *these* to which we must look for a truly impartial and objective history. History must invariably pass through the process of a living, individual, mental moulding, if it is to attract us as a noble work of art, instead of presenting the stiff and graceless aspect of a mummy; and if this is true of any history, it is so, above all, of the history of the Reformation, with its freshness and fulness of life. But the conditions which attach to every work of art hold good in this case also. Everything depends upon a well-considered proportion and a true perspective, upon a right distribution of light and shade. No one man is able to do full justice on all sides to the infinite task; but an earnest will thereto is, if only a relative, yet a consoling guaranty of success.

In this confidence let us proceed to our work! Since we may take it for granted that our readers have already made acquaintance with the church history of the earlier centuries through the preceding volumes of this work, it will suffice here to present a brief synopsis of what has previously been narrated, in order thus to secure a firm basis for that which remains.

We have seen how Christianity, subsequent to its entry as a stranger amongst the ruinous forms of the antique world, had, after many persecutions, become victorious over the powers which opposed it, so far as to have attained, under Constantine and his successors, to public recognition in the Roman state. We have seen it increase, in external scope and internal compactness, with reference to doctrine, constitution, and worship. But in the same degree in which it strove to overcome the world and to fill it with those divine powers by which it was itself upheld, we beheld it exposed to the influences of this world. The external elevation of the Church to power led to a partial diminution of its internal worth. The scientific elaboration of doctrine into dogma, the fixation of the Confession of Faith in the canon of faith, were not accomplished, as we have seen, save in the most passionate conflicts, and frequently at the cost of heart religion, at the cost of love, of inward verity, and of all those virtues which the Saviour enjoined upon His disciples. Yet, notwithstanding all this, we could not refrain from admiring the mighty efforts which fathers of the Church and councils put forth, in order to give to revealed truth an expression which should satisfy the thinking mind, and secure the truth against the corruptions of erroneous doctrine. The simple worship which the first Christians paid to God we have seen gradually develop into a grand and magnificent cult, which, by mysterious symbols, addressed itself to the senses as well as to the spirit, thus opening the doors, however, to a Jewish Levitical system and a heathen ceremonial pomp. In close connection with this phase of Christianity,—with its already hierarchic organization, its dogmatical fixedness, its liturgical precision and elaborateness,—we beheld the preaching of the gospel enter upon its course amongst those peoples who were called by Providence to the founding of new states upon the ruins of the Roman Empire. Out of Rome a new empire over the nations of the West was coming into being, whilst the Church of the East was sinking more and more under the ravages of a newly-risen religion of the sword.

The church history of the Middle Ages coincides with the history of civilisation of the same period. Christianity was not only the religion of the *state*, in the antique Roman-Byzantine sense of the term it became the religion of the *people*, transfusing itself, so to speak, into flesh and blood, and taking complete possession of minds just waking from the night of heathenism, and ready to become the subjects of a nobler civilisation and culture. A long and painful struggle was necessary ere the last remnants of heathenism were removed from the views, manners, and customs of the Germanic and Slavonic races. Apostolic devotion, self-sacrificing love, in conjunction with prophetic energy and a high degree of evangelical wisdom, were requisite for the effective interposition of speech and action at the decisive moment. That some blunders were perpetrated in the missions to which we refer; that, together with the power of love, the less noble impulses of a thirst for spiritual rule were at work; and that the Old Testament zeal of an Elijah supplanted, in some cases, that humble and circumspect conduct which befits the messenger of Christ when he seeks to fish men for the kingdom of heaven, who shall deny? It seemed as if mankind must once more pass through the law school of the "disciplinarian" [παιδαγωγός] in order to arrive in the vestibule of the grace-dispensing church! Yet, after all, we could cite more than one instance in proof of the fact that meantime the salt of the earth was giving unmistakeable evidence of its virtue, and that, beside the seed strewed by the wayside and trodden under foot, the good seed was germinating in the soil of men's hearts and bringing forth fruit. Nor can we withhold from several of the popes our testimony that they apprehended and made good use of the position which God bestowed upon them in those times; whilst among the great ones of this world, kings namely, the form of Charlemagne stands conspicuous, in his world-historic import, as the protector of the Church. This monarch had also, as we have seen, assumed a just relation toward the spiritual head of Christendom, the Bishop of Rome, who saluted him as the new Constantine, and crowned him emperor; with a steady grasp he wielded one of the two swords which, according to the views of the time, God had placed in the hands of sundered authorities, to the end that the kingly and the priestly office might supplement each other in the conduct of God's kingdom on earth. But how speedily did we behold these two powers lift themselves up against each other! The encroachments of the secular power upon the rights of the Church, and, again, the graspings of the ecclesiastical government after the things of this world, to what a long series of controversies have they led!—controversies which have promoted neither the wellbeing of the nations nor the edification of the Church. We will not further follow the course of these disputes. We would only remind our readers that in them we contemplate not merely a battle of personal passion and selfishness, but that here, also, moral powers, such as, doubtless, found in human personalities nobler or more ignoble bearers, grapple with each other and make good their pretensions in a manner in which the right is by no means to be found unconditionally on the one side, and the wrong unconditionally on the other side, but in which antitheses, becoming momently more pronounced and manifest, point to a solution and mediation which were reserved for later centuries. That, in view of the enslavement of the Church, the shameless and conscienceless practice of simony, the hierarchical zeal of a Hildebrand and others like him was a moral necessity, must be admitted even by those who are by no means inclined to defend the exaggerations of that zeal. From the standpoint of this admission we have been enabled to arrive at a proper appreciation of the great qualities which appeared in Gregory VII., in Alexander III., and in Innocent III. and IV., even though we must repudiate their system, as reposing upon false and unevangelical premises. It is true that the ideal element of these premises, the theocracy, interpreted in the spirit of evangelical sobriety, is warranted, inasmuch as it is a fact that all that is human must subordinate itself to the eternal thoughts of God and Christ, and the words of Christ, "Unto me is all power given in heaven and on earth," still form the substance of our Christian confession; but the mixture of the ideal with the temporal and visible, and the violent realization of it through the employment of morally reprehensible means, necessarily perverted the ideal into a caricature, upon which the impress of falsehood was the more plainly to be seen the more rigidly the upholders of this caricature clung to the bare form, even when it was emptied of all internal value. On this account it was impossible for the Papacy to retain its position on the height to which it had been elevated by the favour of circumstances. Circumstances changed in accordance with the law which is inherent in the progress of history. After the downfall of the Hohenstaufens, whose hearts' blood ebbed away in their struggle with the Papacy, the Papacy itself received a deadly wound, from which it has never recovered. Not the ideal might of the German Empire, but the very real and secular policy of France, as exemplified, divested of every romantic feature, in Philip the Fair, was the rock on which the ever higher swelling waves of the Papacy were forced to break. The downward course of the Papacy, from the time of Boniface VIII. to the age of the Reformation, we have already contemplated. The removal of the Papal See to Avignon, the great schism, the ever bolder demand for General Councils which should be *superior* to the pope, the history of these councils themselves and of what followed them, the internal moral corruption which in Innocent VIII. and Alexander VI. recalled the times of the pornocracy in the tenth century, from the pollution of which Hildebrand had saved the Church, may be cited in illustration of the decline of which we speak. And yet at the beginning of the Reformation, the nimbus which surrounded the papal dignity had not disappeared, nor was that dignity the object of the first attack either of Luther or of Zwingle; only when Rome betrayed the trust reposed in her by the Reformers, and shut her ear to their cry for help, was this opposition regarded by them as a proof that instead of the Holy Father of Christendom they had to do with Antichrist. And as it was with the Papacy, so it was with the remaining institutions of mediæval Catholicism. Monasticism also had seen better days. To it Christianity was indebted for its diffusion amongst the nations; to it civilisation, art, and science were indebted for the fostering care which it had exercised over them. It would be ingratitude not to recognise such services. Among the monastic orders, also, we meet with individuals who not only exemplified in spirit and conduct the beneficent ideas of Christianity, but who likewise, from the cloister, exerted an edifying and strengthening influence over the outside world. I need only mention Bernard of Clairvaux. It may be said that monachism occupied toward the secular clergy a relation similar to that sustained, under the old covenant, by the prophethood toward the priesthood. It was the seat of a wholesome fermentation that preserved the Church from corruption. In a social aspect, moreover, the system of religious orders was of high moral importance in view of the rudeness of the times. But as the idea of the Papacy was obscured by the mixture of the spiritual with the secular, so the arbitrary sundering of the spiritual and the secular, and the exaggeration of the antithesis between them, led to the degeneration of monachism. An overstrained asceticism was followed by moral laxity; renunciation of the world was exchanged for luxuriousness, a total lack of discipline, and worldly practices of the worst sort; humility was transformed into pious pretension, and piety into fanaticism. To all this was added the jealousy which the regular clergy cherished against the secular clergy, and *vice versâ*, and, furthermore, the mutual jealousy of the orders amongst themselves, as manifested especially in the two great mendicant orders. What was begun in the spirit not infrequently ended in the flesh. The salt had lost its savour, and the question only too readily suggested itself, Of what further use is it? And yet we must not overlook the fact that many a good and precious grain of salt was to be found even in the convent cells of the sixteenth century. Protestants should bear continually in mind not only that it was an Augustinian monk of the strictest observance from whom the Reformation in Germany, and, from a general point of view, the Reformation as a whole, proceeded, but also that the cloisters in general sent a creditable contingent of the stoutest powers into the field, when it came to a decisive struggle between the old and the new.

The cloistral world was by no means an isolated one. Its influence over the entire Church is sufficiently evidenced by history. How many of the greatest princes of the Church, popes not excepted, came forth from the convents! Cult and science were in great measure under the dominion of monachism. The celibacy of the priests, authoritatively carried into effect since the time of Gregory VII., was based upon monkish views, and the like might be affirmed of many other things. It was from the monastic statutes that the regulations of so-called canonical life were taken, though this, again, notwithstanding all that was praiseworthy which originally lay at the foundation of the institution, was in its decadence. As regards public cult or worship, it was the papal monk Gregory I. who, as the "father of ceremonies," artistically completed the system upon which preceding ages had laboured. We have already expressed our recognition of the grand, the presageful, the overpowering qualities inherent in the symbolism of the mass, as well as in the whole plan of the ecclesiastical year, with its returning festivals. But that, in the elaboration of the symbol, the preaching of the word was pressed farther and farther into the background, whilst the language of Rome — a tongue unknown to the people—prevailed in the cult of the Church; that the external exercise of divine worship, and everything connected therewith, degenerated more and more into a lifeless mechanism, by means of which men even thought that they could render themselves agreeable to the Deity and earn heaven,—these things struck us, perforce, as something foreign, nay, adverse to Christianity, the more we remembered the saying, that God willeth to be worshipped in spirit and in truth. If we fully figure to ourselves the purport of the worship thus rendered by the Catholic Church, we do indeed find that, as is a matter of course among Christians, the Church of the Middle Ages itself theoretically maintained the fundamental principle that to God alone worship is due, and that it is due (in accordance with the faith of the Church) to Him in His quality of the triune God. But the subtile distinction which the Church, or rather the theology of the schools, made between *worship* and *adoration* (conjoined with *invocation*) could not prevent an adoration from being paid, first, to the host of angels and the throng of martyrs, and, next, to the entire and constantly increasing body of saints,—an adoration which, from these objects, was speedily transferred to images, and above all to the holy cross (crucifix), and to relics; an adoration which differed little from the ancient polytheism and the practices therewith connected, since every country, every city, every church, every profession or association was soon provided with its heavenly patron, every evil with its specific "helper." How, above this whole body of saints, the virgin mother of the Lord, the "mother of God," as she has been entitled since the fifth century, claimed for herself the highest honours of the Church, how churches were dedicated to her and festivals instituted in commemoration of her, how knights and monks entered the service of the " Queen of Heaven," how the angelic greeting to the "blessed among women" was placed next to the *paternoster* (in the so-called rosary),—all this we have examined in its proper place.

Mariolatry has for its correlative the worship of the sacrament in the host. In these two forms of devotion the piety of the Middle Ages reached its climax. The adoration of the sacrament found its most solemn expression in the feast of Corpus Christi, whilst it centered in the daily sacrifice of the mass. History has already shown us that this daily sacrifice was next conjoined with intercession for the dead, whose souls were declared to be in purgatorial fires awaiting redemption; that the common celebration of the Lord's Supper (in agreement with its institution) withdrew more and more behind the sacrificial service performed in secret by the priest; that laymen were excluded from participation in the cup and restricted to *one* sacramental element, *i.e.* the bread, which, as it was maintained, was changed into the body of Christ. All this, however, was vindicated in the doctrinal system elaborated by the Scholasticism of the Middle Ages, a phenomenon to which we have also endeavoured to do full justice.

We have not hesitated to compare the doctrinal edifice, striving towards its consummation, rising more and more boldly upon the foundations laid by the Fathers and the Councils, and perfecting itself in every detail, to the gigantic structure of the mediæval cathedral, in which the profoundly significant symbolism upon which the cult of the Church was based is visibly concentrated and embodied for every eye. In opposition to that superficial mode of thought which admires only that which is profitable for the material business of life, I hold that a consideration of the intellectual gymnastics practised by Scholasticism, and remote from our own habits, will always be of service, even if such a consideration appeal merely to our humanity, which should take a human interest in every human endeavour, however different the aim of that endeavour may be from the goal toward which our efforts are directed. And in reference to the very aim that those indefatigable thinkers pursued,—their endeavours to bring divine things nearer to human perception, to mediate a consciousness of the mutual relation of faith and knowledge, to fuse, as far as possible, the dry material of delivered doctrine, and to pour it into new and sometimes, it must be acknowledged, into startling forms,—the Scholastics have, to a greater extent than many are willing to admit, prepared the way for the philosophic and theological speculation which is still practised in our own days by multitudes, both called and uncalled. But the dangers which are naturally connected with such speculations, and with the dialectics employed in them, did not fail to beset the course of those who engaged therein during the Middle Ages, and may serve as a warning to us at the present day.

If the immediate and unqualified rejection of all such thinking as unfruitful must be regarded as inconsiderate prejudice, still the history of Scholasticism has shown us how much that was really unfruitful and crude was conjoined with the good which Scholasticism promoted. In many cases the opposite of what was originally aimed at was accomplished. Instead of the reconciliation of faith and knowledge, the chasm between the two became continually more pronounced; acuteness degenerated into mere cavilling, and the earnestness of investigation was exchanged for sceptical frivolity. Profounder minds had indeed found in *Mysticism* a substitute for that which the subtilizing reason of the wise had been unable to give to the souls that were inquiring after God. In Mysticism, depth and inwardness were restored to that which, under the hands of the Scholastics, had become too much an external thing, and which, with all the schools' display of artistic dialectics, was becoming more and more superficialized. Among the Mystics, in the quiet valleys of contemplative life, we behold those living waters welling, from whose springs Luther himself drew inspiration. But even Mysticism led to abysses into which a reflecting mind, conscious of its limits, gazed only with a secret shudder. In a strained absorption into God, that evangelical sobriety which is needful at all times, even in the investigation of divine things, was lost. That in which Scholasticism and Mysticism agreed was a one-sided tendency toward the transcendental, toward that which lies outside of the domain of what is cognizable by the human mind, and accessible to a simple love of truth. Not only were they both deficient in an unprejudiced observation of natural phenomena,—although the great master of philosophy and logic among the ancients, Aristotle, had long since given an impulse to such observation,—but the historical documents of Christian revelation lacked an exposition which befitted them, an exposition grounded upon philological knowledge and upon history. We cannot say that the Bible was entirely a closed book to the theologians of the Middle Ages. Some amongst them acquired a deep insight into it, and, doubtless, a mind awakened and illuminated by God attained to a knowledge of its true position even in the gloom of these times, and from the Word of Life drew spirit and life. But, on the whole, the interpretation of Scripture was, on the one hand, ruled by ecclesiastical tradition and the canons of the Church, and, on the other hand, lost in arbitrary and oftentimes trifling allegorism. Only a few were familiar with the original languages of the Old and New Testaments. The Latin Vulgate was authoritative and decisive, and hence frequently misleading. There were, indeed, not wanting voices which paved a way for the renewed empirical investigation of nature, so far as that was then possible, as well as for the study of the classical languages, until, immediately before the age of the Reformation, Humanism, starting from Italy, and fertilizing German culture also, pressed Scholasticism more and more to the wall, and prepared a new field for human thought and science.

If we cast one more glance upon the life of the Middle Ages, its manners and customs, a picture exhibiting the most varied mingling of light and shade will present itself to our view. That time has long since passed when men spoke only of the barbarousness of the Middle Ages; but, on the other hand, neither does an enthusiastic predilection for the romance of the same period comport any longer with an upright regard for history. That the moral power of Christianity approved itself a beneficent one in the life of the nations subjected to its influence, must be confessed even by those who deny that Christianity is possessed of any such power in the present. It was, indeed, at first the discipline of the law that, by external means and in the way of compulsion, sought to accomplish that which is reserved for free love alone to perform. But this very free love, with its devotion to the service of God and humanity, is precisely what is touchingly exhibited to us in individual characters and institutions of the Middle Ages. Even whilst the light in which legend presents such figures to the imagination may sometimes be a flattering one, not the sharpest criticism can succeed in erasing fundamental features that have made so deep an impression on the memory of history as the life of a Saint Elizabeth, a Francis of Assisi, a Louis IX., a Thomas à Kempis. Too loud to be disregarded is the testimony borne to the mediæval love of beneficence by numerous charitable institutions, many of which are still in existence; and even though it be admitted that a regard to the forgiveness of sins in this life, and a heavenly reward in the life to come, may have had a large share in promoting such works of mercy, yet the reproach of seeking to establish a holiness of works, which we are so ready to cast at the men of that period, will not shield us from the appeal to the conscience of our own times, to "go and do likewise." Neither, however, will we suffer ourselves to be dazzled by these sunny pictures, which can never be obliterated, and must always be held in honour in our estimation of the general moral condition of the Middle Ages. The degeneracy of the Church must of necessity have been reflected in the popular life. That a prosperous development of human and social relations was impossible under the pressure of the hierarchy, must be admitted by every one who is not prejudiced, at the outset, in favour of a divine prerogative of the priesthood. The tutelage which the clergy exercised over the mass of the laity may, indeed, have been justified at times by the low educational status of the latter. But how often has the Church, that called herself a *mother*, proved to be a step-mother; and how often have the shepherds, instead of leading the flocks to good pasturage, "sought only to shear the wool off the sheep," as Æneas Sylvius, amongst others, openly confessed! What moral scandals have proceeded from spiritual dignitaries, from cloisters and chapters, from the Papal See itself! Not to mention the outrages against men's consciences, the religious tyranny such as was exercised over the noble Countess of Thuringia by Conrad of Marburg, the wars and suits against heretics, the dungeons and stakes of the Inquisition! The iniquitous perversion of moral ideas is most conspicuously exhibited in the fact that whilst the Church was most severe in persecuting those who erred from the faith, her conduct toward vice itself was, under certain circumstances, that of a most indulgent mother. With the same arbitrariness with which she excommunicated and interdicted all who opposed her authoritative commands, she was ready to bestow indulgences upon any who satisfied her avarice or approved themselves serviceable for her purposes. And here we touch upon that foul blot which the traffic in indulgences, the immediate cause of the Reformation of Luther, has left upon the character of the Romish Church. That, however, in which the Church was most sadly deficient, was the proclamation of the divine word to the unlearned by means of a method of instruction suitable to the needs of the people, by preaching intelligible to all. It is true that some few discerning ecclesiastics, as early as in the age of Charlemagne, urged the introduction of preaching in the vernacular, and Charlemagne himself advocated the same; but history has preserved the record of but few instances of such preaching. We are the more thankful for what has been preserved and transmitted to us. From the impression produced by the sermons of Bertholt, the Minorite of Regensburg [Ratisbon], in the thirteenth, and John Tauler in the fourteenth century, upon the thousands who thronged to hear them, we may infer the existence of similar operations on a smaller scale, of which we have no account. But in any case, these preachers were by no means numerous. Such presentations of God's word were always of a pre-eminently missionary character; the regular preaching to which we are accustomed, the expounding of the word in order to the edification of the congregation, did not constitute at all an integral part of the cult of the Church. The religious instruction of youth was also at a low ebb, notwithstanding the earnest efforts in its behalf of certain noble individuals, such as Gerson and the *Brethren of the Common Life*.[1] Public educa-

---

[1] [BRETHREN OF THE COMMON LIFE (*Fratres de vita communi*). This association was founded by Gerard Groot in the latter half of the fourteenth century. Its founder, after a checkered life of worldliness and luxury, and then as a talented and admired lecturer, as the inmate of a Carthusian monastery, and an earnest and fruitful labourer as an itinerant preacher, retired, upon the withdrawal of his licence to preach,—a withdrawal consequent upon his bold denunciations of the corruptions of the clergy,—to his native city of Deventer. He there gathered about him a number of congenial associates, in company with

tion, in the interests of which Charlemagne so ardently laboured, thereby meriting immortal honour, having been for a long time neglected, excited considerable attention only just prior to the Reformation, and, in connection with that event, became the object of persevering care.

That, however, there was at no time a complete lack of reformatory efforts in the Church, has been demonstrated by her history as hitherto discussed. An unedifying dispute is being carried on at the present day by the representatives of different sects, as to what men and what religious associations may be designated as the *forerunners of the Reformation.* Assuredly, even in connection with the Catholic Church, a truly evangelical life has here and there appeared, without, on account of its peculiar views, coming to a rupture with that Church; and, again, not seldom has an opposition been formed against her in which we can by no means perceive the genuine forerunner of the Reformation. Not all that the Church condemned as heresy was justified in its contradiction of the old and the transmitted; there was a heresy that deserved the name, even though the means employed to stifle it augmented the evil instead of healing it. The fanaticism of the official Church was confronted by the fanaticism of the sects, evidenced

whom he applied himself to the religious instruction of the youth of that city, and the copying of the Bible and other good books for circulation amongst the people. It was in consequence of the proposal of one of Groot's companions, Florentius Radewius, that the young men by whom he was surrounded joined their earnings and *lived in common*, acknowledging Gerard as their head. Thus arose a society which rapidly increased and spread throughout the Netherlands and Germany. Its members, without the assumption of any vows, but dwelling together in so-called *brethren-houses*, and ordering their lives after evangelical rules, devoted themselves to the spiritual and physical care of the necessitous people, and especially of the young, and thus performed, during the fourteenth and fifteenth centuries, a work of vast importance. For a more detailed account of the Brethren of the Common Life, see ULLMANN's *Reformatoren vor der Reformation*, vol. ii. pp. 62-201 (translated into English, 2 vols. 8vo, Clark); also a short biography of *Gerhard Groot*, by the same author, in PIPER'S *Jahrbuch* for 1854, pp. 167-173, from which the present note has been derived. Comp. likewise the *New American Encyclopedia*, arts. "Brethren and Clerks of the Common Life," and "Gerhard Groot." It may be stated, in conclusion, that the celebrated Thomas à Kempis was a pupil of Radewius and a member of the order above described.—TR.]

in rude insubordination against everything that was called order and custom. We can trace this battle of the new against things existent, as conducted sometimes with the courage of evangelical liberty,—a courage which is the fruit of conscientious conviction,—and sometimes also with the arrogance of spiritual pride and in alliance with seditious tendencies, back to the first beginnings of Christianity. The Apostle Paul himself had to contend not only with a Pharisaism that clung to the old ordinances of Judaism, but also with those who misused gospel liberty as a cloak for their wickedness. And even in the purer efforts of parties that struggled for the freedom and independence of the Church, much that was impure was mingled. Call to mind the Montanists in Asia Minor and Rome, the Novatians and Donatists of the African Church, and the mediæval sects of the East and West, that appeared under a variety of names which we will not here repeat. It were, indeed, possible for us even here to distinguish between the anti-churchly and the simply anti-papistical and anti-clerical tendencies. But even in the case of the latter, many elements, still in need of purification, were engaged in a process of fermentation; and it will always be a difficult task for the writer of church history to fix the boundary line between justifiable and unjustifiable opposition,—between what is reformatory and what is revolutionary,—between that which was produced by the Spirit of God for the renewal of the Church, and that which, kindled at the fire of fanaticism, led into the wrong ways of heresy. Frequently, moreover, a change from one extreme to the other took place in the same party, in the same individuals. This fact must make us cautious in our judgment, and we shall need the same caution in the treatment of the history of the Reformation itself; for in our discussion of that also, we shall endeavour, as far as in us lies, to distinguish the true and solid from human error and human frailty and sin, attaching even to the men of the Reformation and their followers. Our standard shall be, as hitherto, none other than that with which the gospel of Christ and the preaching and conduct of the apostles furnish us. That any single individual may err even in the application of this standard, who can deny? But if we would never expose ourselves to the danger of erring, we should be obliged to abandon the task of exhibiting to our contemporaries that which has happened before our own eyes, and that to which others have testified.

Once more, therefore, let us confidently set about our work. Let us consider the divine and the human, both in their relation to each other (in so far as the human is serviceable to the divine), and also separate the two where human prejudice stays the free development of divine thoughts, or human passion disturbs and frustrates their operation. Let us, with a mind open to the truth and an honest desire to *learn* of history,—not with an intention of *tutoring* it,—yield ourselves to those impressions which a struggle for the highest blessings must make upon us, so long as an appreciation of those blessings remains alive and waking in our breasts.

CHAPTER II.

PLAN OF THE PRESENT HISTORY—CHRONOLOGICAL LIMITS AND PERIODS OF THE HISTORY OF THE REFORMATION—GENERAL CONDITION OF THE WORLD AND OF RELIGIOUS FEELING.

HAVING taken a final retrospect of the Church's development hitherto, and briefly represented the essential points in the history of the Middle Ages, we stand now upon the threshold of the *History of the Reformation* itself. We will not repeat our preliminary remarks concerning the nature of the Reformation and the task to be performed by its historian. We must, however, arrive at an understanding relative to the *extent* and *limits* of this task. We are accustomed to regard the history of the Reformation of the sixteenth century as beginning with Luther's appearance as an opponent of the indulgence system; and we rightly so regard it. Even the adherents of the Reformed Church[1] must admit this; for though, as we shall see, reformatory ideas had been working in the soul of Zwingle before Luther's name had reached his ears, it cannot be denied that the great world-historic drama began with the bold act of Luther; and everywhere, even in Switzerland, France, and wheresoever else the spark fanned by him had been kindled, the supporters of the Reformation were denominated *Lutherans*, and persecuted as such. The history of the *German* Reformation, which, in its first period, coincides with the history of Luther, must accordingly form the groundwork of our portrayal of the Reformation in general. We do not, however, propose to confine our attention to the

[1 *Calvinists*, in antithesis to *Lutherans*.—Tr.]

Reformation of Germany. Together with it we shall, in the first place, specially consider the *Swiss* Reformation—that of *German* Switzerland, centering in ZWINGLE; and that of *Romanic* Switzerland, of which CALVIN forms the central point.[1]

But beyond this, our plan embraces some account of the Reformation in France, the history of which occupies a relation toward Calvin similar to that sustained toward Luther by the history of the Reformation of Germany and the North, Denmark, Sweden; and we shall also touch upon the history of the same period in England, Scotland, and the remaining countries of Europe, both those which separated themselves from the Romish Church, and those which, although touched and agitated by reformatory ideas, preserved their connection with the Papacy (Italy, Spain). With this plan is connected a difficulty, to which we would call attention at the outset. Whilst the German Reformation must, assuredly, occupy the foreground in this as in every history of the great religious movement to be considered, it cannot constitute a standard of the internal and external course pursued by the Reformation in other countries. The Reformation history of every land has its own peculiar historical structure and physiognomy, its own individual stamp. What order, then, shall we observe in narrating the different histories? Shall we give one *after* another? This course would have the advantage of precluding the necessity for interrupting the narration of events which have an external connection with each other by the insertion of items which are foreign to those events; but, on the other hand, it would present the disadvantage of rendering impossible as clear an exhibition of international relations, and of the reciprocal workings of one Reformation upon another, as these deserve. We believe, therefore, that preference is to be given to a *synchronistic* treatment of the subject. This will, it is true, involve the necessity of turning our eyes now to the right and now to the left, and of transporting our-

---

[1] It should be remembered that these *Lectures* were originally delivered in Basel, before a Swiss audience.

selves, mentally, from country to country; hereby, however, that charm of variety is gained which should not be too lightly esteemed in undertakings of this sort. But with the adoption of the synchronistic treatment, a new difficulty arises. In the *German* Reformation, which resembles an epic poem in its progression, the following periods present themselves naturally to the mind:—I. From the exposition of Luther's Theses in Wittenberg (1517) to the Diet of Augsburg (1530); II. From the Augsburg Diet (1530) to the outbreak of the Smalkaldian War (1546–47); III. and finally, From the beginning of the Smalkaldian War (1546–47) to the Peace of Augsburg (1555). Within this framework, however, the Reformation history of other countries cannot with propriety be adjusted, and in our examination of *it*, it will be necessary to accord such a measure of elasticity to our chronological boundaries as shall be required by the nature of the facts to be narrated. And further, the *concluding period* of the history of the *German* Reformation, corresponding with the Peace of Augsburg, is far from constituting the terminus of the history of the Reformation generally considered. For that of England, for example, the terminus is to be sought at a much later period. Nevertheless, we have resolved, after mature deliberation, to confine ourselves, in the present undertaking, as much as possible to the limits of the German Reformation, it being our purpose to treat further of the Reformation history of other countries in a future work, in connection with the "History of Evangelical Protestantism."[1]

[1] In view of the copious literature belonging to the history of the Reformation, we shall confine ourselves to a mention of those works which are attainable by a more general circle of readers, and to which we shall have occasion to refer:— MARHEINEKE, *Geschichte der deutschen Reformation*, 1817-31, 4 vols.; L. RANKE, *Deutsche Geschichte im Zeitalter der Reformation*, Berlin, 1853, 6 vols.; A. MENZEL, *Neuere Geschichte der deutschen seit der Reformation*, Berlin, 1854, 6 vols.; MERLE D'AUBIGNÉ, *Histoire de la Réformation du 16 siècle*, Paris, 1835 sqq. (1878); L. HÄUSSER, *Geschichte des Zeitalters der Reformation*, 1517-1648, edited by W. ONCKEN, Berlin, 1868; SOUCHAY, *Deutschland während der Reformation*, Frankfort-on-the-Main, 1868. We shall refer hereafter, as we deem it necessary, to the literature on the history of the Reformation in Switzerland and other countries.

Let us now glance at the *general condition of the world* at the commencement of the sixteenth century.

The history of the Middle Ages has shown us that the *political* configuration of national life went hand in hand with the *ecclesiastical* conflicts whose course we have pursued. With *hierarchism* corresponded *feudalism*—a system which checked the free upsoaring and development of individual character. We have seen, however, that the *Crusades* paved the way for a powerful alteration in human affairs, through the fact that the West and East were brought nearer together. The rise of the *cities* awakened the industrial activity of the *burghers*, who steadily increased in reputation and importance as the feudal nobility became impoverished. The cities, in order to protect themselves against the oppressions of the nobles, against whom the Burgher War had been waged in the fourteenth century (1388), leagued themselves together and accorded to one another reciprocal rights of burghership; and emperors as well as popes endowed them with privileges. The system of *corporations* or *guilds*, with their forms of government borrowed from the aristocracy, constituted a healthful counterpoise to the feudal aristocracy. The value of personal life was rated higher than in the times of sword law, and the moral import and prosperity of family life were augmented. The burghers armed themselves in defence of the liberty and security of their cities; but their altered circumstances no longer permitted them to take the field at the command of the emperor. Hence there gradually arose a distinct class, composed of men who made a warlike life their profession; mercenaries or hired troops, the *Landsknechte*, came into existence. The invention of gunpowder and firearms also introduced an essential change in the conduct of war.[1] This invention forms as great an epoch in the political and military world as does the discovery of America in the sphere of material intercourse, or the invention of printing in the

---

[1] BARTHOLD, *George von Frundsberg oder das deutsche Kriegshandwerk zur Zeit der Reformation*, Hamburg, 1833.

realm of intellectual communion. These three great discoveries, in the domains of geography, nature, and art, form, as it were, the three portals through which the spirit of the modern time enters upon that period of history which is assigned to it, and which commences with the Reformation.

Let us now spread the map of the world before our eyes, and take a hasty survey of the countries *in* and *upon* which the Reformation primarily operated.

The two powers which immediately present themselves to our view are AUSTRIA and FRANCE; these, at the time we speak of, were contending for supremacy and measuring their strength against each other. MAXIMILIAN I., who, "as the last knight," occupied the imperial throne of Germany at the beginning of the Reformation, had, by his possession of the Netherlands and his acquisition of Burgundy, attained to a considerable degree of importance. By the marriage of his son, Prince PHILIP, with the Spanish Princess Joanna, heiress of the recently united kingdoms of Castile and Aragon, and by the favour of destiny, the crown of Spain, conjoined with the imperial crown of Germany, descended upon the head of the grandson of Maximilian, CHARLES V., who likewise fell heir to the kingdom of Naples and a large portion of the American possessions, and who, in the summer of 1519, made his debut upon the stage of history as Emperor of Germany.[1] In consequence of this event, the Austrian power might easily have crushed every endeavour that struggled for existence by its side, had not the more concentrated rather than extensive power of FRANCE placed a check upon its movements. France, which after a long and obstinate struggle had expelled the English from the north of its domains, was conscious of a peculiar strength, due principally to the strict unity of the monarchical principle as there dominant, whilst in Germany that principle was limited by the intermediate power of minor princes. Louis XI. had laboured with all his

[1] MAURENBRECHER, *Karl V. und die deutschen Protestanten*, Düsseldorf, 1865.

might to keep down the power of the vassals of the crown, and to strengthen the pillars of the throne. Charles VIII. and Louis XII., called the Father of his people, had, with varying success, turned their weapons against Austria in a war for the possession of Italy. At the period of which we speak, Francis I., a youthful sovereign, had swayed the sceptre of the mighty kingdom since the year 1515. How much the jealousy that existed between Charles V. and Francis I. contributed to the advance of the Reformation—which both were equally anxious to suppress, but which was dealt with by each as it suited the convenience of his private policy—will be seen hereafter.[1]

Together with the powers of Austria and France, that of ENGLAND appears, not yet so important as in later times. Driven back, by the French, upon its own island, it immediately began wisely to recognise and improve the peculiar advantages with which nature had endowed it. As yet, however, the naval power of the Portuguese was superior to its own, and the cleverest artisans who promoted the industry of the country were foreigners. The very peculiar share which HENRY VIII., of the house of Tudor, took in the Reformation, will demand our consideration at a later period. Just now we will remark only, that the political history of England received an impulse from the Reformation, instead of the converse being the case. The same observation applies to SCOTLAND, which, by the marriage of its king, James V., with Marie of Guise, had entered into closer connection with France than with England, toward which it occupied a hostile position.

ITALY, in a political point of view, offers a melancholy spectacle. Divided into a number of petty states, of which some were of a monarchical and others of a republican character, internally riven by a multitude of factions and parties, it was the theatre of war, upon which Frenchmen, Germans, and

---

[1] L. RANKE, *Französische Geschichte, vornämlich im 16 und 17 Jahrhundert*, Stuttgart, 1852.

Spaniards struggled for supremacy, and whither the Swiss mercenaries were decoyed, now by one side, and now by another. And yet, for the history of the Reformation, Italy is of the highest import, not only on account of the antithesis which it presents to the Reformation, in that Rome is the seat of the pope, but also because of the light which went forth from it as the centre of science and art.[1] Both aspects were remarkably reflected in the person of the Medician pope, LEO X., who, so far as his policy allowed, protected liberal-minded effort against brutal assault, although, being utterly wanting in a sense of religion, he scrupled not to hurl the thunders of excommunication against Luther and his work.[2]

But little consideration is due, as yet, to the northern kingdoms of Europe. It was not until somewhat later that SWEDEN, freed from the Danish yoke, became, under the rule of GUSTAVUS VASA (1524), one of the leading powers of Protestantism. Still less need now be said concerning Russia, Poland, and the Slavonic tribes. There is, however, *one* power that we see arising in the East as the foe of all Europe, the arch-enemy of Christendom, and the actual fore-runner of the "antichristian kingdom" (according to the views of its contemporaries); we refer to the power of the Turks (Turkomans, Osmans). Since the capture of Constantinople (1453) under Mohammed II., they had pressed farther and farther into the heart of Europe. Greece, Moldavia, and Wallachia were in their possession. On different occasions, the imperial throne of Germany was imperilled by them. In 1529 they besieged Vienna. Thus the Turkish war is curiously woven into the history of the Reformation, so that continually, together with the "pope," it is "the Turk" whom

---

[1] J. BURCKHARDT, *Die Cultur der Renaissance in Italien*, Basel, 1860.

[2] FRA PAOLO, an Italian, thus criticises Leo X.: "He was a man of extensive acquirements in Belles Lettres, and of uncommon affability and clemency; he was exceedingly liberal, and much inclined to patronize learned and distinguished men. He would, in fact, have been a perfect pope, if he had possessed a well-grounded knowledge on religious subjects and more inclination toward piety; but to both of these matters he attached little importance."

the evangelical are called to oppose with their efforts and their prayers. It was upon the pretext of the Turkish war that Rome proclaimed those indulgences, the resistance to which begins the history of the German Reformation; but this very Turkish war was also, more than once, a wholesome diverter of the storm gathering over the heads of the Protestants, when, at the diets, it was needful to unite the powers of the empire, separated by their variant faiths, in opposition to a common foe.

Such, briefly sketched, was the political condition of Europe in general at the time of the Reformation. Since, however, the reformatory movements in GERMANY and SWITZERLAND are to claim our chief attention, we must devote another glance to the internal figure and constitution of those countries.

GERMANY [1] had, in the fourteenth century, by means of the Electoral League of Rense (1338), and the Golden Bull (1356) issued by Charles IV., received a constitution according to which the right of choosing an emperor was deposited with the seven electoral princes, and thus guarded from the interference of Rome. It was the office of these electors, as the principal members of the imperial body, in the unity of the sevenfold spirit to illuminate the holy empire, "like seven glorious candlesticks" (Rev. i. 12, 13), to quote the expression of the Golden Bull. They were the privy councillors of the emperor. Immediately after his death, it was their duty to assemble, for the choice of a new sovereign, in the free city of Frankfort-on-the-Main, and there to hold a conclave, the opening of which was attended with many ceremonies. The analogy which this imperial election by the prince electors presents to the papal election by the cardinals is so obvious that we cannot fail to remark it. The emperor-elect was obliged to swear that he would support the Catholic faith and the papal apostolic authority. After the election and the taking of the oath, the coronation took place, at first in Aix-la-Chapelle, and subsequently in Frankfort itself, being

[1] For particulars see SOUCHAY, *l.c.*, and RANKE.

accompanied by great solemnities. The imperial insignia consisted of a golden crown, a sceptre, the imperial globe as the symbol of universal dominion, the sword and gospel book of Charlemagne, and a costly mantle. Each of the electors had his special office to perform in attendance upon the emperor, and each was possessed of his peculiar prerogatives. Three of them belonged to the clergy and four to the laity. The former were the archbishops of Mentz, Treves, and Cologne; the latter were the Duke (King) of Bohemia, the Count Palatine of the Rhine, the Duke of Saxony, and the Margrave of Brandenburg. Prominent amongst them all, for the purposes of our history, is the Elector of Saxony at the time of the Reformation, Frederick III., surnamed the Wise; he was the sovereign of Luther, and, as much as in him lay, the promoter of his work. We shall encounter this prince and his successors again in the progress of our history. Meantime, we call attention to the following preliminary remarks relative to his political standing.

After the treaty of Leipsic in the year 1485, the dukedom of Saxony was divided between the sons of Frederick the Mild, subsequent to the death of the latter,—the Thuringian provinces falling to *Ernest*, while those of Meissen devolved on *Albert*. Thus originated the Ernestine and Albertine lines. Frederick III. was the son of Ernest; his cousin, Duke George, whose acquaintance we shall make as the opponent of Luther, was the son of Albert. Twice already, during vacancies of the imperial throne (1496 and 1501), had Frederick III. discharged the regency of the empire, and after the death of Maximilian he was again elected to that office. He came, in fact, within an ace of succeeding to the imperial crown.[1]

With a view to the introduction of greater unity into the imperial body, marvellously joined together as this was, Maximilian I. had distributed all the non-electoral provinces

---

[1] [The imperial crown was offered to Frederick, but he declined it. See D'Aubigné's *History of the Reformation*, vol. ii. p. 57 sq.—Tr.]

into *six* (including the electorates and the Austrian provinces, *ten*) *circles*,—the Bavarian, Swabian, Rhenish, Westphalian, Low Saxon, and Franconian circles. Besides the electoral princes, the remaining dukes, landgraves, and margraves appear as princes and lords over particular districts. Great political affairs were settled at the *diets*. These constituted the centre of legislation and general administration. Here was the imperial tribunal, and here the ban of the empire was pronounced, which latter was the political counterpart of ecclesiastical excommunication. Thus the imperial constitution was, to quote from Ranke,[1] " a mixture of monarchy and confederation, the latter element, however, manifestly predominating." One evidence that such was the fact is furnished by the great importance of the imperial cities: these, like the princes, sent their envoys to the diets, and, conjointly with the former, opposed a compact corporation to the power of the emperor. Amongst these cities there were many, in Middle and Southern Germany, distinguished for art, commerce, and manufactures. Of such, Nuremberg was especially prominent for its skill in the mechanical arts, and it, like Augsburg, Regensburg, Worms, and Speier, had the honour, on different occasions, of beholding the diet assembled within its walls. Ulm, Frankfort-on-the-Main, and Strassburg were, likewise, cities of the first rank, and played, as we shall see, an important part in the history of the Reformation. In the north of Germany, the Hanseatic League had been formed for the protection of the commerce of the confederated cities against piracy, and had, at the epoch of the Reformation, already been in existence for some centuries. In the sequel, it attained to still further political and mercantile importance. To this confederation belonged the cities of Hamburg, Lübeck, Bremen, Brunswick, Anclam, Dantzic, Stettin, Stralsund, Magdeburg, Cologne, and many other places, of greater or less magnitude, whose number has varied at different times. In contradistinction to the flourishing state of the cities, the

[1] *L.c.*, p. 117.

nobility, as has previously been remarked, had, subsequent to the loosening of the feudalistic bands, lost in great measure its original authority. Notwithstanding the "public peace" established by Maximilian I., sword [or *fist*] law, as is well known, continued to prevail, and many of the nobles lived by depredation, making no scruple of falling upon and plundering the merchants of the cities with which they were at feud, and even committing outrages upon the clergy, and upon religious foundations and cloisters. Illustrations of this sort of conduct are afforded even by men of comparatively exalted character,—by the brave Francis von Sickingen, and, in a still greater degree, by his brother-in-law, Götz von Berlichingen of the Iron Hand; even Ulrich von Hutten occasionally (when there were any opponents to be chastised) indulged in this species of warfare. And yet it was "the nobility of the German nation" that, in its worthier representatives, espoused the side of Luther and his cause, although the stout Reformer was on this account none the less earnest and constant in reproving their moral delinquencies, even at the risk of incurring their displeasure. The mass of the nation was composed of the peasants, who were, in great part, still in a condition of serfdom, or, at all events, oppressed with burdens of all sorts, imposed upon them by the nobles, the clergy, and the cities. Attempts to liberate themselves from this state by force of arms had already been made by the peasants, and were renewed in connection with the ecclesiastical Reformation, which they thought to convert into a revolution.

The moral condition of Germany, the general ferment of minds, in connection with the efforts that were put forth in science and art, we shall view to the best advantage as we pursue the thread of our history.

One fact, however, deserves immediate mention—viz., that the mightiest organ of the Reformation, the German language, had just at this time entered upon a new period of its development. The earlier *Minnesong* [*Minnegesang*] had become extinct, and in its stead the *Mastersong* [*Meistergesang*] of the guilds had arisen, a species of poetical composition which in many cities approximated to prose. A happy union of wholesome humour and moral purity meets us in Hans Sachs of Nuremberg. But in this domain, as in others, it was above all the "Wittenberg Nightingale," Luther, who, in poetry and prose, struck a new chord—a chord which, originating as it did in the inmost depths of a breast stirred by religious feeling, made itself intelligible to the German ear of the people without any learned arts of interpretation. As a translator of the Bible and a lyrical poet, we shall, in due time, become more intimately acquainted with him. We would mention in this connection, as a fact of the greatest significance, that the highest affairs of the nation, both in religion and politics, were now publicly discussed in the German language.

Hutten and Luther, in their use of the vernacular, stand on the same platform; and their practice in this respect is one of the points of difference between themselves and Erasmus, who always "stuck to his Latin," handling it, moreover, with an elegance which formed as great a contrast to the rude monkish Latin of the "obscure men" [*Dunkelmänner*], as humanism presented to barbarism.

And now let us glance for a moment at SWITZERLAND. We know that from the time when the Dauphin Louis tested the courage of the Confederates at the battle of St. James-on-the-Birs (1444), the powerful kingdom of France had sought their friendship and alliance.[1] From this very time, however, dates the period of the decay of Swiss independence. The sons of the free country henceforth sold their lives, sometimes to France, sometimes to the popes, and sometimes to other foreign rulers; until at last Francis I., who had become acquainted with their military proficiency in the Milanese wars, concluded, in 1516, a perpetual peace with them. At the epoch of the Reformation, therefore, Switzerland appears as an ally of France against Austria, for which powerful country the Swiss cherished a hatred that was more than

[1] JOH. VON MÜLLER, *Geschichte der Eidgenossen*.

ever increased since the Swabian war, and the ineffectual efforts of Austria, under Maximilian I., to re-annex the Switzers to the empire. The constitution of Switzerland was federative. Subsequent to the Burgundian wars, Freiburg and Soleure had been added (1481) to the eight old cantons. Twenty years later (1501), Basel and Schaffhausen were received into the confederacy, and in the year 1513 this was further strengthened by the Appenzellians, after they had shaken off the yoke of their spiritual ruler. With these thirteen old cantons were connected the "allied cantons,"—the abbot and city of St. Gall, the cities of Mülhausen and Biel, the city of Rothweil in Swabia, the county of Neufchâtel, Valais, the three confederacies of Rhætia, and a few other territories which subsequently united themselves to the Swiss Republic. Finally, since the Swiss had emerged from their defensive position, they had in their turn, by conquest, brought various provinces into subjection to themselves. Swiss governors ruled over the common possessions in Aargau, Thurgau, the valley of the Rhine, and the Sarganserland, just as Austrian governors had formerly ruled over the Swiss. The old simplicity of manners had long passed away. Since the Burgundian wars, the Swiss had acquired wants which the means hitherto in their possession did not suffice to satisfy. And thus, as Johann von Müller remarks, "the poverty of the Swiss became the occasion of their esteeming money the most precious thing next to liberty."

The history of the Reformation will show us how closely Zwingle's reformation in ecclesiastical matters was connected with the abolishment of political abuses, of "foreign mercenary service" and "pensions," and how the evermore passionate opposition of parties ranged confederate against confederate in mortal combat.

Having thus depicted the *political* relations of Europe in general terms, and, so far as it seemed requisite, in detail, it remains for us to glance at the condition of *ecclesiastical affairs* at the epoch of which we treat. In performing this task we may refer in part to the preliminary remarks contained in the last chapter, and in part to the succeeding chapters; for we shall become better acquainted with the ecclesiastical situation when, in the course of the history of the Reformation, we stand on the ground where the conflicts were waged. Let us, in the meantime, first present a general outline of the *religious feeling* of the time.

The period prior to the Reformation has frequently been compared with the period which preceded the foundation of Christianity, and there are, in truth, certain parallels between the two. As, in the earlier time, the ancient divinities, and human faith in them, had become superannuated, so the Catholicism of the Middle Ages had outlived its vigour. As early as in the fourteenth century, the papal schism had inaugurated a process of decomposition. It was with difficulty that the decaying body, whose visible head was exposed to constant vicissitudes, was held together by the great councils. Destroying powers attacked the loose joints of the building on all sides. All this was the occasion of great insecurity of feeling. Confidence in the Church's authority was shaken, but there was no positive foundation laid which could offer a new and firm support to minds invaded by doubt concerning the old order of things. That enlightenment which proceeded from the revival of classical learning could not compensate for the lack of religious inwardness and depth. How was it possible for the ancient philosophy, which, even in the days of heathenism, was no longer able to satisfy the religious wants of the human mind, and which was supplanted by the simple preaching of the gospel, to afford a substitute for Christian truth, darkened and stifled as this was by the rank growth of human ordinance? As, in ancient Rome, two augurs could not meet without exchanging a covert smile, thus it was now in modern Rome—ay, unbelief had seated itself in the very vicinity of the papal throne, had hidden itself behind those ecclesiastical ceremonies at which it was the part of wisdom outwardly to assist. We are not referring now to that audacious unbelief which hesitated not, at the voluptuous banquet, to pour out libations again to Bacchus and Venus; what we contemplate is that more subtile unbelief which surprised even noble thinkers, the more striking the discord became between the philosophic principles which they professed in secret and the public faith which their ecclesiastical position demanded that they should externally uphold. Who shall declare the amount of unconscious hypocrisy that was involved in all this? Whether it is true that Leo x. called Christianity a fable which had brought in a handsome sum to the Roman throne, and which, on that very account alone, should not be dispensed with, we will not undertake to decide. A similar anecdote is related of Cardinal Bembo.[1] When George Sabinus, a poet and scholar of the sixteenth century, was in Italy, the Cardinal asked him a variety of questions concerning the celebrated Melanchthon, *e.g.* as to how much salary he received, how many auditors he had, and, finally, what he thought of the resurrection of the dead and the life everlasting. Upon Sabinus replying to the last question out of the writings of Melanchthon, the Cardinal rejoined, " I should hold him to be a cleverer man if he did not credit this." It need not surprise us that such sentiments did not remain entirely secret, and that even the simple burgher began to imbibe suspicion and to entertain doubts as to the honesty of the priests. We are told that the father of Capito, the future Reformer of Strassburg, did not wish to let his son study theology, because, as he said, an ecclesiastic must necessarily be either a fool or a hypocrite.[2]

The transition from superstition to unbelief is ordinarily formed by *frivolity*—that habit of mind which, whilst it is inwardly estranged from that which is holy, continues its connection with it, according to custom, as a witty game. Sacred things are not derided, but they are, with an earnest mien,

---

[1] ADAMI, *Vita Theol. Germ.* p. 360, in HERDER, *Von der Auferstehung.*
[2] RÖHRICH, *Geschichte der Reformation im Elsass*, vol. i. p. 36.

exposed to ridicule. This is done sometimes purposely, and sometimes unintentionally, and while the one who so presents that which is sacred is unconscious of his unworthy act. Frivolity is the opposite of *naïveté*; it appears where the latter has, through the advance of time, become impossible, just as boyhood succeeds childhood. Thus frivolity had forced its way into theology at the period of degenerate Scholasticism, when men, being no longer capable of a childlike faith, abandoned themselves, with suppressed irony, to the charm of subtle and cavilling discussions, the general bearing of which was far better calculated to excite scepticism than to confirm faith. This same frivolity made itself visible in ecclesiastical architecture—in the fantastic scrolls, and in masks which peer out roguishly from the midst of representations of sacred things.[1] From irony there was but a step to a total profanation of everything sacred. We have already, in our history of the Middle Ages, made mention of the religious plays, the fools' and asses' feasts, and the therewith connected mummeries and banquetings in the churches. In spite of ecclesiastical prohibitions, these disorderly proceedings continued and increased. Let us transport ourselves for an instant to the cathedral at Strassburg.[2] High mass is about being celebrated. The nobles make their appearance, magnificently attired, wearing peaked shoes that clatter as they walk, and accompanied by hounds and falcons, the latter of which they occasionally let fly, by way of pastime, during the service of God. Here merchants are settling their worldly affairs, yonder a magistrate publicly administering justice, in the church. For the sake of shortening the way, sucking pigs, from the market close by, are carried through the sanctuary,

---

[1] The cathedral of Chartres exhibited an ass playing on a harp; one of the pillars of the cathedral of Strassburg was decorated with an ass reading mass; and there were similar representations on the cathedrals of Basel, Ulm, etc. The carvings on the stalls of the canons were of a like nature.

[2] In the description given above we follow the reports of men who lived at this time, viz. Brandt, Weucker, Schott, Wimpheling, as given by RÖHRICH, *l.c.* vol. i. p. 52.

so that the noise and bustle thereby occasioned force the priest to pause in his conduct of the mass. Above the minster-organ was placed a grotesque figure, called the "Ape of the Pipes." During Whitsuntide some wag would conceal himself behind this, and amuse the multitude by howls, coarse jests, and comic songs. From the feast of St. Nicholas to Innocents' Day (to Advent and Christmas time), it was customary for a boy, dressed as a bishop, to read mass; the rest of the people who frequented the church likewise appeared disguised in various costumes within its consecrated walls. Processions were held, and secular songs were sung. Of a still madder character were the proceedings at the feast of the consecration of the cathedral on St. Adolphus' Day (August 29), which was also the time for the annual fair. Casks of wine were placed in the chapel of St. Catharine, the high altar served as a table, and the most immoderate indulgence in wine completed orgies which surpassed those of the heathen in unruliness.

Although there may not have been precisely such mad doings everywhere as have here been described, yet the like folly and extravagance seem to have been very generally diffused at the festal seasons. Thus Bugenhagen laments that in Pomerania, during his youth, the old heathenism bestirred itself ever and anon in seasons of churchly festivity: "When the birth of our Saviour is celebrated, scarcely any one thinks himself religious if he does not, after going only once to church, spend the remainder of each day and a part of the night, until dawn, in the company of Bacchantes, like a devout worshipper of Isis. When the festal beams of the coming of the Holy Ghost arise upon us, we engage in Bacchanalian orgies. . . . And this is done not simply by the common herd of burghers and peasants, but also by the nobles and the most distinguished leaders of the people; ay, even the reverend priests in Christ, whose office it should be to hinder such proceedings so far as they are able, promote them, regardless of their dignity, by making excuses for them, and saying, "Oh, the season brings all these things in its train," when they might perceive the falsehood of their statement from the very prayers that they read when they rise from their foolish banquets.[1]

Preaching was obliged to condescend, more than is right, to the rudeness which dominated the minds of men. Even Geiler of Kaiserberg, the powerful preacher at Strassburg, a man who strove, as did few at that time, to lead souls to Christ, did homage to the taste of the period in linking his earnest discourses to the *"Narrenschiff"* of his friend Sebastian Brandt, and in endeavouring to chain the attention of the masses by mingling trivial proverbs and similitudes with those discourses, by a comic presentation of vices and follies, and by anecdotes which we should look for in a calendar rather than in a Christian sermon. In all this he was vastly exceeded by the French preacher, Michael Menot, who verged on the age of the Reformation (he died about 1518). The latter travestied the sacred records by a burlesque interlarding of the Latin text with French phrases.[2] Pulpit jests were believed to be especially justifiable at Easter, in order that the people might thus be indemnified for the privations of the Lenten season. Œcolampadius gives an account of these Easter fables, and the " Easter laughter" (*risus paschalis*) by which they were attended, in a letter to Capito. There were preachers who, to amuse their auditors, would strive to imitate the voices of different animals. One counterfeited the call of the cuckoo; another cackled like a goose; a third availed himself of the legend of St. Peter by reciting all manner of funny stories about him, as, for instance, how he

---

[1] Vogt, *Johann Bugenhagen*, p. 14.
[2] Comp. his sermon on the Prodigal Son, in Lentz, *Geschichte der Homiletik*, vol. i. p. 397. The history of the pulpit in Northern Germany also affords shocking examples of rudeness. "Suigbertus, a preacher in Brunswick, endeavoured to excite the attention of his hearers by a loud yell, in imitation of a wounded devil, who, according to the preacher, had striven to prevent the Prince of Victory from entering the gates of hell by thrusting his nose in the place of a bolt, and who was, accordingly, mutilated in that member" (Lentz, *Braunschweigs Kirchenreformation*, p. 55).

on one occasion cheated his host out of his reckoning, etc. Other preachers suffered themselves to be guilty of the coarsest and most indecent jokes, so that, as Œcolampadius declares, the more earnest-minded Christians would not go to church at all at this season, whilst others who went were filled with shame and vexation, and hastened out of the house of God. The Neapolitan Dominican monk Gabriel Barletta (who died in 1480) served as an exemplar of this burlesque style of preaching, and gave occasion to the proverb, *Nescit prædicare, qui nescit barlettare.* The following Easter fable was related by him: "When Christ the Lord arose, several offered to carry the glad tidings of His resurrection to His mother. But each one was rejected as unfit for the purpose. Adam said, 'I should be the one to do it, because I was the cause of the evil;' but the Lord answered him, 'Thou likest figs, and mightest tarry on the way.' Abel desired to go, but the Lord said to him, 'On no account; thou mightest meet Cain, who would slay thee.' Then Noah proposed to deliver the message, but the Lord said to him, 'Thou must not go, because thou lovest drink.' The repentant thief would fain have set out on the journey, but he could not, because his legs were broken. And so there was nothing for it but to send an angel, who saluted the queen of heaven with a hallelujah."

Whilst the wild extravagances of paganism thus cropped out at times, the mass of believers were, nevertheless, panting under the yoke of pharisaical ordinances that remind us of the stringency of Judaism. Men's consciences were laden with heavy burdens, and they sought in vain for rest and consolation in the rigorous mortifications to which they subjected themselves. As a sick man turns from one physician to another, so those who were concerned for their eternal health resorted from one saint to another, upon whom they called in their distress,[1] and from one monastic order to

[1] Even the enlightened Erasmus declares (and not in a tone of irony) that he once besought Saint Genevieve for recovery from a fever, and was healed by her, a circumstance which he afterwards celebrated in a poem. See ADOLF MÜLLER, *Leben des Erasmus*, p. 116.

another, in which they hoped to find the satisfaction that they longed for. Zwingle strikingly depicts this state of affairs.[1] "When a man is thirsting after the salvation of his soul, and asks a Carthusian, 'Brother, what shall I do to be saved?' the Carthusian replies unhesitatingly, 'Become a member of our order, and thou shalt assuredly be saved, for it is the strictest.' If thou ask a Benedictine, he replies, 'It is well to mark that a man can with most facility be saved in our order, for it is the oldest.' If thou ask a Preaching Friar (Dominican), he will tell thee, 'In our order one is sure to be saved, for it was brought down to our lady from heaven.' If thou ask a Barefooted Friar (Minorite, Franciscan), he will say, 'Our order is the largest and poorest in the world; judge, therefore, thyself whether salvation is to be found in the other orders more readily than in it.' If thou ask the pope, he will reply, 'The easiest way is to procure an indulgence.' If thou ask them of Compostella, they reply, 'He who seeketh St. James amongst us can never be lost or become impoverished.' Lo, every one recommends a different method, and every one firmly maintains that his opinion is the most correct. But here the thirsty soul exclaims, 'Alas! whom shall I follow? Each so extols his own way that I know not which to follow.' And at last it turns, perchance, to God, crying out in anguish, 'O God, do Thou show me which is right, *i.e.* which of the orders can save me!'"

The disastrous confusion of ideas in matters pertaining to salvation, the uncertainty with which the way of salvation was trodden, notwithstanding the superabundance of means proffered by the Church, is to be regarded as the ground-evil from which this period suffered, and from which it was about to be delivered through the grace of God. Everything else, over and above this, that was felt to be an infirmity,—the oppression of the various nationalities by the overgrown power of Rome, the thousand and one abuses in the disposal

[1] "Of the Glory and Greatness of the Word of God" (*Works*, vol. i. 1).

and administration of benefices, the manifold extortions practised under the cloak of religious purposes, the outgrowths of rudeness, ignorance, and superstition,—all these things, in comparison with that fundamental infirmity, are either secondary considerations, or are so intimately connected with the greater trouble, that the healing of the latter would be accompanied by the disappearance of the symptomatic evils. We will, therefore, refrain from a more detailed description of the ecclesiastical situation, with which we shall have occasion to make ourselves acquainted farther on, and turn to the reformatory endeavours which immediately preceded the act of Luther, and, in part, extended into his time.

Of the so-called forerunners of the Reformation in the fourteenth and fifteenth centuries, such as the Friends of God, Wycliffe, Huss, Jerome, John of Wesel, John Wessel, Jerome Savonarola, we have already spoken in our history of the Middle Ages. These men had not passed away without leaving some trace of their labours. Much of what they had spoken, done, and suffered, still lived in the memories of men. And not alone in memory. The little flock of Bohemian brethren had continued, amidst persecutions, to celebrate the worship of God in wooded glens and caverns (hence they were called *Grubenheimer*, pit-dwellers). Under the merciful reign of King Wladislaus (1472–1516) they ventured forth from their fastnesses, and stood, though but a minute fraction as compared with the great Church, as witnesses to bygone days. In the three Confessions which they submitted to the king in the years 1504–8, they, indeed, proceeded cautiously in regard to those things which they held it to be their duty to reject as abuses; yet they decidedly discarded the worship of Mary and the saints, and avowed their belief in a spiritual presence of Christ in the sacrament of the Lord's Supper, after the example of Wycliffe. Their chief anxiety, however, was to make good their connection with the faith of the old Catholic (Ecumenical) Church. The ideal which they pursued, and to which they strove as far as possible to conform themselves in their congregational constitution, was that of a fraternal fellowship, which should in all things follow the example of Christ and seek for salvation in Him alone. The relation which they subsequently sustained toward Luther and the Reformation will be treated of hereafter.

But not only did those individual congregations that were detached from the great Church, and occupied toward her the position of sects,—in which class we may place the Waldenses, in their valley retreats,—not only did these preserve within them a germ of evangelical doctrine and evangelical life (a germ which, it is true, must needs be fructified by the evangelical *Church*), but—and this fact should not be forgotten—even in the midst of the Catholic Church there were not wanting souls that were longing for salvation, that were susceptive of pure Christianity, and that were waiting in quiet for the "consolation of Israel." There was a confirmation here of the saying of Nicholas Clemange, that, though the whole Church should perish, it could be renewed again from the living faith of one pious woman. Luther's convent cell was not the only one in which fierce conflicts of conscience were waged amid prayers and tears. Amongst the high dignitaries of the Church, moreover, there were always some who strove to discharge the office with which God had entrusted them to the best of their knowledge and ability, and who willingly lent a helping hand to reforms, even when so doing involved personal sacrifice. Many a one there was, in the very days of desolation, who raised himself by the light of the gospel and pointed others to that light. I need but mention the noble John von Staupitz, whom we shall meet with again in the life of Luther. Such men did, indeed, often stand forsaken, finding little support among the clergy, who were for the most part uncultured and frequently immoral. In such a predicament they could but comfort themselves as did Staupitz, who declared, "We must needs plough with the horses that we have, and let him that has no horses plough with oxen."

Before we approach any closer to Luther, we have to direct our attention to those men who, partly as forerunners and partly as contemporaries of the great Reformers, prepared the ground for the Reformation, and are still further woven into its history—viz., Reuchlin, Hutten, and Erasmus. With these and a few of their contemporaries we propose to occupy the next chapter.

CHAPTER III.

REUCHLIN AND THE HUMANISTS—HUTTEN, ERASMUS, WIMPHELING.

THERE are two men who, from their scientific endowments and the light which they diffused about them in their conflict with monkish superstition, pre-eminently claim our attention before we touch upon Luther's Reformation: these two individuals are Reuchlin and Erasmus, the "two eyes of Germany," as Ulric von Hutten called them. The latter himself appears as a third in this friendly alliance, being most intimately connected with each of the others, although he subsequently fell out with Erasmus. His portrait must be inserted between the portraits of his two friends.

JOHN REUCHLIN[1] was born December 28, 1455, at Pforzheim. He was piously brought up by his parents, who, though not wealthy, were in tolerably comfortable circumstances (his father was a servitor of the Dominicans). Speedily distinguishing himself in singing, as well as in other acquirements, at the school of his native city, he was, in his eighteenth year, admitted into the number of the Baden-Durlachian court-singers or choristers. He was next sent, as the companion of the youthful Margrave Frederick of Baden, whose age was near his own, to the University of Paris, where

---

[1] His name [which signifies *Little Smoke*], when translated into Greek, is *Capnio* (from καπνος, *smoke*). Comp. MEINERS, *Lebensbeschreibungen berühmter Männer aus den Zeiten der Wiederherstellung der Wissenschaften*, Zürich, 1795, vol. i.; MAYERHOFF, *Joh. Reuchlin und seine Zeit.*, Berlin, 1830; STRAUSS, *Hutten*, pp. 188 sqq.; LAMEY, *Joh. Reuchlin*, Pforzheim, 1855; KLÜPFEL, in HERZOG's *Realencyklopädie*, xii. pp. 753 sqq.

he became acquainted with the ancient languages, the study of which was there pursued with renewed zeal. John Wessel, whose name we have already mentioned, particularly encouraged him in his ardent application to the classics, and directed him still further in the prosecution of his studies. From him he learned the first elements of Hebrew. Towards the end of the year 1474, Reuchlin encountered this friend again in Basel, and renewed his acquaintance with him upon a still warmer footing. In Basel he also met with the Amerbachs, the celebrated printers of that city. He there explained the Greek classics, instructed the students in the art of writing and in grammar, and laboured upon a Greek lexicon. The general favour with which he was regarded excited the envy of some other instructors, who were more versed in scholastic niceties than in Greek. These had no resource, in their jealousy, save to hold up to suspicion a matter which they did not understand, and to set afloat a charge of heresy against the new teacher. "Of what use is Greek?" they cried; "it is a language that leads to nothing but heresies and schisms." In spite of this outcry, Reuchlin was held in increasing esteem by all who were able to comprehend his unvarnished piety and to appreciate his unusual scientific attainments. Reuchlin's four years' stay in Basel had not been without fruit. Having in 1474 received the degree of Bachelor, and in 1477 that of Master of Arts, he proceeded to Paris, where, under the instruction of a Greek fugitive, he made still further progress in the language of Hellas. In 1478 he removed to Orleans, where he pursued the study of jurisprudence. At Orleans, as well as subsequently at Poitiers, he continued his lectures on the ancient languages, meeting with the same approbation that greeted him at Basel. Many noblemen of high rank, from Germany and of France, who were assembled at the former cities, became his friends, and aided him in the improvement of his external circumstances. After this sojourn in France, he returned, in the capacity of a licentiate of law, to his native country. In the service of Count Eberhard with the Beard he made several journeys, amongst which his journey to Italy proved especially advantageous to him. In Rome he delivered a fine oration, in the presence of Pope Sixtus IV.; and in Florence he was admitted into that circle of learned men whom Lorenzo de Medici had gathered round him. He became the friend of the Platonic philosopher Marsilius Ficinus, and the cabalist Giovanni Pico di Mirandola, both of whom exerted an influence over his mode of thought. Upon his return to Stuttgart, the new residence of Count Eberhard, he was made assessor to the Court tribunal there, and attorney to the Dominican order in Germany. Diplomatic missions brought him into connection with the different princely courts. The Emperor Frederick III. exalted him to the rank of a noble, and bestowed upon him the title of Count-Palatine; shortly afterwards he constituted him imperial councillor. After the death of Eberhard, an event productive of political troubles, Reuchlin gladly accepted a call from the reverend prelate Dalberg, who resided at Heidelberg, as Chancellor of the Elector-Palatine Philip, and who was a zealous patron of the dawning light of science.[1] For this man Reuchlin undertook, amongst other things, a journey to Rome in 1498,[2]—a journey which was of great profit to him in a scientific point of view, and which gained him new friends. After the deposal of Eberhard the Younger, Reuchlin returned, in 1499, to Stuttgart, became a member, and soon after president, of the Swabian confederate tribunal, but retired in a few years to private life. After discharging for a short time the duties of professor in the University of Ingolstadt, he passed the remainder of his days, which were still devoted to study, at Tubingen, and died at last at Stuttgart (1522), in the sixty-seventh year of his age.

Amid all the varied fortunes of Reuchlin, his prominent

[1] The merits of this prelate have been commented on by ULLMANN, in a Latin Programme, 1840.

[2] The elector had been excommunicated by Pope Alexander VI., and Reuchlin was commissioned to negotiate the removal of the ban.

characteristic was an ardent pursuit of learning. Not only did he minister to the revival of classical studies by his efforts in the direction of the Greek language and literature, but that in which his prime importance consisted, as an instrument, in the hand of Providence, of the Reformation, was his zeal in promoting a knowledge of the Hebrew language. It was this very thing, however, that involved him in a conflict with the ignoramuses of his time—a conflict which must be regarded as a little prelude to the great drama of the Reformation.

The study of the Hebrew language, the utility of which in connection with theology is manifest to every layman of the present day, had been totally neglected by the Christian theologians of the Middle Ages. Only the Jewish Rabbins were in possession of the language, whilst the ministers of the dominant Church contented themselves with the Latin version of the Holy Scriptures—the Vulgate. It was, therefore, necessary to acquire the Hebrew from the Jewish, before it could be applied to Christian theology. Great prejudices, however, stood in the way of this apparently simple undertaking. The Jews were universally despised as a people rejected of God, and had on various occasions, as we have mentioned in a former work, been made to experience the utmost harshness and cruelty at the hands of the infuriated Christians. Mere intercourse with learned Jews was, in those days, regarded by the great mass of people as in no whit better than intercourse with heretics and schismatics. Reuchlin, however, did not suffer himself to be detained by such prejudices as these. At the imperial court at Linz he had made the acquaintance of a learned Jew, by name Jacob Jehiel Loans, who was physician-in-ordinary to the Emperor, and who likewise bore the title of knight. This man in particular it was who initiated him into the mysteries of the Hebrew tongue. Reuchlin soon made such progress in the language as to publish, in the year 1506, his *Hebrew Grammar*, of the immense value of which he was himself fully sensible, confessing it openly, without affectation.[1] And, indeed, this work did its part as one of the main levers of the Reformation. With the Hebrew grammar Reuchlin had, as it were, placed in the hands of Protestant theology the key wherewith to open the long-hidden treasures of the Bible. He had kindled the torch which should lead Luther farther into the sanctuary; he had pointed the magnetic needle, by whose aid the bold navigator should press farther out upon the ocean. Luther gratefully acknowledged this, and called Reuchlin his father. Melanchthon and Œcolampadius were also pupils of Reuchlin, and acquired the sacred tongue from him.

If Reuchlin had stopped here, with the preparation of an instrument which should be employed in the building up of a thorough biblical theology, his fame, from this same beautiful simplicity, would perhaps be even greater than it now is. But, unfortunately for himself, he suffered the spirit of the times to seduce him into the turning of the tool into a toy, although the matter in which he engaged was no sport, but serious earnest to him. In his study of the Hebrew tongue he had become acquainted with another branch of learning, from which he anticipated important results, but which, if it had gained the upper hand, would have thrown men back again into the darkness of preceding centuries, rather than have led them forward to the purer light. As the Christian theology of the Middle Ages had degenerated into a barren Scholasticism, which was here and there transformed into an equally obscure Mysticism, so the Jewish theology of the Rabbins had been perverted into a singular species of philosophy, which is known by the name of cabala or cabalism, and which, in brief, principally professed to be able, by virtue of an artificial system of letter-reckoning, to find out all manner of mysteries concerning the universe and the nature of God. Reuchlin eagerly embraced this foundationless, adventurous philosophy; and other celebrated

[1] He prefixed to it the motto, *Exegi monumentum aere perennius.*

men of that period, such as Picus de Mirandola and Agrippa von Nettesheim, anticipated great things from it, as also from alchemy, necromancy, etc. One fruit of Reuchlin's cabalistic studies was a book which was issued in 1494 by Amerbach in Basel, on *The Wonder-working Word* (*De Verbo Mirifico*), a singular mixture of Pagan-Jewish philosophy and Christian religion.

Admitting that Reuchlin erred in searching in the dust and mould of obscure ruins for a magic key to the divine mysteries at the very time when he held the genuine and true key in his hand, yet the impulse whereby he was guided was a pure one; it was a free impulse towards truth, towards light, towards a science which should be able to satisfy spirit and soul, and to promote God's cause amongst men. And does not the bare fact that he could rise above the prejudices which in his time weighed upon the Jews, that he cherished for them in his heart a germ of tolerance utterly foreign to the age in which he lived,—does not *this* testify to a free and untrammelled mind? It is true that in a tractate which appeared in 1505, he himself attributes the proscription (exile, misery) in which the Jews are forced to live, to the hardness of heart with which they continue their blasphemies; but not by violence, but by affectionate instruction, did he hope that they would finally be won to Christianity, and such instruction he, for his part, failed not to offer them.

Totally diverse from the sentiments of Reuchlin were the opinions and the practice of the party of obscure men or ignoramuses [*Finsterlinge*]. To their contracted minds, the Jew and the companion of the Jews were equally hateful, and they swore perdition to them both. For the execution of this dark plan they could employ no better instrument than a man who had himself been a Jew, but who had been led by base motives to embrace Christianity, and who now played the zealot as a proselyte and proselytizer. *John Pfefferkorn* was the name of this worthy. In a production which, with the aid of the Dominicans, he published at Cologne in 1508 and 1509, under the title of *Judenspiegel* [*Mirror of the Jews*],[1] he presented the practices and the doctrine of those whose belief he formerly shared in the most odious light, and advised that their books should all be burned,—a procedure which would indeed have been the shortest way of effecting the overthrow of the whole Jewish theology without any racking of brains. The books referred to consisted principally of the Talmud, the Cabala, and a few other writings.

The Dominican monks, as the professed heretic hounds of the Church, took a prominent position in this affair also, and did not rest until they had (1509) procured a mandate from the Emperor Maximilian I. commanding the burning of these books. Reuchlin had in the meantime been asked for his opinion in regard to the matter. He at first refused to express any, but when constrained by an imperial injunction to give one, he most earnestly advised against the step.[2] He appealed to that natural right by which every man in a civilised community, be he Christian or Jew, must be allowed to defend himself before he can be judged. He then showed that the books indicated were, collectively and individually, by no means as dangerous as they were declared to be;[3] for, observed he ironically, in order to be dangerous for Christians, they must needs be intelligible to them, but in the whole of the Holy Roman Empire there was probably not a Christian to be found who knew enough Hebrew to understand the Talmud. The existence of such books, therefore, even if they could imperil the Christian faith, was, he maintained, a wholesome spur to the sloth of the clergy and the monks. Let them first, said he, arm themselves with such knowledge as is

---

[1] The *Judenbeichte* and the little book entitled *Wie die Juden ihre Ostern halten* were similar in purport.

[2] "*Rathschlag, ob man den Juden alle ihre Bücher nehmen, abthun oder verbrennen sollte.*"

[3] That there were amongst them certain opprobrious writings, which Christendom should not suffer to exist, he, however, admitted, and himself counselled the destruction of such.

requisite for combating the foe before they believe him to be conquered. The simple burning of the books would be a melancholy expedient of ignorance and rudeness. Moreover, it was not known whether there might not be in the books much of good that might be profitable and edifying even for Christians; for, "as the bee sucks honey from every flower, so should the Christian draw from all books that which is best; he should pluck the rose out of the midst of thorns, wherever he finds it." Christ Himself commanded that the tares should be permitted to grow up with the wheat, lest, together with the former, the latter be plucked up also. Should, he continued, the objection be urged that the Jews are strengthened in their error by these books, it should be considered that they may prove to them a guide unto Christ; for Paul, he declared, was led to Christianity by a deeper insight into the essence of Judaism. He finally remarked, with much truth and pertinence, that the suppression of such books would but increase the longing for the forbidden food, and draw attention to the very points that were perilous and injurious. Therefore he, for his part, counselled that the books should not be burned. It seemed to him more advisable that all the German Universities should be obliged to maintain, during ten years, two teachers of Hebrew. Thus Christians would speedily be enabled to meet the Jews upon their own ground, when they might, by convincing them of their errors, convert them to the Christian faith.

These calm and humane ideas—a rare phenomenon in that age—scarcely obtained a hearing with the obscurants. Pfefferkorn, to whom Reuchlin's opinion had been confidentially communicated, published his *Handspiegel*, in which he even held Reuchlin up to the suspicion of having been bribed by the Jews; he also sought to persuade the ignorant that Reuchlin did not understand Hebrew. Pfefferkorn's allies, the Dominicans, likewise tried all possible means of prejudicing the emperor against a man who was so far superior to them in intellect, learning, and hence, also, in clemency of judgment. The theologians of Cologne, with the famous heretic hunter, Jacob Hoogstraten, at their head, were especially busy in this matter. A prolix war of writings now ensued, in which many distinguished literati and vigorous thinkers took part, but which we are unable to follow farther.[1] We must content ourselves with a brief presentation of the subsequent course and final issue of the conflict. The theological faculty of Cologne appointed a committee, headed by Arnold von Tongern, to examine the *Augenspiegel*. Reuchlin tried in vain to change the convictions of these men; he perhaps showed himself only too compliant, thus encouraging his opponents to persist in their insolent treatment of him. The attempt was made to compel him to stop the sale of the *Augenspiegel*, and to recant its contents. On Reuchlin's refusal to comply with this demand, the Cologne theologians hurled against him a condemnatory treatise, to which a wit, named Ortwin Gratius, appended a satirical poem dedicated to the emperor. Reuchlin now laid aside his former timidity, and, carried away by passion, returned insult for insult.[2] The Emperor Maximilian issued an edict enjoining silence upon both parties. At the instigation of Hoogstraten, however, a spiritual judicatory was opened in September 1513, before whose tribunal Reuchlin was summoned. He appeared before this court in the following October. The chapter of Cologne endeavoured to mediate between the contending parties. Reuchlin meanwhile retired to Stuttgart, awaiting the issue of the matter. The affair came before the pope. Leo X., a friend and patron of learning, sought to withdraw Reuchlin from the persecution of his

---

[1] Reuchlin answered Pfefferkorn's *Handspiegel* with the *Augenspiegel*, in which he shows that "baptized Jew" to have been guilty of no less than thirty-four falsehoods against himself (Reuchlin). In regard to the accusation of bribery, he could affirm with a good conscience, "that in all his life he had never received, taken, or procured from the Jews, or for their sake, one farthing, penny, or kreuzer."

[2] He called Pfefferkorn a venomous beast, a scarecrow, a monster; the Cologne theologians he styled crafty dogs, hogs, foxes, wolves, lions, Cerberuses, hell furies. Some of his learned friends—amongst them Pirkheimer and Erasmus—justly censured this tone.

embittered foes by devolving the settlement of the suit upon the Bishops of Speier and Worms. The court of Speier (24th April 1514) exonerated the *Augenspiegel* from the charge of heresy; and Hoogstraten, who in the meantime had, upon his own responsibility, caused the dangerous book to be burned, was sentenced to pay the costs of the procedure. The Dominicans would not recognise the competency of the court. When the sentence was posted up in Cologne, they cut it to pieces. They next had recourse to different Universities, and endeavoured to procure from them opinions favourable to themselves. They applied to Erfurt, Mainz, Louvain, and Paris. To the latter University Reuchlin himself had appealed, and found there, in William Copus, physician-in-ordinary to the king, and a former companion of his own studies in Basel, a warm advocate with the monarch. The Dominicans, however, worked upon the king's confessor to such purpose that the *Augenspiegel* was condemned to the flames and actually burnt. Nothing now remained for Reuchlin save an appeal to the Roman throne. This appeal being made, the Dominicans again exerted every effort to secure Reuchlin's condemnation. They were unsuccessful, however, and experienced a disgraceful defeat, the committee appointed in Rome passing a sentence similar to that of the court of Speier. Only Sylvester Prierias, a Dominican, whom we shall soon see placing himself in opposition to Luther also, espoused the cause of the brethren of his order. The pope, being unwilling to offend this powerful order, issued a mandate *de supersedendo*, by which the suit was temporarily suppressed. In point of fact, however, Reuchlin was victorious. The monks made no attempt to restrain their rage at the issue of the matter, and launched forth into violent invectives against the papal throne. It is said that a few threatened to go over to the Bohemians if they were not better protected by Rome. It has always been found that ultra minds take a revolutionary turn as soon as a check is put upon their fanaticism. Loud was the triumph, in view of all the circumstances, of the friends of Reuchlin and enlightenment, the so-called Humanists.

Before we make the nearer acquaintance of the numerous leaders of the new intellectual current, at the head of whom Hutten stands, permit me to mention a visionary morning dream which Erasmus represents a pious Franciscan as having had at the hour of Reuchlin's death.[1]

At the farther extremity of a bridge, which led over a brook, the sleeper beheld a lovely meadow. Reuchlin, attired in white and shining garments, was advancing toward this bridge, followed by a beautiful winged boy, his good genius. Some black birds, of the size of vultures, pursued Reuchlin, uttering harsh screams as they flew. He, however, turned, made the sign of the cross, and commanded the birds to depart, which they did, after emitting an ineffable stench. At the bridge he was received by St. Jerome, of linguistic fame. The latter saluted him as a colleague, and brought him a robe such as he wore himself, all beset with tongues in three colours, indicative of the three languages which both understood. The meadow and the air were filled with angels; upon a hill which rose from the meadow there descended, from the open heaven, a pillar of fire, in which the two blessed ones, embracing each other, mounted on high, amid the songs of the angelic choirs.

The Reuchlin disputation had set a multitude of pens in motion. The friends of the "good studies"—*i.e.* of classical antiquity—formed thenceforth a close phalanx, the Reuchlinian confederation. To this belonged the celebrated philologists and poets, Crotus Rubianus, Euricius Cordus, Eoban Hesse, in Erfurt; Conrad Mutian, in Gotha; Herrmann von Busche, in Cologne; Count Herrmann von Nuenar, cathedral provost of the archbishopric of the latter place; Wilibald Pirkheimer, in Nuremberg, and many more. The joy of the Reuchlinists at the victory of their champion was expressed by Hutten in his *Triumphus Capnionis.* He describes the triumphal entry of Reuchlin, after the manner of a Roman

[1] *Apotheosis Capnionis*, STRAUSS, *Hutten*, ii. p. 250.

emperor, into Pforzheim, his native town. Before him are borne the weapons of the vanquished—*i.e.*, the sophisms of the antagonistic party, their bloody scourges, their stakes; these are followed by the idols of the adversaries of Reuchlin, —the four monsters, superstition, barbarism, ignorance, and envy. Next come, bound in chains, the vanquished foes,— first, Hoogstraten; then the drunken Ortwin, the hypocritical Arnold von Tongern, and the "Judas" Pfefferkorn, besides others. Now follow the minstrels, chanting an encomium of Reuchlin; and finally the hero himself advances, crowned with a triumphal wreath and surrounded by a throng of jurists and poets, his admirers. Of still greater celebrity than this poem are the *Epistles of Obscure Men* (*Epistolæ Obscurorum Virorum*), a series of productions most intimately connected with the history of Reuchlin. For a long time Hutten was regarded as the author of these. More recent investigations have shown that the first part (1516) was the production of Crotus Rubianus, with whom, doubtless, the idea of the whole originated, but that Hutten, together with others, contributed to a second volume, issued in 1517. These *Epistles* are written in ridicule of the whole monastic clique which had taken the field against Reuchlin and the Humanists, their monkish language, manner of thought, and customs. The greater part of them are addressed to Ortuinus (Ortwin) Gratius, and are couched in the most abominable dog-Latin, amusing from the very fact of its barbarism. The monkish style was so closely imitated in them, that the good "obscure men" regarded the *Epistles* ascribed to them as really coming from one of their number. Erasmus is said to have laughed so immoderately at reading them as to break an abscess with which he was troubled. They would scarcely produce such an effect in our own time.[1] Many of the allusions in them are unintelligible to us, nor did the

---

[1] There is something stiff and school-boyish, to our ears, about the very names of the feigned correspondents—Genselinus, Caprimulgius, Scherschleiferius, Dollenkopfius, Mistladerius.

composers of them spare exaggeration or obscenity. Nevertheless, they are an important document of the history of the time. The learned pedantry of the schools, and the Pharisaical straining out of gnats, prevalent in religious matters, are scourged with equal severity in these *Epistles*. For instance, the question is discussed, apparently in all seriousness, as to whether the eating of an egg in which a chicken may be detected be transgressive of a fast. One asserts that the little creature in the shell may be compared with the worms that exist in cheese and cherries, and which people swallow unhesitatingly [?] during a fast. To this it is responded that the cases are not parallel, since worms rank with fishes, which it is allowable to eat in a fast, whilst the embryonic chicken belongs indisputably to forbidden flesh. The adoration of relics did not escape the satire of the writers of these *Epistles*, and the abuses of the indulgence system were sharply censured. The mocking tone of the great mass of the letters is sometimes exchanged for one of moral and religious earnestness; as, for instance, when the following words, in contravention of the preachers of indulgences, are put into the mouth of the Wurzburg preacher, John Reiss: "Nothing can be compared with the gospel, and he who acts justly will be saved. If a man should receive an indulgence a hundred times, and not live as he ought, he will be damned, and the indulgence will not help him one whit. On the other hand, if a man has lived righteously, or—supposing that he has sinned—if he repents and amends his life, behold, unto him I declare that he will be a citizen of the heavenly kingdom without the need of other aids." Reference is also had to the prophecies of the Old Testament, and the attempt is made to show the imminence of their fulfilment. Thus the following passage from Zephaniah (i. 12) is cited : "And it shall come to pass at that time, that I will search Jerusalem with candles, and punish the men that are settled on their lees," etc.; and the "candles" are interpreted as the learned men of Germany, with whom the new intellectual movement originated,—viz.,

Erasmus, Reuchlin, Mutian, etc.,—whilst in the obscure men are found such as are persistently settled upon the lees of a stale and vapid theology.

The *Epistles of Obscure Men* naturally lead us to Hutten, whose name has for centuries been connected with them. We shall meet with him again in the history of Luther. In the meantime let us sketch his portrait.[1]

On the borders of Franconia and Hessia, in the neighbourhood of the Spessart range, dwelt, from times of yore, the knightly family of the Huttens, represented towards the close of the fifteenth and in the beginning of the sixteenth century by numerous scions. On the 22d of April 1488, there was born to the knight Ulric von Hutten, at the castle of Stackelberg, his first son, who received his father's name. Although the young Ulric was the first-born of his parents, he was destined by them for a clerical life. In his eleventh year he was sent to the venerable and famous Benedictine monastery of Fulda, to be educated. Cloisteral life offered few attractions to the lively spirit of the boy, however, and " it seemed to him that, by reason of his peculiar disposition, he would be able to please God better and to serve the world with more honour in another station." The abbot of the monastery endeavoured in vain to persuade him to enter the order. A friend of the Hutten family, the knight Eitelwolf von Stein, a man of culture and friendly to the Humanists, warned the parents of Ulric against influencing their son to a step which he might afterwards regret having taken. Hutten escaped from the monastery, and, pursuant to the advice of Crotus Rubianus, repaired to the University of Erfurt, proceeding afterwards to Cologne.[2] Subsequently he visited Frankfort-on-the-Oder. Everywhere he formed connections with congenial minds, who rejoiced over his brilliant intel-

---

[1] D. F. STRAUSS, *Ulrich von Hutten*, 2 vols., Leipzig, 1858. The edition of his works issued by E. Münch (1821-23) has been superseded by the newer and better one published by Böcking, 1859-62.

[2] Others say that he went first to Cologne (comp. STRAUSS, i. pp. 23 sqq.).

lectual gifts. He soon published his first poetical attempts; and literary struggles and knightly adventures began for him at the same time. We cannot follow him farther in his wanderings through a great part of Germany, through Bohemia, Moravia, and Italy, nor can we enter into the disputes in which he became involved. We have already learned to know him as the ally of Reuchlin, and will now examine into the position which he occupied toward the incipient Reformation.

We shall anticipate the course of our history in so far as to mention here, briefly, a work which Hutten published *after* Luther's first appearance on the stage of the Reformation, but prior to his own nearer acquaintance with the Saxon Reformer; we refer to the dialogue entitled, "*Vadiscus, die römische Dreifaltigkeit*" [*The Roman Trinity*], written in the year 1519, and issued in print in 1520. This writing, as will readily be seen, is not the outgush of a religious feeling working in the inmost depths of the soul and struggling forth amid the conflicts of an anguished conscience—such a feeling as swelled the breast of Luther; it is the fearless courage, the defiant spirit of the satirist; it is the German's righteous and noble indignation against foreign oppression that here, as elsewhere, has prompted the taking up of the pen as a sword. How this pen was handled, how this sword was brandished, will be shown by the following example.[1]

"*Three* things sustain the dignity of Rome: the reputation of the pope, the bones of the saints, and the traffic in indulgences. *Three* things are innumerable in Rome: harlots, priests, and scribblers. *Three* things are proscribed in Rome: simplicity, temperance, and piety. *Three* things are in universal demand at Rome: short masses, good money, and voluptuous living. Of *three* things people like not to hear: a General Council, a reformation of the clergy, and that the Germans are beginning to come to their senses. With *three* things do the Romans commerce: with Christ, with spiritual fiefs (benefices), and with women. With *three* things they of Rome cannot

[1] STRAUSS, *l.c.* ii. pp. 27 sqq.

be satiated: with money for the palliums, and with the papal monthly and yearly pensions.[1] Of *three* things Rome is subversive: a good conscience, religious devotion, and an oath. *Three* things are wont to be brought from Rome by pilgrims: defiled consciences, vitiated stomachs, and empty purses. *Three* things have hitherto hindered Germany from acquiring wisdom: the stupidity of its princes, the decay of learning, and the superstition of the people. *Three* things are most feared by Rome: the union of the princes, the opening of the eyes of the people, and the coming to light of her deceptions. Only by *three* things could Rome be set right: by the earnestness of the princes, by the impatience of the people, and by a Turkish army at her gates."

And again: "For centuries St. Peter's chair has been occupied by no true followers of him, but by followers and imitators of Nero and Heliogabalus. The papal court is a sink of all corruption. . . . There stands the great granary of the earth, into which are dragged the spoils of robberies committed in every country. In the midst of this granary sits that insatiable corn-worm [the pope], devouring enormous masses of fruit, surrounded by his numerous companions in gormandizing, who first sucked our blood, then gnawed our flesh, and now have come to our marrow, and are breaking our very bones and crushing all that is left of us. Shall not the Germans take to their arms? shall they not storm this place with fire and sword? There are the plunderers of our fatherland, who of yore robbed, and now audaciously and outrageously despoil, the nation that rules the world, who revel in the sweat and blood of the German people, who fill their bellies and feed their lust from the bowels of the poor. To these men we give gold; at our expense they keep horses, hounds, mules, and (oh, shame!) women and men for the gratification of their lust. With our money they practise their iniquity, live in luxury, array themselves in purple,

---

[1] The pope had reserved to himself the right of filling the bishoprics which were vacated in the six odd months of January, February, etc.

bridle their horses and mules with gold, build palaces of marble. They who should be the guardians of religion, not only neglect it,—which alone would be sinful enough,—but they despise it—ay, they outrage it, pollute it, profane it! And whilst, formerly, they baited us with blandishments and charmed our money from us by lies, inventions, and deceptions, now they arm themselves with terrors, threats, and violence, that they may strip us like hungry wolves. And we must still caress them; we dare not stab them nor pluck [our goods from] them—nay, we dare not so much as lay a finger on them. When shall we come to our senses and avenge our shame, our common loss? If supposed religion and pious awe have hitherto withheld us, necessity now compels us and constrains us."

That such productions, apart from Luther's protests, which at first made no assault upon the Roman chair, not only created a hubbub among the decided adherents of Rome, but also excited serious scruples in the minds of Hutten's friends, amongst whom Erasmus was still numbered, may be readily conceived. Nor did Erasmus, with his usual prudence, fail paternally to admonish the youthful presser and stormer to moderate his zeal.

Let us now turn to Erasmus himself, who forms, in the whole phenomenon of his being, the opposite of Hutten. In many respects, it is true, the career of the one reminds us of that of the other. Both withdrew from the imprisonment of the cloister, which offered no attractions to their free natures. Both gained a wide field of view and made for themselves a famous name by numerous travels and manifold connections. Both declared war against the monkish and priestly system, and favoured the enlightenment of the century. Both wielded the weapons of ridicule and satire. Notwithstanding all this, however, the paths of the two were widely divergent,— that of the knight, whose breast was always bared to the view of the world, and with whom it was at all times 'a word and a blow; and that of the cautious man of books, anxiously calculating the consequences of each step, and refraining from cutting too deep into the flesh of his contemporaries, and exposing himself to embarrassments.

Desiderius Erasmus,[1] the fruit of an illicit and unfortunate love, was born at Rotterdam in October 1467. The romantic story of his father Gerard[2] is out of place here; be it observed, only, that a disinclination to a monkish life, which Gerard had been forced against his will to embrace, and which was the source of much misery to him, was transmitted to his son, and that the latter thus literally "imbibed a hatred of the monks with his mother's milk." In spite of this, however, the youthful Erasmus was, by the policy of his guardians, destined to enter a convent as soon as he should have received the first rudiments of learning at the schools of Utrecht and Deventer. He was not one of those remarkable children of whom we sometimes hear; he is even said to have given evidence, in his earliest years, of a rather dull intellect,—a fact which has since, it is declared, afforded much consolation to many a Dutch mother whose son did not make as rapid progress in learning as was desired. In his later boyhood, however, his rare capacities developed in so surprising a manner, that the learned Agricola, on visiting, upon one occasion, the school of Deventer, prophesied that he would become a great man if he persevered in the course he was pursuing.

Any one who critically considers the history of this great man's youth, will more leniently judge his later errors, especially that weakness of character with which he is so frequently reproached. The only comfort of an unhappy

---

[1] ADOLF MÜLLER, *Leben des Erasmus von Rotterdam; eine gekrönte Preisschrift*, Hamburg, 1828. Comp. also older descriptions by Jortin, Burigny, Hess; the article by Bayle in his *Dictionnaire*, and that of the author of this work in Herzog's *Realencyc.* iv. pp. 114 sqq.

[2] The name DESIDERIUS ERASMUS is in reality but a Latin and Greek translation of the name GERHARD = *Gernhaber, Liebhaber* [lover]. The name of ERASMUS, however, was already in existence as the appellation of a popular saint (of the time of Diocletian), who was ranked among the Church's helpers in time of need.

mother, by whom he was fondled and indulged to excess,—whilst at school, on the other hand, his teachers intimidated him by their severity,—his inner life had become the scene of cruel discord, and the free development of his mind had thus been early stunted and neglected. Then, after the death of his mother, came his confinement in the cloister—a thing repugnant to his whole soul. Though to stronger natures, such as Luther's, a youth so hard, being more in unison with their ruder home training, might prove a wholesome school for after life, yet upon the weakly Erasmus, effeminated from his infancy, such a discipline must necessarily have a pernicious effect. His mind could not fail to elaborate, unobserved, the dangerous weapons with which weakness so often seeks to protect itself against its rude opponents—I refer to an ignoble pliancy, and, where this avails not, artifice and dissimulation.[1] Ignorant of the world, whose acquaintance he did not make until a later period of his life, dissatisfied with his surroundings, and thrown upon his books as the sole companions that afforded him pleasure, for him passed joyless that blooming time of youth from which stronger souls draw profit even amid unfavourable circumstances; and there were developed in him a vanity that exerted itself most strenuously to win the favour of men, and an unnatural affectation—qualities which made him more of a closet student, a servitor of lofty patrons, than an independent man of the world, a *free* man.

In the monastery of Stein (Emaus), near Gouda, he had unwillingly passed five of the best years of his youth, from the age of eighteen to twenty-three, when he was freed from his prison-house by the Archbishop of Cambray. From this time we behold him, the many-gifted and highly-lauded one,

[1] An instance of the cunning of Erasmus is given in the well-known anecdote (MÜLLER, p. 105) of the pear theft committed by him during his residence in the monastery. In the perpetration of this, he endeavoured to cast suspicion upon a lame monk by imitating his limping gait, thus deceiving the prior, who was on the look-out for the thief. The punishment for the crime fell upon the innocent one.

placed upon the stage of the great world, in connection with popes and cardinals, with princes and their ministers, with the greatest scholars and artists of his time. We should be well repaid if we could accompany him on his journeys to Paris, England, Italy, and home again to the Netherlands,—if we could observe him in the circle of his numerous and often aged pupils at Oxford, or in the houses of his illustrious hosts,—Cardinal Wolsey, Sir Thomas More and Warham, in England; Aldus Manutius in Venice; Frobenius and Amerbach in Basel; or at the courts of Henry VIII. and Prince Charles of Brabant,—or if we could examine in detail his literary achievements. But the pleasure that we have unwillingly denied ourselves in Hutten, we must forego in this instance also, since it is our intention not to furnish a complete biography of these men, but only to give prominence to those traits of character or life that have a bearing upon the history of the Reformation, or that exhibit some particular aspect of the reformational spirit. Let us now, as a pendant to the sturdy figure of Hutten, examine the physiognomy of Erasmus.

We have several portraits of Erasmus; of these the one by Holbein, in the museum of Basel, many copies of which are extant, is the most successful. In reference to these portraits, Lavater remarks:[1] "The countenance of Erasmus is one of the most speaking, one of the most expressive [in respect to the character of the man] that I know. Different as are the faces of these various portraits, there is common to them all a pose of feature indicative of timidity, hesitancy, circumspectness; there is in all a humorous curve about the mouth, a free glance in the eye. They all bear the same expression of manifoldness of thought, of timidity, of naivete, humour. There is nowhere to be seen a trait telling of a boldness that would rush upon an adversary and crush him. There is in the eye the calm serenity of the acute observer who perceives and takes in all things. That half-closed eye, of such a depth and shape, is surely such as always belongs to the subtile and

[1] In his *Physiognomy* (comp. ADOLF MÜLLER, p. 108).

clever schemer. That nose, according to all my observations, is assuredly that of a man of keen intellect and delicate sensibilities. The gentle compression of the lips, the broad chin which is yet neither flat nor fleshy, the multitudinous expression about the entire face, correspond excellently with the rest, and are indicative of reflection and quiet activity. The furrows on the brow are usually no very favourable token; they are almost invariably the sign of some weakness, some carelessness, supineness, or laxness in the character. We learn, however, from this picture that they are to be found in some great men."

The physiognomist's last remark about the furrows on the brow applies with equal force to the furrows in character; these also may not unfrequently be found in great, or at least in celebrated, people, and they are, unfortunately, present in Erasmus. Yet let not the furrows hinder us from recognising the more delicate groundwork of his soul, nor let the shadows that we may observe make us forget the light that from his mind streamed forth over Europe.

Erasmus was, to complete his picture,[1] small in stature, weakly, but well formed, with fair complexion, light hair, and blue eyes. He was dignified in his bearing, and dressed with neatness and elegance. His face and voice were agreeable and full of expression. He had an antipathy to everything rude, awkward, or common. A finer kind of sensuality was naturally connected with his sensitive nerves, whilst those grosser excesses which in his day were not uncommon even among the clergy disgusted him. His delicate health and pampered youth made him dependent upon a thousand little minutiæ; and instead of vigorously overcoming these peculiarities, he seemed with egotistical vanity to delight in them. The mere smell of fish, for instance, made him ill; he could not endure any wine but Burgundy. The atmosphere of our stove-heated rooms set his nerves on edge. Every draught

---

[1] Much of the above is taken from Müller; some is the result of personal study of Holbein's portrait of Erasmus; and some is drawn from passages in his letters.

occasioned him a fever. Riding on horseback was a necessity to him, but every other physical exercise he shunned. He himself confesses that in his youth he shuddered at the bare name of death; it was natural enough that he should in later years jestingly declare that he was not born to be a martyr.

And yet, who has not felt attracted by the grace of his polished intellect, the tender sensibility of his soul, his enlightened and moderate way of thinking, which was only occasionally, and by reason of a morbid untuning of his nature, exchanged for a momentary bitterness, whereby the most disagreeable contrast between his conduct and his amiable maxims was called forth? We use the word "maxims" purposely, because "principles" appears to us too strong; the latter were precisely what he lacked, if by them we understand not simply the uppermost intellectual tenets of his moral system, but the pillars of his soul, the bearers of his will. His powerful memory, his facile grasp of a subject and skill in its presentation, his versatile fancy, and, above all, his wit, more playful and sparkling than striking and trenchant,[1] were the qualities that made him the most fertile and ingenious author of his time, the favourite of all persons of culture. Erasmus was no man of the people.

If we ask what was the quality of this man's Christianity, it may be replied that it was verily neither the fiery, vigorous Christianity of Peter and Paul, nor the profound, clear, fervently-loving Christianity of John. It was more an external connection with the Church, the result of education, habit, and a certain respect for everything good, than an internal, vital connection with Christ, that made Erasmus a Christian. He was almost entirely deficient in what we call *mysticism*, taking the word in a good as well as in a bad sense; in him the rational faculties were decidedly predominant. At the most he had but a few dashes of mysticism in his composition, as a

---

[1] The view of MÜLLER, who (p. 112) denies that he possessed any claim to wit, may, in accordance with indications furnished by that author himself, thus be modified. His was, we admit, not the trenchant and sarcastic wit of Hutten.

fruit of his many-sided reading. His *feeling* was of a moral and æsthetic rather than of a purely religious character. By virtue of this nice moral feeling, however, he was able to grasp and to represent the moral ideas and relations of Christianity in a delicate manner, and one which was often beneficial to the inner life. His piety, when he shows us the man, is as frequently childlike and honest, as it is strained and ambiguous when he exhibits the cautious theologian. In cases where religion relates simply to his own individual personality, it serves, in those better moods in which he was not lacking, to glorify his being. He is moved with gratitude at the reception of benefits, and on such occasions shrinks not from the reproach of superstition.[1] But to grasp religion as the supreme yearning of mankind after God, to resign himself entirely to religion, to think of himself only in connection with the grand whole—in connection with the kingdom of God—and to sacrifice all things to that, to subordinate his own individuality to the public good, was something to which neither his *con amore* study of the ancients nor his philosophical Christianity had led him.

Nevertheless Erasmus did, in various modes, prepare the way for the Reformation, although more indirectly than directly. If the revival of learning was in general favourable to the Reformation (although not the exclusive cause of it), Erasmus was, in his relation to this revival, of essential service to the Reformation. He it was who, like the Humanists, who looked up to him with admiration, still further perfected the study of the Greek language and literature, in the interests of which Valla and Reuchlin had already laboured, and who, especially by his Greek edition of the New Testament,—prepared in Basel, and the original of Luther's translation,—aided in placing the divine word, in its primitive purity, once more in the hands of men. He it was who revived a sense for the beauties of Roman and Greek antiquity, and who set the grand and godlike traits which are to be found even among the

[1] Comp. the *Ode to Saint Genevieve*, already referred to, MÜLLER, p. 116.

heathen—in Cicero and Plutarch, for instance—in a friendly light. He it was, again, who freed the study of theology from the shackles of Scholasticism, and introduced a more elegant treatment of sacred themes. He it was, also, who, like Reuchlin and other contemporaries, with satirical sharpness laid bare the doings of the monks, against whose calling and character he entertained a peculiar prejudice, and brought ridicule upon a multitude of the infirmities of the age. Mere ridicule, it is true, is not medicine—nay, it may often effect more harm than good. But where it precedes a more serious treatment, it is like the aquafortis that the engraver uses to prepare the way for his burin, in order that he may more distinctly and permanently trace upon the surface before him the objects which he wishes to represent.

One of the most celebrated works of Erasmus is *The Praise of Folly*. This he is said to have composed partly in the saddle and partly on shipboard, on the occasion of his second journey to England, where he completed it in a few days in the house of the Chancellor, Sir Thomas More.[1] In this book he ridicules the follies of the different classes, and especially those of the clergy and the monks, as well as the pedantry of the Schoolmen and the superstition of the common people. Although Erasmus in this work transgresses the bounds of decency far more seldom than many of his contemporaries, the book is, nevertheless, not free from obscenities; and at times his sarcasm in regard to religious matters so nearly approaches frivolity, that an inexperienced person might be doubtful as to whether his irony is aimed at the abuses of religion or at religion itself. The library of Basel possesses the copy in which are the pen-and-ink marginal sketches by Holbein.

Basel became the second home of the great man, after many wanderings through the half of Europe. He frequently had the

---

[1] Sir Thomas More was himself one of the men who lashed the follies of the age with a Lucian-like satire. In his *Utopia* (1516) he treated the monks as worthless vagabonds.

offer of important situations. In Rome the pope wished to confer upon him a high and lucrative ecclesiastical office, merely to keep him in his vicinity. England and the Netherlands disputed for the honour of possessing him. But Erasmus, with his inclination for personal independence and undisturbed leisure, preferred to spend the evening of his days in a city which was free both in its relations to the outer world and in its constitution, which was surrounded by a rich and beautiful country, enlivened by a burgher population made flourishing by its industrial activity, and at the same time the seat of learning and, together with a few of its equals, the ornament of the century. The University was now at the height of its bloom. Erasmus did not, indeed, enter it as a professor; he was, however, on friendly terms with its professors, and was visited by all who repaired to Basel on account of its University.[1] From the year 1516 Erasmus was an inmate of the house of Frobenius.

He writes thus to a friend:[2] "I seem to myself to be in the most delightful museum, not to mention to you all the numerous and great men of learning (with whom I hold intercourse). Every one understands Latin and Greek, and the generality are acquainted with Hebrew also. This man is distinguished in history, that one in theology. Here is a fine mathematician, here a diligent antiquarian, there a (distinguished) jurisconsult. How rare such an assemblage is, you yourself know. For my own part" (thus speaks the travelled Erasmus), "so happy a meeting has never before fallen to my

[1] At that time, Wyttenbach and Capito were professors of theology, Glareau (Loroti) of philosophy, Pellican of the Oriental languages, Amerbach of jurisprudence, etc.

[2] *Ad Sapidum* (*Epp.* lib. i. p. 58, in the edition of Frobenius): "Nam mihi prorsus in amoenissimo quopiam Museo versari videor, ut ne dicam eruditos tam multos et eruditos tam non vulgari more. Nemo Latine nescit, nemo Graece nescit, plerique et Hebraice sciunt; hic in historiae cognitione praecellit, ille callet theologiam; hic mathematices peritus est, alius antiquitatis studiosus, ille juris consultus. Jam hoc quam sit rarum, ipse nosti. Mihi certe hactenus non contigit in aeque felici versari contubernio. Verum, ut haec sileantur, qui candor omnium, quae festivitas, quae concordia! Unum omnibus animum esse jures."

lot. But setting aside this (these scientific advantages), what candour rules over all, what friendliness, what concord! You would swear that they were all of one mind."

In Basel, however, where he experienced such happiness, the storms of the Reformation reached him as he was already beginning to advance in years. On the theatre of that grand event we shall again behold him in collision with Luther.

In a similar, and yet, again, in an entirely different mode from that of Hutten, Erasmus also had laid bare the mischiefs of the age[1] and pointed out their appropriate remedies. These latter he found not in the heart of the *German* people (as a Netherlander he was an alien to them, and did not even understand their language; he spoke and wrote in Latin), but in the thorough culture of science, above all in a theology purified from Scholastic rubbish and united to a grammatico-historical understanding of the Bible. Contrasted with the defiant language of Hutten, the reformational ideas of Erasmus certainly appear very tame; but we shall always consider with sincere delight the hints which, in his preface to the second edition of the New Testament, he gave to the student of theology of his own time,[2] and in which he recommended a comprehensive study of the Holy Scriptures, supported by a

[1] In his ridicule of the monks and of superstition, he stands upon the same ground with Hutten and the *Letters of Obscure Men*. In the dialogue entitled *The Corpse*, he describes two dying men. One, a quondam warrior, the owner of much unrighteously acquired property, sends for a body of monks, dies under the cowl of the Franciscans, bequeaths all his possessions to that order, in whose church he directs that he shall be buried, and compels his wife and children to devote themselves to a religious life. The other, an upright, decent man, dies without any parade, trusting in the merits of Christ, and, having already done much good in his lifetime, leaves not a penny to the cloisters. Conscientious scruples relative to fasting he also presents in a ridiculous and extravagant light. Thus he depicts a sick man who, in spite of the advice of his physician, refuses to eat eggs, or food of which milk is a component part, because he will break his vow, whilst, at the same time, he has no scruples about committing perjury to clear himself from accusation. Finally, no one has more effectually than Erasmus exposed the degeneracies of Scholasticism to the ridicule of rational minds.

[2] *Ratio seu methodus compendio perveniendi ad veram theologiam*, 1519 (at the same time at which Hutten wrote his *Vadiscus*); published singly in 1522.

knowledge of the exact and historical sciences. His sole aim in this recommendation was not the acquisition of learning, as might be suspected; he claims that all theological study should result in the passing into the life of the person engaged therein of all that he has read and pondered over in pious moods; for, as he says, it is not the correct presentation of a syllogism, but, rather, the life of morality and piety, that makes the theologian. Erasmus desired, moreover, that the better knowledge of salvation should not be confined to theologians; he, too, had a heart for the needs of the Christian *people*. Accordingly, in his preface to the *Paraphrase of the New Testament*, he characterises as Jewish narrow-mindedness the desire to conceal the mysteries of the gospel from the people. It is true, he says, that in former days the high priest alone went into the holy of holies; now, however, the veil is rent, and there is access for all unto Christ, the true high priest. Some are disturbed, he continues, because women and cobblers now converse about the Holy Scriptures. " I would rather hear unlearned maidens talk of Christ than certain rabbins who pass for men of high attainments." Erasmus even expressed the wish that the Scriptures might be translated into all languages. He was also equally desirous, however, of as wide a diffusion of that enlightenment which springs from a study of the classics. "Amongst all writings," he declares, in his *Familiar Conversations*,[1] "the Holy Scriptures are, indubitably, entitled to the first and highest consideration; but there is also in the writings of the heathen and the ancient poets so much that strikes me as so chaste, so holy, so truly God-like, that I am constrained to suppose that the hearts of the men who gave utterance to such things were the subjects of divine influence. The Spirit of Christ is, perchance, more widely diffused than we imagine, and many [will] appear amongst the saints whose names are not written in my calendar. I often can scarce refrain from exclaiming, ' O holy Socrates, pray for us!' "

[1] *Colloq. famil.* (*Convivium religiosum*).

Erasmus was the most lauded man of his time—the *king*, to whom the princes of learning, the Humanists, came from all directions, to do him homage. He was almost, indeed, exalted into a divinity. Eoban Hesse, prince of the poets of that period, actually called him a "divine being." In the year 1518, Hesse, accompanied by a friend, travelled on foot to the Netherlands in order that he might see face to face the great Rotterdamer, who was ill and suffering at that time; and a similar pilgrimage was undertaken a year later by the subsequent friend and associate of Luther, Justus Jonas, also in company with a friend. They shrank not from the hardships of the journey, which "led through so many forests, and so many cities smitten with contagious disorders," and would, as the travelling companion of Jonas, in his extravagant letter to Erasmus, affirms, have visited him "if he had been sojourning in the uttermost borders of India, or in distant Thule, instead of in the Netherlands."

Camerarius, the biographer of Melanchthon, thus writes concerning the Erasmus worship which prevailed in Erfurt: "He was applauded like a learned and artistic player on the stage of letters. Every one who would not be thought a stranger in the kingdom of the Muses admired, glorified, and extolled him. The age was congratulated on its possession of him. If any one was able to charm forth a letter from him, vast was the fame of that person and great the triumph that was celebrated. But if any was so lucky as to be favoured with a personal encounter and conversation with Erasmus, he esteemed himself one of the blessed of the earth."[1] It will be seen from this that even superior men of sprightly intellect, and fitted to take an active part in the affairs of the time, were travelling the down-hill road of human deification and of a new hero worship, second in no particular to that of the heathen. And yet all who devoted themselves to this worship would fain be accounted good Christians. Not one

[1] Pressel, in his *Life of Jonas*, p. 8.

would in any degree renounce Christianity. Each soul would have shrunk back in horror at the very thought of so doing. Here, certainly, there is a discord — one, however, which escaped the consciousness of even the most penetrating minds of the period.

A mingling of the humanly beautiful and great, that attracts us in the philosophers and poets of antiquity, with that which is peculiarly divine in its character, and which is to be found in biblical revelation,—or, we might rather say, that immediate juxtaposition of the two which reminds us of the temple of Alexander Severus, in which the statue of Christ stood side by side with the heathen divinities,—meets us almost universally in the "Humanists" of the fifteenth and sixteenth centuries.[1] Not even Hutten was free from it. And we can well imagine that susceptible and excitable minds felt a drawing toward both sides—toward the classics and toward biblical Christianity—as contrasted with what the fallen Church had been able to offer to souls that were yearning after higher ideals. It was a long time before the separation of the two was effected, before each was duly appreciated in its proper place and connection, before the thoughts of God were understood—those thoughts which are visible in the revival of letters as well as in the restoration of the gospel, but which are by no means mingled together in an arbitrary manner, destructive of all historical propriety.

Accordingly, we have felt constrained to reckon all the historical matter that we have hitherto presented, even though it might lie on this side of the boundary which separates the time of the Reformation from the Middle Ages, as belonging to the *pre-reformational* or *transition* period. The next chapter will bring us nearer to the Reformation of Luther. In the meantime there is one other man whom it is proper for us

---

[1] It is well known that works of art of this period, even tombstones, exhibit this mongrel compound of styles—a compound improper even when regarded only from an æsthetic point of view. Comp., in regard to *tombstones*, the *Christliches Kunstblatt* for 1869, ii. pp. 23 sqq.

to mention,—one who, by his restless activity in educational matters, and by many wholesome reformatory tendencies, has won the right to be numbered among the forerunners and first contemporaries of the Reformation,—we refer to the excellent Alsatian Humanist, Jacob Wimpheling. Born at Schlettstadt, 24th July 1450, he was educated in the school of the Westphalian Dringenberg, agreeably to the mode of those institutions which the Brethren of the Common Life had established in the Netherlands, and which in measure occupied in that period, so greatly deficient in educational advantages, the place of Christian normal schools. The instruction and the impressions which he there received exercised a decisive influence over his entire life, and his character was further stimulated by Geiler of Kaisersberg, to whom he listened in Freiburg. In Heidelberg, Wimpheling commenced the study of canon law, by the aid of which he might easily have succeeded in obtaining a lucrative benefice. But, mindful of the saying of the Lord, "What shall it profit a man if he shall gain the whole world and lose his own soul?" he turned his attention to theology. The mysticism of Gerson was especially attractive to him. Impregnated with his ideas, he could calmly witness the controversies of Realists and Nominalists without participating in them himself. He also formed a connection with the Humanists, but was withheld by his piety from a one-sided worship of classical paganism. He recommended a cautious use of the classics even in the schools, and laid more weight upon the fact of their contributing to the formation of style than upon their being promotive, in any manner, of the moral advance of humanity. Virgil alone, he, like so many churchmen of the Middle Ages, regarded as standing almost in the same rank with Christian writers.

After preaching in the cathedral of Speier and lecturing before the Faculty of Arts in Heidelberg, he again took up an idea, which he had previously entertained, of retiring from the world, in company with his friend Christopher of Utenheim, the subsequent Bishop of Basel. At a later period, however, he assisted the latter in the preparation of the synodal statutes, which were designed to introduce an ecclesiastical reform in the diocese of Basel. The reformational domain in which Wimpheling displayed peculiar talent and adroitness was that of schools and education. Amongst his Strassburg pupils we observe one Jacob Sturm, the afterwards celebrated burgomaster, who eventually turned more decidedly to the Reformation than his former teacher, to whom age brought an increase of caution. When warned against heresy by Wimpheling, Sturm replied, "If I am a heretic, you have made me one." It fared with Wimpheling as with many others at that time. He had deeply felt the failings of the Church; he had disputed with the monks;[1] he had even helped the Emperor Maximilian I. to compose a treatise complaining of the encroachments of the papal court, and urging the abolition of various abuses. But the movement which began with Luther, and which was at first joyfully greeted by Wimpheling, grew beyond the latter, and left him standing midway between the old and the new. Toward the end of the year 1515, he retired to the house of his sister at Schlettstadt, where, surrounded by a circle of aspiring and diligent youths, he passed the remainder of his years. He died, weary of life, on the 17th of November 1528. He was wont daily to pray, "Gracious Jesus, be merciful to me, a poor sinner, who am a lover of the common weal, the unity of Christians, the Holy Scriptures, and the good education of youth." Of the three great men whose characters we have just been considering, each one, in his own manner, expressed his recognition of the merits of Wimpheling. The learned Reuchlin extolled him as a foundation pillar of religion; honest Hutten declared that he strove only after the holy, and that not only himself, but all the youth of Germany,

---

[1] The dispute turned, amongst other things, upon the highly important question as to whether St. Augustine was himself a mendicant monk and wore a hood, or not!

owed much to him; and even the penetrating Erasmus, who, in the lifetime of Wimpheling, ridiculed his reformational zeal (because he fought so vehemently against the concubinage of the priests), bestowed the amplest encomium upon him after his death.[1]

[1] Comp. C. SCHMIDT, art. "Wimpheling," in Herzog's *Realenc.* xviii. pp. 168 sqq.

CHAPTER IV.

THE DUMB COMEDY—LUTHER: HIS HISTORY DOWN TO THE POSTING OF HIS THESES AND THE COMMENCEMENT OF THE REFORMATION.

WHILST the Emperor Charles v. was in attendance at the Diet of Augsburg in 1530, some persons (so the story runs) were announced who desired that they might be allowed to perform, for the after-dinner amusement of the emperor and his brother Ferdinand, a *dumb comedy*, or pantomime. Permission being granted them, there first appeared on the scene a masked individual, habited in the ordinary garb of a doctor, and having the name Capnio (the Greek name of Reuchlin) written on his back. He carried a bundle of straight and crooked sticks, which he threw down in the middle of the room, and retired. He was followed by another person, clad as a secular ecclesiastic, and bearing the name of Erasmus, who endeavoured to arrange the scattered sticks in an orderly manner, and to bend the crooked ones straight. Perceiving the fruitlessness of the attempt, however, he shook his head with vexation and departed. Upon this there appeared, in the attire of a monk, Dr. Martin Luther, who set fire to the crooked sticks, and when the flame shot up withdrew. Next entered a person dressed as the emperor, who, when he saw the fire consuming the crooked sticks, thrust at it with his sword, which, instead of extinguishing the flame, did but fan it into greater violence. Finally the pope appeared. Clasping his hands above his head in terror, he looked about for means to quench the conflagration. At some distance stood two pails, one filled with oil and the other with water. In his anxiety he seized the oil and poured it upon the flame. The fire gained ground; the actors availed themselves of the confusion which arose among the spectators to make good their escape, and when inquiry was made for them they were nowhere to be found.

Be the anecdote true or false,[1] the pantomime here described represents, in a brief and striking manner, the history of the German Reformation. Reuchlin and Erasmus, who occupied our attention in the preceding chapter, had gathered the sticks together for the flame, and fruitlessly striven to make the crooked straight. But the spark that Luther cast into the midst of the dry and rotten fuel, ignited, and neither emperor nor pope was able to restrain the giant flame, which they did but steadily increase by their opposition.

Parables and images such as the above were rife at this period. Amongst other things, it was said that Erasmus *laid the egg* and Luther *hatched it*. Erasmus maintained, however, that the chicken egg which he had laid was developed by Luther into a bird that differed totally from the tame and gentle chicken; the man who has gone as far as the bank of a river cannot possibly, said he, be regarded as the predecessor of him who plunges headlong into the midst of the flood.

Hence it is that we, as we have already remarked, begin the *actual history of the Reformation*, in the narrower sense of the term, with Luther himself.

We stand at present at the portal of that history, and standing thus, our feet are on the threshold of a poverty-stricken house in Eisleben, in the county of Mansfeld. Here, on the 10th of November 1483,[2] Martin Luther was

---

[1] Its first appearance, so far as I am aware, is in the *Vita Reuchlini* of MAJUS (Durlach, 1687), p. 546; it is found also in MAYERHOFF, p. 79, and in ADOLF MÜLLER, p. 358. Majus does not mention the scene of the occurrence, but the year (1530) warrants the inference that it happened at Augsburg. At that time comedies were frequently enacted, upon solemn occasions, by the burghers of cities.

[2] There is no proof that the parents of Martin were, at the time of his birth, attending the *annual fair* at Eisleben, as was for a time supposed. Comp. LINKE, *Martin Luther's merkwürdige Reisegeschichte zur Ergänzung seiner*

born.[1] His father, Hans Luther, a native of Möra, near Salzungen, was a miner. He seems, at a later period, to have raised himself to circumstances of some comfort by the acquisition of a smelting furnace of his own, and this supposition is further strengthened by the fact that he was made a member of the council of Mansfeld. In earlier life, however, Luther's parents (the maiden name of his mother, the daughter of a burgher of Eisenach, was Margaret Lindemann) were country people, and in needy circumstances. Martin himself, moved by filial gratitude, relates: "My father was a poor peasant, and my mother has repeatedly carried upon her back the wood that my father would cut, by the sale of which they brought up us children. They spared no toil in our behalf." The home training of the Luthers was, in accordance with the spirit of the age, pious and honest; they were brought up in obedience to the precepts of the Church, but rough and severe. Luther says, in his *Table Talk*, that his father

Lebensumstände, Leipsic, 1769, p. 3. The stay of the Luthers at Eisleben was, however, in any case a short one, for Martin himself says that he was born at Eisleben, but brought up in Mansfeld. In modern times (1867) the hypothesis has even been advanced that the family was a noble one; it is claimed that a Fabian von Luther was, in 1413, raised by the Emperor Sigismund to the rank of baron, and created count-palatine. In order to harmonize the contradiction which this story presents to that which is known of Luther's parental house, and which savours more of the plebeian than the patrician order, it was assumed as a historical certainty that Hans Luther, upon one occasion, slew, in anger, a peasant who was working in the field, and was in consequence obliged to become a fugitive from his home—a romantic incognito!

On the life of Luther, compare, in addition to the *Sermons* of MATTHESIUS, and older works, together with the biographies of SPIEKER, UKERT, TISCHER, etc., GUSTAV PFIZER, *M. Luther's Leben*, Stuttgart, 1836; JÜRGENS, *Luther's Leben*, 1846 (unfinished, alas!); GELZER, *Dr. Martin Luther, der deutsche Reformator. Mit bildlichen Darstellungen von* GUSTAV KÖNIG, Hamburg, 1851, 4to; D. SCHENKEL, *Die Reformatoren und die Reformation*, Wiesbaden, 1856, and *Luther und seine Kampfgenossen*, Lahr, 1868; HOFF, *Vie de Martin Luther*, Paris, 1860; J. KÖSTLIN's article in Herzog's *Realenc.* viii. pp. 568 sqq.; H. W. J. THIERSCH, *Luther, Gustav Adoph und Maximilian I. von Baiern*, Nördlingen, 1869. Of the different editions of the works of Luther, the one published at Erlangen is now the most generally diffused. We have sometimes adopted the citations given by WALCH. Luther's *Letters* are quoted from DE WETTE's edition.

[1] The name [of *Luther*] imports the same as *Lothar*, an appellation borne as early as in the third century before Christ by the chief of the German tribe called the Tectosages. Even in Luther's day, the spelling of the word was not fixed; it fluctuated between Lutter, Lotter, Luder, etc.

once chastised him so harshly that he ran away from him, and it was some time before his resentment could be appeased; whilst his mother on one occasion beat him until the blood came, for stealing a nut. He remarks, in this connection, that too much severity in the training of children is not good. "My parents," says he, "had the best intentions in the world, but they possessed none of that discrimination of character by which punishment should be regulated;" the apple [reward] should, he thinks, always accompany the rod.

After having acquired, from a crabbed schoolmaster[1] in the town of Mansfeld, the first elements of human learning, he was sent, in his fourteenth year, to the school of the Franciscans at Magdeburg. One of the lecturers of this institution was Andreas Proles, a liberal-minded man. Whether Luther had the benefit of listening to his instructions cannot be ascertained.[2] In Eisenach, whither he soon afterwards repaired, to be near some relatives on his mother's side who were residing there, he was forced to earn his bread by singing from door to door. Frau Cotta, a pious woman whose name is well worthy of being preserved in history, admitted to her table the young student, by whose fine alto she had been edified, and constituted herself his patroness. And, truly, what she did unto this *little one* amongst the servants of the Lord, she did unto *Him*, the Lord of the Church. Luther remained four years in Eisenach at the Franciscan school, where, under the guidance of the learned rector Trebonius,[3] he distinguished himself far

---

[1] The surliness of this schoolmaster may be inferred from the fact that in one forenoon Luther was flogged by him fifteen times in succession. "The schools," says Luther at a later period, "were, previous to this time, regular dungeons and hells; the poor children who attended them were beaten immoderately and incessantly. They studied with great labour and excessive diligence, but with little profit."

[2] H. A. PRÖHLE, *Andreas Proles, Vicarius der Augustiner, ein Zeuge der Wahrheit, kurz vor Luther*, Gotha, 1867.

[3] This man treated his pupils humanely, in antithesis to the prevailing tyranny of the schools. When he went into the classroom he was accustomed to take off his hat to the scholars, remarking, upon one occasion, to his assistants, "There are boys sitting here of whom God will make burgomasters, chancellors, and doctors."

above his fellow-students. Upon reaching the age of eighteen, he entered the University of Erfurt, the fame of which was just then very great, insomuch that all the other schools of Germany sank into insignificance beside it, being, in comparison with it, "mere primary schools" ["*kleine Schützenschulen*"], as Luther says. His stay at this University had, in various respects, a decisive influence over his future life. In the first place, it was here, in the library of the University, that he for the first time met with a whole copy of the Bible. This circumstance gave him extraordinary joy, and his desire for a complete and thorough knowledge of the holy book continually increased with its perusal. Again, it was here that, in 1503, he was afflicted with a severe illness, which became for him a rigorous trial school. An aged priest visited him during this illness, and comforted him with the following words: "My baccalaureate, be of good cheer, you will not die this time; our Lord God will yet make a great man of you, and you will comfort many people." Luther did indeed recover, and afterward remembered these words, which the religious feeling of the time regarded as a prophecy. Finally, he here met with an experience which suddenly gave to his choice and inclination a different direction from that contemplated by his parents. In accordance with the wish of the latter, he had purposed becoming a jurist, and hoped one day to fill a public office. But Luther had a friend, Alexis by name, to whom he was united by the tenderest affection. On the day before the Visitation of Mary (1505), this young man was violently torn from his side—some say by lightning, whilst others relate that he was stabbed, but that shortly afterwards a flash of lightning struck the ground close by Luther's side—as he was in the vicinity of Suternheim. However this may be, the powerful impression which both events—the death of Alexis and his own narrow escape from death by lightning—made upon his mind caused him to recognise in them an intimation from on high that he should henceforth consecrate his life to God. He, therefore, after giving a farewell entertainment to his friends, entered a cloister of the Augustinian order at Erfurt, without the consent or knowledge of his father, to whom the reception of the secular raiment and the master's ring of his son occasioned no small grief. Luther himself, after he had become acquainted with the full extent of the injury which monkish self-righteousness inflicts upon the soul, repented of this step, and, although a man of recognised importance at the time, formally asked his father's forgiveness in a letter.[1] He represents his action as a work of Satan, who blinded him with spiritual pride, and led him to lose sight of God's greatest commandment, that enjoining reverence and obedience toward parents. It is admissible for us to think that Luther judged himself, in this instance, with undue severity. In the course of time, when he had acquired a clearer insight into his own heart, it doubtless occurred to him that he might have acted, upon that occasion, from an impure impulse; and being accustomed to use severity in his judgment of the moral motives of men,—his own as well as others,—it may readily have appeared to him that it would be a wholesome humiliatory exercise to lay bare the secret blemishes and failings of even the more noble impulses of his youth. If, however, Luther was justified in passing such a sentence upon himself, *we* have no right to imitate him in this respect. We are constrained to the supposition that he took this decisive step from a true zeal for the service of God; that it was an unenlightened and misguided zeal we do not pretend to deny. We must go still farther, however, and recognise in his action the leading of a higher power; for it was precisely by his experience of the hard school of convent life that Luther was prepared to become the earnest and thorough Reformer that he was. There is usually nothing that we combat with more success than a thing which we at first embraced with love and enthusiasm, from which we anticipated everything fair and good, but by which we at last perceived ourselves to have been terribly deceived. How different was

[1] *Luther's Briefe, Sendschreiben und Bedenken von* DE WETTE, vol. ii. No. 348.

Luther's course in this particular from that of Erasmus! The latter had always, from worldly-mindedness, entertained an aversion to a cloistral life; he was never heartily and thoroughly a monk—he did but play the monk for a time whilst he wore the monkish hood; and so his subsequent attacks upon monasticism were chiefly those of wit and pleasantry, or of a worldly vexation at things with whose *innermost* and *deepest* nature he was unacquainted. But Luther had, I might say, passed through the very soul of monasticism; he had surrendered himself completely, in all love, to the cloistral mode of thought and life; and when, at a later period, he, not in levity, but with a bleeding heart, cast from him the member that offended him, he stood a proven hero on the battle-ground, and spoke from his own experience. Luther was not to hasten to his goal on the smooth and pleasant path of science and art, or on the light wings of jest; *he* was to climb the steep and rugged ascent to the stars, to enter through sorrows and tribulations into the kingdom of truth, the kingdom of God. Let not this be forgotten by those who regard the Reformation as the offspring of mere mental illumination, and as consisting purely in negation. As of old the Apostle Paul could say that he had been the most zealous Jew, the most zealous champion of the law, but that through the grace of God he had died unto the law *through* the law, so Luther could testify concerning himself that he had, from conviction, been a good Catholic and pious monk until God caused the scales to fall from his eyes.[1]

Brother Martin[2] was, in his novitiate, treated with great

---

[1] Here is his own testimony concerning himself: "Of a truth, I have been a pious monk, and kept, more strictly than I can tell, to the laws of my order. If ever a monk reached heaven by monkery, I also would have got there. All who knew me in the cloister will bear me witness that this is so; for had I persevered much longer, I should have killed myself with watching, praying, reading, and other labours" (*Luther's Werke*, T. xxi., Lips., p. 21; comp. KEIL, *Lebensumstände*, etc., pp. 15 sqq.). "Our adversaries do not believe," he remarks in another place, "that we toiled so heartily, and even to the death, only that we might secure rest and peace for our hearts and consciences in the sight of God; and yet that peace we could nowhere find in such horrible darkness."

[2] Subsequently he assumed, as a monk, the name of Augustine.

harshness in the cloister. He was obliged to perform the most menial offices, and to wander through the city with a bag, begging. Everything that was required of him he did, true to his vows of poverty and obedience. But the third vow—that of temperance—he observed with still greater strictness. He macerated his body to the utmost by fasting and night-watching. Often he contented himself for an entire day with a little bread and a herring. At the same time he kept his mind constantly exercised, either by prayer and meditation or by scientific speculation. The Church Fathers, and especially the works of the patron of his order, St. Augustine, were read by him with great eagerness, as were also the works of the previously mentioned mystics, the writings of Tauler and Thomas à Kempis, and the *Theologia Germanica*, which last he published in 1516 with a preface. His favourite book even now, however, was the Bible, an entire copy of which he found in the library of the convent also: *it* was the treasure from which he nevermore parted; *it*, the sacred thing into whose spirit he sought to press further and further; *it*, that higher wisdom, the meaning and consistent tenor of which he strove to realize more and more fully in his life. And thus it became also the foundation-stone of Protestantism!

The infallible result of the strenuous exertions and rigorous abstinences of Luther was the prostration of his body, and in the sufferings of the physical man the soul took part. Luther was attacked by a severe illness. His imagination, disordered by weakness and disease, painted the terrors of hell in glowing colours to his mind. The anguish of his soul rose often to the highest pitch, his whole body trembled feverishly; his condition was fearful. Whilst he was thus afflicted, the Vicar-General of his order, John von Staupitz, a Misnian nobleman, visited him. This man, who possessed "high intellectual powers and an honest, upright, noble disposition,"[1]

---

[1] It is thus that MATTHESIUS, in his twelfth sermon on the life of Luther, describes Staupitz. Even MAIMBURG, the Roman Catholic, speaks of him in

had, as a true "experimental theologian and a biblico-practical mystic," himself discovered and appropriated the foundation upon which the soul needs to rest; and he lifted up the despairing young man with gentle words of encouragement and consolation, and taught him to look in faith to the end of his trials, the conqueror's crown that awaited him.¹ He strengthened him, moreover, in his purpose of reading the Holy Scriptures, and gave him such directions as might enable him to do this in an intelligent manner and in connection. Nor did this noble helper rest here. The fine abilities of Luther and his pure and pious zeal had not escaped his eye, and he sought to provide him with a sphere of action better fitted to these gifts. An opportunity for the accomplishment of this desire speedily presented itself.

Not long before (in 1502), the University of Wittenberg had been founded by Frederick the Wise, Elector of Saxony. In this enterprise Staupitz had been of essential service to his prince, and it was in the new University that he now sought to establish his favourite, an endeavour in which he was finally successful. In the year 1507, Luther was consecrated to the priesthood, and thus obtained the right to enter the pulpit. This, however, he dared not do. Luther, who subsequently preached with so much power,—who gave a new direction, and a force and elevation never before attained, to the whole system of German preaching,—who is still the

---

this wise: *Erat hic vir ingenio pollens, magnæ dignationis, industrius eloquens, corporis forma conspicuus, multumque a Friderico, Saxoniæ duce, æstimatus, a quo in consilium adhibebatur.* Comp. in regard to him, ULLMANN, *Reformatoren vor der Reformation,* ii. p. 257, where also other books that have reference to him are mentioned.

¹ Staupitz jestingly and good-humouredly remarked to him, "Thou wouldst fain be sinless, and thou hast no real sins; thou shouldst have a register with genuine sins in it: if Christ is to help thee, thou must have something else to show than such botchy and baby sins as these" [*Humpelwerk und Puppensünden*]. This pleasantry had, however, no more effect upon Luther, in his deep affliction, than had the consolation offered him by his confessor: "God is not angry with thee; thou art angry with God." Greater success attended the efforts of an old monk to whom he confessed, and who, instead of recommending penances and mortifications, pointed him to the Saviour of sinners and His all-sufficient merits. Luther often afterwards spoke of this monk with cordial gratitude.

unparalleled master of all who hope to effect more by the internal demonstrativeness of a discourse than by its external ornamentation,—this Luther was too modest, too humble, to take the place of a preacher. It was only at the solicitation of Staupitz that he finally ventured to preach—at first in the oratory of the convent, and then in church. This natural timidity and bashfulness of the great Reformer are important as throwing light upon his character and work. They prove him not to have been one of those forward declaimers who think that they cannot soon enough begin to teach others, before they themselves have learned; nor of those who, trusting in their own understanding and wit, press forward where talent can shine, but draw back where *courage* should achieve. Luther was weak and timid in the flesh, but great and mighty in spirit. When he once laid aside his natural timidity and came forward as a bold combatant, he did it because he believed it to be his duty, because God commanded it, because his conscience urged it. That which is beautiful and truly great in his life, is the fact that he did not stand in his own strength, as a frail and finite creature of his time, but that he was carried and uplifted by the divine idea which animated him. This combination of maidenly modesty and manly defiance, this union of the simplicity of the dove with the boldness of the lion, give to the character of Luther that genuine *Christian* stamp which manifests the exceeding mightiness of God in the weak. Luther, if any, could say with the Apostle Paul, "When I am weak, then am I strong" (2 Cor. xii. 10).

In 1508 Luther received a call to the University of Wittenberg. He was not yet to teach theology, but was to give instruction in those branches of learning which, in accordance with the views then prevalent, were preparatory to the study of theology, viz. physics and dialectics, or, as *we* would say, the purely philosophical sciences. To this restriction, likewise, he submitted himself; but his heart burned, as he assures us, soon to be permitted to teach theology, which, to his mind, was the highest and dearest of studies.[1]

In this particular, also, Luther's inclination is, at first view, seen to be very different from that of Erasmus. The latter regarded science as the highest pursuit, and when he occupied himself with theology, he studied it more as a philologist and philosopher. But to Luther, theology, in its connection with religion, was the final and supreme aim of life; and even when he busied himself with other sciences, it was as a theologian that he engaged in them. We have no intention of saying that all should have the same preference as Luther. It was well that the critico-philosophical tendency of the Humanists and of Erasmus ran parallel with the predominantly theological bias of Luther, and even to the present day the two tendencies must supplement each other in the Church as well as in the scientific world. Nor can we regard Humanism as a heathenish anti-Christianity, as some partial minds consider it. One thing, however, is incontestable—namely, that the Church of Christ, in all times, is profited, not by science, not by culture, wit, and learning alone, but by the true theology of heart and conscience.

Luther was soon permitted to deliver theological lectures on the Bible, and thenceforth laboured, with ever increasing ardour, to advance himself in the study of theology and in the languages requisite for its successful prosecution. Greater and greater became his antipathy to Scholasticism—an antipathy which extended even to Aristotle, who was guiltless of any connection therewith;[2] whilst his preference for the Mystics became continually more positive, although that

---

[1] Compare the letter to Johann Braun in Eisenach (DE WETTE'S *Collection*, vol. i. No. 2).

[2] Luther's harsh strictures upon Aristotle, as well as his unfavourable deliverances concerning the application of philosophy to theology, are explicable on the ground of the impressions which he had received. To those, however, who at the present day, believe, upon his authority, that it is their duty to reprobate the use of the rational faculties in theology, we would say, *Duo cum faciunt idem, non est idem.*

preference was overbalanced by a love for the divine word itself as given in the Holy Scriptures. In 1512 he received his degree of doctor; this, also, it required the persuasions of his friend Staupitz to give him courage to accept.[1]

An event which happened still earlier in the life of Luther, and which we regard as of particular moment, was the journey to Rome which he undertook, in the interests of his order, in the year 1510. This visit gave him an opportunity to inspect, in person, the doings of the Roman court, against which he subsequently directed his attacks. "There he sees," as Matthesius, his biographer, remarks, "the holy father, the pope, and his golden religion and impious courtesans and courtiers—a sight which afterwards strengthened him for his earnest assaults upon Roman abominations and idolatry." When he arrived within sight of the holy city, he fell upon the earth, lifted up his hands, and exclaimed, "I salute thee, holy Rome!" He made the round of all the churches and cloisters, visited the places of pilgrimage, and climbed Pilate's Staircase on his knees. That, at the last place, a voice called to him as from above, "The just shall live by faith," we agree with modern critics in considering doubtful. It does not accord, moreover, with the following remark of his: "I said mass several times at Rome, and I regretted that my father and mother were still living, for I should have liked to release them from purgatory by my masses."[2]

Luther, during his sojourn in Rome, had sad experience of the unbelief and levity of the superior clergy. He, in his

---

[1] The two had a confidential conversation on the subject under a tree in the garden of the convent. When Luther declined, on the plea of being "a sick and weak brother," to accept the proffered dignity, Staupitz answered, in his genial way, "It is plain to be seen that our God will soon have a great deal to do, both in heaven and on earth, and He will therefore be obliged to have many young and industrious doctors through whom He may transact His business. So, whether you live or die, God has need of you in His council" (MATTHESIUS' Sermon i.; ULLMANN, l.c. p. 262).

[2] They still show the little church of Maria del Popolo, where Luther preached, as the guest of the Augustinians in their adjacent inn.

innocence, was as a lamb among wolves. A sincere Catholic at heart, and a zealous son of the Church, he could not understand how the very persons who ought to have been the most pious, could trifle so shockingly with the holy work of God. Upon one occasion, for instance, he was reading mass at Rome, and performing the service with all devoutness, in the most solemn mood, for he was a true believer in the doctrine of transubstantiation. The attendant priests, growing weary, however, whispered to him, "*Passa, passa!* send our dear Mother her Son back speedily," thus alluding, in mockery, to the transubstantiation, in which they did not believe. An equally offensive allusion to this doctrine—which he still regarded as an important one—came to his ears at table; some one related an anecdote of a priest who said to the elements in the Lord's Supper, "Bread thou art, and bread thou shalt remain; wine thou art, and wine thou shalt remain" (*Panis es, panis manebis; vinum es, vinum manebis*), whilst he yet represented to the people that it was the true body and the true blood of Christ that were partaken of. Who knows whether these scoffs, which so deeply wounded the spirit of Luther, may not eventually have contributed to disincline him to the Zwinglian doctrine concerning the Lord's Supper, he confounding it with the unbelieving views above illustrated? Luther subsequently regarded his visit to Rome as a good providence of God; for he said to his friends that he would not have missed this journey for a thousand florins. On the other hand, however, he likewise recognised the danger of a lengthy stay in that city, on which account he was, in after years, accustomed to say, "He who goes to Rome for the first time, seeks a knave; the second time, he finds him; the third time, he brings him back with him." So far as his feelings at the time of his visit are concerned, however, we may say, with Dorner,[1] that he returned home "with his enthusiasm for Rome, as it then was, damped, but still without having inwardly broken with her, or having become

---

[1] *Geschichte der prot. Theologie*, p. 81 (Eng. Trans., 2 vols., Clark).

conscious of any personal dissent from the ways of the Church."

If Luther's journey to Rome was useful in affording him a near view of the Papacy, a visitation of the Thuringian and Misnian cloisters which he undertook in 1516, during the absence of Staupitz, must have served to procure him a closer acquaintance with convent life than he gained during his own abode in a cloister.

This year, 1516, was in all respects a rich year for him—rich not only in external, but also in internal experiences. From it a considerable number of letters have come down to us, which testify both to the order of his studies and to his great humility. He writes thus, under date of 7th April, to George Spelein, an Augustinian monk at Memmingen:[1] "Learn to know Christ the crucified; He is the righteousness for our sins. Strive not after a holiness that would make you seem pure [in your own eyes], so that you would no longer recognise yourself to be a sinner. It is in sinners that Christ wills to dwell." Luther reminds his friend that the more he dwells on this thought, the more patient and forbearing will he be to the brethren. He admonished him to bloom like a rose or a lily amongst thorns, and not himself to become a thorn in impatience.[2] On another occasion he recommends an escaped monk to the prior of an Augustinian monastery in Mentz. He begs him to receive the fallen one again. That a man should fall, he declares, is no wonder; but that, having fallen, he should rise again and remain upright, *is* a wonder. To the fact that Luther had found that peace of God which he so long sought, the following letter (dated 22d June) to Michael Dressel, an Augustinian in Neustadt, testifies:[3]— "You seek peace," he writes, "and strive after it, but not in the right way. You are seeking peace as the *world*, not as *Christ* gives it. Do you, then, not know, dear brother, that the reason why God is so marvellous in His people is because

---

[1] DE WETTE's *Collection*, vol. i. No. 9.   [2] *Ibid.* No. 11.
[3] *Ibid.* No. 15.

He has not placed peace in the midst of peace, but in the midst of all temptations, when He says, 'Rule in the midst of thine enemies!' It is not, therefore, he whom none disquiets that has peace, for such is the peace of the world; but *he* has true peace whom all men and all things (*omnes et omnia*) disquiet, and who, nevertheless, bears all things calmly and joyfully. You say with Israel, 'Peace, peace,' where there is no peace. Say rather with Christ, 'Cross, cross,' and there is no cross; for the cross ceases to be a cross when you can cheerfully say, 'Blessed cross, there is no tree so dear to me as thou!'" The clear views which Luther had already arrived at concerning the doctrine of justificative faith —in which particular he differs from Erasmus—are exhibited in his exceedingly important letter, of 19th October, to Spalatin.[1] He allows, even at this time, of no righteousness save that which proceeds from faith. The virtues of the noblest men—such, for example, as a Fabricius and a Regulus —are in themselves, according to him, as destitute of that righteousness which is well-pleasing in the sight of God as a bramble bush is of figs. We become righteous, he declares, not by doing right, as Aristotle teaches, but only *after* we become righteous *can* we do right. *The man himself must first be changed;* then his works will become different. Abel pleased God before he brought Him offerings and gifts. Well may it seem like boldness that he should venture to dictate to Erasmus in theological matters; his profound earnestness in such matters, however, would not suffer him to bend to human authority.

These and the like deliverances of Luther, dating from the time before the conflict, must be well pondered if we would have a right appreciation of the conflict itself. Prior even to Luther's inauguration of the struggle, he had expressed his reformational principles so far as to declare that the true regeneration of the Church must be the issue of *faith, upon the basis of the word of God.* When, in the autumn of 1516,

[1] DE WETTE's *Collection*, vol. i. No. 22.

the Lateran Synod convened at Rome, Luther sent this programme of reformation to the Provost of Leitzken, who was about to repair thither: above all things, said he, the clergy must commence the reformation by reforming themselves.[1]

The humble opinion which Luther entertained of himself may likewise be gathered from his epistolary effusions of this period. There is no affectation of modesty, but perfect seriousness, in his deprecation, in a letter (of 27th January) to Christopher Scheurl, a jurist of Nuremberg, of all the commendations which the latter had bestowed upon him, whilst he regards the praise accorded to Staupitz as perfectly just and proper.

Let us now follow Luther to the field of battle.

"Nothing in history," says Johann von Müller,[2] "is more remarkable than the spectacle of a single man who, simply through means that lie within the reach of any of us, victoriously combats all the gifts of fortune and all the terrors of human authority. . . . Dr. Martin Luther, professor in the University of Wittenberg, a private individual possessed of intelligence and courage, but having neither extraordinary learning nor a cultivated taste—this man, we say, by dint of sheer heroism, with no other might than that of common sense in his consideration of many weighty subjects, and of truth where he attacked abuses, *gave a new soul and an invincible energy to the half of Europe.*"

It was no will of his own, but the force of circumstances, that led him into the conflict, and duty commanded that he should not shrink from it. The idea of becoming a general reformer of the world never entered into the mind of this modest man. Whilst he found so much still to correct in his own heart and life, why should he concern himself about the business of others? Not even the corruption which he had beheld in Rome, or his observation of the abuses which had elsewhere crept into the Church, suggested to him the thought

[1] HOFF, p. 101.   [2] *Allg. Geschichte*, vol. iii. p. 4.

of becoming a reformer. It was only when he encountered such abuses within his own department, within the sphere of action which God had allotted him, that he felt it to be his bounden duty to oppose those abuses to the full extent of his judgment and ability. Here, also, the truly reformatory character of Luther is exhibited. He does not rummage about in the domains of others and ferret out deficiencies and failings which he thinks himself called upon violently to remove. But when the corruption of others hinders him in the conscientious discharge of his own office,—when the enemy endeavours to make a breach in his own wall,—then he acts upon the defensive. Once upon the battle-field, however, he continues to pursue the enemy, on account of the impossibility of defining with precision the limits of the defensive; and the defensive line of action is then, indisputably, exchanged for the offensive.

It was within his own sphere of duty as a pastor that Luther first encountered the nefarious system of indulgences, together with their mischievous results; the *duty* of interfering, in such case, in defence of the souls committed to his care, was the warranty for his *right* so to do.

Hitherto we have seen Luther quietly and unpretendingly waiting upon his office in Wittenberg. The enemy approaches from without. We have already a general knowledge of the character of this enemy, but are at present called upon to make his nearer acquaintance. It will doubtless be recollected, from our history of the Church in the Middle Ages, that, subsequent to the Crusades, but especially since the time of Boniface VIII., the inventor of the papal jubilee, and under his successors at Avignon, particularly John XXII., the traffic in indulgences had become a regular systematic trade. The more the popes became involved in pecuniary embarrassments, —owing partly to their own fault, and partly to stress of unfavourable circumstances,—the greater became the necessity for the contrivance of artificial means of procuring funds. The popes, moreover, really needed money for several great undertakings. The borders of Christendom were continually harassed by the insidious stratagems of the Turks: it was needful, therefore, that the charitable hearts of Christians should be disposed and won in favour of a Turk tax—*i.e.*, an impost for the conduct of the war that was about to be waged against the Turks. Leo X. was also, as we know, a prince who loved magnificence, a patron of the arts, an encourager of talent. Whilst he permitted the inner structure of the Church of Christ to fall to pieces through religious indifference, he thought it necessary to earn the approbation of men by prosecuting the external construction of the superb Church of St. Peter at Rome, the foundation of which had been laid by his predecessor, Julius II. Thus the building of this gigantic edifice and the waging of war against the Turkish power were the two leading pretexts for the trade. The principles upon which this trade was conducted were as admirable as those governing any financial speculation in the political world of our own day. As the state sometimes finds it expedient to rent out her revenues to collectors, so there was a formal farming of indulgences.[1] Of three commissions amongst which the German districts were distributed, the first embraced the greater part of the upper and lower German dioceses. This commission was superintended by a member of the Roman prelacy, Arcimboldi. The second embraced Austria and Switzerland, and was under the supervision of the Franciscan general, Christian Numai da Forli. The third, finally, embraced the archiepiscopal provinces of Mentz and Magdeburg, and was under the direction of the archbishop and prince-elector, Albert of Mentz. Arcimboldi resigned his commissariat in Germany as early as 1516,[2] whereupon it also devolved upon Albert. The archbishopric of Mentz had, by reason of frequent vacancies, and the yearly pensions

---

[1] For particulars in regard to this matter see RANKE, vol. i. pp. 309 sqq.

[2] Arcimboldi went from Germany to Denmark and Sweden. He subsequently received the bishopric of Novara and the archbishopric of Milan. A proof of his abilities as an extortioner may be found in the fact that he had made for himself at Lubeck a silver salver and silver kettles and pans.

whose payment was thereby rendered necessary, as well as through the expenses of the pallium, incurrred a considerable amount of debt. In the liquidation of this indebtedness, the indulgence monies were to aid. The chief farmers had sub-commissioners under them. Thus Forli had Bernard Samson, whilst the Dominican monk John Tetzel was in the service of the Archbishop of Mentz.

Tetzel (Diez, Dezel), a native of Leipsic, and son of a goldsmith, was a man of unusual talents, and not entirely without learning. He had previously served as sub-commissioner under former commissioners, and had thereby amassed a large fortune; for he was excelled by none in his loud and extravagant recommendations of the indulgences, although his unbridled and scandalous course of life made him odious to all the more religious portion of the people.[1]

We should make a great mistake if we were to conceive of this seller of indulgences as a common pedlar—as a monk who went about on foot and spread his wares before common people at their convenience. This was by no means the case. Tetzel conducted himself, on his commercial journeys, like a high prelate. He drove into the cities in superb style, amidst the pealing of bells. The papal indulgence bull was carried before him on a velvet cushion. Solemn processions, bearing crosses and banners, went to meet him and escorted him into the church. Then a red cross, upon which were the pontifical arms, was set up, and this Tetzel affirmed to be as efficacious as the cross of Christ Himself. One of his train[2] even tried to make the multitude believe that he saw the blood of Christ flowing gently down over it (the red colour of the cross, if steadily gazed upon by the credulous, might easily engender

---

[1] He was, in conformity to the law, to have been drowned for adultery, but his life was spared through the interposition of the elector of Saxony. Comp. in regard to him, F. C. HOFMANN, *Lebensbeschreibung des Ablasspredigers Joh. Tezel*, Leipsic, 1844—on the Protestant side ; on the Catholic side, in defence of him, GRÖNE, *Tezel und Luther*, Soest, 1853.

[2] The Dominican monk Bartholomew (see MARHEINEKE, vol. i. p. 50, and LÖSCHER, vol. i. p. 398).

such an optical illusion). Indulgences were offered upon every condition—even for *future* sins.[1] The little couplet of which the indulgence vendors made use is well known: "When in the chest the coin doth ring, the soul direct to heaven doth spring" [" *Wenn nur das Geld im Kasten ringt, die Seele gleich gen Himmel springt*"].

In the year 1517 Tetzel arrived at Jüterbogk, in the neighbourhood of Wittenberg, in which latter place Luther was acting as doctor of theology and pastor. It was in the confessional, whilst he was attending to the cure of souls, that Luther's first sad experiences of the effects of this traffic were made. The people, instead of confessing themselves to him and afterwards conversing in a friendly manner concerning their spiritual condition,—which is the real and true design of confession, even according to the views of the Church,—simply presented to him the indulgences which they had purchased, thinking that they were thus discharged of all further guilt. This grieved Luther deeply. Accustomed as he was to perform all his priestly functions with the utmost conscientiousness, he pursued the same course in reference to the confessional. He held it to be his duty to instruct those whose confessor he was in regard to the true nature of indulgences. This he did in several sermons, in which he demonstrated that a change of heart constitutes the sole condition upon which a man can receive forgiveness. He concluded one of these sermons[2] with the following words:—" If some, to whose coffers such truth is prejudicial, call me a heretic, I make little account of their clamour, for it proceeds only from a few muddy-brained fellows who have never so much as scented the Bible, never read the doctrines of Christianity, never understood their own teachers, but are well-nigh rotting in their ragged and tattered opinions;

---

[1] This operated disadvantageously for Tetzel upon one occasion. A nobleman bought an indulgence for a highway robbery that he intended to commit; he then attacked the indulgence seller himself, and gave him a good thrashing. Tetzel's complaint against him was dismissed.

[2] Sermon on the indulgence and grace, published at Wittenberg, 1557, and frequently reprinted (*Luther's Werke*, vol. xviii. p. 533).

for had they understood, they would have known that they should not slander any one unheard and unconvicted. But may God give us and them a right understanding! Amen."

It was the aim of Luther, however, to oppose the shameless works of the obscurants not only as a preacher and pastor, but also as a servant of science, a doctor of theology. And thus it was that, at noon on All Saints' Day, the 31st of October 1517, he affixed his ninety-five propositions or theses against indulgences to the door of the castle church of Wittenberg. This church was just at this time a favourite resort of pilgrims, and an indulgence was offered to all who should perform a pilgrimage thither.[1] Instead of citing the whole of the ninety-five theses[2] individually and collectively, I will content myself

---

[1] Pope Julius II. had, in the years 1502 and 1510, proclaimed a hundred days' indulgence to all who should visit this church (the construction of which was completed in 1499) from the Monday after Misericordias Domini until after Jubilate. Not long prior to the time of which we write (viz. 31st March 1516), Leo X. had not only confirmed this indulgence, but ordered that it should take effect on the feast of All Saints. The church also possessed numerous and costly relics.

[2] These theses may be found in LÖSCHER's *Reformationsacten*, p. 438, and in *Luther's Werke*, vol. xviii. p. 254. Extracts from them are contained in most histories of the Reformation [see MERLE D'AUBIGNÉ's *Hist. of the Ref.* vol. i. pp. 204 sqq.]. We quote the following in illustration of them :—1. When Christ says, "Repent," we are to understand thereby that the whole life of Christians should be a repentance. 6. The pope can remit no guilt, but only declares and confirms what is remitted by God. 8. The laws of the Church in regard to penance are imposed only upon the living, and can have nothing whatever to do with the dead. 21. The preachers of indulgences are mistaken when they say that men are, through the indulgence of the pope, freed from all punishment, and made the recipients of eternal salvation. 27. They are preachers of human ordinance who affirm that *as soon as the money rings in the chest, the soul is released from purgatory*. 28. This, on the contrary, is assuredly true, that as soon as the money rings in the chest, the thirst for money and gain is increased. 32. They who believe that they are sure of their salvation on account of the letters of indulgence that they have procured, will go to the devil, in company with their teachers. 36. Every Christian who feels true contrition receives perfect absolution from punishment and guilt without any letter of indulgence. 37. Every true Christian, living as well as dead, takes part, through the grace of God, in all the riches of Christ and of the Church without a letter of indulgence. 41. Caution should be used in the preaching of indulgences, lest the common people think that they are preferable to the other good works of *love*. 43. Christians should be taught that he who gives to the poor or lends to the needy does better than if he buys an indulgence; for (44) through the work of love, love grows, and the man increases in piety; whereas a man does not become better through an indulgence, but is only released from the penalty of his sins.

with saying that the general purport of them was that Luther placed true repentance in a *change of heart*, and repudiated every mechanical expungement of sin by mere external works or by the payment of money. According to him, the works of love are the only really good works by the practice of which a man continually grows better. The Church can remit external ecclesiastical punishments only; the true forgiveness of sins lies with God alone. At that time Luther still earnestly believed, and stated this belief in his theses, that the pope had no intention of deceiving and seducing souls. Thus he says in the 50th thesis: "Christians should be taught that if the pope knew of the extortions of the preachers of indulgences, he would rather burn St. Peter's Church to powder than have it built of the skin, flesh, and bones of his sheep." He likewise demonstrated that the Church contradicted herself in granting indulgences in this world, and for future sins, and still continuing her masses for the souls of the dead. This, in truth, was a remark whose justice could not fail to be patent to the most ordinary understanding. In fact, it is related of a shoemaker[1] who had bought indulgences for himself and his wife, that upon the death of the latter shortly after, he refused to have masses read for her soul, because, as he claimed, she had already been advanced to heaven by her ticket of indulgence. Either, then, correctly argued the man, the indulgence is really profitable for this life and the life to come—in which case I have no need of soul masses; or it is of no avail—in which case I can put no confidence in the masses either, for both amount to nothing but deceptions.

55. The pope must surely be of opinion that if men celebrate the indulgence, which is the lesser matter, with one bell, one pageant and ceremony, they should, on the other hand, much rather honour and magnify the gospel, which is the greater matter, with a hundred bells, a hundred pageants and ceremonies. 62. The true treasure of the Church is the gospel of the glory and grace of God. 94, 95. Christians must be admonished that they should seek to follow Christ, their Head, through punishments, death, and hell, and that they may therefore be certain that they will enter into heaven through many tribulations rather than through assurances of peace.

[1] LÖSCHER, vol. i. p. 42.

Luther, meantime, did not rest satisfied with the posting of his theses, but addressed himself by letter to the high clergy of Germany, with a view to calling their attention to the disorderly and pernicious traffic that was, in part, carried on under the abused sanction of their names. His applications, which were addressed chiefly to the elector Albert of Mentz himself, and to the Bishops of Brandenburg, Misnia, Merseburg, and Zeitz, met, however, with but little success. Only the Bishop of Brandenburg, Hieronymus Scultetus, sent him a reply, through the Abbot of Lenin, stating that he found the theses to be in perfect conformity to Christian Catholic truth, but at the same time recommending moderation.[1]

[1] For Luther's letter to Albert of Mentz, see DE WETTE, vol. i. p. 42. On the result of his letters, see the letter to Spalatin (November), No. 43.

CHAPTER V.

CONTROVERSY CONCERNING THE THESES—LUTHER AT AUGSBURG BEFORE CAJETAN——MILTITZ——CARLSTADT——MELANCHTHON ——DISPUTATION OF LEIPSIC.

LUTHER'S sermon on indulgences and his theses, copies of which were multiplied by the press, had, in the space of a month, traversed a great part of Christendom and excited universal attention. To some they brought joy, whilst apprehensions of danger were called forth by them in the minds of others. A number of pens, the property of the monks and their allies, were set in motion, being urged on by the recollection of the Reuchlinian controversy, which was still fresh in the memory of all. Luther, for his part, failed not to answer every attack that was made upon him. Interesting though these pen-and-ink wars may be, as exhibiting traits that are conducive to a more accurate knowledge of the age and of the people who figured in it, we are unable to give a circumstantial account of them. Let the following sketch suffice. The first who appeared upon the scene as the shield-bearer of Tetzel was Conrad Koch, called Wimpina, professor of theology at Frankfort-on-the-Oder. *His* taking up of the gauntlet is partly attributable, doubtless, to the jealousy which subsisted amongst the German Universities, Wittenberg and Frankfort being at that time rivals of each other. Tetzel himself next published a German sermon and a Latin treatise, opposing to the scriptural proofs, brought forward by Luther in support of his tenets, the authority of the Church, and also interpreting Scripture in accordance with that authority. This wounded Luther to the quick, and he thus breaks forth in his reply to Tetzel: "Would that I alone had been the object of his ill-treatment! He might call me a heretic, apostate, evil-speaker, and whatever else his displeasure might dictate, and I would willingly submit to it, and never bear him enmity, but pray for him as a friend. But it is utterly insupportable that he should treat the Holy Bible, our consolation, as a sow does a sack of oats." He next invited Tetzel to a personal disputation: "Here am I, Doctor Martin Luther, monk of the Augustinian order at Wittenberg. If there is any heretic hunter who has a mind to devour iron and rend rocks, to him be it known that, through the gracious promise of the worshipful and Christian prince, the Elector of Saxony, a safe conduct, an open door, and free board and lodging await him here. . . . I make no pretensions to any ability to soar over the tall fir trees, but I doubt not that I may be able to crawl over the dry grass."

Tetzel did not see fit to accept this invitation. He had a fire lighted in the street, and publicly burned Luther's theses. The Wittenberg students, on the other hand, bought a quantity of Tetzel's propositions, and announced that whoever was desirous of being present at the burning and funeral of the Tetzel tenets must be in attendance at two o'clock in the afternoon.[1] Luther disapproved of such proceedings.

Besides Tetzel and Wimpina, the field was taken by a third antagonist from Rome; this was the Dominican Sylvester Mazzolini di Prierio (Prierias), *Magister Sacri Palatii* and professor of theology. He had already been active in the Reuchlinian dispute. Luther speedily disposed of him.[2] Finally, a fourth opponent appeared in the person of James von Hoogstraten, the celebrated heretic hunter of

---

[1] Comp. the letters to Lang and to Jodocus at Erfurt, DE WETTE, Nos. 58 and 64.
[2] Comp. letters Nos. 51, 74, 76, 77, in DE WETTE.

Cologne, whom we have already encountered in the history of Reuchlin. Luther treated this man as being himself the worst heretic who had arisen for four hundred years. "Away," he writes, amongst other things, " thou bloodthirsty murderer!— thou who canst not get thy fill of the blood of Christian brethren! Go, hunt for beetles on a dung-heap, until thou learn what error, sin, and heresy are! I have never seen a greater ass than thee, notwithstanding thou boastest of having studied dialectics for so many years."[1]

On the polemical tone of Luther and his contemporaries, the indelicacy of which has been illustrated above, and will be still further exemplified from time to time, I will remark, once for all, that we are apt, in judging it, to make one of two mistakes. Those, assuredly, are wrong who believe that the power of the reformatory word consists in *roughness*, and who appeal to Luther to justify them in the use of a rude and abusive style in an age which has progressed in culture and taste. This is a wretched species of rhodomontade, and a thing which Luther himself would be as far from approving in our own day as any other well-bred man. On the other hand, however, it would be a misapprehension of Christian meekness and clemency to regard every vigorous opposition of wrong, every ebullition of a righteous and manly indignation against the doings of obscurants in certain periods, as incompatible with an earnest Christian cast of sentiment. In this particular our ears have been too daintily educated. I prefer the roughness of the sixteenth century to that over-refinement which holds that God gave language to man in order that he might *conceal* his thoughts, not *reveal* them. That, however, Luther might, even in his day, occasionally have moderated his expressions, far be it from us to deny. In this respect, how far is he behind the lofty example of Christ and the apostles!

Most lengthy and most violent was the dispute which was carried on between Luther and John Eck, doctor of theology

[1] *Luther's Werke* (Walch's edition), vol. xxi. App. p. 118.

and chancellor of Ingolstadt. This man, whom we shall frequently see opposed to Luther on the field of battle, was not destitute of talent—Luther himself did not deny his possession of this;[1] he was, however, narrow-minded and false-hearted. In a writing entitled *Obelisks*, he attacked the principles of Luther. Luther's reply was the pamphlet which he issued under the name of *Asterisks*. We can devote but a glance, in passing, to the other literary labours of Luther, prosecuted by him for the good of the Church, in the midst of the conflicts in which he was engaged.[2] Nor can we be more diffuse in reference to his journey, in 1518, to the Augustinian convent in Heidelberg, where the voices of the Reformation of North and South Germany were just beginning to be heard, and where there was a meeting of congenial minds for discussion on the 26th of April. Let us turn our attention to the main current of events, and consider the impression which the actions of Luther had produced at Rome.

Leo X. seemed at first to regard the affair as a mere monkish quarrel, similar to the Reuchlin dispute, and vouchsafed no attention to Hoogstraten's proposal that Luther should

---

[1] Compare Luther's letter to Sylvius Egranus in DE WETTE's *Collection*, vol. i. p. 59. Eck is there described as *insignis vereque ingeniosæ eruditionis et eruditi ingenii homo*, and the context forbids the supposition that there is irony in these words. The true name of Eck was Maier. He received the appellation by which he is generally known, and which flowed more glibly from the popular mouth, from his birthplace Eck, in the Swabian county of Mindelheim, where his father for some years discharged the office of sheriff. He was born November 13, 1486, and was therefore only a few years younger than Luther. From his ninth to his twelfth year he resided in the house of his uncle, the pastor of Rothenburg, where he became acquainted with the Bible; at least he affirms that he had read it through by the time he was eleven years old. In Heidelberg and Tübingen he had the benefit of listening to the instructions of Reuchlin. At the University of Cologne, to which he afterwards repaired, he studied the writings of Thomas Aquinas, and seems in his devotion to Scholasticism to have somewhat lost sight of the Bible. At all events, his theology was not nurtured on that holy book. Eck was an ever ready and skilful disputant. After teaching philosophy for some time at Freiburg in Breisgau, Duke William of Bavaria called him to the chair of theology at Ingolstadt (1510). He made the acquaintance of Luther through the Nuremberg patrician Christopher Scheurl. Compare SCHENKEL's art. on Eck in Herzog's *Realenc.* vol. iii. pp. 626 sqq.

[2] *Erklärung der zehn Gebote; Auslegung des Vaterunsers*, etc.

be burned. Luther, however, through his friend Staupitz, addressed a humble letter (30th May 1518) to Leo, accompanying it with an explanation of his theses.[1] Both in the letter and in the pamphlet the person of the holy father is treated with the utmost consideration, and the regret is expressed that so good a sovereign should reign in such sad times. The letter closes with the following words:—"Therefore, holy father, I prostrate myself at the feet of your holiness and resign myself, with all I am and have, to you. Spare my life or take it, pronounce me in the right or in the wrong, as it pleases you. *I shall recognise your voice as the voice of Christ,* who rules (the Church) in you and speaks by you. If I have merited death, I will not seek to escape it; for the earth is the Lord's, and all that is therein. To Him be praise throughout eternity; and may He for ever preserve you. Amen."

We see that Luther had by no means broken with the papal chair as yet. For him the authority of the pope had still an ideal import, and the reigning pontiff, Leo, possessed his real and entire confidence.

Leo, however, was deaf to the representations of Luther. The system of the Curia [court][2] was more powerful than his personal tendency, and acting in the spirit of this system, he, instead of quenching the fire, poured oil upon it, as we have already seen in the "dumb comedy."

Even before the arrival of Luther's missive, the affair had taken a graver turn in Rome. It was at first ordered that Luther should appear in person at Rome and answer for himself before the pope. Through the mediation of the Elector of Saxony, however, this command was modified, and Cardinal Cajetan (Thomas de Vio of Gaeta) was despatched to Augsburg, with orders there to examine Luther in regard to what

---

[1] DE WETTE, vol. i. No. 67 sq.; comp. MARHEINEKE, i. 72.

[2] [The Roman *Curia* or court is composed of the pope, the cardinals, and the prelates. See the valuable work of the Rev. S. P. BARNUM, entitled *Romanism as it is,* p. 199.—TR.]

had transpired. Just at this time the Diet was in session at Augsburg, and the elector himself was in attendance there; the business of the empire was, however, already finished. The cardinal is described as haughty and fond of ostentation. At his nomination to the cardinalship, he stipulated that a white palfrey with reins of crimson velvet should be allowed him, and that his apartments should be decorated with hangings of crimson satin.[1] Before his birth his mother is said to have dreamed that St. Thomas Aquinas himself instructed her son and took him to heaven.[2] In honour of this saint he was baptized Thomas. He was really a man of great learning. His extensive erudition and blameless walk gained him the confidence of the brethren of his order, so that he became procurator and general of the order even before he received a cardinal's hat. At the councils of Pisa (1511) and Rome (1512), he defended the strict hierarchical system against the advocates of a more liberal policy.

Frederick the Wise, who had returned from the Diet at the time of Luther's departure for Augsburg, provided the latter with recommendations to the councillors of greatest note in the city. Luther performed the most considerable part of the journey on foot. After a number of precautionary measures had been taken, he finally met with the cardinal, who at first received him with perfect friendliness, merely requiring from him, as if it were the easiest thing in the world, the recantation of his theses. Upon Luther's not immediately complying with this demand, however, and especially upon his appealing to the Scriptures, and by proofs from them nonplussing the cardinal, who based his arguments upon tradition, that spiritual dignitary became choleric, and at last, after three different interviews, dismissed him with the threatening words, "Go, and come no more to me until you are willing to recant." "I can dispute no longer with this beast," said the cardinal afterwards; "it has a couple of wicked eyes and marvellous thoughts in its head." Luther, for his

[1] RANKE, vol. i. p. 326. [2] *Ibid.* p. 384.

part, came to the conclusion that the cardinal was a bad theologian, and about as well qualified to be a judge in spiritual things as an ass is to play on the harp.[1] In spite of Luther's safe-conduct, there was really as little safety for him in Augsburg as there had been for Huss, years before, at Constance. His friends were anxious to get him away. Staupitz provided him with a miserable nag without any bridle, and Christopher Langemantel, the councillor, ordered that a little gate in the wall should be opened for him, and gave him a guide who was to go with him as far as Nuremberg.[2] At his departure he left an appeal from the pope, ill informed, to the same personage when he should be better instructed; two days after Luther left Augsburg, this appeal was posted up on the door of the cathedral. In Nuremberg he learned that he had not taken his departure too soon, for he saw the papal brief which the cardinal carried with him, and which empowered him to throw Luther into prison as a heretic. But even now he was not secure. Who would protect him from the power of the pope? from the anger of the cardinal? from the snares of the Inquisition? The Elector of Saxony, Frederick the Wise, although he had favoured him from the beginning, was as yet far too undecided in the matter to espouse with vigour the cause of the proscribed monk. Nay, he even wished that he would quit his territories; and Luther, who observed this desire on the part of his prince, really entertained the idea of going away, without, however, knowing whither. He was half inclined to trust himself to France and the University of Paris, but was still desirous of remaining in his beloved Wittenberg, where the flourishing scientific

---

[1] Compare the letters to Spalatin and Carlstadt, in DE WETTE, vol. i. Nos. 83 and 85, and the letter to the Elector of Saxony, No. 95.

[2] "Dr. Staupitz had furnished me with a horse, and advised me to take an old outrider with me who knew the roads; and Langemantel (the councillor) helped me to get out of the city by night through a little gate. Then I hurried away without breeches, boots, spurs, or sword, and arrived at Wittenberg. The first day I rode eight German (thirty-two English) miles, and on reaching the inn that evening I was so tired that when I dismounted in the stable I could not stand, but fell down on the straw."

spirit of the University gave him great pleasure, where excellent and noble men had already joined themselves to him, and where the heart of the youth belonged to *him*. The thought of parting was a sad one; nevertheless he made his preparations to leave the electoral domains, and was just enjoying a farewell repast with his friends when he received a letter from the court preacher, Spalatin, informing him of the elector's surprise that he had not yet gone. At this Luther exclaimed, "Father and mother forsake me, but the Lord will take me up!" On the very same day, however, the elector changed his intentions with regard to Luther. The latter remained at Wittenberg; and Frederick, having, upon the death of Maximilian I. in the beginning of the year 1519, become administrator of the empire pending the election of a new emperor, had more courage to protect him. Luther himself somewhere writes that the storm visibly abated during the regency of the elector, and the thunder of papal excommunication began to appear contemptible.

In the meantime new negotiations were being entered into at Rome in the affair of Luther. The popes had long been accustomed to consecrate a golden rose on mid-Lent Sunday, and to send it, as a token of their favour, to the princes of Europe. This rose was emblematic of the body of Christ, as the flower of flowers. The papal legate, Charles von Miltitz, canon of Mentz, Treves, and Meissen, was now chosen to convey this token of the pontifical favour to the Elector of Saxony, and on this occasion the affair of Luther was likewise to come under discussion. In December 1518 Miltitz arrived in Saxony; he, however, did not bring the rose with him, since it was desirable that he should first discover how matters stood. When the gift itself arrived somewhat later, the elector had become so indifferent to it as to receive it through three of his nobles. This occasioned Luther to remark that had the rose come in 1515 (when the elector petitioned for it), it would have retained its fragrance; now, however, it had lost it on the long journey.

The commission of Miltitz was aimed not only against Luther, but also against Tetzel. The impudence of this man had excited the indignation of the pontiff himself, and Miltitz speedily gained a knowledge of his practices. He learned that Tetzel had every month drawn on the then famous house of the Fuggers at Augsburg, managers of the indulgence monies for the Elector of Mentz, for 80 florins for himself, and 10 for his servant, besides numerous other sums, independent of the peculations and thefts which he had committed in other ways. Many particulars of Tetzel's scandalous course of life in other respects had also reached the ears of Miltitz. Suffice it to say that Tetzel had so much to fear from the displeasure of the pope, that he at first concealed himself in a monastery, and when he was at last compelled to submit to an examination, he resorted to the most wretched subterfuges. Shortly after this he died. Luther wrote him a letter of consolation prior to his death,[1] telling him not to be troubled, that he was not the originator of the matter [*i.e.* the indulgence system], but that the child had another father. Luther cherished no resentment against individuals; and when he was obliged to wound them, he did it always for the sake of the cause that was sacred to him.

Miltitz had a conference with Luther at Altenburg, in the house of Spalatin. That which Cajetan had failed to accomplish by arrogance and overbearing, Miltitz was confident of attaining by flattery and gentleness. He embraced Luther, kissed him, and said all manner of engaging things to him about himself. For instance, he remarked: "Dear Martin, I thought you were an old doctor who had taken up some queer fancies beside your stove; but I see that you are still in the prime of life. Had I five thousand tried men with me, I would not undertake to deliver you up at Rome; for I have been inquiring all along the road what the people think of you, and I have found that where there is one for the pope

[1] This letter is no longer extant; comp., however, the letter to Spalatin, DE WETTE, vol. i. No. 120, and Seidemann's Appendix to DE WETTE, vi. p. 18.

there are three against him and for you." Luther, however, did not suffer himself to be ensnared by such speeches, although he was inclined to make amends for any harm that he might have done through his vehemence.[1]

He again wrote a very humble letter to the pope,[2] assuring him that if it were in *his* power to restore peace, even by the recall of his disputation, he would willingly do it, but that the affair was no longer under his control. " I testify before God and all creatures," the letter concludes, " that I have never intended, and do not now intend, to encroach in any way upon the authority of the Romish Church and of your holiness, or to abate anything of it by artifice. Ay, I freely confess that the authority of that Church is superior to everything, and that nothing, either in heaven or on earth, can be preferred before it, *save only Jesus Christ, who is Lord over all.*"

In this letter Luther still exhibits a strong attachment to the Romish Church, which he sincerely held to be the one true and only saving Church, and he therefore still appears as a submissive son of the supreme pontiff. There was one thing, however, of which he was already firmly convinced—namely, that the authority of Christ was superior to the authority of the Church and the pope; and this truth became subsequently the point of departure for all his conclusions against the papal government. There is nothing more contrary to historical fact than the belief that Luther arrived *at once* at his clearer views; nor would it have been well if this had been the case. A good conscience and a clearer insight into truth must always preserve a perfect balance if our work of reformation is to have a happy and blessed course. If mere knowledge hasten ahead with the torch of enlightenment before a warning conscience overtakes her, she may easily produce a conflagration, and occasion misery instead of blessing. Luther was so great a Reformer because he was so conscientious.

---

[1] On Luther's discussions with Miltitz, comp. Letters 108, 109, 115, in DE WETTE's *Collection*, vol. i.

[2] DE WETTE, i. No. 124; comp. MARHEINEKE, i. 114.

Well might the responsibility which he had assumed in attacking, or even seeming to attack, what men had hitherto considered sacred, weigh heavily upon him. Well might he be startled at the conflagration which he had kindled, and anxiously query with himself, "Hast thou power to say to the flames, 'Thus far shalt thou come, and no farther'?" Such hours of painful solicitude are to be found in the apprenticeship of all who undertake great things in the service of humanity. Such feelings are no evidence of cowardice and a fear of man; they are rooted in the fear of God, which is the beginning of wisdom.

It is from this point of view that we must judge the conduct of Luther, when we learn that besides his letter to the pope, he issued at this time another production,[1] in which, before all the world, he professed his attachment to the Roman Catholic Church, and indeed avowed his reverence for several doctrines to which he subsequently found it impossible to adhere, as, for instance, the doctrines of the invocation of saints, of purgatory, etc. "To separate from a Church in which St. Peter and St. Paul, forty-six popes, and 100,000 martyrs have shed their blood and overcome hell and the world," was a hard thing for him; he feared that it might be a sin.

The mighty Reformer almost seems, in truth, to have experienced a shade of sorrow that the matter should have progressed so far, although he firmly persisted in combating actual and clearly-recognised abuses. But man proposes, God disposes. Luther was but an instrument in the hand of the Supreme Being. It was no longer in his power to take back the words which, impelled by the Spirit of truth, he had spoken before all the world. Those words, uttered at the right time, were too true, too striking, not to find a harmonious echo in congenial minds. God had now, as it were, Himself taken the matter in hand; Luther might have resigned all connection with it, and it would have still pro-

---

[1] "Information on some articles which are laid to his charge by his enemies."

gressed to maturity. But Luther was bent upon being faithful to it, and he therefore, in God's name, pressed onward in a conflict of whose ending he had no conception when he unsuspectingly began it. Setting aside his personal interests, carried forward only by the common feeling of all the better men of his time, supported by the power of a faith which was daily increasing, we now behold him rushing into the battle, blind to all danger, with bandaged eyes, but an open heart. Such are the qualities that made Luther so great, raising him above the ordinary sphere of humanity and exalting him into proximity to the prophets and men of God.

As often, after a spring rain, the blossoms, which before have been slumbering in germ, suddenly open, and we seem to be transported into a new world, so there are in the spiritual world such fructifying movements which, as by the stroke of a magic wand, reveal the counsel of hearts, and call into visible existence a multitude of talents and aspirations that hitherto have seemed to slumber. But when the blossoms have once burst forth, who shall force them back into their discarded cases? who shall say to the heaven, "Take back thy rain and let the night of winter return"? Thus it was at the time of which we speak. The words that went forth from Luther were the fertilizing spring rain; where a drop fell, there opened a blossom that had been slumbering underneath its winter covering—the spring began its sway in the valleys of the Alps and in the broad lands of Germany, and the warmth increased and spread. Where ice was still lying, it began to melt, and the streamlets swelled and rushed roaring into the valleys, where, in truth, their passage was not always unattended by danger to such frail dwellings of men as stood in their way.

From this time forth a multitude of heterogeneous spirits, unequal in their gifts and diverse in their modes of working and warring, may be seen to range themselves upon the battle-field. Gentleness allied itself to strength, rudeness to vigour, impurity to purity, and of all this we shall hereafter perceive the effects. Immediate mention, however, must be made of two men whose personalities differed exceedingly, so that in one of them the vehemence of Luther appears augmented to its extreme, whilst in the other it is beneficently softened—I speak of Karlstadt and Melanchthon. Let us, before proceeding farther in our narrative, tarry awhile with these two.

Andreas Bodenstein, called Karlstadt from his birthplace in Franconia, was born in 1483, and was, therefore, of just about the same age as Luther. In 1504, six years earlier than Luther, he was installed at the University of Wittenberg as professor of Scholastic philosophy. When Luther became his colleague, he speedily constituted himself his friend and adherent. Through him he was drawn away from the barren system of Scholasticism and directed to the fountain of truth. Although he subsequently abandoned that fountain and turned to the turbid waters of fanaticism, this fact should not hinder us from recognising the zeal with which he embraced the cause of Luther as one of its first champions. At a time when Luther was almost too ready to yield, it was he who took up the gauntlet which Dr. Eck had thrown to the friends of the light. It was he who called forth that discussion at Leipsic which we shall soon have occasion to examine.

Philip Melanchthon, the other of the two individuals whom we have mentioned, forms a perfect contrast to the fiery Karlstadt. Philip Schwarzerd[1] (this was his German name), a native of Bretten in the Rhenish palatinate, was born 16th February 1497. He was the son of an armourer (called "the locksmith of Heidelberg"),[2] but lost his father at an

[1] The principal source of information in regard to the life of this remarkable man is still the charming biography compiled by his contemporary CAMERARIUS. Comp. besides, TISCHER, *Melanchthon's Leben*, Leipzig, 1801 ; FACIUS, *Melanchthon's Leben und Charakteristik*, Leipzig, 1832 ; *Reformationsalmanach*, i. p. xxviii.; the most recent descriptions of the life and character of Melanchthon by MATTHES, GAILE, and Dr. C. SCHMIDT (*Leben und ausgewählte Schriften der Väter und Begründer der luther. Kirche*, i.), Elberfeld, 1861. Comp. also LANDERER in Herzog's *Realenc.* ix. pp. 252 sqq.

[2] He is described as a very honest and peace-loving man, who never had a law-

early age. He received his first instruction at the school of Pforzheim, where he was frequently visited, and encouraged to persevere in his diligent application to study, by his relative Reuchlin, whose acquaintance we have already made.

The teacher of this school, George Simler of Wimpfen, was a fine grammarian, and versed not only in Latin, but also in Greek and Hebrew. Reuchlin, who was a friend of Simler, jestingly presented the promising eleven-year-old scholar of the latter with a doctor's red hat, and likewise gave him books—some, amongst others, of which he was himself the author. Out of gratitude for this kindness, the youthful Philip, together with his companions, learned one of the comedies of Reuchlin and enacted it at the next visit of the author. Upon this occasion Reuchlin, agreeably to the custom then prevalent, translated the German name of the boy into Greek, and from that time forth he was called Melanchthon.

Melanchthon's mind was one of those that early arrive at maturity; it did not, however, belong to the class that suddenly shoot up, only to fade as speedily. Anything that he had once learned, he did not readily forget. In his twelfth year (1509) he, already a young man in earnestness of sentiment and maturity of judgment, repaired to the University of Heidelberg, and received the degree of Bachelor of Arts in his fourteenth year. The degree of Master of Arts was denied him on account of his youth. Somewhat chagrined at this, he betook himself, in 1512, to Tübingen, where, in addition to Scholastic philosophy, he studied ancient literature and history, both of which were just reviving under the touch of Reuchlin and Erasmus. At Tübingen he enjoyed the benefit of the stimulating instructions of Heinrich Bebel. Here, in his seventeenth year (1514), he obtained the coveted degree of Master of Arts, having already, a whole year earlier, published his *Greek Grammar*. He himself subsequently

suit in his life, never was drunk, and never swore. The mother of Philip was also a God-fearing person, after the old style of the Church.

disapproved the youthful ambition which had, in his earlier life, tormented him more than was reasonable. "It is sometimes well," he remarks, "when the desires of young people are denied them. By the refusal of the University of Heidelberg to grant me my master's degree, I was but spurred on to increased diligence."

Melanchthon was not only profound and thorough in his studies, but also many-sided. With his extraordinary natural gifts, and in the condition in which science then was, he found it possible to embrace, in the circuit of his learning, the several faculties of medicine, law, and theology. His decided preference was always for the latter, although he never became an ecclesiastic. In this respect Melanchthon forms a connecting link between Erasmus and Luther. He exhibits a more decided theological tendency than the one, and possesses, on the other hand, a wider culture and greater elegance of style than the other. Erasmus himself highly esteemed the learning of Melanchthon, and publicly testified his appreciation of it.[1] "Immortal God," he exclaims with reference to the youth who had excited his admiration, "what promise is there in this young man, this *boy!* His attainments in both literatures are equally valuable. What ingenuity and acumen, what purity of language, what beauty of expression, what a memory for the most unfamiliar things, what a wide extent of reading!"

In 1518, at the age of twenty-one, Melanchthon, who had hitherto been lecturing on rhetoric at Tübingen, entered upon the professorship of Greek literature at Wittenberg. Reuchlin had been instrumental in securing his appointment to this chair. In his inaugural address he professed his adherence to the following hermeneutical principle—viz., that the Scriptures should be interpreted in accordance with their wording, all Scholastic rubbish being left out of consideration: Christ, he

---

[1] In the annotations to the First Epistle to the Thessalonians, Basel edition (1522), p. 515. In the later edition of Erasmus' works (Basel, 1541), T. vi., the passage is wanting.

declared, is the sum and substance of true theology. He speedily had cause for rejoicing in the golden opinions which were showered upon him. "Like an overflowing river" (to use the simile of Luther), his fame attracted students from all parts of Europe. Even Italy, the seat of learning, sent its representatives to Wittenberg. Often did the lauded teacher have an auditory of two thousand, some of those who composed it climbing up on the windows that they might obtain places. It was here that he speedily entered into bonds of eternal friendship with Luther, and this relationship forms a lovely and brilliant pearl in the garland of the history of the Reformation.[1] If it were admissible to trace back the diversity of gifts in conjunction with the one Spirit, as manifested in these two friends, to that apostolic period when the first-fruits of the Spirit were exhibited in diverse vessels, well might we be tempted to compare Luther with Paul, and Melanchthon with John. But, without executing any such comparison, which, considering the different state of the times, might be somewhat hazardous, suffice it to say that, in various ways, Melanchthon, according to the gift which he had received, formed a supplement to Luther. Not only did he subdue the vehement ardour of Luther by his mildness and gentleness, but with his greater and more extended learning he served as a bright lamp to the former, and by his scientific methodization he was as active in the internal promotion of the Reformation by the establishment of a doctrinal system, as Luther was in the external furtherance of it by his strong practical sense and his personal character. Let us hear what Luther himself says concerning his later relations to Melanchthon: "I must," he declares,[2] "uproot the stocks and stems, cut

[1] Luther, in different passages of his letters, speaks enthusiastically of his friend. He thus expresses himself to Spalatin (31st Aug.), DE WETTE's Collection, No. 76; to Prior John Lang, No. 80; to Reuchlin, No. 102. To him, Melanchthon is a man worthy of all admiration, almost all of whose qualities transcend the measure of humanity, and he glories in his friendship; but with still greater veneration did Melanchthon look up to Luther.

[2] In the preface to Melanchthon's exposition of the Epistle to the Colossians, translated into German in 1529; MARHEINEKE, i. p. 136.

down the briars and hedges, drain the marshes. I am the rough-hewer and pioneer. But Master Philip comes gently and quietly after me, tills and plants, sows and waters at his leisure, according to the gifts wherewith God has richly endowed him."

John Kessler, the Reformer of St. Gall, who, in the year 1522, was a student at Wittenberg, gives us, in his *Sabbata*, the following description of the exterior of Melanchthon:— "He is in person small and insignificant: you would think him but a boy of eighteen should you see him with Martin Luther. As these two walk together—and their ardent love for each other constrains them to be always together—Martin is a whole head and shoulders taller than Melanchthon. But in intellect, learning, and ability, Melanchthon is a great and mighty giant and hero, so that one might wonder how so vast a mountain of ability and wisdom can be enclosed in so small a body."

In company with these two colleagues, the Rector of the University, Duke Barnim of Pomerania, and other professors and doctors, Luther arrived at Leipsic on the 24th of June 1519, there to take part in the dispute with Dr. Eck. The students, armed with long halberds, marched along beside the carriage. All were most anxiously expectant of the issue of the affair. Duke George of Saxony established himself in the castle of Pleissenburg, and on the 27th of June the public debate began. In order to the worthy opening of this momentous business, mass was celebrated in St. Thomas' Church at six o'clock in the morning, after which the actors and spectators moved, in solemn procession, to the castle. Here a numerous watch was stationed to ensure order. In the saloon two pulpits had been erected facing each other. Peter Mosellanus, president of the assemblage, mounted one of these, and, in a fine Latin oration, reminded the disputants of their duties, admonishing them not to let the debate degenerate into a vain war of words, but continually to keep their eyes fixed upon the truth as the prize of the contest. At the close of this discourse, music resounded through the hall, and whilst the whole assemblage knelt, the ancient hymn *Veni Sancte Spiritus* was chanted. Thus the forenoon glided away in the introductory solemnities. Let others, if they will, regard these as empty ceremony, a remnant of mediæval formalism. I cannot do away with the impression which the recital of these formalities has ever made upon me. Let us recollect that many of those present brought an agitated and anxious heart to the ground where earnest battle was to be made, and that the thought, "What will the end be?" doubtless passed through the mind of more than one in that great company. The lots were cast; the point at issue was no mere Scholastic fancy, but a vital question—the existence or the non-existence of that which had hitherto been the doctrine of the Church and the prescribed way of salvation. Such, at least, may have been the feelings of some who had secretly reflected on the turn which the times might take. At this moment, the one bond of the Church that had endured so long stills holds all together; prayer to the Lord of the Church, to the common Father of all, still ascends as from one mouth; and though with many it might be only a prayer of the lips, doubtless here and there a troubled heart was throbbing with anxiety and grief, and praying fervently for the coming of the Spirit of truth and love.

And now for the disputation itself! Eck and Karlstadt disputed for eight days on free-will, Karlstadt maintaining that everything good that a man does is a work of divine grace, and Eck defending the human freedom, and in part also the meritoriousness of good works. In the following two weeks Eck disputed with Luther about the primacy of the pope, purgatory, repentance, and absolution. In reference to human freedom, Luther was entirely on the side of Karlstadt. He compared the will of man to a *saw*, moved only by the master's hand (Isa. x. 15)—a figure which others had used before him. This absolute dependence of man on God, however, involved his independence of human authority in cases in which his internal position toward God was concerned. Christ alone is the true Head of the Church, Luther declared. Under this invisible Head he could conceive of a Church without a pope, just as the Greek Church subsists without a pope. He discarded more positively than before the doctrine of purgatory, etc. The entire disputation consumed twenty days, and it would have lasted still longer, had not tidings arrived of the proximity of the Margrave of Brandenburg, who was returning from the imperial election in Frankfort. Duke George being obliged to yield his quarters to him, the disputants were forced to separate.

People wonder now at the patience with which theological disputations were listened to in those old times, when even secular dignitaries gave their most earnest attention to the discussion of matters of religion. It should not, however, be forgotten that the period of which we speak was wholly interpenetrated with religion; that civil life was most closely interwoven with ecclesiastical life; and a change in dogmatics was followed by as weighty consequences as are attendant, in the present day, upon a change in the political constitution. I will not say that our forefathers were, on this account, more pious than their descendants; it even seems to me to be a defective arrangement to make the public peace of mind and civil happiness too dependent upon particular doctrinal definitions of theologians. Great disadvantages always attach to the confounding of religion and dogmatism, of Christianity and ecclesiasticism. But I do maintain that the defects of that period should not lead us to overlook those of our own time; for truly, as *we* wonder that the men of *that* age could dispute for twenty days on dogmatical propositions and make the prosperity of the states dependent upon them, so might our fathers wonder if they could see us of the present day, with our frequent utter disregard of the treasures of eternity, with our utter ignoring of the higher interests of the spirit, directing all our attention to material advantages, and disputing, not weeks, but years, about things which doubtless have their weight as bearing upon the public weal, but upon which *all* prosperity is very far from being dependent.

Let us review a few characteristic traits of this discussion. Amongst other things, Eck reproached Luther with entertaining views of the Church similar to those of the Bohemians or Hussites. This Luther denied; he is even represented by eye-witnesses as having taken all possible pains to remove from himself all suspicion of being connected with the Bohemians; nevertheless he even then confessed that of the doctrines held by them and condemned by the Church, some were Christian and evangelical—a declaration which occasioned a great stir in the assemblage. Duke George exclaimed, so loud that he could be heard throughout the hall, "A pest upon him!" ["*Das walt' die Sucht !*"], shook his head, and rested his hands upon his sides. Duke George of Saxony took the liveliest interest in the whole dispute, which, however, only increased his disinclination to Luther; he continued throughout his life to be an antagonist of the Reformation. Other witnesses of the contest Luther won over to his mode of thinking; one of the most important of these acquisitions was Duke George of Anhalt [then a lad of twelve], who subsequently espoused the cause of the Reformation, and, as reigning prince, preached the gospel to his peasants. Upon Melanchthon also, who was no friend to such disputations,[1] and whose position at this discussion was that of a mere spectator, the deportment of Luther made a deep impression. The Rector of the University of Wittenberg, Duke Barnim of Pomerania, was also deeply impressed; he did not miss an hour of the dispute, and was a much more earnest listener than any of the Leipsic theologians. For, that the attention of which we have previously spoken was not invariably accorded by the witnesses of the discussion, is a fact of which we are informed by contemporary authorities. It is related of those who were on the side of Dr. Eck: "They were

[1] In this he agreed with Œcolampadius. He declared that it was at the Leipsic disputation that he first learned what the ancients meant by sophistry.

wrapped in gentle slumbers; so diligently did they listen and so sweet did they find the disputation, that when the disputants ceased for a time, they had all to be roused, in order that they might not lose their dinners."[1]

The debate was at times very sharp. It was the constant effort of Eck to elude the texts of Scripture which Luther brought to bear upon him, and to take refuge behind the human ordinances of tradition. Luther, observing this, exclaimed, provoked, "Thou fleest the Bible as the devil flees the cross!" Karlstadt declared that during the disputation a Dominican monk sent Eck a note, instructing him to demand that Luther should lay aside a little cylindrical ring which he wore on his finger, as it contained a familiar spirit to whom, it seems, a magical inspiration was attributed. A bunch of flowers that Luther held in his hand was also regarded with suspicion.

At the close of the disputation both parties claimed the victory. Neither had convinced the other, for their very principles were at variance, — the one side placing the authority of the Church above that of the Scriptures, and the other holding the contrary opinion; a circumstance which of itself rendered it impossible that a union should be effected by disputation, often as this mode was tried. Luther expressed himself much dissatisfied with the result of a discussion which, having begun badly (for Eck and the Leipsic theologians had sought only their own glory, and not the truth), had also ended badly.

Before bringing the account of the Leipsic disputation to a close, we deem it proper to portray the men who distinguished themselves in this encounter, as sketched by the pen of a contemporary and eye-witness.

Peter Mosellanus, president of the disputation, writes as follows concerning Luther, Karlstadt, and Eck:[2]—

---

[1] MARHEINEKE, vol. i. p. 131, after the report of Sebastian Fröschel.

[2] Mosellanus has given two accounts of the dispute, one addressed to Wilibald Pirkheimer and the other to Julius von Pflugk. The latter is the source whence

"Martin Luther is of medium size. His meagre body is so exhausted by care and study that upon a closer view you could count his bones.[1] He is still in the full vigour of manhood; he has a clear and melodious voice; his learning and knowledge of the Scriptures are admirable—he has almost everything at his fingers' ends. He has a sufficient acquaintance with Greek and Latin to qualify him to be a judge in matters of exegesis.[2] He is never at a loss for material for discourse; a vast forest of words and ideas is at his disposal. In ordinary life and in his manners, he is courteous and easy; there is nothing stoical or haughty about him; on the contrary, he understands accommodating himself to all circumstances. In company he is a cheerful and agreeable conversationist, always lively and free from care; serenity blooms perennially upon his countenance, although his opponents give him plenty to do, so that one could hardly believe that this man could undertake such great things without the assistance of God. But nearly every one reproaches him with being somewhat too impolitic and tart in his censure, more so than is advisable for a reformer or proper for a theologian. . . . All the qualities of Luther are found in a lower degree in Karlstadt; the latter is shorter than Luther, and has a swarthy and sunburnt face, a harsh and disagreeable voice, a less faithful memory, and greater irascibility than Martin. (The sequel will show how exactly applicable this description is to the subsequent conduct of Karlstadt.) Eck, finally, is tall, fleshy, and square-built (*corpus quadratus*); he possesses a full and truly German voice, which, supported by a strong pair of lungs, would do not merely for an actor, but even for

---

we draw the description given above. Comp. besides on the Leipsic disputation the report of Melanchthon to Œcolampadius (LÖSCHER, vol. iii.), that of Cellarius (*ibid.*), and several letters of Luther. On the opposite side, Eck wrote to Hoogstraten. See also SEIDEMANN, *Die Leipziger Disputation*, etc., Dresden, 1843.

[1] It was not until Luther advanced in years that he became corpulent. Comp. KIRCHMAIER, *Disquisitio historica de D. Martini Lutheri oris et vultus habitu heroico*, Wittenberg, 1750. On different portraits of Luther (the best were by Lucas Cranach), see the *Reformations-almanach*, i.

[2] In the knowledge of these languages Melanchthon was far superior to Luther.

a public crier; it is, however, more hoarse than distinct. He is thus very deficient in that charm of address which was natural to the Romans, and was so greatly lauded in Fabius and Cicero. His mouth and eyes, his whole countenance, in short, is of such a cast that you would take him to be a butcher or a Carian warrior rather than a theologian. As regards his mental qualities, he has a stupendous memory, and if his understanding were equal to it, nature's work in his behalf would be complete in all its parts. He, however, lacks that swift perception and acuteness without which all other gifts are vain; and hence it is that in disputing he heaps so many arguments, so many Scripture passages, so many learned quotations, one upon another, without any attempt at selection, not observing the quantity of dead matter in all this,—matter which, though full of meaning in its place, is inapplicable as he uses it. How much that is hypothetic and sophistical may be found in his oratory! His only aim is, by heaping up a huge mass of learning, to weave a blue haze before the eyes of his, for the most part, stupid hearers, and thus to make them believe that he is the victor. To all these qualities he adds an incredible effrontery, which he is able to conceal by an admirable cunning. When by means of this cunning he perceives that his opponent is about to entangle him in a net, he gradually gives a new turn to the dispute, after which he sometimes adopts the view of his antagonist as his own, only giving it a different expression, and, with admirable subtlety, attributes his own absurd affirmation to his antagonist. Thus it seems as if he could conquer any number of Socrates', only with this distinction, that whilst Socrates, adhering to irony, decided nothing, Eck manifests a complete reliance on the peripatetic school of learning, and thus exposes his parasitic nature."

In accordance with this description, we may behold in Luther that true *genius* which made him paramount amongst the men of his time; in Karlstadt, a one-sided, subordinate, and limited *talent;* and in Eck, the ludicrous presumption of the bully.

CHAPTER VI.

RESULTS OF THE LEIPSIC DISPUTATION—THE GERMAN NOBILITY AND LUTHER'S RELATION TO IT—HIS WRITINGS ENTITLED, "TO THE CHRISTIAN NOBLES OF THE GERMAN NATION;" "CONCERNING THE BABYLONISH CAPTIVITY;" AND "CONCERNING THE LIBERTY OF A CHRISTIAN"—THE ROMISH BULL—DIET OF WORMS—LIFE IN THE WARTBURG—TRANSLATION OF THE BIBLE.

THE issue of the Leipsic disputation was of a dubious character, inasmuch as each of the contending parties claimed the victory. Its result was, however, really favourable to the cause of the Reformation, since it was instrumental in procuring fresh adherents to the evangelical tendency and the new order of things. A certain jealousy had for a long time prevailed between the Universities of Leipsic and Wittenberg, and this circumstance must have rendered it peculiarly trying to the former city when a number of students deserted its University for that of Wittenberg, in order that they might enjoy the instructions of Luther and Melanchthon.

Of special encouragement for Luther was the position assumed by a large portion of the German, and particularly the Franconian, nobility toward the Reformation. Francis von Sickingen, Ulrich von Hutten, and Sylvester von Schaumburg ranged themselves in full armour on his side, ready either to wield the sword in his behalf or to protect him, in their castles, from the attack of the enemy. The strongholds of Sickingen were ever open, as "harbours of righteousness," to all whose safety was threatened by Rome.[1] But he whose sure fortress was his God, whose best defence and weapon was the two-edged sword of God's word, declined such warlike aid with hearty thanks; for "I would not," said he, "have the gospel maintained by violence and bloodshed. Through the word, the world has been overcome; through the word, the Church has been preserved; through the word, it will also be restored; and, as antichrist has gained his power without violence, so he will fall without violence." The valiant sentiments of these knights, however, cheered the spirit of the great Reformer, who wielded the sword of the word with increased boldness and joy, and more openly defied the adversaries of the gospel. "The die is cast," he writes; "the favour and the displeasure of Rome are scorned. I will nevermore be reconciled to the papal party, or have any fellowship with them. They may condemn and burn my books; I, on the other hand, will condemn and publicly burn their whole system of laws, that hydra of heresies, and will put an end to our vain humiliations before them." Luther kept his word. Until this time he had defended his cause chiefly in theses and polemical tracts, written on the spur and inspiration of the moment, or in sermons and oral disputations. He now issued books upon the subject. Of these the first two were of a warlike character, but were followed by a third of a more pacific nature. They all appeared, in quick succession, in the summer and autumn of 1520. The first, which was published in June, bore the following title:—*To his Imperial Majesty and the Christian Nobility of the German Nation;*

---

[1] On Sickingen and his relation to the Reformation, see the *Reformations-almanach* for 1819; also the writings of SCHNEEGANS (1867), HOLLENSTEINER (1868), and KLIPPEL, in Herzog's *Realencyc.* xiv. pp. 330 sqq. The Reformer of Zweibrück, JOHN SCHWEBEL, who enjoyed the hospitality of Sickingen for a time, thus testifies concerning him: "There is no member of any order, however religious he may think himself, and no theologian, however highly he may estimate his learning, who speaks as constantly and as intelligently concerning the things that pertain to the praise of God and the salvation of souls as he. Formerly, men learned the law of God from the priests; now, it is needful for the priests to learn of the laics."

concerning the Reformation of the Christian Body. This book was issued with the intention of drawing the laity into the combat. In it Luther primarily directs his attention to the head of the secular government, the newly-chosen emperor, Charles v., "that young and noble person whom God has placed at the head of Christendom, in order that many hearts may be aroused to a great and good hope." He then turns to the princes, who had hitherto relied far too much on their own power, and admonishes them "to seek the help of God by earnest prayer, and ever to bear in mind the distress and necessity of wretched Christendom." Under the figure of *three walls,* which he asserted that the Romanists had thrown up around themselves, he presents the Romish system, to break and destroy which he claimed that he had come. To the tenet that the secular power has no authority over the spiritual power, he opposed the apostolic idea of universal priesthood; for "we are all consecrated priests by baptism, although it does not become all men to discharge the priestly office." The fall of this first paper wall was, he declared, accompanied by the overthrow of the second, viz. the assertion that none but the pope may interpret the Scriptures: "Every Christian possesses the right of reading the Holy Scriptures, and the power of tasting and judging what is right and wrong in the faith" [of the Church]. Furthermore, the third wall —the asseveration that the pope alone is entitled to call a council—must, he maintained, fall of itself; "for when the pope acts in a manner contrary to Scripture, it is our duty to reprove him in accordance with the saying of Christ, Matt. xviii. 15-17."

In this same publication Luther further developed his ideas on the subject of reformation. He demanded, with justice, that the reformation should begin at the papal chair itself; for, said he, "it is horrible to behold that the chief of Christendom lives in a style of such worldliness and magnificence that no king or emperor can equal him." . . . "He wears a triple crown, whilst the highest kings wear but one crown."

"An ordinary bishop's crown [or mitre] would be sufficient for the pope; it is in ability and holiness that he should surpass others." He then censures the wicked and worldly life of the cardinals, and the custom of filling German bishoprics and pastorals with foreigners. He demands a curtailment of the monastic orders, the abolishment of celibacy, the reform of the indulgence system, the diminution of masses for the dead, and a thorough reform of the Universities and schools.

This book of Luther's was, with incredible rapidity, diffused throughout Germany. In the month of August alone four thousand copies were sold, so that it became necessary to prepare a second edition, to which some few additions were made. The success of this production furnished the enemies of Luther with fresh occasion for invective, whilst his friends encouraged him with their plaudits.

Soon after (in October) the second book appeared, entitled, *Concerning the Babylonish Captivity*. In this Luther particularly attacked the Romish Church's doctrine of the Seven Sacraments,—the Reformer recognising as true sacraments only baptism, repentance, and the bread of the Lord's Supper. He demanded that the cup should be restored to the laity, and combated the idea of the sacrifice of the mass.

Of a more pacific character was Luther's sermon, *Concerning the Liberty of a Christian*. He here, in the spirit and tone of ancient mysticism, elaborated the beautiful thought that whilst a Christian is constantly engaged in the service of God and humanity, he is, nevertheless, a lord of all things. By the advice of Miltitz, with whom he had another conference at Lichtenberg (11th October 1520), he transmitted this last production to the pope, accompanying it with a letter which was at once honest and humble.[1] In this letter he expresses his hearty regret that Leo, whom he still personally esteems, should have been obliged to live at this particular time, when he was worthy of a better one. He compares

---

[1] Under date of 6th September. The letter was purposely ante-dated, with a view to the ignoring of the papal bull already suspended over Luther's head.

him to a sheep in the midst of wolves, to Daniel amongst the lions, to Ezekiel amidst the scorpions; for it is now evident to him that the Romish chair has fallen under the wrath of God, it being more iniquitous and more pernicious than any Sodom, Gomorrah, or Babylon.

Eck, meantime, did not rest until he had procured, in Rome, a bull of condemnation against Luther and his doctrine. This he brought with him to Germany in the year 1520.[1] In it, forty-one of Luther's propositions were condemned as unchristian, as "scandalous and corrupting," though they contained nothing but the pure truth of the gospel. Amongst these were such as the following,—viz., that the best repentance is a new life, and that the burning of heretics is contrary to the will of the Holy Spirit. The bull excited much disgust in Germany, and many tribunals refused to publish it. The students of Erfurt tore the paper in pieces and threw it into the water.[2] Luther would not recognise it as emanating from the pope, but regarded it as the product of the lying arts of Eck, or at least designated it as such.[3] Ulrich von Hutten published it with some caustic comments.[4] He laid hold of the matter at first from the national standpoint, stating that not only Luther, but all the people of Germany were interested in this bull. He then issued a special letter to the Elector of Saxony,[5] containing, amongst other things, the following: "Would ye, beloved Germans, know what is done with our money at Rome? A part the pope divides among his relations; another part is squandered by the cardinals, of whom the pope created thirty-one in a single day. Then there is such a quantity of assessors, prothonotaries, abbrevia-

---

[1] The two legates, Caraccioli and Alexander, were officially commissioned, however, to deliver it to the Archbishop Albert of Mentz for promulgation.
[2] See Luther's letters, DE WETTE, i. No. 267. *Bulla Erfordiæ a studiosis discerpta et in aquam projecta, dicentibus: Bulla est, in aqua natet.*
[3] Comp. Luther's pamphlet, *On the New Bulls and Falsehoods of Eck.*
[4] See *Hutten's Werke*, edited by BÖCKING, vol. v. pp. 301 sqq.
[5] September 11, 1520; BÖCKING, vol. i. pp. 383 sqq. Comp. also *Hutten's Lamentation and Warning against the Power of the Pope* (in German verse, with the motto, *Jacta est alea*), BÖCKING, vol. iii. pp. 473 sqq.

tors, secretaries, nuncios, chamberlains, copyists, beadles, room-warmers, ass-drivers, grooms, and an innumerable throng of prostitutes of both sexes. . . . Besides all these, they keep dogs and horses, apes and monkeys, and many more curious beasts in which they delight; they build houses of marble, and decorate themselves with jewels to their hearts' content; they live and dress magnificently, gormandize, revel, and follow the dictates of their lusts. In fine, our money maintains many useless persons in idleness at Rome. There is there no care for religion, and no fear of God, but only rioting, security, contempt of God and man, to an extent scarcely to be found among the Turks."

Luther himself wrote "against the bull of antichrist,"[1] complaining especially of the malicious misrepresentation of his doctrines: "As the spider sucks poison from the rose, to the detriment of the same flower whence the little bee draws innocent honey, so that wretched generation of vipers, as Christ calls them, have done with my sermon on *Repentance*, in which I taught that contrition should proceed from a love of righteousness—the identical doctrine that they themselves write and teach, and yet do not understand." The burning of books is an easy thing, he said; even children could do that. Let men think what they would of the bull, he proceeded, he knew that, by the grace of God, he was independent of it,—he knew where his consolation and confidence were to be found, and that they were assured to him in the face of men and of devils. In conclusion, he recommended that earnest prayer should be made to God that He would turn away His anger from the adversaries and redeem them from the evil spirit that possessed them.

That, however, which occasioned the greatest stir was the symbolical act whereby Luther set forth his separation from the papal ordinances and the laws of Rome in a manner that was intelligible to every one, but whereby he also kindled a fire which it was beyond his power to quench. On the 10th of

---

[1] *Contra execrabilem Antichristi Bullam (wider die Bullen des Endechrists).*

December 1520, he publicly announced, by a placard, that it was his intention to burn the papal decretals and bulls at nine o'clock of the same morning. A large number of doctors and students accompanied him to the Elster Gate. A preceptor of the University applied the torch to the pile, and when the fire was kindled, Luther cast into it the papal decretals,[1] together with the bull of the pope, and some few writings of his opponents, John Eck and Jerome Emser, pronouncing meantime the following words suggested by Joshua vii. 25 :—" Because thou hast troubled the Holy One of the Lord, may the eternal fire trouble and devour thee."

Different opinions have been expressed in regard to this step of Luther's, and it is fitting that we should enter upon a somewhat closer examination of it. Some have regarded it as the most heroic of his actions, whilst others look upon it as mere empty rhodomontade. Either view appears to me to be extreme. That Luther did not himself regard the burning of books as a particularly heroic act, is perfectly evident from his own utterances; for the day after the event described, he admonished the students to whom he was lecturing, that they must not think that everything was accomplished with the burning of those papers, but must continually be on their guard against the pernicious errors of the pope, and vigorously combat them. But, on the other hand, neither should we judge the step too harshly. It must be remembered that the Romish Church had itself taken the initiative in the matter of *burning*, and that not merely in regard to *books: men* had, for the sake of the faith which they held, been consumed by thousands in fires of its kindling. Luther's books themselves had shortly before been given to the flames.[2] The burning of the bull, therefore, was rather a sort of ironical comment on the conduct of Rome than of any special importance in itself.

[1] [The Canon law was burned at this time. See D'AUBIGNÉ, vol. ii. p. 106. —TR.]

[2] Comp. Luther's tract, " Why the Books of the Pope and his Disciples have been burned by Dr. Martin Luther. Let who will show why *they* have burned Dr. Luther's Books ;" also, *Grund und Ursach aller Artikel, u.s.w.*

It was designed to intimate that the time for such burnings had gone by; that if the papal party could build piles, the reforming party could do so likewise; and that if the former had no better arguments than such fires, Luther and his friends would not fear them. Such, manifestly, was the meaning of the act. The proceeding was, moreover, by no means an unexampled one. Jerome of Prague and his associates had, a century before, burned the bull which condemned Huss; and that which was issued against Luther was treated with much indignity in other places besides Wittenberg. At Döblin, for instance, it was soiled and torn, and the following words were inscribed upon it:—" The nest is here; the birds are flown."[1] Hutten satirically celebrated the destruction of the bull and decretals in a German requiem.[2] " Weep and howl," he cried to the Romanists; " Be glad and rejoice," to the Germans and all true Christians. " The toils of human laws and ordinances in which we were held, are, by the will of God and with His help, cut through as with a sharp axe. Thank God, we are loosed from them. Now may the healing waters of the divine law, so long troubled and poisoned by the foul slough of the Romish decretals and papal ordinances, flow pure again. Now may the truth be spoken freely and with impunity. Now may we with impunity be Christians. The heaven has again opened over our heads through the goodness and mercy of God. The thunderbolts of papal excommunication have been dashed in pieces like glass. May they rest eternally (*requiem æternam dona eis Domine*)."

Had Luther performed no greater action than the burning of the bull and the issue of a few polemical writings, his fame would deservedly have been small, and he would have shared it with those who in every age have sounded the tocsin. But if a man, and especially a Christian, appears *greatest* upon occasions when pure enthusiasm lifts him above

---

[1] Comp. Letters 293 and 294 in DE WETTE, vol. i.
[2] *Hutten's Werke*, edited by BÖCKING, vol. iii. pp. 470 sqq.

passion and its paroxysms; when the pure consciousness of right alone gives him that loftier courage which not even passion, at its highest point, is able to bestow; when, in the patient bearing of his cross, he follows his Lord and Master, then is he great indeed; and it is upon such an eminence, attained by few, that we are now about to behold Luther, on the occasion of his appearance before the *Diet of Worms*.

This Diet had assembled toward the end of the year 1520. The Emperor Charles, whilst at Oppenheim, had requested the Elector of Saxony to bring Luther with him to the Diet, in order that the Reformer might there undergo examination. This, however, was not agreeable to the papal party, and especially the legates, because it did not seem to them proper that a matter which belonged exclusively to the ecclesiastical tribunal should be decided at a secular diet. The effort was therefore made to hinder, by any means, Luther's appearance at Worms; another bull had even been launched against him, in which his excommunication was declared in such wise that every Catholic Christian was bound to regard the mere holding of intercourse with him as a sin.[1] Notwithstanding this, Luther was cited to appear before the Diet, and a free imperial safe-conduct was offered him; and Luther showed himself inclined to obey the citation.[2]

At this Diet a number of complaints, emanating from secular quarters, and amounting in all to 101, had been urged against the pope; and even those who were unfavourable to the cause of Luther—Duke George of Saxony, for instance—agreed in these complaints. The relation which the Diet sustained toward Luther resembled the relation sustained by the Synod of Constance toward Huss. Men wished for a reformation, but hated the reformer; they were desirous of

---

[1] The bull *Decet Romanum Pontificem*. Soon afterwards the third bull, *De Cœna Domini*, appeared, and was answered by Luther in his pamphlet entitled, *Vom Abendfressen des allerheiligsten Herrn, des Papstes* ["On the Supper of the Most Holy Lord, the Pope"] (1522).

[2] Compare on this subject several glorious letters of Luther's in DE WETTE, vol. i. Nos. 277, 288, 302, 305-307.

victory, but shunned the conflict. Luther, indeed, anticipated a fate similar to that of Huss, but, nevertheless, went resolutely to meet it. "If I do not return," said he to his beloved Philip Melanchthon as he took leave of him,—"if I do not return, and my enemies murder me, I conjure thee, dear brother, not to cease to teach and to stand by the truth. Work, meantime, for me also, because I cannot be here; thou canst do better than I. It is not of much consequence what becomes of me, if thou remain. The Lord has a learned warrior left in thee." Luther then tore himself from the arms of his friend and set out for Worms. He was accompanied by his colleague, Nicholas Amsdorf, and by the learned professor of law, Jerome Schurf, who was his advocate at the Diet; a nobleman and his own brother, James Luther, also went with him. The imperial herald, Caspar Sturm, in his robes of office, and bearing the imperial eagle, rode on horseback, with his servant, in advance of Luther and his party. Justus Jonas, who had recently received a call to Wittenberg, travelled from Erfurt to Weimar to meet the Reformer.[1] Luther's journey resembled a triumphal procession, although he was under the ban of the pope. His reception at Erfurt was particularly brilliant. The Rector and the professors of the University met him at Nora, a village on the borders of the Erfurt territory, at a distance of about two leagues from the town; in this party there were forty men on horseback, besides a number who followed on foot. The Rector, Crotus Rubianus, and the learned Eoban Hesse greeted the distinguished guest with orations and poems. Surrounded by a mass of human beings, the waggon which contained Luther and his friends drove into the city, whose streets, gates, and roofs were crowded with spectators. After much persuasion, Luther preached a sermon in the church of the Augustinians, in presence of a numerous audience. In this sermon, which was against work-righteousness, he declared that among three thousand priests it would be difficult to find four upright

[1] See PRESSEL, *Justus Jonas*, Elberfeld, 1862, p. 19.

ones. During the sermon there was some confusion in the gallery, which threatened to fall on account of the crowd. Luther, remarking this, exhorted the congregation to pay no regard to this "devilish sport," nor to suffer their minds to be drawn off from their devotion. Tradition afterwards affirmed that the devil on this occasion moved a stone from the gable of the church. A similar anecdote is related concerning a sermon preached by Luther in Gotha. At Eisenach he fell sick, but recovered "upon the letting of some blood and the taking of a cordial that the physician gave him." "When he entered a town," says a contemporary, Frederick Myconius,[1] "the people flocked together to see the wonderful man who was so brave, and who dared make a stand against the pope and all the world, that held him to be a God, in opposition to Christ. Some gave him poor comfort, telling him that, because there were so many cardinals and bishops at Worms at the Diet, he would speedily be burned to powder, as Huss had been at Constance. But Luther answered such men as follows: 'And if they should build a fire between Wittenberg and Worms that would reach to heaven, in the Lord's name I would appear, and step into Behemoth's mouth, between his great teeth, and confess Christ, and let Him do His pleasure.'" As the friends of Huss had once been anxious to turn him from his purpose, so the friends of Luther were desirous of dissuading him from carrying out his intentions. At Oppenheim he was met by Bucer, who was then in the service of the Knight Francis von Sickingen, and who offered him the castle of the latter, the Ebernburg, as a secure residence. It was thought that he might there come to an understanding with Glapio, the confessor of the emperor, who was commissioned to dispute with him, without its being necessary for him to go to Worms. But Luther answered: "I will go on; if the emperor's confessor has anything to say to me, he can say it at Worms." Spalatin also, the court

---

[1] See WALCH's edition of *Luther's Werke*, vol. xv., and MARHEINEKE, vol. i. p. 155.

preacher of the Elector of Saxony, and the intimate friend of Luther, advised him, by a post messenger, that he must not go immediately to Worms. It was then that Luther uttered his ever memorable speech: "And if there were as many devils at Worms as there are tiles upon the roofs, I would go thither." This, manifestly, is the moment in Luther's life when he appears at his greatest; he has reached the culminating-point of manly strength and decision; he is far removed from all visionary fanaticism and arrogant assumption, and elevated above all the considerations of human weakness. He stands forth a hero in the hand of God, resting only on that faith which is mighty in the weak. He was, subsequently, himself unable to comprehend this boldness, and looked upon it as a miracle, due entirely to the grace of God. "I was undismayed" (he declared at a later period, in regard to his condition of mind, so incomprehensible to himself) "and afraid of nothing. God is able, I doubt not, to make a man so mad-brained. I know not whether I should be so joyous now." And Matthesius, his pious biographer, adds: "Thus does the heart expand within the body, giving strength and courage to both preachers and warriors." On the 16th of April 1521, at ten o'clock in the morning, Luther entered Worms in company with his escort; many of the nobility had met him outside of the city, and over 2000 persons escorted him to his lodgings. Let us hear his own description of his arrival: "Thus, with my hood on my head, I drove into Worms in an open waggon. All the people poured into the streets, desiring to see Doctor Martin, the monk. I drove to the hotel of Duke Frederick, who was troubled on account of my having come to Worms."[1]

On the morning after his arrival, he was cited by the hereditary marshal of the empire, Ulric von Pappenheim, to appear before the assembled Diet. Pappenheim himself called for him at four in the afternoon, and went before him in company with the imperial herald. They had to work their way

---

[1] *Luther's Werke*, WALCH'S ed., vol. xv.

through an immense crowd, and, because the streets were overflowing with human beings, were frequently obliged to pass through the adjoining gardens to reach the "house of judgment," as Luther called the place where the Diet was convened.[1] At the door of the hall, the grey-haired warrior George Frundsberg was stationed. This veteran tapped Luther on the shoulder, saying, "O little monk, little monk! thou art marching now to make such a stand as was never known either by myself or many another officer in the hottest battle. If thou art in the right and sure of thy cause, go forward, in God's name, and be of good cheer, for He will not forsake thee." Thus greeted, Luther entered the hall, and found himself in the midst of the assembled lords of the Diet. Near the emperor sat the Archduke Ferdinand, his brother; and besides these two high dignitaries there were six electoral princes, twenty-eight dukes, thirty prelates, a number of landgraves and margraves, archbishops, bishops, abbots, deputies from cities, and ambassadors from almost all the kingdoms of Europe, making an assemblage of about 200 illustrious personages. The two papal legates, Marino Caraccioli and Jerome Aleander, were also present. Several thousand persons were assembled in the passages, the neighbouring streets, and about the windows. On a table in the middle of the hall lay Luther's books. John von Eck, chancellor of the Archbishop of Treves (not to be confounded with Eck of Ingolstadt), asked him if he acknowledged these books to be his, to which Luther replied in the affirmative. He was then

---

[1] The locality in which the examination of Luther took place was recently made the subject of discussion, viz. on the occasion of the query as to where the Memorial of Luther by Rietschel should be erected, in "the Town Hall or the Bishop's palace." That the examination did not take place in the Town Hall, but that it was held in the Bishop's palace, was proved conclusively by Dr. Friedrich Eich (in opposition to Dr. Hohenreuther), in his article on the subject published in 1863. To this paper a plan of the city is attached, by means of which it is possible to follow the route of Luther from his lodgings to the assembled Diet. The memorial was finally put up in neither of the above-mentioned localities, but in a place that was still better fitted for it, where it was solemnly unveiled 25th June 1868. Comp. Dr. Eich's account of the celebration, published at Worms, 1868.

asked whether he would recant them. This question he desired time to consider. The next day he was again sent for at four o'clock in the afternoon to attend the Diet; but it was not until six that he gained admission to the hall, the crowd outside being so great. Permission to speak was now granted him, which he accordingly accepted. He began by excusing himself with much modesty for any offence against form that he might commit during his discourse, or for any mistake that he might be guilty of in the use of the titles of those in whose presence he stood, " not having been brought up," as he said, " in courts, but in the cloister, and being therefore unaccustomed to speak before great lords." He then defended himself in regard to the books which he had written, showing that it was impossible for him to retract any of these, so far as the essential contents of them were concerned, although he acknowledged that he might now and then have used more vehement expressions than were consistent with his station. " But," he continued, " I, being a man and not God, cannot help or defend my poor books in any other way than that pursued by my Lord and Saviour with reference to His doctrine. When He was questioned by the high priest Annas concerning His doctrine, and when He had received a blow from the high priest's servant, He said, ' If I have spoken evil, prove that it is evil.' Now if the Lord, who knew that He could not err, refused not to listen to testimony against His doctrine, even from a mean and contemptible servant, how much more should I, who am but dust and ashes, and apt to err, challenge testimony against my doctrine? Wherefore, by the mercy of God, I entreat your imperial majesty, your electoral and princely graces, or any other person, of high or low degree, who may have the requisite ability, to bring testimony against me, to prove by prophetic and apostolic Scriptures that I have erred. If I be convinced of this, I shall be willing and ready to recant all error, and will be the first to fling my books into the fire."

These words and many besides were spoken by Luther, at

first in German, and then, at the emperor's request, in Latin. But his opponents were not satisfied. The electoral official Von Eck demanded that he should give a short and positive answer as to whether he would recant or not. Upon this Luther said: "Since your imperial majesty and your electoral and princely graces desire a plain, simple, and positive answer, I will give you one which shall have neither horns nor teeth, —namely, Unless I am conquered and convinced by the testimony of the Holy Scriptures, or by open, clear, and distinct grounds and reasons,—for I believe neither pope nor councils alone, because it is manifest that they have often been mistaken and contradicted themselves,—unless, therefore, I am convicted [of error] by passages that I have myself cited, and my conscience is thus taken captive by the word of God, I can and will recant nothing, for it is neither safe nor prudent to do aught against one's conscience. *Here I stand. I can do no otherwise. God help me. Amen!*"[1]

After having thus spoken, he was dismissed, with an escort of two men. Some noblemen who thought that he was being led away prisoner made emphatic demonstrations against such a procedure, but professed their satisfaction when they heard that he was only about being convoyed to his lodgings.

Luther's discourse made a powerful impression upon the minds of those who heard him, and several of the princes and counts who were present at the Diet visited him at his inn. Duke Eric of Brunswick sent him a can of Eimbecker beer by a page. Luther, upon seeing that no harm was meant him, took a draught of the beer, and said, "As Duke Eric has this day remembered me, so may our Lord Jesus Christ remember him in his last struggle." Eric thought of these words upon his deathbed, and desired a page who stood by— Francis von Kramm by name—to refresh him with the consolations of the gospel. The young landgrave, Philip of

---

[1] According to recent investigations, Luther made use of the last words only, "God help me. Amen!" Comp. BURKHARDT, *Ueber die Glaubwürdigkeit der Antwort Luthers, u.s.w.*, in *Theol. Stud. u. Krit*, 1869, Part iii.

Hesse, afterwards one of the most active promoters of the Reformation, was among the number of those who visited him; at his departure he shook Luther by the hand, saying, "If you are in the right, Doctor, may God help you!" That which was of special importance to Luther, however, was that his own sovereign, the Elector Frederick the Wise, was won over entirely to his side, and being, as it were, mailed and armed by Luther's speech, he henceforth took more vigorous measures in defence of his cause. The very same evening, before supper, the elector sent to Luther's inn for Spalatin, received him in his cabinet, and made the following remark to him: "Father, Doctor Martin spoke well before the emperor and all the princes and estates of the empire. He was but far too bold for me."

Notwithstanding the decided answer of Luther, there were further attempts made to induce him to recant, and several private conferences were held with him,[1] the result of which was that Luther appealed to the counsel of Gamaliel: "If the work is of men, it will speedily come to nought; but if it is of God, ye cannot overthrow it."

After Luther had passed a fortnight at Worms, he was dismissed from the Diet. He was enjoined not to preach on his way home. Declaring, however, that the word of God was free, he preached, despite the injunction, at Hirschfeld and Eisenach. As he was making a little detour from the latter place, in order to visit some of his relatives and friends at Möhra, near Salzungen, he was suddenly fallen upon, in the neighbourhood of Altenstein and Waltershausen, by a company of horsemen, lifted out of the waggon, and, whilst his companions, Nicholas Amsdorf and James Luther, were suffered quietly to go on their way,[2] he was set upon a horse, driven about for some hours in the forest, and finally, at eleven

---

[1] Comp. MARHEINEKE, vol. i. pp. 268 sq.; MENZEL, i. pp. 96 sq.; RAUMER, *Neuere Geschichte der Deutschen*, vol. i. pp. 262 sq.

[2] He had previously parted from his other companions; even the imperial herald had taken leave of him at Friedsberg.

o'clock at night, brought to the castle of Wartburg, near Eisenach, which had formerly been the seat of the old landgraves of Thuringia. It soon became evident that this sudden capture, which in all probability was ordered by the elector,[1] was intended to secure the wellbeing and personal safety of the Reformer; for, although he had been permitted to leave Worms with a free escort, there was issued against him on the 26th of May an edict of proscription, which was chiefly the work of the papal legate Aleander. Thus was Luther, in accordance with the imperial decree, declared to be under the ban of the empire; his books were interdicted, and all persons "who should house him or give him food or drink, or aid him, secretly or openly, by word or work," were threatened with the ban of the empire. The same punishment was to extend to the relations of Luther, if they did not give evidence that they had turned from the wrong path and received papal absolution. The same penalty was likewise to be incurred by any who should read, sell, copy, or print Luther's writings, and every one was enjoined to burn and destroy these writings. The decree gives a fearful description of the character of Luther. He was a man, it declared, who taught the propriety of a life of perfect licence and complete conformity to one's own selfish will and desires—a life of utter disregard of all law, and of thorough bestiality; a man who reprobated and overturned all laws; in fact, he was no man, but the devil himself in the form of a man, and clad in the hood of an Augustinian, etc.

When Luther arrived at the Wartburg, he found secular garments ready for him to put on. He also let his hair and beard grow, after the manner of the laity, and was known in the vicinity by the name of Knight George [*Junker Jörg*]. Now and then, that he might do honour to his supposed knighthood, he engaged in worldly pursuits. He relates that

---

[1] Luther's own suspicions in regard to the plan may be gathered from the letter which he wrote during his journey from Worms to his friend Lucas Cranach. See DE WETTE, vol. i. p. 311; comp. PFIZER, pp. 232 sqq. [see also D'AUBIGNÉ's *Hist. of the Ref.* vol. ii. p. 257].

he went hunting, but, amidst the nets and the dogs, cherished theological thoughts, comparing the poor beasts of the chase with human souls, for which the devil lies in wait with his hunters and his hounds, whilst Christ, the Good Huntsman, has such difficulty in seizing a soul for Himself.[1]

Luther's life at the Wartburg is a romantic episode in the history of the German Reformation. This period of the Reformer's life is enshrined within the memory of the German people, and song and story have in many instances contributed to confirm the reminiscences of it and to decorate their subject. Who does not know the tale of the inkstand which Luther is said to have flung in the face of the devil, as he stood by the wall, mocking him with malicious grimaces, whilst the Reformer was engaged in his translation of the Bible? and what wanderer through Northern Germany does not boast of having seen the stain occasioned by this exploit, and renewed from time to time by an industrious hand in honour of the great name of its author?

Protestants as well as Catholics have their legends, but those of the former are less connected with *religious* belief, and more closely confined to the realm of harmless popular wit; the Protestant Church, moreover, contributes less to the maintenance of faith in the legends. Now whilst something of a real and deeper nature lies at the bottom of most popular traditions and popular belief in general, we need not wonder that Luther's sojourn at the Wartburg should have given rise to marvellous and extravagant stories. A significant turning-point is here visible in the life of Luther, as well as in the general history of the Reformation. Hitherto the hero of our drama has marched steadily forward, unchecked, and as though borne by a foreign and higher power. As the mist disappears before the sun, so evil spirits, exorcised by his

---

[1] Comp. Letter 325 in DE WETTE, vol. ii. Luther's letters from the Wartburg, dated sometimes "from l'atmos," sometimes "from the wilderness," sometimes "from the kingdom of the air and the birds," are exceedingly important in assisting us to form a just estimate of the Reformer; they give us profound insights into his character.

word, flee before him to the place of darkness. The mouth of slanderers is stopped by the pure word of truth, and the thunderbolt of excommunication rebounds, powerless, from the triple mail that shields the bold breast of the hero. He dares defy even the prince of darkness and his hosts; for the declaration, that if there were as many devils at Worms as there were tiles upon the housetops, was, in Luther's mouth, no mere figure of speech; it was possessed of full import for him who believed in the *substantiality* of the devil and his comrades as firmly as he believed in the existence of his own person. And the devil bowed before the mighty one. The stronger had come and had bound the strong one; Luther had set his foot upon the dragon's head. Must he not sometimes have seemed to himself to be an extraordinary vessel of the Lord—a being of a higher sort, whom the spirits obeyed? a hero, a saint, who merited heaven by the strength of his faith, by the greatness of his courage? History bears witness to the fact that this bold thought never attained to maturity in the soul of Luther; and if it be true that he who subdues his own heart is greatest, Luther's greatest triumph still consists in the humility with which, to the end of his life, he regarded his work. Never did he presume to appropriate to himself the name and dignity of a prophet even (in the eminent sense of the word), much less of a saint. In his own opinion of himself he was always the unworthy instrument by which God had served Himself—the impure vessel of honour into which, notwithstanding its own utter demerit, heaven had poured the fulness of its grace. But such sentiments as these could gain strength and firmness only in conflict. It was in the wilderness that the tempter once approached the Lord; over Him, however, Satan had no power. Should it fare better with the servant than with the Master? Or have we any right to exact from one who was but a sinful child of humanity, as perfect a victory as was gained by the Author and Finisher of the faith? Can we wonder that the assaults upon Luther waxed hotter, the lowlier the station which he took at His Master's feet? And truly these assaults came not merely from his own flesh and blood; outside of him there were temptations, trials, and dangers enough. The die was cast, the fire was kindled, the flame was spreading—who could restrain it? All around friends of the new doctrine were rising, and to many, doubtless, it was welcome only because it was—or, rather, seemed to be—a new one. What a sad turn might be given to the whole affair! The work had been begun in the Spirit, but who could guarantee that it should not end in the flesh? Might not the bold language uttered before the emperor and the empire strike a harmonious chord in the breasts of those who desired a new order of things only from love of licence? Might not the doctrine that a Christian is lord of all things [1] be misunderstood and abused? In one word, might not the *Reformation* which Luther designed to bring about be followed by *revolution?* Might not the latter, should it gain the upper hand, destroy in the germ all that was noble in the former, and cause mischief instead of the meditated good? And should the better principle be crushed, would not a reaction, more fearful than the preceding state of things, necessarily set in? would not the kingdom of darkness raise a shout of triumph louder than before? and, in case of all this, was not the door shut and the bolt drawn against any, even the best-intentioned, reform for centuries?

These and many similar thoughts may well have passed through the breast of Luther; and if he did not think them in these words, he thought them after his own fashion—vigorously, vividly, not in abstractions; nay, in bold, gigantic images that thronged before his exhausted soul, that menaced him in the form of embodied devils, with lifted finger and hideous grin! What marvel is it that, sojourning in the midst of a wild and gloomy solitude, left to his own sad thoughts, sick and weary in body, at war in the innermost recesses of his soul, he believed himself to be actually struggling with the powers of darkness? What marvel that Luther, not accustomed, as we

[1] Comp. LUTHER's treatise, *On the Liberty of a Christian,* Wittenberg, 1520.

are, to regard the external and the internal of life as separate things, but looking upon one as the mirror of the other, became possessed with the idea that the devil was mocking him and jeering at him at the very time when he was engaged in the holiest work, viz. in preparing, by the translation of the Bible, the weapons with which he hoped to combat the kingdom of evil with assured success?

The *translation of the Bible* into the vernacular may be regarded as the key-stone of the Reformation, in so far as the latter was dependent upon the person of Luther. The Bible once given to the people, the foundation of the new building laid,—the old and firm foundation that none can move,—other builders might come and finish the work. Luther's task was accomplished. We may therefore designate the time of Luther's sojourn at the Wartburg as the epoch from which his personality begins to retire behind the further history of the Reformation. Henceforth the work is no longer in his hand; it is the property of his time, his people, and the spirit of the times; a spirit, which he himself is unable to restrain, takes possession of it and urges it on, for evil as well as for good. Not that Luther was not continually making noble efforts to influence this spirit of the times, not that his influence did not continue to be a mighty one—ay, on some occasions it was even too great; but he now manifestly withdraws within the ranks of other men who were labouring upon the new structure with equal enthusiasm and frequently with greater discretion and circumspection. If it is a law of history that every personality bears within itself a measure which it is not permitted to exceed, Luther reached his meridian at the Diet of Worms; and had Providence been pleased, in removing him to the Wartburg, to withdraw him for ever from the eyes of the world, his end would have been like an apotheosis. But history is not a play; and not those things which the idle spectator would pronounce effective, but such as are for the profit of every man in the situation in which God has placed him, are carried out in joy and sorrow, in poetry and prose, with all their lights and shades, as a higher wisdom sees fit. We must therefore speedily accustom ourselves no longer to perceive in Luther the extraordinary man of God solely; shades in his character will soon appear, and we shall meet with some things that will disturb and annoy us in the further course of his life and works. But before this comes to pass, let us once more view him advancing with all the power of a *true* prophet against the false prophets who have pressed into the sanctuary of God. Driven by the Spirit, he returns from the Wartburg to Wittenberg, and quenches the flame of riot with words of authority and holy earnestness.

Just now, however, we will examine neither the shadows of the Reformation in general nor those of the great Reformer in person. Rather let us collect in one focus all the rays which stream upon us from different directions, and draw from this new light all the edification that we can, before turning our eyes to the less cheerful portions of the picture.

We remarked, a short time ago, that by the translation of the Bible Luther placed the key-stone upon his personal work in the Reformation, and laid the foundation for the further development of the latter, whose centre of gravity is now no longer to be sought for in his person, but in its own essence. Before proceeding farther, we must devote a little space to the consideration of this great deed of faith and learning.

It needs but a passing glance at Dr. Martin Luther's translation of the Bible, found to-day in every peasant's hut as one of the necessaries of life, to effect the conviction that such a work could not have been accomplished in as short a time as was comprised in the sojourn of Luther at the Wartburg. Tempting as it may be to the fancy to picture Luther in his solitude as busied with the Bible in much the same manner as John on Patmos was with the Apocalypse, we find that in historic actuality the matter is somewhat modified. Only the New Testament and the five books of Moses were translated at the Wartburg, and even of these it was for the most part but the first draft that was there prepared. The remaining books of the Old Testament appeared later, and the entire translation was not completed until 1534. This, however, need not hinder us from here reviewing the whole work, and estimating it with a due regard to the standpoint of the time in which it originated.

Any one who is acquainted with the difficulties which, even at the present day, beset the most learned philologist in a translation of the Old and New Testaments, will not only find it comprehensible that several revisions were necessary before the work arrived at that degree of perfection in which we possess it, but he will be amazed that it attained to such a degree at all. I do not intend to say that Luther's translation is in all respects one that it is impossible to improve upon. Every unprejudiced person recognises its defects, and nought save a senseless fanaticism could entertain the idea of embellishing even the errors of this translation by assuming them to be the product of divine inspiration. But despite the many errors in detail, which can readily be corrected by the learning of our own day, in the present advanced stage of philological aids,[1] the *whole* is imbued with such an unction of the Spirit, such vigour and impressiveness of language, such an inner harmony, that we are at once convinced that none but a mind filled with the spirit of Christian piety could succeed in apprehending and representing the word of life with such freshness and vitality. Regarded as a merely human work, what great linguistic knowledge it displays, what tact in the choice of expressions, what felicity of style, what naturalness, what simplicity, what true genius! The high value which attaches to Luther's version of the Bible from a mere *linguistic* point of view has long been recognised by philological scholars. As is the case, however, with all intellectual works of high merit, men are not wont to consider the difficulties amidst which it arose. As a fine poem, in which the verses flow along smoothly and easily, seeming as if they had spontaneously suggested

---

[1] We take pleasure in referring here to the excellent version of DE WETTE, which, in respect of philological accuracy, far surpasses that of Luther.

themselves to the mind of the poet, has occasioned the latter far more research than we who hear it can imagine, so many of the readers of Luther's Bible might not readily believe how much time and trouble were spent upon the minutest points. It will therefore be better to cite a few instances in illustration of our statement. Luther himself wrote thus in later letters to his friends: "We are now at work" (he thus expresses himself to Wenceslaus Link, in 1528[1]) "on the prophets, turning them into German. What a tremendous and vexatious work it is to force the Hebrew writers to speak German! How they struggle against it, and will not quit their Hebrew to follow the rude German; it is as if one should strive to make a nightingale leave off her lovely melody and imitate the cuckoo." And in another place he remarks concerning the same difficulties: "It has been my constant effort to render the Hebrew into pure and clear German, and it has often happened that we have worked at a single word for two, three, and four weeks, and yet have sometimes not found a satisfactory translation for it. In Job, Master Philip, Aurogallus, and I were sometimes four days in getting off three lines. Well, now that it is turned into German and finished, any one can read and master it. One may run his eyes over three or four pages without a single stumble, and without guessing how many rocks and stocks once lay there—there where it is now as smooth as a planed board, but where we had to sweat and toil. It is good ploughing when the field is cleared."

Luther displayed wonderful tact as a translator in keeping the true mean between too wide a departure from the original and a pedantic punctiliousness alien to the spirit of his vernacular. He designed making a translation for the German *people;* he therefore introduced German terms in measures,

---

[1] Comp. on this entire section J. G. MÜLLER's *Reliquien,* vol. iii. pp. 291 sqq., and several letters of Luther relating to this subject in vol. ii. of DE WETTE's *Collection.* See also HOPF, *Würdigung der Lutherischen Bibelverdeutschung, mit Rücksicht auf ältere und neuere Uebersetzungen,* Nuremberg, 1847; WETZEL, *Die Sprache Luthers in seiner Bibelübersetzung,* Stuttgart, 1859.

weights, and coins—for instance, such as *Groschen, Scheffel* [= bushel], etc.; he also translated the word proconsul by *Landpfleger* [= governor of a province], and did many other things of a similar nature. He also occasionally inserted the word *Lieber* [= dear, good] when he thought that the insertion of it would give a milder turn to the sentence. To illustrate: In speaking of the angel's greeting to Mary, he remarks that the literal rendering of it is as follows: Mary, full of grace.[1] "But," says he, "when does a German thus speak? He thinks of a cask full of beer, or a purse full of money. I have therefore thus Germanized it: Thou gracious [or lovely] one! [*du Holdselige*]. And if I had used the best German I should have translated it: God greeteth thee, thou dear Mary; for this is what the angel means, and just what he would have said if he had wanted to greet her in German. Whoever understands German knows what a sweet and affectionate word that is: Thou *dear* Mary! [*du liebe Maria*]; the dear God! the dear emperor! the dear man! I know not whether they have aught so affectionate and heart-satisfying in the Latin and other languages as the word *Liebe*—aught that so presses and rings into the heart through all the senses as that word does in our mother tongue."

The unutterable pains that Luther gave himself, with a view to fully mastering the treasury of the German language, are interestingly illustrated by his own letters and the records of contemporaries. In order that he might correctly designate the precious stones mentioned in the Revelation of John (chap. xxi.), and that he might himself have a just conception of what he was writing, he procured, through his friend Spalatin, the loan of a selection of such jewels from the cabinet of the elector. He likewise obtained minute and circumstantial information in regard to the names of certain animals, birds of prey, and reptiles mentioned in the Bible. He frequently mingled with the common people on the market-place, that he might catch their manner of speaking from their very

[1] [Κεχαριτωμένη, *much graced*, as the margin of the E. V. has it.—Tr.]

mouths, as it were; and he commissioned his friends to furnish him with a supply of good popular expressions, for, he declared, he could not use "the words of castles and courts." Upon one occasion (according to Matthesius) he made a butcher kill a sheep before him and explain to him the whole anatomy of the animal, in order that he might employ the appropriate terms in the translation of such passages in the Bible as speak of the Levitical sacrifices, the entrails of animals, etc.

Such labour Luther underwent that he might plant the precious Bible in the heart of the German people, and that he might make it, to use his own expression, not a mere reading-book, but a book and word of everyday life. In thus doing, it was not his idea to put forth a work that should be complete for all time; for, to the end of his days, he, in company with the other theologians of Wittenberg, was occupied in making corrections on his translation. Nor was it his intention to furnish theologians with an excuse for slothfulness, a substitute for the study of the original languages of Holy Writ; on the contrary, he desired that his work should be an incentive to such study. And if the German version had continued to be amended in accordance with his views, his aim would have been most fully attained; for he wished that every town might have its own translator of the Bible, in order that it might be on the tongues, and in the hands, eyes, ears, and hearts of all.[1] But it seems as though all times were not equally favourable for such pious undertakings. As spiritual song flourished most in the season of conflict and religious enthusiasm, so the Word of Life can be successfully translated only when it is experienced in the heart and proved in the life; and as the original is a work of the heavenly Spirit, so a translation also must be the issue of the promptings of the same Spirit. For where such is not the case, we may sing with Klopstock:[2]

[1] Compare the letter to Joh. Lange, DE WETTF, vol. ii. p. 354.
[2] The German Bible (*Odes*, vol. ii.).

"*Heiliger Luther, bitte für die Armen, denen Geistes-beruf nicht scholl und die doch Nachdolmetschen, dass sie zur Selbsterkenntniss endlich genesen!*"[1]

In concluding the present chapter, I will say a few words in relation to the external history and the reception of the work which we have been considering.

The books of the New Testament *first* appeared in the year 1522: two successive editions of them were issued by Melchior Lotter, the first in September, and the second in December; and in the same year a reprint of them was put forth by Adam Petri in Basel. The different portions of the Old Testament, the Pentateuch taking the lead, appeared from time to time, until in the year 1534 the entire Bible was completed and in the hands of the Christian people of Germany. The diffusion of this precious acquisition was very rapid. Three presses were daily employed in the printing of 10,000 sheets. Hans Luft, of Wittenberg, was the name of the printer. To the eagerness with which the Bible was received, the lamentations of the opponents of the evangelical doctrine afford a testimony that is beyond suspicion. John Cochlæus[2] complained bitterly that shoemakers and women, and in fact all the uneducated, who knew *nothing but German*, magnified the New Testament as the source of all truth, carried it about with them, and learned it by heart; and Jerome Emser[3] published, in 1523, a pamphlet, which Duke George of Saxony invited him to prepare, and in which he charged Luther with no less than 1400 heretical errors. The pretended heresies, however, were chargeable mainly upon the

---

[1] ["O holy Luther, pray for the poor souls to whom no spiritual call has e'er resounded, but who still insist upon translating Holy Writ, that they at length unto self-knowledge may attain!"]

[2] His real name was Dobeneck; he also for some time called himself "Wendelstein," after his birthplace in the neighbourhood of Nuremberg. Luther, in allusion to his Latin appellation, called him "Rotzlöffel" [Snivelspoon].

[3] Emser, who was several years the senior of Luther, was at first one of his friends. The Leipsic disputation, however, gave rise to an open breach between them, leading to a lengthy literary feud. Emser was at Leipsic in the service of Duke George of Saxony.

fact that Luther had ventured, in his translation, to depart from the Latin version recognised by the Church, viz. the Vulgate. In later times the Protestant Church has seen the day when departures from the Lutheran translation have been censured with almost equal harshness. And yet Luther never thought of giving to the Church a translation to which it should be bound for all time. That his translation has hitherto been as a whole unexcelled, remains a fact, although from this it does not follow that the work is in every respect unimprovable. Much has been done in our own day for the *spread* of the Bible. May the time come when, in pursuance of the laudable preparatory steps which have already been taken, the immortal work of Luther may be renewed in his spirit,—the spirit of popular and wholesome piety,—and a thoroughly revised translation of the Bible be presented to the people of the Church, as a memorial of the fruits of a Reformation which, in its effects, shall ever continue to live!

CHAPTER VII.

EXAMINATION OF LUTHER'S TRANSLATION OF THE BIBLE CONTINUED—HIS IDEAS IN REGARD TO THE BIBLE GENERALLY—MELANCHTHON'S "LOCI COMMUNES"—LUTHER'S FURTHER LITERARY LABOURS AT THE WARTBURG, AND THE CONTINUATION THENCE OF THE CONFLICT.

IT has often been remarked that one point of difference between reformatory and revolutionary operations consists in the fact that, whilst the latter restrict themselves to overthrowing and tearing down, the former are equally anxious to build up and to preserve.

Of this truth Luther afforded us a striking illustration in the preceding chapter. In the midst of the war that he was waging against abuses which he mercilessly combated, he prepared a *positive* remedy for the ills of his own time and of all succeeding ages in his translation of the Bible. According to his own expression, he did indeed "uproot thorns and brambles;" but in their stead he also planted the tree of life, under whose shade future generations might dwell in peace, and with whose fruit the traveller might regale himself. He did indeed "drain the marshes," but, like Moses, he also caused a fountain to spring from the rock, at which the thirsty might drink and be refreshed.

The benefit which Luther, by his translation of the Bible, conferred upon the German-speaking peoples cannot be sufficiently estimated. Not that he was the only person, or even the first, who had ever translated the Bible into German; for German versions had existed before his time, and his opponents set on foot a work similar to his own shortly after the completion of the Lutheran translation. If *all* were done with the simple doing of the *words* of the original into German, Luther might not merit all the praise that is now deservedly his. But none have so rendered the *spirit* of the Bible into German as he; and hence it is not so much the *letter* of his translation by which he has laid claim to our highest admiration (for in that he was most liable to err), but the *living mode of his apprehension* of the Bible. As the pious artists of that day frequently represented the subjects of sacred history in the costume of the current age, and introduced portraits of themselves kneeling, with folded hands, before the Redeemer, so Luther has given us in his translation of the Bible a picture painted in living colours on the ground of his own time, and thus he has sketched in the midst of it his own figure, his own physiognomy. Ay, Luther lived so entirely *in* and *with* the Bible, he was so bound up in its modes of thought and conception, as to reproduce it, so to speak, in his own personality, thus impressing a biblical stamp not only upon his own individual character, but also upon the character of the whole German people and language. It is therefore not merely the Bible *translated into German* that he has given us; it is the *German Bible*, the Bible *of Luther*—a monument of *his* spirit, *his* people, *his* age, a Bible of the sixteenth century, yet containing (as far as was possible) the one true Christian Bible, the pure and eternal word of God. This very meeting of the general and the individual, the mingling of the Christian and the popular, the spiritual link that here unites the worlds of the sun-rising and the sun-setting, is that which constitutes the significance, the grandeur, and the vital power of the work, in the contemplation of which qualities we are willing to forget its individual errors and drawbacks.[1]

---

[1] Comp. on this subject HÄUSSER, pp. 69 sqq. This author justly gives prominence to the blessing resultant to German national life from Luther's translation of the Bible. "The full magnitude of this blessing," he remarks,

On account of these considerations, it will be seen that we have not fully satisfied the requirements of our task in ascertaining, as we did in the preceding chapter, how Luther translated the Bible in detail; we must also discover what opinions he held in regard to the whole mass of this sacred book, which to him was the fountain and root of life. We must, if we are to comprehend his work, transport ourselves into the sphere of his living faith in the Bible, and feel with him the blessing which he experienced thence. Let us, therefore, abandon our chronological scheme, and examine a few of the various utterances of Luther concerning the Bible,

"did not become manifest until the centuries succeeding Luther." . . . "We are often tempted to inquire," he continues, "how it is that this German nation, which, since the sixteenth century, has been so terribly visited by internal and external convulsions, has conserved within its depths an indestructible kernel of national religious and moral training,—a kernel not always to be found amongst the higher ranks of the people, who only too readily subjected themselves to foreign influences, but retaining its vitality in the lower classes, untouched by the desolations of the Thirty Years' War or the flood of foreign customs and tastes [*Ausländerei*] which rushed in in the succeeding generations. The cause of this phenomenon is, that there was amongst us no cottage so small, no household so poor, that this book did not find its way to it; that Luther's Bible became for the *people*, in the peculiar sense of that term, not merely a book of prayer and devotion, but the reading and family book—in fact, their whole intellectual world, in which the young grew up, to which the old recurred, wherein the common man inscribed his family history and anniversaries, and from whose contents the weary and heavy laden drew comfort and alleviation for their sorrows in the day of need. The wars that made of our fair fatherland a great churchyard, a smoking waste of ashes, were unable to destroy this treasure; it continued to be the inalienable possession of the kernel of our nation at a time when our learned men had returned to the use of the Latin, and our men of polish and refinement spoke and wrote in French. For the conservation of our wholesome popular spirit, which no foreign fooleries or modish extravagances could corrupt, this book was an unequalled panacea. From the simple homes of our country pastors, our burgher and peasant families, by whom Luther's Bible was prized above all else, came the reformers of our national culture in the eighteenth century; and when these commenced their work of purifying our beautiful tongue from the disfiguring foreign elements which had been introduced into it, they had recourse to the inexhaustible treasury of this book: they recognised, with Lessing, that our language has become impoverished when we compare it with the riches of this work, and they found the most vital understanding of the Holy Scriptures not amongst the distinguished divines of the pigtailed pedant school [*Schriftgelehrte des correcten Zopfes*], but in the circles in which Luther's Bible had continued to be the *organum* of theology since the sixteenth century. In it the depth of feeling, the soul of the German nature, found full satisfaction."

as we find them scattered through his writings;[1] we shall thus attain, at the same time, a convenient resting-point in the history of the German Reformation, whence we may take a general survey of events, and afterwards present a view of contemporaneous occurrences.

Luther justly regarded the Bible not as a uniform system of theology, but as a rich mine of divine and human wisdom, as a living collection of books of various times, by different authors, in different styles, but all permeated by the same Spirit. The Bible, he declares, is a vast forest in which many trees of every species are found. From these trees we may gather all kinds of fruit; and, he continues, there is no tree in this forest at which he himself has not rapped, and broken or shaken thence a couple of apples or pears. In the wonderful preservation of this book he beheld the hand of Providence; and although he did not for its sake despise human books, the Bible was always to him the book of books. He found the proof of its divinity in its internal thoroughly religious character rather than in any outward marks. "The great, fine, and useful books of Homer, Virgil, and the like are *ancient* books, but they are nothing when compared with the Bible; for the books of the heathen teach nought of faith, hope, and love. They regard only present things, which we can feel, and which we can grasp and comprehend with our reason. But there is nothing in them about trusting and hoping in God. Such matters we must look for in the Psalms and the book of Job, which both treat of faith, hope, patience, and prayer. In short, the Holy Scriptures are the highest and best book of God, full of comfort in all tribulation; for they teach concerning faith, hope, and love many more things than the (mere) reason can see, feel, comprehend, and experience; and when we are in trouble, they teach us how these virtues should shine forth, and that there is another eternal life above this poor and wretched one." The highest aim in the investigation of the Bible is, according to him,

[1] Comp. especially his *Table Talk*, *Letters*, and J. G. MÜLLER'S *Reliquien*.

growth in the knowledge of Jesus Christ. To Him, the living Son of God, the whole of Sacred Writ directs us, and in His Spirit it must be understood. Never can man entirely exhaust its depths, never can he learn all that there is to be learned in it. We can get no farther than the A B C of the Bible. Beggars we are, and must remain."

Luther's laws of exegesis were as widely removed from that visionary fanaticism that pretends to explain the Holy Scriptures without the aid of human science and ability, and solely in accordance with assumed inspirations of the Spirit, as they were distant from that prosaic narrow-mindedness which fails to enter into the spirit of the Scriptures, from being completely taken up with minute and learned criticisms upon the words. He everywhere insists upon the so necessary knowledge of the original tongues, even beholding in these an instrument of the Holy Spirit. "The greater our love for the gospel," he declares, "the more importance should we attach to the languages." "Where there is an understanding of the languages, the work of expounding goes forward vigorously and powerfully; a familiar acquaintance with Scripture is gained, and faith is constantly renewed by fresh words and works." Despite the great importance which he attached to this useful branch of learning, however, he was far from believing that a mere grammatical knowledge of the sacred languages was alone sufficient to constitute the biblical exegete, if the unction of the Christian spirit were absent. In one place he expresses his wonderment at the young Hebraists of his time. He had anticipated much from their labours, he states; but it had fared with him as with King Solomon, who, after expecting precious things from India, had received apes and peacocks. "The Spirit of God must, therefore, Himself be our master and preceptor." Even in human things, like perceives like. "Whoso would rightly understand the *Pastorals* of Virgil," he remarks in another place, "must be a shepherd for at least five years; he who would understand his *Georgics* must busy himself for at least five years with agriculture; and no man will have a correct appreciation of Cicero's *Epistles* but he who has been for twenty years in a fine regiment. Nor can any one rightly understand the Holy Scriptures who has not reigned a hundred years with the prophets, John the Baptist, Christ, and the apostles of the Church." "For interpreting the Holy Scriptures," he says somewhere else, "a right pious, cheerful, diligent, God-fearing heart is needed—a heart, moreover, that is instructed, experienced, and practised in Christianity."

Luther was well aware that some who were wise in their own conceit would take offence at the simple form of the Bible—its childlike mode of presentation. For these over-clever persons he remarks: "I faithfully beseech and admonish every pious Christian not to be offended or stumble at the simple discourses and histories that are in the Bible, and not to doubt them; plain and foolish though they may seem, they are all words, works, histories, and judgments of the high Divine Majesty, Power, and Wisdom." . . . "In this book thou wilt find the swaddling-clothes and manger wherein Christ lay, and to which the angel directed the shepherds. The swaddling-clothes are plain and mean, but precious is Christ, the treasure they contain."

To Luther, apprehending the divine things with this clear and childlike mind, the strivings of those who believed themselves able, by their human intellect, to gauge and interpret the infinite fulness of Divine Wisdom must necessarily have appeared vain and idle; hence his frequent warnings against the one-sided application of reason [1] to matters of faith, and especially to the exposition of the Scriptures. With this supernatural view of the Bible, a purely human and natural mode of contemplating it was harmoniously combined. He was far from removing this sacred book to such a distance

---

[1] He calls it "Old Madam Storm-brewer" [*die " alte Frau Wettermacherin"* = sorceress]. In order that false inferences may be avoided, it should never be forgotten that he frequently applies the name of *reason* [*Vernunft*] to that which we more correctly call understanding [*Verstand*].

from the range of human vision that it could be only wondered at and admired; he desired that every individual portion of it should be tested and appreciated to the fullest extent possible to the human faculties, and that the proper place should be assigned to each of the different elements which compose it.

Whilst he regarded the whole Bible as the word of God, and perceived in it the living breath of the Holy Spirit, he did not shrink from recognising the *human idiosyncrasies* of the various writers, or from taking into consideration the different times in which they lived and for which they primarily wrote. Not every book of Scripture engaged his affection to an equal degree, or was accounted by him as of equal importance; on the contrary, he undisguisedly expresses his preference for some portions of the Bible, and his doubts and scruples in regard to others. In the Old Testament the Psalms were most prized by him; and truly the heat of the conflict in which Luther himself stood may be discerned throughout his translation of this book. The foes against whom David's petitions are indited are to him the never-extinct enemies of the kingdom of God, with whom *he* still has to fight; the strong fortress in whom *he* trusts is the same on whom Israel's faith was built. To him everything in the Psalms is prophetic, everything present, everything Messianic; everything is in connection with the grand course of the world's history. Let us listen to his own utterances: " Where do we find more glorious words of joy than in the psalms of praise and thanksgiving! In these thou lookest into the hearts of all the saints, as into fair and pleasant gardens—nay, as into heaven; thou seest what fine, lovely, and pleasant flowers, of all manner of beautiful and joyful thoughts of God and His benefits, grow up therein. Again, where dost thou find deeper, more lamentable, more grievous words of sadness than in the psalms of lamentation! In those again thou seest into the hearts of all the saints, as into death—nay, as into hell. How gloomy and dark it is with all sorts of troubled views of the anger of God! I hold that there has been and that there can be on earth no finer book of examples or legends of the saints than the Psalter; for there we find not only what one or two saints have done, but what the *Head of all* the saints has done, and what all the saints are still doing—how they comport themselves toward God, toward friends and foes, how they behave themselves in all dangers and sorrows. More than this, we there find all manner of divine and wholesome doctrines and commands. Hence it is that the Psalter is the *book of all saints*, and every man, in whatever circumstances he may be, can find a psalm and a word applicable to those circumstances, *and as appropriate for him as if they had been composed solely for his sake, insomuch that he could not himself write, or find, or wish for anything better.*"

In the New Testament, the Pauline Epistles, especially the Epistle to the Romans, and the Gospel of John possessed the highest esteem of Luther; next to these he valued the First Epistle of Peter. These, he declared, a Christian should study most, and assimilate them as he does his daily bread. John writes more concerning the preaching (doctrine) of Christ, whilst the other three Evangelists treat more extensively of His works and miracles. "Hence the Gospel of John is *far, far* preferable to the others; it is the unique, tender, true, main Gospel." The accounts of the miracles scattered throughout the Bible were in general not so highly valued by Luther as they have been by later theologians. Although a sincere believer in the miracles, he did not regard them as the objects of prime importance; more to him were the personal appearance and character of Christ, His doctrine, and the inner spiritual life. External miracles are the apples and nuts which God gave to the childish world as playthings; *we* no longer have need of them. We should let external miracles lead us to the far greater daily wonders of the inner world—wonders of faith and love.

Luther had, as is well known, a very unfavourable opinion of the Epistle of James; he called it an "epistle of straw," and declared that there was "nothing evangelical about it;" he, indeed, did not regard it as of genuine apostolical origin. That he carried these sentiments too far, will be confessed by every one who examines, with unprejudiced eyes, this epistle, so rich in practical Christian truths. Granting, however, that Luther was deceived in this point, his example will serve to show that what we call biblical criticism was practised even by the Reformers, and that the deepest reverence for the Bible as a whole is compatible with a liberality of judgment concerning individual portions of it and their relation to the whole. For Luther was as well aware as we should be that the collection of our sacred writings was of gradual growth, and was arranged by the Church of the first centuries, and that it is consequently the privilege of historic investigation to seek after an increasingly clear understanding of the external scope of this collection. There existed even in the first centuries disagreements relative to the reception of certain books into the canon. Why, then, should we strive to conceal what cannot be concealed? Luther was no friend to such hushings-up of doubts for pious ends. He would have every doubt fully agitated and discussed; and this freedom of investigation and trial continues to be the undiminished inheritance of the Protestant Church as contrasted with the Catholic Church, which lies benumbed and torpid in its positive decrees. He who would here curtail the right of investigation has to do with Luther and the rights of Protestant theology.

Luther disliked not only the Epistle of James, but also the Revelation of John, which latter book he did not regard as a work of the Evangelist and apostle. A knowledge of his views in reference to the last-mentioned book should be welcome to us at the present day, when a variety of opinions are rife concerning it,[1] although we need not think ourselves

---

[1] Luther himself says: "Some have concocted many ridiculous things out of their own heads" (in the *Preface* to the Apocalypse).

in any manner bound to fall in with his sentiments. He says: "In this book there are wanting more things than one to make me believe it either apostolic or prophetic. First, and principally, the apostles do not deal in visions, but prophesy in clear and plain terms, as do Peter and Paul, and also Christ in the Gospels; for it pertains to the apostolic office to speak clearly, and without figure or vision, of Christ and His work. There is no prophet in the Old Testament, much less in the New, who deals so entirely in visions; I therefore put this book almost on a par with the fourth book of Ezra,[1] *and I certainly cannot detect any trace of its having been inspired by the Holy Ghost.* Many of the fathers of the Church long ago rejected this book. Finally, let every one think of it as his own mind inclines him, *my* mind can take no pleasure in the book; and cause enough to me for my low estimation of it is that Christ is therein neither taught nor recognised, though it is the first duty of an apostle both to recognise and to teach Him. . . . On account of such uncertain interpretation and concealed meaning, we have hitherto suffered the book to lie untouched, but would prevent no one from thinking it the production of St. John the apostle, or whom he will."

Thus we see that Luther, with all his high and unbounded veneration for the Bible, in which he is surpassed, we venture to say, by no believer of our own day, scrupled not to leave some few trees in the great forest *unmarked*, contenting himself with the fact that there was still a sufficiency of fruits with which he might refresh his heart and strengthen his spirit. And the right kind of faith is precisely such as he manifested—the kind which does not demand documentary evidence for every particular, which does not regard the salvation of souls as dependent upon the genuineness of this or that individual letter, but which is satisfied with the plenitude—so rich in any case—of divine revelation. Where there is such faith, such a sense of the Divine, wherever and

[1] [= Second Esdras.]

however that may manifest itself, there is no danger that investigation will lead to unbelief; truth cannot but gain, and will never lose, by investigation conducted in such a spirit.

Luther held, as the Christian faith has always held, the Bible to be the work of the *Divine Spirit*. But he did not with scrupulous anxiety strive to hold this Spirit captive to the letter. And although, in contradistinction to fanatic enthusiasts, he rated the *written* word of God above all else, he also took it for granted that the Spirit of God bloweth where He listeth; and, in conformity to this belief, he regarded the beautiful songs of the Church, which contributed to his edification, as promptings of the Holy Spirit, they having originated in impulses similar to those which gave birth to the pious songs of the prophets and the psalmists. This grand inspiration doctrine of Luther, which recommends itself to every believing soul, was subsequently narrowed down by Protestant theologians into an iron formula, a painful juridical fetter of conscience, to be imposed, perforce, upon the mind and heart of Christendom, to the detriment of fresh religious life, and to the destruction of a just appreciation of and taste for the Bible. In strict truth, Luther himself, in a degree, undoubtedly paved the way for this scrupulous literalism in the deplorable controversy respecting the sacraments; but of this, as constituting a portion of the darker side of his character, we shall speak hereafter.

Whilst the Bible formed the foundation of Protestant theology,—a foundation laid pre-eminently by the hand of Luther,—there appeared in the year 1521, during Luther's sojourn at the Wartburg, a work, of which Melanchthon was the author, corresponding to the translation of the Bible. The publication to which we have reference, and which must be regarded as the first Protestant system of doctrinal theology ever drawn up, was a *systematic digest of the doctrines of faith as presented in the Scriptures.*[1] The Bible, as we are aware,

[1] *Loci communes.* Comp. GALLE, *Charakteristik Melanchthons*, Halle, 1840; and SCHMIDT, *Philipp Melanchthon*, pp. 64 sqq.

is not a connected system of divinity. To deduce such a system from the Holy Scriptures, it is necessary to discover their leading ideas, to join to these kindred conceptions, and to link all together in a whole. This Melanchthon endeavoured to do in his Latin work, in the preparation of which he placed upon the foundation laid by Luther the first stone towards the future edifice. For such a purely scientific and speculative task Melanchthon was better adapted than Luther, his mind being more systematic and contemplative than that of his more practical friend.

Luther set an exceedingly high value upon this book of his friend, and even esteemed it worthy of a place in the canon—another proof of his liberal views in regard to the latter! The book was universally disseminated, and translated into all languages. It was at various times revised by Melanchthon, and it has long been the guide of the doctrinal manuals of the Lutheran Church. The author confines himself in his first edition (and it is of this that we have primarily to speak) to the actual kernel of evangelical doctrine. Instead of beginning with speculative inquiries concerning God and His essence, and concerning the Trinity of God, of which latter he says that it can better be "adored" than "apprehended," he assumes at the outset an anthropological standpoint, and discusses, with psychological acuteness, the religious nature of man, his capacity for divine things, his ability to know and to love the same. And this, we think, is the true mode of procedure in dogmatics, if we wish to escape the danger of losing ourselves in arbitrary tenets. The human soul has, according to Melanchthon, the two leading faculties of knowing and willing. That which the legislative power (the senate) is in the state, the reason of man is in reference to his personal life, whilst the will may be likened to the executive power. But since the Fall, the will of man has been incapable of performing that which is truly reasonable and good. (Upon this latter doctrine Melanchthon insists with Augustinian rigour and pertinacity.) The relation which the caprice of a tyrant occupies toward the law is occupied toward the same by the will of an individual; he does not order himself in accordance with the law, but acts according to his own pleasure. Melanchthon was far from absolutely denying the free agency of man. In all terrestrial and natural things man acts freely. We are at liberty either to greet such a person in the street or not to greet him, to put on this coat or another, etc. But the great question is, whether it lies in our power *of ourselves to love God*—to love Him as He wills to be loved, unselfishly, with all our heart, with all our soul, and with all our strength. The idea that we possess this ability Melanchthon combats. That *moral* freedom by which we avoid a vice or practice a virtue subsists, according to him, more in appearance than in substance. We can, of course, for the moment suppress certain of our affections for the sake of another and stronger passion. The voluptuary may be able to bridle his lust, for the sake, perchance, of his avarice; but of ourselves we are not able *perfectly to subdue* the evil that is within us. What seems at a superficial glance to be virtue, is, when examined by broad daylight, hypocrisy. According to these views, the virtues of the heathen must necessarily have appeared to Melanchthon, as they did to Augustine, as shining vices, gentle and charitable though the sentiments of the first-named personage were wont to be. And yet this very Melanchthon, with the acuteness and delicacy of perception of a Humanist, appreciated all that was great and noble in the ancient world as few others have done; everything that is truly good, he insists, we owe *purely to the grace of God*. And thus (before the days of Calvin and the reformed system of theology) he advanced the doctrine of the *election of grace*, just as Luther defended the same doctrine against the Pelagianizing Erasmus. In agreement with Augustine, he teaches concerning hereditary sin: As the magnet attracts iron, so there is to be found in man an inborn propensity to evil. *Selfishness* is the source of our actions. All that is born of the flesh is flesh. By flesh, however, we are not to understand gross sensuality simply; but even the noblest motions of the soul, so long as they are not adopted into the divine life and interpenetrated by it, are of a carnal sort. The natural man has indeed a law, and the laws of the ancient states were by no means arbitrary inventions of man. But the law given by God upon Sinai should be regarded as supreme and of the highest moral authority. Melanchthon here branches out into a consideration of the ten commandments. He apprehends the transgression of them not merely in a literal, but also (in accordance with his time) in a mystical sense. Thus those who undertake to effect their salvation in their own strength (when God would have His work alone in us) are violators of the Sabbath. Work holiness had attained its development in the system of monasticism especially; Melanchthon therefore attacks this, for nowhere has antichrist more iniquitously revelled than in the monasteries and nunneries. In the ceremonial laws of the Old Testament, Melanchthon beholds mere types of what has been fulfilled in the New Covenant; although he admits that typological and allegorical exegesis has been greatly abused. The Old Testament is not law *alone*; the *gospel* may be found even in *it*, although in the form of promise. Saul was under the law; David was a child of promise. One who is under the law may set his hands, his feet, and his mouth in motion to fulfil the law, but his heart is far from it. God, however, demands the *heart*. This leads to a consideration of the operations of grace ([*Gnade*], $\chi\acute{\alpha}\rho\iota\varsigma$), which is better represented by the Latin word *favor* than by *gratia*, a term subject to Scholastic misinterpretation. The gifts of grace are gifts of the Holy Spirit; amongst them shine pre-eminent the Christian virtues of faith, love, and hope. *Faith* is no mere historical belief, as we put faith in the narratives of Livy and Sallust, nor is it simple opinion (*opinio*), but it is a firm reliance on the mercy of God as promised to us in Christ. Such was the faith of Abraham and all the saints of the Old Covenant. Works are the indices (*indicia*) of faith. Where there is faith, there are also works. When James speaks of faith without works as being dead, he means that purely historical faith which even the devils can have. The genuine believer is no longer under the law—nay (mark this), he is not even under the moral law of the decalogue, so far as that appears in the form of law. We must not understand this to mean that the believer is permitted to transgress the commandments of God. On the contrary, he will, out of free-will and the pure impulse of love, do that which one who is under the law does from compulsion. Here it is that we first touch the soil of *freedom*. The firmer we stand in faith, the freer are we; the more unbelieving we are, the more certainly do we, as unfree and bound, stand under the curse of the law. Whatsoever is not of faith is sin [Rom. xiv. 23]. Here is an end, therefore, to the Scholastic distinction of mortal and venial sins. Unbelief is the true and real mortal sin; in Christ alone is life. Venial sins, on the other hand, are the infirmities that still cling even to believers. With this view of faith and its operations, Melanchthon's view of the sacraments is connected. He desires that the very name of *sacrament*, which is unbiblical, should be discarded. He prefers the use of the word *sign* (*signum*). Precisely the thing for which Zwingle was subsequently censured, therefore, is here to be met with in Melanchthon, the friend of Luther; yet the latter never raised an objection to the doctrine of his friend. Neither baptism nor participation in the Supper of the Lord possesses any saving efficacy in and by itself, but those two ordinances *testify* the gracious will of God toward us, and confirm the consciences of those who doubt His grace.[1]

Two sacraments were instituted by Christ—baptism and the Lord's Supper. Repentance, which Melanchthon subsequently (*Apol.* p. 100) cited as a third sacrament, is here treated of in connection with baptism, and the Scholastic theory of repentance is shown to be untenable and pernicious.

[1] "Baptismus nihil est, participatio mensæ nihil est, sed testes sunt voluntatis divinæ erga te, quibus conscientia tua certa reddatur, si de voluntate Dei erga te dubites."

He also repudiates auricular confession, but retains private confession, which should be distinguished from the former. Satisfaction by a man's own works (*satisfactio operis*) he further declares to be void and nothing worth, since there is no other satisfaction than that which was once made by the death of Christ. The Lord's Supper is treated of as a *sign* of the grace of God, and participation in it is regarded as a *confirmation* of faith; the sacrifice of the mass is repudiated.

In conclusion the author discusses the powers that be, and the obedience which we owe them. This was the more necessary, because revolutionary tendencies were already developing in the train of the Reformation. We are to render obedience not only to the secular powers, but also to the spiritual authorities (bishops), so long as they demand nothing contrary to Scripture. We are to avoid giving offence to any, to bear with the weak, and to conform even to human traditions in so far as they are consistent with Christian truth. This little book, which, with all its evangelical decision, breathes the mild spirit of its author, closes with the saying of St. Paul: "The kingdom of God is not in word, but in power."

We have anticipated the progress of our narrative in according to Luther's translation of the Bible—the history of which is most closely connected with the history of the Reformer's captivity at the Wartburg—an attention extending to later years. The same remark applies to Melanchthon's *Manual of Doctrine.* Let us now return to Luther at the Wartburg. The translation of the Bible was not the only thing which occupied him. Several pamphlets, having a powerful bearing upon the Reformation, were the product of his pen at this time. Amongst these we may enumerate a little book, entitled, *Concerning Confession*, and dedicated to Francis von Sickingen, and his work on *Religious and Conventional Vows*, dedicated to his father, Hans Luther. We are aware that his entrance upon convent life was contrary to the wishes of his father. This transgression of the commandment, "Honour thy father and thy mother," he had now come to regard as a flagrant sin, and he begs his father's pardon for it, declaring, "On your side are divine commandment and authority, on my side is human sacrilege." He shows, however, that through the gracious providence of God his monasticism was overruled for good. "God, whose mercies cannot be numbered, and of whose wisdom there is no end, caused these errors and sins to be productive of higher good to all. Methinks, Satan must from my youth have foreseen the things which he now suffers." God, he believes, had willed that he should by his own experience become versed in the wisdom of the Universities and the sanctity of the cloisters, but God had now taken him away from the monastic life. It was true that he was still (as regarded his outward station) a monk; but he belonged not to the pope, but to Christ. "Christ" [says he] "is my Bishop, Abbot, Prior, Lord, Father, Master; I know none other, and I hope that He thus took your son from you in order that He might now through me begin to help many other of His sons." It is impossible, however, for us further to examine this little book, which is divided into seven parts. Luther shows that conventual vows are contrary not only to the word of God and to faith, but also to Christian liberty, love to our neighbour, and reason, or, as he expresses himself, "the dark and gross light of nature."

The indulgence abomination, which had at the first summoned Luther to the battle-ground, drew him, at this time, once more into the lists. Careless of the Reformer's warnings, the archbishop, Albert of Mentz, had again, in November 1521, issued a proclamation of indulgence at Halle. He had at the same time imprisoned a pastor for taking a wife, and had forced him to let her go. Upon this, Luther composed his tractate against the *Idol at Halle*. Before publishing it, however, he made trial of a more pacific way of removing the nuisance. He addressed a sharp and spicy letter to the archbishop, earnestly admonishing him to suppress the abuse, and threatening him with his already completed tractate if he should neglect to comply with this demand, a respite of a few days being granted him. And, behold! the exalted prelate actually condescended to write to Luther in a friendly tone, seeking to appease him by the assurance that the scandal was already suppressed, and making a humble confession of his impotence.[1] If Luther was satisfied with this letter, he was, on the other hand, not a little vexed by an epistle which accompanied the archiepiscopal communication. This was the production of a man whom we shall encounter hereafter as a Reformer at Strassburg, who, however, was at that time at the court of the prelate of Mentz, and who felt himself constrained to censure Luther for his inconsiderate attack, and to recommend to him moderation. The person to whom we have reference was *Fabricius Capito* (Köpfli) of Hagenau. Luther, in his reply to him, made the following open declaration:—" I was as greatly afflicted by thy letter, my dear Fabricius, as I was rejoiced by that of thy cardinal." He would have nothing to do with a false forbearance or a charity that was detrimental to faith. "In a few words, this is the conclusion of the matter. My love is ready to die for you. But whoso meddleth with faith, toucheth the apple of our eye. Here is love; ye may deride or honour it, as ye will; not so faith. Ye are to adore the word [of God] and to hold it to be most sacred; this is what we would have of you. Expect of our love all that ye will, but fear our faith in all things."

In order justly to appreciate such language as this, we must bear in mind the inward conflicts through which Luther passed prior to his appearance on the stage of action; and,

---

[1] " And, God willing, I will so comport and show myself as befits a pious, spiritual, and Christian prince, so far as God gives me grace, strength, and wisdom, for which I will also faithfully make, and cause to be made, supplication; for of myself I am able to do nothing, and I confess that I stand in need of the grace of God, being a poor sinful man, prone to sin and to err, and daily, as I deny not, sinning and erring. I know well that without the grace of God there is nothing good in me, and I, as well as another, if not more than any other man, am but unprofitable and stinking dung. . . . Brotherly and Christian rebuke I can assuredly bear, and I hope that a merciful and gracious God will give me further grace, strength, and patience, in this and other points to live according to His will."

remembering these, we shall sympathize with him in the consciousness of victory that even now thrilled his breast. The greatness of Luther consists, we would here observe, in this heroism of faith. He who is untouched by this, will never thoroughly comprehend the character of Luther; he will be repelled by his roughness of expression, where others, despite certain undeniable asperities, are edified by the fundamental tone of the Reformer's whole nature.

We will not further follow the literary labours of Luther.[1] A few words more and we have done. Once, in the dull November days, he ventured to steal away from the Wartburg and to visit his friends in Wittenberg, especially his Philip (Melanchthon), and Nicholas Amsdorf, in whose house he was concealed. Here (according to his own testimony) he experienced "much pleasure and entertainment," but learned, to his sorrow, that the books which he had sent to his friends from his "Patmos" had never reached their destination. They were (he conjectured) either intercepted on the road or lost through the carelessness of the messenger.[2] He comforted himself with the thought that the enemy might destroy the inanimate paper, but would never be able to quench the Spirit of the living God. Refreshed and strengthened, he returned to his solitude, which he quitted for ever only when he believed that he was called thence by a higher power.

[1] To these belong a commentary on a few of the psalms and the German postils, which we should find more edifying than the polemical writings. Amongst the latter we may mention the tract against Latomus, the theologian of Louvaine, that against the Dominican, Ambrosius Catharinus, and the polemical tracts against the "he-goat" Emser and the Parisian theologian whom Melanchthon despatched (and upon whom Luther bestowed the name of "ass"). All these polemical writings are pervaded by a tone which is not of the finest.

[2] Letter to Spalatin, No. 6, DE WETTE, vol. ii. No. 351.

CHAPTER VIII.

PROGRESS OF THE GOSPEL—PROCEEDINGS AT WITTENBERG—KARLSTADT AND THE PROPHETS OF ZWICKAU—LUTHER LEAVES THE WARTBURG (HIS INTERVIEW WITH TWO YOUNG SWITZERS AT JENA)—HE SUBDUES THE STORM—HIS STRIFE WITH HENRY VIII.—ADRIAN VI.—DIET OF NUREMBERG (1523)—CLEMENT VII.

THE revived gospel had, meantime, made visible progress. In various quarters men appeared preaching in Luther's spirit. The mouths of the heralds of the truth were opened. Several princes, who had admired the lofty courage displayed by Luther at the Diet of Worms, inclined to the new doctrine. Nobles and knights offered it the support of the secular arm; cultured laymen and statesmen joined themselves more closely to the evangelical preachers, and represented their cause amongst the people. The latter, also, felt their yearnings go out toward the new light, though but dimly conscious of the reasons which made that light desirable. Youth pressed from all quarters to Wittenberg, eager for a personal sight and hearing of the men from whom the light streamed forth. Pupils of these men were already proclaiming the gospel in the spirit of their teachers. Frederick Myconius (Mecum), who, as a student, had been a witness of Tetzel's audacity, and, after him, Nicholas Haussman, preached at Zwickau; Eoban Hesse, Joachim Camerarius, Euricius Cordus, and Joachim Lange, at Erfurt; and Wolfgang Stein set forth the word of God at Weimar. At Annaberg, a Saxon mining town recently built by Duke George, such zeal was prevalent, that, when it was found that the Duke would not tolerate the new doctrine, the people repaired to Buchholz in Electoral Saxony to hear the lectures of Wenceslaus Link and Gabriel Didymus.[1] The spirit of the Reformation prevailed mightily throughout the electorate of Saxony, and especially in Wittenberg; and even the brethren of Luther's order, the Augustinian monks, lent a willing hand to the innovations. The Misnian and Thuringian Augustinians held a convention at Wittenberg, at which they abolished private masses and abrogated all vows that were contrary to the gospel. Luther and the Wittenberg theologians, whose opinions had been procured, approved this step, and the elector, who was at first apprehensive that disorders might thereby be occasioned, was also satisfied.

On the part of the evangelicals, everything had thus far proceeded orderly and harmoniously. When violence had been employed, it had emanated from the dominant Church, which, in accordance with its principle, had from time to time persecuted the heretics. Minor disturbances there may have been, reactions against the violence of Rome, which are not worth the mention. On the whole, it may be said that *a reformation had been introduced in a national and law-abiding manner*, on the principle of instruction and the most perfect liberty of conscience. The progress of such a reformation, however, was too tardy for the impetuous spirit of some.

Andrew Karlstadt, whom we have seen associated with Luther at Leipsic, was one of those who, possessing mediocre powers of intellect and an upright but rugged and biassed will, considered it their vocation to anticipate the prudent and deliberate work of Luther and begin where the Reformation should have ended. In his ambition he could not forget that Luther had forced him to take a second rank at Leipsic, and had borne away from him the laurels of the day. Like all Reformers of the inferior sort, he and his associates laid much stress on externalities, believing that reformation consisted principally in negation, in the abolition of forms, in

[1] Seckendorf in Roos, pp. 87 sqq.

the removal of images, and in a turbulent abandonment of fasts and hitherto existent ecclesiastical regulations. Ay, in their zeal for liberty they went, as ultra-Liberals are wont to do, to the extent of making their liberty a law to others, of forcing it upon them, and striving to impose upon them a new yoke in lieu of the old one. Karlstadt had married in the April of 1422—a step which Luther himself approved. But he did not rest satisfied with this. He gave a useless publicity to his marriage, boasting of it as if it had been a heroic deed. He now regarded the marriage of priests as the sum of all good, and would therefore fain have constrained all clerics to enter into the matrimonial state; he even threatened to rebuke and assail, by word of mouth and by act, every priest who would not follow his example. He also conducted himself in a most indiscreet manner in relation to the public worship of God. He admitted people to the Lord's Supper, which he administered in both kinds, without preparation or confession, and, in company with some students, wantonly injured the pictures and images that were in the churches. On being warned by the elector, through Chancellor Brück, to discontinue these proceedings, he replied that he should abide simply by the word of God, that he could regard the person of none, and that his work could be displeasing to none but those who were not Christians. According to this, Luther, in his eyes, was no Christian, for Luther it was who most decidedly disapproved his actions. Nor did Karlstadt stand alone. He found a congenial companion in the Augustinian monk called Gabriel Didymus (Zwilling), who was born in the year 1487 at Joachimsthal in Bohemia. From Prague, where he had studied, Didymus had come to Wittenberg. He was a little man with a weak voice, but an energetic and defiant brain,—a Hotspur, in whom something of the old Hussite fire burned. When he preached, his auditors would rise from their seats and station themselves about the pulpit, in order that they might hear him the better, and he was able to hold them spell-bound thus for hours. He, with twelve other monks, quitted the cloister and exchanged the cowl for secular garments.

At this time Wittenberg was the resort of a company of fanatics from Zwickau, to whom the name of the Prophets of Zwickau had been given. The most important of these individuals were Nicholas Storch, a cloth-weaver, Martin Cellarius (Borhaus, afterwards professor at Basel), Mark Stübner of Elsterberg, and the notorious Thomas Münzer. These persons, not satisfied with the restoration of Christianity to the historic foundation of the Bible, pretended to have received new revelations surpassing the Bible, and regarded themselves as having been awakened and privileged by the Lord in a peculiar manner. That which Luther had already done seemed to them a small matter in comparison with what the Lord was about to accomplish through *them*. They affirmed that they were in direct communication with God, and that they were under the inspiration of the Holy Ghost. Accordingly they predicted things to come. " God's judgments," said they, " will soon burst upon the world ; the Turk will speedily take possession of Germany, and all priests will be slain even if they take to themselves wives. The world will come to an end in from five to seven years. Then no godless man or sinner shall be left alive. Then there shall be one faith and one baptism." In regard to the last clause, the Zwickau prophets declared that it was wrong to baptize children, that infant baptism was a mere farce. These people, moreover, despised everything that rested upon tradition and custom in ecclesiastical and civil ordinances ; and, what was still more dangerous, they condemned the light of science and even the most necessary school instruction as something profane. A schoolmaster named George Mohr, who was an adherent of theirs, stationed himself at his window one day and sent home the boys when they came to school ; he also admonished parents to remove their children from school. When some one asked Stübner if he had written any books, he answered, " No ; our Lord God has forbidden me!"

That this fanatic and radical movement did not owe its origin to the Reformation, but that it has appeared in the Church, in different modes, from the earliest times, may be seen from the history of the Novatians and Donatists, and from that of the sects of the Middle Ages, the Beguins, Fratricelli, Lollards, Spirituals, and the later degenerate Taborites. It is true that it was through the Reformation that the latent fever in the body ecclesiastic was revived; but a similar statement may be made in regard to all important crises. The spark that slumbered beneath the ashes was fanned into new life by the storm that Luther raised. The Reformation, however, was not to blame for this. On the contrary, in it fanaticism found a mighty wall, against which the dark power of the mistaken movement must sooner or later be spent.

Good Melanchthon was placed in circumstances of no little embarrassment by the appearance of these men. Though more learned than Luther, and more scientific in theory than he, he was far from possessing the unfailing tact and practical sharp-sightedness of the latter in the ordinary affairs of life. With what delight he would have hailed the proximity of his friend! He applied to him by letter, advising the elector, meantime, to take no hasty steps, and admonishing the students to throw no obstacle in the way of these singular persons, but to bear patiently with them. Melanchthon even thought that there might be somewhat of truth in the matter, and believed that he should be sinning against God were he to quench the Spirit in them.[1] The true spirit of the Reformer is manifest in this refusal of Melanchthon to decide hastily upon extraordinary movements in the spiritual world, and in his subjecting to trial even that which has appearances against it. Luther

---

[1] "I have heard them myself," he writes to the elector; "they claim wondrous things for themselves—namely, that God has clearly called them to teach, that they have confidential intercourse with God, that they behold things to come, and, in short, that they are prophetic and apostolic men. *The effect which all this has upon me I cannot well describe. I have, in truth, weighty reasons why I should not despise them;* none but Martin Luther, however, is competent to pass sentence upon the case."

also most earnestly recommended such a trial, although he was less inclined than Melanchthon to recognise anything prophetic in these people. He was not to be captivated by any pretence of visions and marvellous occurrences. He set little value at any time upon these things, so imposing to the multitude. As he found the main evidence of the truth of Christianity not in the miracles, but in its demonstrations of the Spirit, in its truly moral and sanctifying power, so at the present juncture he conceived that everything depended upon the *fruits* borne by the tree which had occasioned so much commotion—the sure criterion in every age. "We must try the spirits," said he, "to determine whether they are of God." Hitherto, he declared, he had heard nothing of them that Satan could not do and imitate. They must make proof of their vocation, for God sends no one without calling him through men. No account should be made of mere revelations which they pretended to have received. It should first be seen whether they suffer spiritual anguish—whether they know aught of a divine birth, of death, and hell. Though we should hear nothing but lovely, devout, and holy things of them, though they should say that they had been caught into the third heaven, yet should we not regard them. The Divine Majesty speaks not so immediately with man, least of all can God have intercourse with the *old* man before it is slain and destroyed.

Luther applied to the elector, however, through his friend Spalatin, and conjured him not to stain his hands with the blood of the prophets. In this he followed the true evangelical principle, *to which he adhered throughout his life*—namely, that truth cannot be disseminated, or error be checked, by violence; and when, at a later period, Calvin and Beza held the tenet that it is right and necessary to inflict capital punishment upon heretics, *i.e.* those who hold mistaken opinions on the subject of religion, Luther's better and humaner sentiment recoiled affrighted.

In the meantime the disorder was daily increasing at

Wittenberg. Several students withdrew from the University on account of the disturbances. Duke George of Saxony, the bitter opponent of Luther, pursued the course ever taken by the foes of amendment, and seized the occasion presented by casual abuses and mistakes to cast blame upon the Reformation itself. Luther, it was claimed, was the author of all that was wrong. "Why was the liberal doctrine suffered to spring up? Here we have the consequences of it!" was the cry of short-sighted mortals then as now. We can imagine the painful position of Luther. He saw the edifice burning that he himself had constructed; from the Wartburg he could descry the heavens glowing with the conflagration; he heard the peal of alarm and the cry of distress, but was unable to hasten to the rescue and to extinguish the flames. His way was barred by the Edict of Worms and the stringent command of his sovereign. But must he look on and see beam after beam and rafter after rafter fall? Must he hear the cry of his friends for help, without at least attempting to burst the bars which kept him, the only one who could here be of assistance, from the conflagration? His decision was made. He quitted the Wartburg. Conscience, that inward monitor, commanded his departure. *To him* it was clear that the voice of conscience *was at this time the voice of God.* That voice he must obey rather than men. In order, however, that he might not be wanting in the respect which he owed to his prince, who had most strictly forbidden him to leave his place of retirement, and also to disengage that prince from any unpleasant consequences which might ensue, he wrote him from Borna, on Ash Wednesday of 1522, a letter unfolding a vigour of spirit that leads us to forget the form in which the epistle is couched, which is somewhat blunter than that ordinarily employed in communications addressed to princes. He writes, amongst other things, that he takes for granted the elector's good intentions in forbidding him to leave his abode; but neither must the elector have any doubts as to *his* [Luther's] good intentions. That, however, was neither here nor there. It was not a personal thing, but the cause of God, which called him to Wittenberg. Cherishing such a belief, he had courageously gone to meet the devil at Worms, and he would now give further proof of the same spirit in proceeding to Wittenberg. ... The elector had particularly warned Luther against the machinations of Duke George, to which he would expose himself in abandoning his retreat. To this warning he answered: " I know well my peril. But if affairs in Leipsic were at the pass they are in Wittenberg, I would gallop into the former city, even—may your electoral grace pardon my foolish speech—though it should rain nothing but Duke Georges for nine consecutive days, and though each were nine times more furious than the actual one now is. His lordship the duke holds the Lord Christ to be a man of straw. My lord and I can put up with this for a time, but misfortune shall at last pour upon him in an unbroken stream."

In reference to the elector's protection, Luther writes as follows: " I go to Wittenberg under higher protection than that of the elector. Nor have I any intention of asking the protection of your electoral grace. Nay, I hold that I am better able to protect your grace than your grace is to protect me. Furthermore, if I knew that your electoral grace could and would protect me, I would not go to Wittenberg. The sword has no right to intermeddle, or power to aid, in these matters. God alone must work here, without the care or the intervention of man. Therefore, whoso has the strongest faith will be the best protector in this case. Now, perceiving, as I do, that your electoral grace is as yet but weak in the faith, I can by no means look upon your grace as a man who could protect or save me."

These words have a ring of defiance. Yet Luther, in employing them, was far from forgetting that consideration which he owed to the prince as his sovereign. He declares to him that he will submit to whatever arrangements the elector might make with regard to his person, in case he should be compelled to deliver him up to the opposing party. He even exhorts the elector to obedience to the emperor as *his* sovereign, "*for none should commit any breach against the authorities, or offer any resistance to them, except He alone who instituted them; aught else is rebellion, and opposition to God.*" He hopes that the emperor and the princes will be reasonable, and consider that the elector was born in too lofty a station to be made the jailor of Luther. Finally, he commends the elector to the grace of God, and concludes with the following words:—" I am dealing with a different person from Duke George; it is One who knows me well and Whom I know not slightly. If your electoral grace believed, you would see the glory of God; but because you do not yet believe, you have as yet seen nothing. Unto God be love and praise to all eternity. Amen."[1]

This letter, which De Wette justly calls an admirable monument of that courage of faith with which Luther was filled, made a peculiar impression upon the elector. He honoured Luther's personal courage, and yet did not feel strong enough to take up his cause before the empire. The Diet of Nuremberg was in prospect; at its assemblage the elector was desirous of presenting a manifesto from Luther, announcing that the latter had left the Wartburg without the permission of his prince. Luther readily complied with this desire of the elector, and wrote the manifesto, although not exactly in the proper tone; hence he was obliged to submit it to a revision, in which certain strong passages were altered. For instance, he had expressed himself as follows: " Doubtless, Heaven's decrees differ in many points from those of Nuremberg." He was constrained to tone down this forcible expression and to use more general terms, to the effect that Heaven's decrees differ in many points from those of earth. He had, moreover, to call the emperor his *most gracious* lord, although, as he writes to Spalatin, all the world knew that the emperor was anything but gracious to him.

[1] See DE WETTE, vol. ii. No. 362.

Let us now endeavour to conceive of Luther in the frame of mind in which he quitted the Wartburg. On the one hand there were the spiritual perils which awaited him at Wittenberg, and on the other the physical personal peril of being captured and delivered up to the empire. In addition to all this, he was tried and tempted in body and soul, and he must needs appear doubly great to us when we see him preserve his cheerfulness and good humour in the midst of these storms, and carry out his incognito with a roguishness and complaisance which make it seem as if he had assumed it as a mere jest.

The chronicle of Kessler, the Reformer of St. Gall, records a noteworthy scene from this portion of Luther's life; we will quote the main particulars.[1]

Attracted by the fame of the University of Wittenberg, and especially by the names of Luther and Melanchthon, two young Switzers, Kessler and Spengler[2] by name, hitherto students at Basel, set out for the former city. At that time the journeys of travelling scholars were rich in adventures, as every one who has read the well-known history of Thomas Plater is aware.[3] More interesting, however, than such rude features of a rude age may prove the following narrative, which will interrupt the gravity of our drama by a pleasant interlude. The two youths, who, of course, were journeying on foot, arrived at Jena weary, and wet to the skin by a terrific thunderstorm. Here they sought in vain for a night's lodging. They were just about to leave the city and pass the night in an adjacent village, when they were met by a

---

[1] BERNET, *Johann Kessler genannt Ahenarius* (St. Gall, 1826), p. 27. The above-cited incident has frequently been quoted before, for the last time in GUSTAV FREITAG's *Bilder aus der deutschen Vergangenheit*. Since the appearance of the last work the Historical Union of the Canton of St. Gall has issued a complete edition of Kessler's chronicle in its original form (*Joh. Kessler's Sabbata*, edited by E. Götzinger. In two parts. St. Gall, 1866 and 1868).

[2] It is probable, at least, that Spengler was the companion mentioned in the narrative. See the note in BERNET, *l.c.*

[3] Kessler himself relates that he was attacked in sport by strolling vagabonds, and that his travelling companion, Spengler, was tossed in a blanket.

man, who asked them whither they were going so late, and, upon learning their embarrassments, directed them to an inn situate in the suburbs, and bearing the sign of "The Black Bear." Upon entering the public room they saw, seated in a corner by the table, a man dressed in the habiliments of a knight, with a sword at his side, upon the pommel of which his right hand was resting. In front of him on the table lay a little book which he was studiously perusing. He soon, however, bestowed a friendly greeting on the young men, who, on account of the soiled condition of their garments, had not ventured to approach the table, but had seated themselves on a bench in a remote corner of the apartment. The seeming knight, after requesting them to draw nearer to him, asked them whence they came. Without waiting for their answer, however (he probably knew them by their dialect), he said to them, "You are Switzers. From what part of Switzerland do you come?" They replied, "From St. Gall." He remarked that they would find a couple of their countrymen in Wittenberg, Jerome Schurf and his brother Augustine. "We have letters to them," said the students. They then asked him if he knew whether Luther had returned to Wittenberg. The stranger replied, "I know of a certainty that Luther is not yet at Wittenberg, but it is said that he soon will be there. Philip Melanchthon, however, is there and is teaching Greek." He then admonished the youths to give good heed to the languages, and especially to Hebrew, saying that they would have a fine opportunity for acquiring them at Wittenberg. The young men assured him that there was nothing that they more longed for than to be speedily initiated into evangelical truth, and that they rejoiced above all at the prospect of making the personal acquaintance of the man who had attacked the priesthood and the mass; for they had themselves, they said, been destined for a religious life by their parents, and they were therefore anxious to know the truth about these things. "Where have you been studying hitherto?" asked the knight. "At Basel," replied the students. "Well, how are things going on at Basel? Is Erasmus there still? and what is he doing?" "My lord, so far as we know, all is going on well at Basel. Erasmus is still there; but what he is doing no one knows, for he keeps himself very quiet." "And what think they of Luther in your Switzerland?" "My lord, there are a variety of opinions about him there as elsewhere. Some cannot sufficiently extol him, and thank God for having manifested His truth and discovered errors through him. Others, again, condemn him as an *insufferable heretic*, and before the clergy." "I see," interrupted he, "the priests are against him." Such conversation made us feel quite at home, says Kessler, also remarking, however, that he and his companion were struck with the learned language of the knight, and especially with his acquaintance with Erasmus and the ancient tongues. Their astonishment was increased when Kessler's companion chanced to take up the book that was lying on the table in front of the stranger. It was a Hebrew Psalter. The student put the book down again and the knight took possession of it. "I would give one of my fingers," said the student, "if I could understand that language." "That you will certainly do in time if you apply yourself diligently to the study of it. I also am anxious to know more of it, and practise myself in it every day."

At this point the host came into the room, and, remarking the young travellers' eagerness to see Luther, said, "Had you been here two days ago, you would have seen him; for he sat here at this very table." The students were much vexed at this, and at first gave vent to their anger at the expense of "the bad roads" which had deprived them of a sight of the Reformer; they, however, expressed their pleasure at seeing at least the place where the great man had sat. At this the host laughed and went out. After a little he called Kessler to him. "I was frightened at first," says Kessler, "and bethought me whether I could have been guilty of any breach of good manners, or be innocently suspected of any offence." The host, however, spoke to him in a friendly manner, and informed him (what you will already have guessed) that it was Luther who was sitting at the table with them. But Kessler thought that the host was wishing to amuse himself at his expense; he therefore said to him, "You are trying to make game of me and to satisfy my longing with the mention of Luther." When the host, however, repeated his assertion, begging him not to act as if he suspected anything, he went into the room again, and could not refrain from whispering the secret to his companion. The latter was as incredulous as Kessler had been, and declared that his friend must have misunderstood the host, who doubtless had said *Hutten* instead of *Luther*. This explanation seemed a very probable one to Kessler himself, for the knightly attire of the stranger agreed far better with the supposition that it was Hutten than with the idea that it was Luther. (They did not know that Hutten was just then visiting Basel.) Two merchants now entered the inn, and after they had removed their outer garments and taken off their spurs, one of them laid an unbound book upon the table. Luther asked by whom the book was written. "It is Doctor Luther's *Exposition of the Gospels and Epistles,*" was the reply. "Have you not seen it?" continued the merchants. "I shall soon get it," answered Luther. The host, meantime, announced that supper was served. The poor students, however, who had not a superabundance of cash, did not wish to sup with the others, who were evidently more favoured of fortune, and begged the host to give them something at a separate table. The host, nevertheless, bade them be seated, and promised to be "reasonable with them;" whilst Luther, who was pleased with the young men, said to them, "Sit down, and I will settle the bill with the host." "This," remarks Kessler, "gave us great delight, not on account of the money and the delicacies, but because *this* man had invited us to be his guests. At supper Martin spoke much in a godly and friendly manner, so that the merchants and ourselves lapsed into silence, and paid more attention to his words than to the dishes before us."

They spoke of the approaching Diet of Nuremberg, saying that nothing of importance would issue from it, for "the princes and lords that composed it were more fond of passing away their time in costly tournaments, sledging, debauchery, and magnificence, than in hearing and receiving the word of God," etc. "But I hope," continued Luther, "that evangelical truth will be productive of more fruit in our children and later descendants." The merchants now expressed their opinion, and one of them remarked that he, to be sure, was only a layman, but, so far as he could understand, Luther must be either an angel from heaven or a devil from hell. He would, he said, gladly give ten florins if he could confess to him, for he believed that Luther could and would instruct his conscience. Supper being ended, the merchants withdrew, and Luther was again alone with the students. These returned their thanks for his hospitality, and gave him to understand that they took him for Ulrich von Hutten. At this Luther jestingly observed to the host, "Look you, I have this night become a nobleman, for these Switzers take me for Ulrich von Hutten." "That you are not," said the host, "but you are Martin Luther." Luther smiled and said, "They take me for Hutten, you for Luther; I shall soon be Marcolphus."[1] After thus saying, he took a tall beer glass and drank the health of the Switzers, asking them to drink also. When Kessler, however, was about taking the glass, Luther handed him a glass of wine instead, saying, "I know that beer is an unaccustomed beverage to you Switzers; drink the wine." With this he slung his cloak over his shoulder, took leave of his young friends, and said, "When you get to Wittenberg, greet Dr. Schurf, your countryman, for me." "With pleasure," said the students; "but from whom shall we say the greeting comes?" "Say only, '*He who is coming sends you greeting,*' and he will understand," and with these words he withdrew.

"This took place at the first night's lodging between the

[[1] The name of the jay in fable.—TR.]

Wartburg and Wittenberg, at a time when the ground was hot under Luther's feet, when he was approaching the most terrible dangers, the most desperate undertakings, and when his soul was filled with all the grand thoughts of faith and confidence which he expressed a day or two later in his letter to the elector."[1]

It is only great souls that are capable of such cheerful equanimity, and even harmless sportiveness, in moments of peril. Such a friendly smile, met by the tears of sadness, is like the genial sunbeam piercing the black clouds of the gathering storm. Happy is the man the sun of whose spirit is never entirely darkened!

Gloom now gathers over the picture that we are contemplating, and the pleasant interlude is followed by scenes of tragic earnestness.

Arrived at Wittenberg, Luther found everything in the greatest confusion. For a whole week he preached with great power, and yet with the utmost possible regard for persons, against the rioters and fanatics.[2] He showed the impropriety of too much haste in executing reforms, and the necessity of giving milk to the weak; he also demonstrated the impossibility of " dragging any one to the gospel by the hair of his head;" for it is not in the power of man, but in the hand of God alone, to change the heart. That must be left to God. " *The word* must operate everywhere; *the word* alone, and not violence,"— this was the glorious motto of Luther, and this is and always will be the motto of the reformatory principle. " *Through the word the world is overcome;* " he had already proclaimed this with emphasis, when several German knights had offered him their swords, and he had refused them, on the ground that God's cause is not to be decided with the sword. And it was to this alone sure principle of all true

---

[1] Remark of Füsslin in BERNET, p. 37.

[2] His sermons on this occasion were printed separately: "Seven Sermons by Dr. Martin Luther, delivered from Invocavit Day to the following Sunday, upon his return from his Patmos to Wittenberg." Ranke ranks these sermons among the most important ever preached by Luther.

liberty that he now recurred. "The Word created heaven and earth and all things; the same Word must be operative here, and not we poor sinners. *Summa summarum:* I will *preach* the Word, I will *speak* it, I will *write* it; but *force* and *constrain* any one by violence I will not." He cited himself as an example, showing that he had *preached* and *written* against indulgences, but had used no violence, and the *Word* had quietly effected all the results that had come to pass. "When I was sleeping," says he, "when I was drinking Wittenberg beer with my Philip and Amsdorf, *the Word* worked so mightily that the Papacy has become weaker than any prince or emperor has ever made it. *I* have done nothing to it; the Word has accomplished all. If I had wished to make trouble, I might have turned all Germany into a field of bloodshed—ay, I might have set on foot such a game at Worms that the emperor would not have been safe. But what would it have been? A fool's game, and perdition to body and soul." . . . "I cannot drive any one into heaven (by violence), or beat any one into it with cudgels. This is plain speaking; methinks you have understood me." Luther further showed that nothing was gained by the mere external removal of abuses, by the violent abolishment of images and ceremonies, especially if the people were not aware of the true reasons for such innovations, but merely followed the multitude blindly. "St. Paul," he continued, "on arriving at Athens, and seeing the numerous altars there, did not worship the idols, it is true, but neither did he tear down the altars." "There are many people," he remarks, "who worship the sun, moon, and stars; shall we therefore go to work and tear the stars down from the heavens? That be far from us." [1]

Luther also endeavoured to come to an understanding with the fanatics by means of private conversations with them.[2]

[1] See *Luther's Werke*, WALCH's edition, vol. xx.; PLANCK, *Geschichte des protest. Lehrbegriffs*, vol. ii. pp. 67 sqq.; MARHEINEKE, vol. i. p. 322.

[2] Camerarius (in his *Life of Melanchthon*, ch. xv.) narrates the following incident as having taken place in one of these interviews. Mark Stübner, wishing to give Luther a proof of the prophetic gift which enabled him to see into the

He treated them with gentleness and condescension, but became more and more convinced that their claims were utterly without foundation. In their spiritual pride they regarded Luther as a man blinded by learning, and destitute of true simplicity of heart. They looked upon themselves as far more enlightened than he, and disdained to dispute with him. Luther, for his part, saw that nothing could be done with such blockheads. They therefore left Wittenberg after loading Luther with invectives. Karlstadt retired to Orlamünde, where he made common cause with the peasants and played the demagogue. He renounced all the prerogatives which his doctor's title bestowed upon him, assumed the garb of the peasantry, studied to acquire their manners, and fraternized generally with the country people, by whom he would be called nothing but " Brother Andrew" and "Dear neighbour." To this sublime liberality Dr. Luther, indeed, did not attain; he held that the difference of culture is a sufficient reason for a distinction of ranks in civil life. Hence the ultra-Liberals regarded him as an aristocrat, a prince-server, and a petty pope; and the rage of that party was especially directed against him after Karlstadt's dismission from the electoral domains. Luther published upon this occasion a tract bearing the following title: *An Admonition to all Christians to keep themselves from Riot and Rebellion.* We cite from this tract a few golden words: " Those who rightly read and understand my doctrine are guilty of no riotous act; they have not learned such things from me."

And he spoke truly. Neither the tempestuous spirits of the sixteenth century, nor those of the eighteenth and nineteenth centuries, drew their principles of action from Luther.

hearts of men, declared that he knew, by a revelation of the Spirit, that Luther was at that time conscious of a favourable inclination towards him. That such was the fact Luther afterwards himself confessed. The Reformer, however, immediately braced himself, and, beholding in this affection of his mind a temptation of the devil, cried out, "May God rebuke thee, Satan!" "Setting aside the harshness of his expression," says Ranke, "this struggle between two opposed spirits, a malignant and a protecting genius, contains a grand and deep truth."

There is a wide and eternal distinction between reformation and revolution, and whoso regards the former as the mother of the latter has not yet learned to know the tree by its fruit. That Luther, with all his reverence for the established powers, was no prince-server, but that, without regard of persons, he fearlessly proclaimed the truth even to princes, is beautifully evidenced by his letter to the elector. A less gratifying proof of the fact is afforded us by his combat of the same year with Henry VIII. of England. When a prince enters upon the slippery path of scientific authorship, he must himself bear the blame if he is judged in accordance with the law that prevails, or should prevail, in the republic of letters —the law of unvarnished truth, without respect to the author's person or external position in society. Now Henry had a longing to distinguish himself as a theological writer, and especially as a polemical writer, against Luther; and, throwing down his gauntlet to the latter in his tractate on the sacraments, he must needs put up with the somewhat sharp blows with which his opponent met him. On the other hand, however, this does not excuse that opponent for so far forgetting the respect which he owed the attacking party as to fall into vulgarities and extravagances. If the defiant spirit of Luther, with whose manifestations hitherto we, considering his situation, can find no fault, and which was perfectly compatible with a noble and manly soul, ever degenerated into a blameable arrogance, such was surely the case here. The tract which Luther wrote against the king exhibits an exasperation and a coarseness that are almost without parallel.[1] This coarseness even runs into a mocking derision, which, coming from the mouth of so earnest and worthy a witness for the truth, cannot fail to be offensive. It is true that the king had previously attacked Luther with very unkingly words:

---

[1] There is a pamphlet by Luther (dated in the year 1541), addressed to another Henry, Duke Henry of Brunswick, whom he calls "Jackpudding" ["*Hanswurst*"]; in this Luther, if possible, surpasses himself, and produces a perfect masterpiece of coarseness.

he had called him a blasphemer of God, a limb of Satan, a horrid, hellish wolf; he had urged the emperor and the empire to persecute the new doctrine with fire and sword. But how edifying it would have been if, in face of all this, Luther had still confronted the railing king in his prophetic dignity and apostolic station! He might have told him the truth boldly, without becoming coarse and unmannerly. Instead of this he returns invective for invective, thus lowering himself in the eyes of even his admirers.[1] In his reply to the king he continually calls the latter Hal [*Heinz*]—Hal by the *dis*favour of God; he reviles him as a miserable fool, a rake, a blockhead, a king of lies, an impudent liar whom he will rid of his itch for falsehood—whose lies, which he has vomited forth against Christ, he will cram down his own throat again, and whose crown he will daub with the filth wherewith *he* has defiled the crown of Christ, etc. How was it possible for Luther to dream of apologizing for such language by the plea that Christ and the apostles preached without respect of persons! It is not thus that Christ spoke to Pilate and Herod, or Paul to Felix, Festus, and Agrippa.

We turn now from this unprofitable dispute with the humiliating reflection that even the greatest men have their weak hours, in which passion has power to lead them into errors that they never would have committed had they not forgotten themselves and their own dignity.

Leo X., who had been led by King Henry's zeal for the faith to bestow upon him the title of *Defender of the Faith* at about the time when Henry became involved in a war with the king of France, had died in the midst of these political and ecclesiastical storms, on the 1st of December 1521, and Adrian VI., a Netherlander and the former instructor of Charles V., had, on the 9th of January 1522, been chosen

---

[1] Luther's colleagues, especially Bugenhagen, disapproved his sharp language. See ZIETZ, *Johann Bugenhagen*, pp. 79 sqq. This is a proof that Luther's roughness considerably exceeded that usual in the age. See also RAUMER, *Neuere Geschichte*, vol. i. p. 341.

pope in his stead. Adrian was far from possessing the taste and culture of his predecessor, and the arts and sciences failed to find in him the liberal patron that they had enjoyed in the splendour-loving Medici. On the other hand, however, Adrian, with a more limited intellect, had a more earnest will than Leo. The reformation of the Church was really a subject that lay near his heart. His disinclination to the works of the Italian artists was in part owing to the fact that the heathenish tendency of their art excited his displeasure, and even the most lauded antiques found no favour in his eyes. He beheld in them, without excepting even the Laocoon, nothing but heathen idols. He also (and with more reason) disapproved the luxury of the papal court, and himself set the example of diminishing it, thus drawing upon himself the hatred of the epicurean cardinals. Indeed, his early death is, not without probability, ascribed to poison, which is thought to have been administered by the direction of the opponents of his beneficent measures. At least, the house of his physician was found, shortly after the death of the pope, adorned with a garland and the inscription, "To the saviour of his country."[1] Notwithstanding Adrian's peculiar views, he was no less antagonistic to Luther and his doctrine than his predecessor had been. He desired a reformation of the Church, but he wished it to be *through* the pope, and not *against* or *without* him. Adrian, moreover, with his limited mental culture, was a slavish adorer of Scholasticism and the gloomy monastic theology, and the fact that Luther combated these was that which grieved him most. Soon after his assumption of the Papacy, however, he showed the most unexpected favour to Zwingle, to whom he sent, by the legate Ennius, an obliging

---

[1] On Adrian's tombstone in St. Peter's Church were inscribed the following words: "Here lies Adrian vi., who regarded it as the greatest misfortune that he reigned." The Netherlander Eukevord, the only cardinal whom he created, caused a monument to be erected to him in another church in Rome, on which were engraved some words that Adrian himself had been wont to use: "*Of how great importance is it to the very best and most honest man, in what time his life falls.*" SOUCHAY, *l.c.* p. 207 (after Menzel and Mignet).

letter, praising his piety and seeking by all means to win him, and the Swiss through him, to his own side—an obvious stroke of policy, which, however, was without avail. But against Luther he thought it needful to take more decisive steps.

The Diet had assembled at Nuremberg. To it the new pope despatched his legate Chieregati, with bitter complaints that the edict promulgated against Luther at Worms had been so laxly observed, and with the demand for a more punctilious fulfilment of it. The states of the empire had, meantime, become partially enlightened in regard to the cause of Luther, and some of them were more leniently disposed towards it, whilst others, as especially Duke George, had been all the while nourishing their hatred of Lutheranism. The complaints of the German nation against the Romish See, formerly preferred at Worms, had, however, remained the same. And so the Diet could give the pope no other consolation than such as might be derived from the assurance that all possible caution should be observed in regard to what was taught and printed, and that restrictions should be laid upon the arbitrary abandonment of the cloisters. As for the rest, it was expected that the Papal See would at length, for its part, consider the grievances of the German nation.

The pope had, in his letter to the states, brought forward, amongst other things, the plea that the Catholic faith is the oldest—an assertion which has been so frequently alleged by the opponents of Protestantism. Against this plea, Luther justly demonstrated that where truth is concerned, it is not a question of age, but of truth itself, with which we have to do. " If custom and long usage are sufficient in themselves, why do we not believe with Jews, Turks, and heathen ? Why do we not cleave to the tenets of the devil, who has always been *accustomed* to be wicked ? Why do we not inquire into the origin of a custom, whether it be right or wrong ? *The name of our God is not custom, but truth, which God Himself is.*"[1]

---

[1] See RAUMER, *l.c.* p. 354 (from *Luther's Werke*, vol. xv. p. 2659).

How sadly neglected by Protestants themselves did this truly Protestant maxim, that antiquity and custom are not *alone* decisive (although a due regard must always be paid to historical development), afterwards become! How frequently did dead historic tradition take the place of living progress! True it is, as Luther further declares, that truth must sometimes die with Christ; but it shall, as he likewise affirms, also rise with Him.

Upon the death of Adrian, another Medici, Clement VII., a nephew of Leo X., ascended the pontifical throne. This pope was disposed to act entirely in the interests of the Papal See, and was destined to play an important part in the political affairs of the world. He sent his legate Campeggi to the Diet, but the latter was coldly received and reminded of the yet unfulfilled promises of the pope. At the Diet there was a manifest inclination to protract, as far as possible, the settlement of Luther's cause, and to await its further course. The following abstract of the resolutions of the Diet was therefore published in the spring of 1524:—" The Edict of Worms shall be fulfilled *as far as possible;* all necessary preparations for a council shall be made; disorders and violent measures shall be suppressed until such time as the council shall meet; and further arrangements shall be deferred until the convention of the new Diet at Speier." The clause "*as far as possible*" afforded free scope for the pleasure of individual princes, and furnished them with a backdoor of escape in case of the nonobservance of the edict. This very fact, however, rendered the decree of the Diet most obnoxious to the papal legate and the emperor. The latter, to whom the decree had been sent, issued, at Burgos in Castile, 10th July 1524, a letter to the German princes, expressive of his indignation that so little attention was paid to the Edict of Worms, and commanding its better observance. Even at this time, however, he thought it advisable to proceed cautiously, and he therefore gave his brother, Duke Ferdinand, to whom he entrusted the letter, secret instructions to produce it only in case he should perceive an inclination to obedience on the part of the states.

The legate Campeggi, meantime, had quitted Nuremberg and repaired to Ratisbon, where he concluded with a few of the states that were attached to the old faith a close compact for the support of the Edict of Worms.

Thus was the foundation for a division of the states in matters of religion already laid, and the cause of the Reformation had become a thing of diplomacy. What mighty changes had taken place within a brief period! When, in 1517, Luther posted his theses against indulgences, the affair seemed but an insignificant monkish controversy. But seven years have scarce elapsed, and the monkish quarrel has become a momentous question of European politics. From this time forth, it is true, the purely human interest of the matter decreases. The figure of Luther, great only when it stood alone, as it were, retires more and more into the background. Luther was anything but a diplomatist. He despised—nay, he not seldom totally misunderstood—even those more innocent paths of policy which it was sometimes thought expedient to follow. Hence the disfavour with which he invariably regarded the proceedings of the empire; hence, too, the often misplaced indignation and derision with which he was wont to greet them. He was highly dissatisfied, for instance, with the decree of the Diet of Nuremberg, unexpectedly gracious as that had proved, considering the circumstances of the time, to the work of the Reformation. His straightforward soul hated all *half-measures*. He was, however, not sufficiently mindful of the difficulty of the circumstances which gave rise to such half-measures. He did not sufficiently consider the difference between the regeneration of an individual and that of a state, and especially such a sluggish and unwieldy body as the German Empire. Himself contemning all violent action in favour of the gospel, he was equally displeased with an evasive and hesitating policy. Suffice it to say that he found himself in that painful condition of mind in which great, noble, and enthusiastic souls are often placed, when they see that what appears to them so simple in idea meets with a thousand obstacles in its execution,—when they see that which is most beautiful and venerable dragged down into the sphere of human, oftentimes inadequate, and hence unworthy, calculation. In this state of irritation, Luther was even seized with an actual repugnance to the German people, to whom he nevertheless altogether belonged in heart and soul. Thus in printing together the two Edicts of Worms and Nuremberg,—edicts contradictory beyond a doubt, but *happily* contradictory,[1]—and remarking upon the inconsistency of the decrees of the Diet, in accordance with one of which he was placed under the ban of the empire, whilst more or less consideration was shown him by the other, he stated in the preface that he had had these commands printed by reason of his great compassion for the poor Germans, in order that they might have palpable and sensible evidence (for of seeing there was no need[2]) of the blindness and stupidity of their conduct. "Well," he continues, "we Germans must continue to be Germans, and the pope's asses and martyrs; though (as Solomon says) we be bruised in a mortar like grain, yet will our foolishness not depart from us. Unavailing are all lamentations, teachings, entreaties, and supplications—ay, even our own daily experience of their manner of flaying and devouring us."

But matters did not stop with a few passing fits of ill-humour. Hell actually seemed to have conspired against Luther. From all quarters trials press upon him; he feels himself wounded and assailed on every side, and the dark period of his life begins, over which his shortly succeeding marriage diffuses, through the medium of the quiet joys of domestic life, some mitigating beams, it is true, but which never again passed into perfect brightness. And yet amidst all the outbreaks of passion we still discern the beating of the

---

[1] "*Zwei kaiserliche uneinige und widerwärtige Gebote, den Luther betreffend*" (*Luther's Werke*, vol. xv. p. 2712). Comp. MARHEINEKE, vol. ii. pp. 33 sq.

[2] "Hogs and asses could see it," is still in the text.

old, faithful, and affectionate heart; from the midst of the dark clouds that surround his brow we behold the old love shining forth in heavenly radiance; we see an unshakeable faith lifting its standard high above the billows of the raging whirlpool; and as a noble man becomes doubly dear to us when misfortune overtakes him, let us not withdraw our love from the man whom we are considering, even when, blinded by a mistaken zeal, he coldly pushes honest Zwingle from him.

But before entering upon the unedifying controversy at which we have just hinted, it will be necessary for us to glance at the extension of the Reformation within and outside of Germany, in doing which we shall reserve Switzerland for separate consideration.

CHAPTER IX.

VIEW OF THE EXTENSION OF THE REFORMATION WITHIN AND OUTSIDE OF GERMANY—THE FIRST MARTYRS—PUBLIC FEELING AND THE PRESS.

RANKE[1] admirably says, in reference to the rapid spread of the Reformation in its first years: "No arrangements needed to be made, no plan had to be agreed upon, no mission was necessary. As the seed which the husbandman has sown shoots up in every quarter of the field under the first warm rays of the spring sun, so the new convictions, prepared for by all that had been experienced and heard, now pressed forth to the day, either independently or upon the smallest provocation, throughout the German-speaking realm." The same author likewise draws attention to the fact that there existed undeniably various sorts of connecting points for the diffusion of the new doctrine, and states, with truth, that the confraternity of the Augustinians especially lent their aid to the spread of evangelical ideas. Not, however, the Augustinians alone, but also the Franciscans, in whom a reformatory ferment had been working for a considerable period, exhibited a susceptibility for reformatory ideas; and even amongst the Dominicans, although these last were more inclined to take measures of inquisitorial severity against the innovations, some few were found who joined themselves to the movement. It would, moreover, be taking a one-sided view of the case to suppose that the democratic element of the Church alone sympathized with the Reformation, whilst the ecclesiastical aristocracy kept

[1] *Deutsche Reformationsgeschichte*, vol. ii. p. 67.

at a distance from it. Occasionally we see men of high position—bishops and abbots—leading the way into its ranks, and thereby setting a good example to the inferior clergy and the laity. Even amongst the inhabitants of the cloisters the decisive motive for embracing the reformatory cause was not always, as is generally supposed, the longing to be freed from cloistral restraints.

Without binding ourselves strictly either to a geographical or a chronological mode of procedure, let us gather, from the abundant special histories of individual states, the most salient pictures, in order that we may gain as vivid a view as possible of the whole.

Taking Wittenberg as our point of departure, we will begin with Southern and Middle Germany. Here we meet with one who, despite repeated and violent opposition, laboured with blessed results in various cities—in Dinkelsbühl, Würzburg, Salzburg, Vienna, to the borders of Bohemia and Moravia. This is the Swabian Paul Speratus, a scion, it is believed, of the noble family of the Sprettens, and the same who gave to the evangelical Church the hymn beginning, "*Es ist das Heil uns kommen her*" ["To us salvation now is come"]. He subsequently repaired to Prussia, and thus belongs to the north as well as to the south of Germany. His ministry in Prussia extended over a period of twenty-seven years, six of which he passed in Königsberg in the capacity of court chaplain; during the remaining twenty-one he laboured, to an advanced age, in Marienwerder as Bishop of Pomesamia.[1] At Ulm, Anthony Eberlin of Günzburg (on the Danube) preached. Driven from the former place, he proceeded to Basel and the neighbouring Rhine provinces in hither Austria. Hence also he was driven by the Austrian Government in Ensisheim. Already the friend of Hutten and Sickingen, he formed still closer ties of friendship with Melanchthon at Wittenberg. We encounter him again at Rottenburg on the Neckar, at Erfurt, and elsewhere. At Ulm, Jost Höflich followed in the footsteps of

[1] ERDMANN in Herzog's *Realenc.* vol. xiv. pp. 626 sqq.

Eberlin, and, the churches of the city being shut against him, preached to large audiences, consisting of about 500 men and women, on the "Engelsplatz" or "Drachenfels," outside of the gates of Ulm. One day, however (shortly before Whitsuntide of 1524), he was taken prisoner and driven on a cart to Constance, there to undergo a judicial examination. He was kept in close confinement at Meersburg and put to the rack, but could not be induced to recant. The peasants of Meersburg are said to have assisted him to make his escape. Before his time the Franciscan Henry of Kettenbach appeared as a Reformer at Ulm. The language of this man was bold and defiant. We cite as a specimen of his style the following: "Fear ye not the monks; they are the hirelings and Scripture perverters of antichrist. They blare, and lie, and blaspheme against that Christian, Martin Luther, and yet are not able to answer, from the Holy Scriptures, one in a thousand of his words." "If but the hundredth part of the priests were priests, there would still be too many of them.[1] Three finches in a bird-cage praise God more by their joyousness" (we might think we were listening to a modern naturalist) "than a hundred monks in a cloister praise Him." "There is better preaching in the taprooms and burgher homes of Ulm than can be heard from all the pulpits in the town." It was not only an earnest and edifying discourse that took possession of the minds of men and bore them along with resistless power, dry native wit had also its share in effecting the change in popular sentiment, and not unfrequently cast its vigorous shadows across the picture. By the year 1524 matters had made such progress that the town council of Ulm acceded to the petition of the burghers, and permitted the pure gospel to be preached throughout the city. In that same year Konrad Sam (Sohm) repaired to Ulm and occupied the post of preacher there, and it is he who must be regarded as the true Reformer of the city.

---

[1] EBERLIN had previously given similar advice to the citizens of Ulm: "Let all your priests except six or seven die out; you will have enough with these, and if they do not behave themselves, even they will be too many."

But the man who, in a wider sense than any other, deserved the name of the Swabian Reformer, was John Brenz.[1] He was born 24th June 1499, in the town of Weil on the Würm, and studied at Heidelberg. He learned Greek from Œcolampadius, and Hebrew from Dr. Adriani, a Spanish Jew who had embraced Christianity. He spent whole nights in the study of Aristotle. He had attended the discussion which took place during Luther's presence at Heidelberg (1518),[2] and what he then heard was impressed upon him for life. Thenceforth Luther's writings were his daily study.

This well-schooled man we meet in the spring of 1522 as a preacher at Schwäbisch-Hall. In 1523 he desisted from the reading of mass, and preached against the idolatry practised by the worship of saints. He was a zealous opponent of the clergy "falsely so called," whose connection with the Church was the occasion of mere external ostentation and pageantry. He had already gained a clear conviction of the distinction between the visible and the invisible Church. His preaching was not without effect. The mendicant friars were speedily obliged to leave the city; the worst of them were sent in carts to Würzburg, and the rest received stipends in the hospital, or married. Their convent was turned into a school, and with its revenues teachers in the ancient languages, etc., were hired. We shall encounter this Swabian Reformer again.

At Heilbronn, John Kröner and John Lachmann preached; at Reutlingen, Matthew Alber. At the latter place public feeling became so violent that, in the year 1523, any priest who did not preach agreeably to the Bible was forcibly compelled to withdraw from the pulpit. In Esslingen,[3] also,

---

[1] C. W. KEIM, *Reformationsgeschichte der Reichsstadt Ulm*, Stuttgart, 1845.
[2] [At the Augustinian convention.]
[3] The pope had hitherto commended the people of Esslingen for their constancy to the old faith. The churches were full of wonder-working images and relics. The city was the centre of the cloistral system of Swabia. It is said that the whole world did not contain within an equally narrow compass another such collection of convents and Beguin houses as were to be found in Swabia, in

another Swabian town, the seat of the court of the Imperial Chamber, there were many friends of the Reformation. Amongst them we see a member of Luther's order, Michael Stiefel (Styfel), a native of Esslingen, and thirty-five years of age at the time of which we speak. He was in outward appearance a delicate and courtly little man, of noble origin,[1] but bold and somewhat eccentric in his actions, and chiliastic in the tincture of his mind. Among the biblical books he was most attracted by Daniel and the Revelation of John. He regarded Luther sometimes as Elijah, and sometimes as the Apocalyptic angel flying through heaven. He chanted the praises of the Reformer of Wittenberg in a spiritual song "to the tune of Brother Vitus:"

> "Nun grüss ich dich von Herzen,
> Du edles Wittenberg!
> Viel Frommer litten Schmerzen,
> Dir ging es überzwerg."[2]

This song was received with much favour. Murner answered it by another, to which Stiefel did not fail to reply. When the clergy of Esslingen issued a number of articles against the Reformation, Stiefel sent them to Luther at Wittenberg; whereupon Luther, under date of 11th October 1523, addressed an affectionate letter to the people of Esslingen, encouraging them to be stedfast in the faith, and directing them to the Pauline Epistles, from which they could learn, far better than from his writings, what was profitable for their salvation.[3] Stiefel, after meeting with a variety of fortunes, sank more and more into a downward course.[4] By

a circuit of ten miles from the imperial city of Esslingen. See KEIM, *Reformationsblätter der Reichsstadt Esslingen*, Esslingen, 1860.

[1] He is thus described by MURNER, his opponent.
[2] [The stanza may thus be rendered:
> "Brave Wittenberg! a greeting
> Now sends to thee my heart.
> Pangs all the saints were meeting,
> But thine the bitterest part."—TR.]
[3] DE WETTE, vol. ii. No. 808.
[4] Being banished from Esslingen, Stiefel resorted first to Hartmuth von Kronberg, and then proceeded to Wittenberg. At the solicitation of Luther, he

his daring prophecies of the speedy end of the world, by which he excited much disturbance amongst the credulous, he drew upon himself the reprimand of Luther, who continued, however, to be a fatherly friend to him. The city of Esslingen retained its connection with him even after his banishment thence. At all events, the Reformation did not die out there with his departure. The chaplain Fuchs was the first to tread in his footsteps. Others followed; and as a result of the first Diet of Nuremberg (1523), the town council commanded all preachers to proclaim the pure gospel. Hereafter we shall meet with Ambrose Blarer as a Swabian Reformer.

In 1519 a young preacher called John Schwebel (Schwäb-lin) assumed a prominent place in his native city of Pforzheim, having laid aside the garb of his order and joined himself to the Reformation. At the command, however, of the Margrave Philip, who was related by marriage to the Bishop of Speier, Schwebel was obliged to leave his birthplace and home. Like many others, he found an asylum in the "refuge of the just," with Sickingen. Through his friend, Knight George of Leutrum (Luthrumer), he still maintained his connection with Pforzheim. He caused a tractate to be printed there, in which he attacked the abuses that prevailed in the administration of alms. On a woodcut accompanying the tractate, the pope was pictured, in his triple diadem, and seated beside a sack full of money; in the background might be seen the dealers in indulgences, with their chest filled with coin, and a boy attracting buyers by ringing a bell. Schwebel was finally permitted to return to Pforzheim, and preached in the hospital church on "the Good Shepherd." From Pforzheim he was called to Zweibrücken as court chaplain and superintendent. Ludwig II., the count palatine, was a patron and promoter of the Reformation, and therefore

preached in Upper Austria. He was next pastor at Mansfeld, and subsequently occupied a similar position at Lochau (near Wittenberg), which place he was also obliged to leave. He died at an advanced age in 1567. Comp. GÖSCHEL in Herzog's *Realencyc.* vol. xv. pp. 88 sqq.

raised no objections to various innovations which Schwebel introduced into the public celebration of divine worship— such, for instance, as church singing in German. Schwebel (in 1529) prepared a liturgy on the basis of these innovations.

At Strassburg there had existed for a long period a soil favourable to the reception of the Reformation. We would call to mind Tauler and the Friends of God, Geiler of Kaisersberg, and Wimpheling. The place of the first Reformer (in the sixteenth-century sense of the word Reformation) was occupied by Matthew Zell (Cellius), born in 1477 at Kaisersberg in Upper Alsatia. In 1521, having been powerfully affected by Luther's theses, he began decidedly to preach the gospel. He explained the Epistle to the Romans, and developed thence the programme of the Reformation. Many listened to him with approbation; others opposed him. Threatened by the priesthood, he sought and found protection among the better portion of the burghers. In the year 1523 the bishop caused to be affixed to the chapter-house of the cathedral a complaint against Zell, which he, for his part, did not leave unanswered. On the 1st December of the same year, the municipal authorities issued a decree commanding that all preachers should "in future preach nothing but the holy gospel and the teachings of God, and whatsoever promoteth the love of God and of our neighbour, and that they should freely and openly proclaim these to the people." A few months after this, the bishop pronounced sentence of excommunication upon all married clergy. The burghers, however, cared nothing for the episcopal ban, but, on the contrary, there ensued a visible declension from the Papacy. The monks were pensioned, and the revenues of the cloisters were applied to the support of schools and beneficent objects. Zell was soon joined by other Reformers, whose names were Capito, Bucer, and Hedio, and whom we shall meet again farther on. Among the learned laymen of this time, the jurist Nicholas Gerbel (Gerbelius) already occupied a prominent position. He was the recipient of various letters from Luther, in the first of which (under date of 6th May 1524) the latter expresses his joy at the prevalence of the pure word of God at Strassburg.[1]

At Frankfort-on-the-Main, Pastor Hartmann Ibach had, since the Diet of Worms, borne open testimony to the Reformation. The clergy on this account made an accusation of heresy against him to the Archbishop of Mentz. Stirring scenes followed. Peter Meyer, a pastor who maintained his allegiance to the old faith, vehemently opposed Ibach and his learned friend and fellow-combatant, Otto Brunfels, from the pulpit. The latter were obliged to leave the city. The knight Hartmuth von Kronberg now arose as a defender of evangelical liberty. On the 16th of May 1522, he affixed to the Main Gate a challenge " to the false prophets and wolves," and Hutten sent a letter of defiance to Meyer, in which he gave him notice that he would no longer be at peace with him if he did not permit Ibach to preach.[2] The emperor, upon this, in a rescript of 4th July, had recourse to the town council of Frankfort, commanding the protection of the clergy from the threats of the nobles. But the council issued, 5th March 1523, a direction to all the preachers in the city to proclaim the pure word of God, and that alone. Meyer now gave vent to his anger in invectives against the Government. He thus, however, exasperated the people of Frankfort, and was finally turned out of the city.

At Fulda, Adam Kraft (Crato Fuldensis) preached, and promoted the Reformation in Hesse. He had become acquainted with Luther and Melanchthon at the Disputation of Leipsic (1519), and had since been one of their decided adherents. Melanchthon, on his journey to his native place,

---

[1] DE WETTE, vol. ii. No. 601. On Zell comp. the article by C. SCHMIDT in Herzog's *Realencyc.* vol. xviii. p. 484 ; on the Reformation in Strassburg and Alsatia, the writings of JUNG (Strassburg, 1830) and RÖHRICH (Strassburg, 1830-1832), vol. iv.

[2] There is extant a letter from Luther to Hartmuth von Kronberg. See DE WETTE, vol. ii. No. 375.

visited him at Fulda (1524), and previous to this Luther wrote him a letter of encouragement (1522).[1]

Among the cities in which the light of the Reformation shone betimes, Nuremberg claims a distinguished place. The most respected patricians of the city—Wilibald Pirckheimer, Lazarus Spengler, the learned Christopher Scheurl, and the unlettered cobbler, but richly gifted poet, Hans Sachs—were counted among the friends and admirers of Luther. Hans Sachs hailed him, in the summer of 1523, as " Die Wittembergisch Nachtigal, die Man jetzt höret überall,"[2] and wrote the following verses in his honour:—

" Wach auff, es nahend gen dem Tag,
 Ich hör' singen im grünen Hag
 Ein wunnigkliche Nachtigal,
 Ihr Stimm durchklinget Berg und Thal,
 Die Nacht neigt sich gen Occident,
 Der Tag geht auff von Orient,
 Die rotbrünstige Morgenröt
 Her durch die trüben Wolken geht,
 Daraus die lichte Sonn thut blicken,
 Des Mondes Schein thut sich verdrücken,
 Der ist jetzt worden bleich und finster
 Der vor mit seinem falschen Glinster
 Die ganzen Herd Schaf hat geblendt,
 Dass sie sich haben abgewendt
 Von ihrem Hirten und der Weyd,
 Und haben sie verlassen beid',
 Sind gangen nach des Mondes Schein
 In die Wildniss den Holtzweg ein."

And then it continues:

" Wer die lieblich Nachtigal sei,
 Die uns den hellen Tag ausschrei',
 Ist Dr. Martinus Luther,
 Zu Wittenberg Augustiner,
 Der uns aufwecket von der Nacht,
 Darein der Mondschein uns hat bracht."

The poem closes with an exhortation to Christendom:

" Darauf ihr Christen, wo ihr seid,
 Kehrt wieder aus des Bapstes Wüste,
 Zu unserm Hirten Jesu Christe,

---

[1] DE WETTE, vol. ii. No. 422.
[2] [The nightingale of Wittenberg, whose voice is heard throughout the land.]

Derselbig ist ein guter Hirt,
Hat sein Lieb mit dem Tod probiert,
Durch den wir alle sind erlost,
Der ist unser einiger Trost,
Und unser einige Hoffnung,
Gerechtigkeit und Seligung,
All die Glauben an seinen Namen,
Wer das begert, der spreche Amen."[1]

In the year 1522, Andrew Osiander preached the gospel at Nuremberg. The Margrave of Brandenburg, when attending

[1] [The Translator subjoins the following imperfect rendering of the "Wittenberg Nightingale," in the hope that it may afford those who do not understand German some slight idea of the meaning and style of the original:—

"Awake! the day is drawing near,
And singing in the hedge I hear,
So wondrous sweet, a nightingale.
Her voice resounds o'er hill and dale,
The night drops toward the Occident,
The day springs from the Orient.
The ruddy glow of early morn
Flushes the clouds, erst black,—now torn
By the sun's rays, that, flashing brightly,
Make the moon veil her beams unsightly;—
Pallor and dimness now o'erspreading
Her who, while late false radiance shedding,
Did the whole flock of sheep so blind,
That, turning from their Shepherd kind
And from the mead where once they fed,
They to the wilderness all sped,
Chasing the beams that them beguiled
Into the forest dark and wild.

"Who is that lovely bird whose strain
Proclaims, The bright days comes amain?
'Tis Doctor Martinus Luther,
An Augustinian brother.
He wakes us from the gloomy night,
In which we erred by pale moonlight.

"Then, Christians, up! where'er ye be.
Quickly forsake the popish waste,
And to our Shepherd Jesus haste.
He a Good Shepherd is and kind;
To prove His love He life resigned.
'Tis through Him that we have salvation,
He is our only consolation,
Our only hope, our righteousness,
Eternal life and blessedness.
All who upon His name believe,
Say Amen, if ye'd those receive."]

the Diet (1523), listened to him with much pleasure. Others there also were who preached in a similar tone. At Easter of 1524, over three thousand communicants partook of the Lord's Supper in both kinds. The priors of St. Sebald and St. Lorenz, Besler (Pessler) and Böhmer, abolished the abuses of the mass, and defended this measure in a tractate.

At Hof, in the Voigtland, Kasper Löhner preached; at Baireuth, John Brückner. At Bamberg the enlightened bishop, George von Limburg, showed himself favourable to the Reformation; and the gospel early took root in the city, notwithstanding the admonitions of the pope. At Augsburg, in 1521, John Frosch made a stand against the Papacy, and was joined by Stephen Agricola, Urban Regius, and others. At Ratisbon several monks fell under suspicion of heresy, and were driven out of the city. With them was banished a certain Hans Planmacher (Plohanus), so called because he was a blue-dyer by trade. A portion of the burghers, however, had already decided in favour of the evangelical doctrine. These had recourse to Luther, who issued a written injunction to the town council of Ratisbon, requiring them to protect the gospel and to check superstition—in its rampancy about an image of the Virgin Mary especially.[1]

Erhard Schnepf of Heilbronn, having first preached the gospel in Weinsberg, the birthplace of Œcolampadius, and been expelled thence, gathered about him in the Kreichgau, under the protection of the lords of Memmingen, a confraternity of congenial country pastors. He then, subsequent to 1523, preached in the free imperial city of Wimpfen. Later, in 1526, he was called by Count Philip III. of Nassau to Weilburg, with a view to his superintendence of the progress of the Reformation there.

At Memmingen, Christopher Schappeler, preacher at St.

---

[1] Not long before this time the Jews had, at Hubmaier's instigation, been expelled from the city, and their synagogue had been destroyed. On its site a chapel was erected to the "beautiful Mary," the fame of whose miracles attracted a great number of pilgrims. It is to this fact that Luther's letter refers (see DE WETTE, vol. ii. p. 525). Comp. chap. xviii.

Martin's, had introduced the reformatory principles. This man was a native of St. Gall, and took an interest in the fortunes of the Swiss Reformation;[1] his type of Reformation was, moreover, that of Switzerland rather than that of Wittenberg. The Bishop of Augsburg called him to account, and pronounced sentence of excommunication upon him. Schappeler, upon this, drew up seven articles, to which he subsequently made additions, and a religious conference ensued. In his third article Schappeler denied the justice of the tithes. We need not here examine into the extent of his share in the Peasant War of 1525.[2]

At Alt-Oetingen, in Bavaria, Wolfgang Russ was zealously attacking the practice of making pilgrimages and of trusting to work-holiness for salvation. Even in Ingolstadt, the spiritual domain of Eck, a journeyman weaver was reading Luther's books to assemblies of the people.

On the whole, however, the Reformation in South Germany nowhere met with more opposition than in Bavaria. At the instigation of Eck, a sharp eye was kept upon all who were suspected of heresy throughout the land. Luther complained bitterly of these persecutions on the part of the "raging swine," as he called the Romish party, who were "wallowing in the blood that they had shed."[3] Duke William IV. and his brother Ludwig had, as early as Ash Wednesday 1522, issued the most stringent orders against any who should desert the faith of their fathers. More than one convert to evangelical ideas perished by the hand of the executioner.[4] To such a fate did the youthful Arsacius Seehofer expose himself. He

---

[1] He presided at the second religious conference at Zurich, in October 1523. See chap. xii.

[2] On the fact that he was not, as is often claimed, the author of the Twelve Articles of the Peasants of Swabia, see STERN, *Ueber die 12 Artikel der Bauerschaft*, pp. 18 sqq.

[3] Letter to Gottschalk Crusius, 30th October 1524, DE WETTE, vol. ii. No. 628.

[4] To anticipate a little, George Carpentarius was, in 1527, burned at Munich as a heretic, and Bernard Käser (Kaiser) died a martyr's death at Schärding on the Inn. Numbers of heretics were at the same time drowned at Munich.

was the son of a burgher of Munich, and had sat at the feet of Luther and Melanchthon. He had written some theses, in the year 1523, that were condemned by the University of Ingolstadt, and he himself was compelled to abjure his teachings as "arrant arch-heresy and knavery," and was punished by being shut up in the convent of Ettal. Luther, in the same year, issued a tract "Against the blind and foolish condemnatory judgment of the wretched and infamous University of Ingolstadt." But the great Reformer was forestalled by a woman. Argula von Staufen, Baroness von Grumbach by marriage, addressed, on the 19th of September, a letter of censure to the high school, and challenged the whole University to a disputation. "I indeed," she wrote, "can speak no Latin, but ye can speak German, having been born and bred in that tongue." Her sex, she demonstrated, by no means condemned her to silence; St. Jerome did not scorn to exchange letters with women, and our Lord Christ Himself permitted Mary Magdalene and "the woman at the well" to speak. Ungallant Dr. Eck is said to have sent her a spindle and distaff in return for her literary present. From other quarters, also, satirical verses were sent her, advising her to occupy herself with spinning, embroidery, and lace-making, rather than with literary pursuits. Argula answered the "fool according to his folly," in the same tone and measure. She was, however, not only competent for a battle of wits with men of learning, but also knew how to speak an earnest word to princes when there was need for earnestness. To Duke William she recommended the exercise of justice and clemency toward those who were persecuted, and conjured him to give free course to the gospel. "O ye princes," she wrote, "would God that your eyes might be opened!" Eck could not forgive the "Grumbach woman" her forwardness in writing to the University. He sought to influence William's brother, Duke Ludwig, to dismiss from his service the husband of Argula. Still "the disciple of Christ," as Luther called her, was undismayed. "The Lord will provide for my little ones," said she; "He will feed them together with the birds of the air, and clothe them along with the flowers of the field. He has said it: He cannot lie." She was finally—it being found impossible, either by warnings or threats, to move her from her faith—banished from the country, and her son, Hans George, was discharged from his situation. The husband of Argula had shown a less courageous spirit than his spouse; he, in fact, as she once complained to her cousin, Adam von Törring, "aided in persecuting Christ in her." She, however, was firm in her determination "to abandon everything—father and mother, sisters, children, property, and life"—rather than be false to her convictions.[1]

If we turn now to the cities of the Rhine, we shall find that the seed that Luther had sown by his appearance at Worms was joyfully springing up. Meetings for evangelical worship were at first held in the open air, a portable pulpit being employed. To the Christians of Worms Luther writes, 24th August 1523, as follows:[2]—"With joy have we heard from our dear lord and friend in Christ, that God, the Father of our Lord Jesus Christ, has caused to rise among you and upon you the glorious light of His grace and the brightness of the knowledge of Himself, through His Son Jesus Christ, through whom, being reconciled, we have peace with God and a joyful conscience, being purged from all our former sins and falsely magnified good works, in respect to which the apostles of darkness and preachers of Belial have so grievously misled us hitherto. We therefore rejoice concerning you and with you, offering the sacrifice of praise and thanksgiving to God, the Father of all mercies, and praying that He who has begun the good work both in you and in us will continue to glorify Himself in us all more and more unto the end, that we may be found the new and unblameable work of His grace at that day. Amen." He next admonished the citizens of Worms to stedfastness: "Ye, dear brethren, have special

---

[1] Comp. SIXT'S beautiful notice of her, in Piper's *Evangelical Calendar* for 1860, pp. 163 sqq.
[2] DE WETTE, vol. ii. No. 524, p. 392.

need to cleave fast to the gospel of grace, and to send many labourers into the harvest; for ye dwell, as did Ezekiel, among scorpions."

"Be firm, then, beloved brethren," he says in conclusion; "edify and comfort one another in the strength of God—that is, with God's word, that conquers all things. . . . That which comes of God must endure the enmity of the world—nothing else is to be expected; and if the world do not hate and persecute it, it is surely not of God. May the same God our Saviour and Lord Jesus Christ strengthen you, together with us, in His holy light, to the eternal praise and glory of His holy name! Amen."

At Miltenberg on the river Main, a city of the electorate of Mentz, John Draco (Drach, Trach, Draconites), called also John Carstadt from his birthplace, taught the gospel and made application for the administration of the sacrament in both kinds.[1] This demand occasioned some disturbance. The clergy of the town, in connection with that portion of the burghers who adhered to the old faith, procured from the electoral governor an order that the pastor should be deprived of his office. The order not being obeyed, excommunication ensued. When the edict of excommunication, dated 8th September 1523, was about to be read in church, a tumult arose. Draconites was himself obliged to protect the priest, whose duty it was to read the edict, from the violence of the people. He left the city, being accompanied beyond the gates by the weeping burghers, and sought refuge in Wittenberg.[2] In February 1524 Luther despatched a letter of consolation to the deserted congregation at Miltenberg.[3] He admonishes them not to cherish vengeful feelings against their enemies, and comforts them with the thought that it is for God's sake

---

[1] He had made the acquaintance of Luther in 1521 when the latter was on his way to Worms, had been expelled from Erfurt on account of his Lutheran heresy, and had repaired to Wittenberg. Whilst at the latter place he received his call to Wittenberg. See Herzog's *Realenc.* vol. iii. p. 495.

[2] For a further account of him, see Herzog, *l.c.*

[3] DE WETTE, vol. ii. No. 580, p. 475.

that they are suffering shame and persecution. "That only is a joyous victory that is gained without the sword or the hand of man." He also sent them for their edification an exposition of Psalm cxix. (cxx.) Though, he continues, the gospel be suppressed in one place, as it is at Miltenberg, it will break forth in a dozen other places; the more they blow the fire, the stronger it will burn. At the same time he wrote to the Elector of Mentz, begging him to give justice a hearing.

We shall hear on a future occasion of the first movements of the Reformation at Cologne, and of the martyrs' blood that was shed there.

Let us now turn to *Northern* Germany.

At Husum in Schleswig there stood in the churchyard two linden trees, "mother and daughter."[1] Under the larger of these trees—the mother—Hermann Tast, one of the twenty-four papal vicars of Schleswig, preached, because the churches were closed against him. Upon each occasion of his holding forth, his armed followers proceeded to his house and escorted him to the place of meeting, and conducted him thence again at the close of the service. His adherents speedily became so numerous, that as early as 1524 Frederick I. issued an edict of tolerance in favour of the Lutherans, with special reference to Husum. The Reformation began with the year 1525 in the city of Schleswig also. Its commencement here was peculiar, being due to a monk (called Crazy Frederick) who had eloped from his convent, and whose preachings were at first productive, doubtless, of more offence than edification. Better things, however, soon ensued. The gospel meantime began to prevail in Flensburg, Hadersleben, and other towns besides. In August 1524 Duke Frederick I. published, as we have already stated, an edict of tolerance sanctioning the preaching of the evangelical doctrine, but also protecting the rights of bishops, chapters, and cloisters.[2]

---

[1] Ranke, vol. ii. p. 72.
[2] See the article on "Schleswig-Holstein," by Lau, in Herzog's *Realenc.* vol. xx. pp. 782 sqq.

At Emden in East Friesland, "Master George von der Düre" (Aportanus) was driven from the church for daring to preach in the spirit of Luther. The people, however, adhered to him, and listened to him in the open air, never resting until the halls of the great church were again opened to their preacher. The magistracy found it necessary to station a guard in the church to protect both the adherents and the opponents of the preacher from violence.

Before Luther's appearance as a Reformer, Albert Krantz, a learned and pious theologian, had laboured at Hamburg, in advance of the Reformation, in the double character of preacher and syndic. He had, however, reaped but little fruit from his labours; so that, after reading Luther's theses, which reached him shortly before his death (4th December 1517), he laid them sadly down, with the sorrowful words: "Thou speakest truth, good brother, but thou wilt accomplish nothing. Go into thy cell and say, 'God have mercy on me.'" Facts, however, soon gave the lie to this despondent utterance. In 1522 the vicar of the cathedral and pastor of the church of St. Catharine, Otto Stimmel (Steynmeel, Stiffel), ventured, incited probably by Krantz, publicly to oppose the traffic in indulgences and the licentious life of the clergy. Though his success in this undertaking was comparatively small, better fortune attended the exertions of Stephen Kempe from Rostock, whom, after a sermon delivered upon his arrival at Hamburg, the burghers invited to remain with them and preach to them the pure word of God without human additions. From this time the number of evangelical preachers in Hamburg increased in a most gratifying manner. John Bugenhagen of Wittenberg was called to the church of St. Nicholas, and to him it was reserved to carry out the work of Hamburg's reformation.[1]

Events of a similar character took place at Bremen. Here, also, a large portion of the burgher population cherished feelings favourable to the Reformation. At precisely the right time in the year 1522, Henry Moller made his appearance in

[1] KLIPFEL in Herzog's *Realenc.* vol. viii. p. 49, and vol. v. pp. 496, 497.

the city, having been driven by persecution from the Netherlands. Moller, who was born in 1488, in the county of Zütphen, and was hence ordinarily called Henry of Zütphen, wore the garb of the Augustinian order. The representatives of the congregation of St. Ansgarus visited the fugitive at his inn on the market-place, and urgently petitioned that he would preach the word of God to them. The approbation which his first sermon met was so general, that the congregation forthwith made choice of him for their preacher. But the more considerable the influence of his sermons became, the more vehemently did the clergy demand the expulsion of a heretic so disagreeable to them. On the other hand, however, the magistrate declared that as long as the monk remained in the service of the city, and was not confuted from the Scriptures, the burghers would not desert him. And Henry, for his part, declared that he would not leave Bremen unless he should be forcibly expelled. Despite all the machinations of the Archbishop Christopher and the chapter of the cathedral, the Reformation continued to gain ground in the city—a fact which Luther rejoices over in a letter to Spalatin.[1] The number of preachers increased. Jacob Spreng (Propst) was called from Antwerp to the Liebfrauen Church, and John Timan was summoned from Amsterdam to the church of St. Martin. At the expiration of a ministry of two years in Bremen, Zütphen accepted a call to Meldorf in the Ditmarshes, where he suffered martyrdom.[2]

In the free city of Goslar, in the Hartz Mountains, the evangelically minded had (like the same class at Husum) assembled under a lime tree, and were hence called the Lime Brethren. In Brunswick, also, the burghers and a portion of the preachers were favourably inclined toward the Reformation; on the other hand, Duke Henry the Younger sought to hinder its spread as far as possible. Luther had in vain

---

[1] May 11, 1524; DE WETTE, vol. ii. No. 602.
[2] KLIPFEL, *l.c.*, vol. ix. pp. 704 sqq. [See D'AUBIGNÉ's *History of the Reformation*, vol. iii. pp. 168 sqq.—TR.]

cherished the hope of winning him for the gospel. The work of carrying out the Reformation here was reserved for a later time.[1] At Rostock, Joachim Slüter preached the gospel after the manner of Luther, and won over to the reformatory principles one who had previously been a defender of the old doctrine, Valentine Curtius, preacher at St. Catharine's.

Pomerania counts John Bugenhagen (Dr. Pommer, Pomeranus) among the first and most eminent of its Reformers. He was born 24th June 1485, at Wolin, where his father was a member of the council, and educated at Greifswald under the Humanist, Hermann Busch. Prior to the Reformation he had, as rector of the monastery of Belbuck, already earned the gratitude of his country by editing a Pomeranian chronicle (*Pomerania*). In this book he had pointed out the abuses of ecclesiastical life, although at the time of its publication he was still an adherent of the old Church and its doctrine. He confesses that he loved the Holy Scriptures from his youth, but says that he was unable to use them aright until the precious gospel of the grace of God was once more brought to light. " Brought up in the doctrine of the pope, we have been such blockheads that we have not known the gospel, and, moreover, so wicked that we have not wished to know it." In 1520 Luther's treatise on the *Babylonish Captivity* fell into his hands. It at first shocked him exceedingly, so that he thought that since the death of Christ there had arisen no worse heretic than the author of this book. But, reading it repeatedly, he soon arrived at the opposite conviction, and maintained that until this time the world had lain in utter blindness, and that this man alone had pointed it to the true light. Thenceforth he was a decided adherent of Luther, and even won over the abbot of his monastery to the new doctrine. In 1521 he repaired to Wittenberg, desiring personally to hear the great Reformer. He was himself detained in the city as a teacher. The lectures on

[1] LENZ, *Braunschweigs Kirchenreformation im 16 Jahrhundert*, Wolfenbüttel, 1828.

the Psalms which he delivered in his room to Pomeranian peasants met with such hearty approval that he was obliged to have them printed. Luther declared that Dr. Pommer was a better expositor of the Psalms than any other man on earth. Bugenhagen remained at Wittenberg, co-operating from time to time, however, in the spread of the gospel in other places, as his help was required. We shall meet with him again at the house of Luther, in the circle of friends there assembled. Returning now to Pomerania, we find two names deserving of mention next to that of Bugenhagen,—they are those of Andrew Knophen, whose piety and theological learning were highly esteemed by Erasmus,[1] and Christian Ketelhudt. At Pyritz in farther Pomerania, the Franciscan monk John Knipstro was delving deep into the Bible and into the writings of Luther. He compared them conscientiously with each other and found that they agreed. He also soon gained his brethren in the monastery to which he belonged to his way of thinking. He, however, was obliged to flee to Stettin; in 1525 he became assistant preacher in the church of St. Mary at that place, thus gaining a scanty living, and subsequently found a wider field of usefulness as superintendent at Stralsund. His academic labours at Greifswald belong to a still later period. Paul Rhodius (of Rhoda) preached the gospel, meantime, at Stettin.

In 1521, the year in which Bugenhagen removed to Wittenberg, the Bishop of Camin, Erasmus von Mandüwel (Manteuffel), inaugurated a persecution of the evangelicals; but the old Duke Bogislav showed himself not disinclined to the Reformation, although adhering, for his own part, to the old faith.

Among the German cities in Polish Prussia, Dantzic is prominent as one of those in which the more liberal doctrine early found adherents. It was professed as early as the year 1510 by James Knade, preacher at St. Peter's Church. Entering into the matrimonial state, he was imprisoned.[2]

---

[1] *Mentem istam tuam piam tamque avidum Christianæ doctrinæ studium vehementer exosculor* (in a letter to Knophen of January 1520).

[2] He is said to be the first evangelical clergyman who took this step.

After his release, he preached at Thorn, and afterwards at Marienburg. He was succeeded in Dantzic by John Böschenstein, Bernard Schulz, and James Hegge. The latter preached in the open air on the "Hagelsberg," or under the shade of a lime tree in the churchyard of St. Gertrude; subsequently, however, the doors of St. Mary's Church were opened to him. He went somewhat too far, it must be confessed, and kindled the zeal of the iconoclasts. At Elbing, the town council and the burghers decided in favour of the Reformation in the year 1523.

In Silesia, Luther's writings were early diffused amongst the people. They were distributed to the guests in the Schweidnitz cellar. The first evangelical pastor of Breslau was John Hess (Hesse) of Nuremberg.[1] He was the canon and private secretary of the Bishop of Breslau, John Turzo, whom Erasmus designated as a model bishop,[2] and who, in this character, hailed the reformatory ideas as a step in advance. Luther, in a letter to Hess of the 25th of March (Annunciation of the Virgin Mary) 1522, expressed his great joy at the happy progress of the Reformation, and invoked upon his fellow-labourer the blessing of God in the discharge of his office of evangelist.[3] He also commended the honest zeal of the bishop, adding, however, a warning against the supposition that the essence of the Reformation consisted in externals. He exhorted Hess to do everything that could promote faith and love, remarking, for instance, that what constitutes a Christian is not a participation in the Lord's Supper in both kinds, but faith and love, and these can exist as well when the sacrament is partaken of in the old way, in one form. Hess returned to Nuremberg. But the burghers of Breslau, and not these alone, but also the monks in the

---

[1] Comp. JULIUS KÖSTLIN's article in Piper's *Evangelical Calendar* for 1865.

[2] In a letter to Turzo of September 1520, *Erasmi Epp.*, xv. p. 473.

[3] This letter is No. 373 of DE WETTE's *Collection*. At its date Bishop Turzo was dead (he died in 1520). The praise [noted further on] must therefore belong to his successor, James von Salza, who, however, was less favourable to the Reformation.

monastery of St. James, pressed forwards, the more persistently the rest of the clergy clung to the old customs. Hess was recalled by the magistrate, and even the successor of Turzo, Bishop James von Salza, gave his consent to this step, although it was opposed by the cathedral chapter. A public discussion ensued on the 20th of April 1524, in consequence of which the council commanded that the pure word of God should be preached, and, with the help of Hess, gradually introduced the Reformation (1525). Hess was assisted by Ambrose Moiban, who was called to the church of St. Elizabeth. Both of these Reformers married.

The Reformation also early gained access (1524) to the principalities of Liegnitz, Brieg, and Wohlau, which were under the government of Frederick II., a grandson of George Podiebrad.

In Lower Lusatia the Francisan monk John Brismann, born at Cottbus (1488), proclaimed the word of God according to the gospel. Drawn by Luther to Wittenberg, he thence addressed a cheering letter to his former congregation at Cottbus. He soon accepted a call to Königsberg, and preached his inaugural sermon in the cathedral of that city, 27th September 1523. "He ministered the word of God," according to the testimony of a chronicler, "with great mildness, but all possible earnestness." In this he was favourably distinguished from another preacher who laboured at his side— Amandus, whose stormy zeal not unfrequently overstepped the boundaries of propriety. Brismann received a worthy co-labourer, however, in the person of Paul Speratus, with whom we are already acquainted, and whom Luther warmly recommended.[1] George von Polenz, Bishop of Samland, did not disdain to be instructed by Brismann in the gospel; this prelate also lent the whole weight of his authority and example to the support of the Reformation. In a Christmas sermon of the year 1523, he bore witness to his own faith,[2]

---

[1] In a letter to Brismann, DE WETTE's *Collection*, vol. ii. No. 609.
[2] *George von Polenz, der erste evangelische Bischof*, Halle, 1858.

and on the 15th January of the succeeding year he issued an ordinance, commanding that henceforth sermons should be delivered and baptism be administered in the language of the country. He recommended Luther's translation of the Bible and his other writings, especially the treatise on *Christian Liberty*, and the *Postils*. Luther in return dedicated his Latin commentary on Deuteronomy to the bishop in 1525. In the dedication he extols him as the only real and true bishop in Christendom. Entirely different was the position assumed toward the Reformation by Bishop Mauritius of Ermeland. He was most anxious to crush the "Lutheran monster." He addressed a pastoral letter to his flock, admonishing them to walk, as they had done hitherto, in "the laudable footsteps of their pious sires and progenitors;" and issued, in the beginning of the year 1524, a mandate against the Lutheran heresy. It appeared simultaneously with the mandate of the Bishop of Samland, which latter, as will be remembered, was favourable to the Reformation. Luther published these two mandates with a preface and marginal glosses: "Two Episcopalian Bulls; the one by a godly, the other by a popish bishop." Bishop George at this time ceded the secular government of his diocese to the Grand Master of the Teutonic Order of Knights, Albert of Brandenburg, who in pursuance of the Peace of Cracow had been acknowledged hereditary Duke of Prussia.[1] Duke Albert renounced his connection with the clergy, to whose ranks he had hitherto belonged as Grand Master of a religious order of knights, and married. Thus a religious state was transformed into a secular dukedom.

Besides Speratus, whom we have already mentioned, John Poliander (Graumann) contributed, in connection with the two evangelical bishops [George von Polenz and Erhard von Queiss], to the establishment of the ecclesiastical conditions of Prussia and the remodelling of divine worship. At the

[1] A similar course was pursued by another bishop favourable to the Reformation, Erhard von Queiss, Bishop of Pomesania.

Diet assembled in December 1525, the new ritual ("Articles of Ceremonies and other Ecclesiastical Ordinances") was submitted, approved, and adopted. No one was more delighted at these advances of the gospel in Prussia than Luther. He declared it to be a miracle that the gospel should be thus pressing on with all sails set.[1]

Among the cities of North Germany, one has, by its varied fortunes, attained a historical celebrity above many others— we have reference to Magdeburg. The inhabitants of this place manifested from the first a favourable disposition toward the Reformation. Its burgomaster, Klaus Storm, had made the personal acquaintance of Luther whilst the latter was attending the Franciscan school at Magdeburg, and, presuming upon this acquaintance, ventured to write to the Reformer, remonstrating with him on account of his rough treatment of the great, and the epithets of fool and ass which he bestowed upon them.[2] Luther, however, defended himself against the honourable gentleman, his worthy friend [*den ehrsamen, lieben Herrn und Freund*], by protesting that he practised patience and humility long enough, and had earnestly entreated God that his enemies might amend, but in vain. His adversaries were like the hardened Pharisees, on whom the goodness and gentleness of Christ Himself had had no effect. This explanation seems to have satisfied the burgomaster. At least it may be conjectured that it was partly through his influence that, on the 23d of June 1524, the burghers of Magdeburg, in conjunction with seven preachers, presented certain articles to the council, entreating that thenceforth the pure word of God might be preached, that the sacrament of the Lord's Supper might be administered in both kinds, that the celebration of the mass might be discontinued, that the funds of the religious foundations might be made over to the treasury of the Church, and that an annuity might be settled upon the monks in case they should resolve to lay aside their religious dress

---

[1] Letter to George von Polenz, April 1525, DE WETTE, vol. ii. No. 696.
[2] See the letter of 15th June 1522, DE WETTE, vol. ii. No. 409.

and receive instruction in the evangelical doctrine. The magistracy not only granted the petition of the burghers, but applied to the Elector of Saxony with the request that he would send them Nicholas von Amsdorf for a year as preacher. This was done, to the great vexation of the chapter. The canons persuaded the imperial solicitor to impeach the magistracy of Magdeburg before the court of the Imperial Chamber. Dr. Schurf, however, the Wittenberg jurist, conducted the cause of the council so ably that the threatened storm was happily averted.

Beyond the borders of Germany, as well as within its limits, the Reformation made visible progress as early as the first half of the third decade of the sixteenth century. It was at first propagated directly from Wittenberg. In the year 1519, the brothers Olaus (Olaf) and Laurence [Lars] Peterson scattered the seed of the new doctrine—received by them on German soil—in their native Sweden. They were the sons of a well-to-do blacksmith of Oerebro. Dedicated to a religious life, they had gone for the completion of their studies to Wittenberg, instead of to Rome, and had devoted themselves with entire confidence to their teachers, Luther and Melanchthon. The elder brother had even been permitted to accompany Luther on his visitation journey through Misnia and Thuringia. Many a good word may have dropped from the mouth of the teacher during this journey, and found warm lodgment in the young heart of the pupil. It was not in vain that Olaf took Luther for his model. He had scarcely returned to his native country before he found an opportunity to oppose the traffic in indulgences, carried on by an Italian called Antonelli (brother to the papal legate Arcimboldi), in a manner similar to that pursued by Luther in the case of Tetzel. This occurrence took place at the town of Wisby, in Gothland. From there Olaf repaired to Strengnäs. The episcopal chair at that place was occupied by Bishop Matthias, one of those men to whose minds the new ideas found ready access. He made the young man his chancellor, and gave him a canonship in his cathedral. Olaf employed the leisure hours afforded him by these offices in imparting to the younger clergy, through the medium of lectures, some of the treasures which he had gathered in Wittenberg. Here, as elsewhere, biblical exegesis formed the central point of theological studies. In the same year (1520) the two brothers accompanied Bishop Matthias to Stockholm to the coronation of Christian II. This was the bishop's last journey—his journey to death. He fell a sacrifice to the treachery of the tyrannical king, and it was with difficulty that his two followers escaped a similar fate. They returned to the chapter of Strengnäs. Here, Archdeacon Laurence Anderson was temporarily acting as administrator of the bishopric. He also was favourable to the Reformation, and under his protection the two brothers were able to preach the new doctrine unhindered. They did it with success.

In the meantime, Gustavus (Ericson) Vasa had, shortly after the massacre at Stockholm, arisen as the deliverer of the land. He had already, during his stay at Lubeck (1519), learned to know and love the evangelical doctrines. He was elected king at the Diet of Strengnäs in 1523. At the same Diet, Olaf Petri delivered a powerful discourse. The king, who made Laurence Anderson his chancellor, appointed Olaf to the position of preacher at Stockholm and town syndic. His brother Laurence was made professor of theology at Upsala. It was resolved that a disputation between the respective adherents of the old and the new faith should be the means of bringing about a final decision in regard to the comparative merits of the two systems. This discussion took place at Upsala at the end of the year 1524. Peter Galle, the professor who defended the old doctrine, was defeated by his opponent Olaf. A positive decision was, however, not yet attained. The Latin mass was, nevertheless, abolished at the capital of Sweden, and in 1525 Olaf, with the permission of the king, took to himself a wife. Here, as elsewhere, the translation of the Holy Scriptures into the vernacular constituted an essential aid to the progress of the Reformation. The king's chancellor, Anderson, was commissioned to prepare such a translation, and the brothers Peterson assisted him in the task. In 1526 the New Testament appeared. It was not until the following year, at the Diet of Westerås (1527), that the Reformation was carried into effect.

In Denmark,[1] the way of the Reformation had been prepared by Paul Eliä, a Carmelite monk. This man was distinguished for his classical culture, and was president of a royal college in the University of Copenhagen. He is said to have opposed Arcimboldi's traffic in indulgences. He stood high in the favour of King Christian II. This sovereign, who was related to the princely house of Saxony, was an assiduous follower of everything that emanated from Wittenberg. In the year 1520 he called a pupil of Karlstadt's, Martin Rynhart by name, the translator into Danish of Luther's treatise on the *Babylonish Captivity*, to Copenhagen. Karlstadt himself was for a brief period at that city. Upon the king the Reformation had, unfortunately, made no morally ennobling impression. His tyrannical yoke was cast off, and the crown passed to his uncle, Frederick I. Notwithstanding his altered fortunes, the exiled monarch remained constant to his reformatory principles for a time, and even caused a Danish translation of the Bible (by Hans Michelsen) to be printed at Leipsic in the year 1524. As the legitimate sovereign of Sweden, his cause was espoused by Luther, who exercised some influence over him. Subsequently, however, Christian, who was in general governed by political motives rather than by anything higher, returned to Catholicism. As for the new king, Frederick, he, indeed, was at first bound by a muniment to co-operate to the extent of his ability in the extermination of the heresy; but in his heart he was faithful to his reformatory sentiments, and as reigning king speedily found means to make them efficacious. We have already seen how the Reformation had gained ground in the German dukedoms

[1] See PANTOPPIDAN, *Kirchengeschichte von Dänemark*, Copenhagen, 1741-1753.

connected with the crown of Denmark. From them a retro-action upon Denmark ensued. Hermann Tast, the vicar who had preached at Husum, became chaplain to the king. Liberty of religion was declared in 1524, and thus, after long struggles, a way was made for the new doctrine.

Owing to the displeasure cherished by Henry VIII. against Luther, England, though in many respects prepared for the Reformation, was for a time shut off from it.

In the Netherlands, one of the first adherents of Luther was that James Spreng (Propst, Praepositus) whom we have already mentioned in our sketch of the Reformation in Bremen.[1] In 1519 Erasmus wrote concerning him to Luther as follows:—"There is at Antwerp a prior of an Augustinian monastery who is a true Christian, and who loves you above all others whom he knows; he says that he was once a pupil of yours. Amongst all the clergy of that city, he is almost the only one who preaches Christianity; the rest preach the fables of men, or seek their own profit."[2]

The convent church at Antwerp, in which Prior Spreng preached, was always crowded to its utmost capacity. In 1522 the convent was destroyed by order of the regent, Margaret of Austria, and the church was converted into a parish church. Spreng, who in 1521 had repaired to Wittenberg in order that he might there, in a public discussion at which Karlstadt presided, obtain the rank of a licentiate, was, at the instigation of the professors of Louvaine, enticed from Antwerp to Brussels, and detained a prisoner at the latter place. In an hour of weakness he was even persuaded to make a public recantation. He, however, soon gained courage to testify anew, and preach the gospel as before. After a variety of fortunes, he arrived, in 1524, at Bremen. Like him, Henry of Zütphen had there found an asylum. But though these two had thus escaped a martyr's death, this was not to prevent the first drops of heretical blood from being shed in the

[1] Comp. Klose's article on Spreng, in Herzog's *Realenc.* vol. xiv. p. 689.
[2] *Erasmi Epistolæ*, Basel, 1538, vol. iv. p. 235.

Netherlands — we have reference to the martyrdom of the two stedfast confessors, Henry Voes and John Esch. The most incorrigible of the inmates of the destroyed convent at Antwerp had been sent to the castle of Vilvoorde. A few of these, through fear of the stake, yielded to the efforts made to constrain them to recant. Voes and Esch not complying with the demand of their persecutors, however, but rather persisting in their faith, were, together with another stedfast companion, Lambert of Thorn, taken to Brussels and confined in one of the prisons of that city. The spiritual judges (heretic masters), amongst whom were especially distinguished Hoogstraten, with whom we are already acquainted, and Nicholas van Egmont, made inquisition of them concerning their faith. They replied, "We believe and hold the Twelve Articles (of the Apostles' Creed), and all that is contained in the evangelical and biblical writings. We believe also in a Christian Church, but not in such a one as ye believe in." When questioned further as to whether they also believed in the statutes of the councils and in the fathers, they answered, "As far as they accord with the Divine Scriptures." To the third inquiry, as to whether they did not think they were committing a mortal sin in not accepting the decrees of the popes and fathers, they responded, "We believe that the commandments of God, and not the statutes of men, confer eternal salvation and damnation." When it was found that they could not be prevailed upon to recant, they were delivered to the secular judge, and Henry Voes and John Esch were condemned to be burnt. The sentence was executed 1st July 1523, on the public market-place, in front of the Council-house Square. The superior of the Franciscans addressed the assembled populace on this occasion. Henry Voes, the youngest of the three prisoners, was first stripped of his religious apparel; John Esch and Lambert of Thorn were then treated in a like manner. Hoogstraten then advanced toward the three, and exhorted them to recant. Upon their stedfast refusal, nothing remained but to execute the sentence.

Voes and Esch were led to the stake. They praised and blessed God in the face of death. Once more they were admonished to recant, in order that they might not become the prey of the devil. They replied, "We will die in the truth of the gospel." The pile was kindled. As Voes beheld the flames shoot up at his feet, he exclaimed that it seemed to him as though roses were scattered round him. The two chanted responsively the Apostles' Creed and the Te Deum. When wrapped in the flames, they were heard to cry aloud, "Lord Jesus, Son of David, have mercy on us!" Their adversaries, however, diligently spread the report that they had recanted in the hour of death.

Lambert of Thorn, the third of the prisoners, had, in the face of the fearful death imminent upon him also, asked for a respite of four days for consideration, and had been led back to prison. Not even he, however, could be induced to recant.[1] It was supposed by many, on the authority of contemporaneous statements, that Lambert suffered, a few days later,—on the 4th of July,—the same death that had been inflicted on his companions in tribulation; and even Luther at first credited this report.[2] But we find, under date of 19th February 1524, a letter of consolation addressed by Luther to this very man. In it the great Reformer expresses the sympathy excited in him by the death of the "two brethren," who, as he says, "had been a sweet savour to all Christendom and a glorious ornament to the gospel of Christ." To Lambert he says: "Do you ask how I come to burden you with my cold and powerless consolations? Who knows wherefore the Lord *willed not that you should perish with those two?* It may be that He has preserved you *because He designs yet to accomplish some great thing through you.*" It is clearly evident from this that Lambert must have escaped death at this time. Of his subsequent fate we know nothing.[3]

---

[1] See SPÖRLEN's article in Piper's *Evangelischer Kalender*, 1858, pp. 150 sqq. According to this account, Lambert also suffered martyrdom.

[2] See DE WETTE, vol. ii. No. 511, under date of July 1523.

[3] See critical remarks in DE WETTE, vol. ii. No. 576, p. 462; and SEIDEMANN, vol. vi. p. 627.

Luther's letter, of July 1523, to the Christians in Holland, Brabant, and Flanders, is also rich in consolation.[1] "The time is come," he writes, "when we hear the voice of the turtle-dove, and the flowers spring up in the land;" he congratulates the Netherlanders on being permitted to be the first to suffer shame and loss, anguish and tribulation, imprisonment and peril, for Christ's sake, and also upon being allowed to testify to the truth with their own blood. His most touching tribute to the two martyrs, however, is the hymn he composed in honour of their death.[2]

[1] DE WETTE, vol. ii. No. 512, p. 362.
[2] " Ein Lied von den zween Märtyrern Christi zu Brüssel von den Sophisten zu Löwen verbrannt, geschehen im Jahr 1523," Dr. Martinus Luther :—

Ein neues Lied wir heben an,
Das walt Gott unser Herre,
Zu singen, was Gott hat gethan
Zu seinem Lob und Ehre.
Zu Brüssel in dem Niederland
Wohl durch zween junge Knaben
Hat er sein Wunder macht bekannt,
So reichlich hat gezieret.

Der erst recht wohl Johannes heisst,
So reich an Gottes Hulden,
Sein Bruder Heinrich nach dem Geist,
Ein rechter Christ ohn Schulden,
Von dieser Welt geschieden sind,
Sie ha'n die Kron erworben,
Recht wie die frommen Gotteskind,
Für sein Wort sind gestorben;
Sein Märt'rer sind sie worden.

Der alte Feind sie fangen liess,
Er schreckt sie lang mit Dräuen,
Das Wort Gott's man sie leugnen liess,
Mit List auch wollt sie täuben;
Von Löwen der Sophisten viel,
Mit ihrer Kunst verloren,
Versammelt er zu diesem Spiel,
Der Geist sie macht zu Thoren;
Sie konnten nichts gewinnen.

Sie sungen süss, sie sungen sau'r;
Versuchten manche Listen,
Die Knaben standen wie 'ne Mau'r,
Verachten die Sophisten;
Den alten Feind das sehr verdross,
Dass er war überwunden
Von solchen Jungen, er, so gross,
Er ward voll Zorn, von Stunden
Gedacht, sie zu verbrennen.

Sie raubten ihn'n das Klosterkleid,
Die Weih, sie ihn'n auch nahmen;
Die Knaben waren dess bereit,
Sie sprachen fröhlich : Amen.
Sie dankten ihrem Vater Gott,

Dass sie los sollten werden
Des Teufels Larvenspiel und Spott,
Darin durch falsch Geberden
Die Welt er gar betreuget.

Da schickt's Gott durch sein Gnad' also,
Dass sie recht Priester worden,
Sich selbst ihm mussten opfern da
Und gehn in Christen Orden,
Der Welt ganz abgestorben sein,
Die Heuchelei ablegen,
Zum Himmel kommen frei und rein,
Die Möncherei ausfegen
Und Menschentand hie lassen.

Man schrieb ihn'n für ein Brieflein klein,
Das hiess man sie selbst losen,
Die Stück sie zeichn'ten alle drein,
Was ihr Glaub war gewesen.
Der höchste Irrthum dieser war :
Man muss allein Gott gläuben,
Der Mensch leugt und treugt immerdar,
Dem soll man nichts vertrauen;
Dess mussten sie verbrennen.

Zwei grosse Feu'r sie zündten an,
Die Knaben sie herbrachten,
Es nahm gross Wunder jedermann
Dass sie solch Pein verachten :
Mit Freuden sie sich gaben drein,
Mit Gottes Lob und Singen,
Der Muth ward den Sophisten klein
Für diesen neuen Dingen,
Dass sich Gott liess so merken.

Der Schimpf sie nun gereuet hat,
Sie wollten's gern schön machen,
Sie durft'n nicht rühmen sich der That,
Sie bergen fast die Sachen :
Die Schand im Herzen beisset sie
Und klagen's ihr'n Genossen ;
Doch kann der Geist nicht schweigen hie :
Des Habels Blut vergossen
Es muss den Kain melden.

Although the Swiss Reformation, and especially the person of Calvin, formed, at a subsequent period, the central point of reform for those countries in which the Latin tongues were spoken, it was nevertheless from Luther that they received their first reformatory impulse.

In France we first meet with the Erasmian-Humanistic tendency as displayed in a James Faber Stapulensis (Lefèvre d'Etaple). This man—born in 1450, and deriving his name from a little town in Picardy—had obtained his Humanistic culture at Paris and in the most famous cities of Italy, at Florence, Rome, and Venice. He was equally familiar with Plato and Aristotle. After having taught in Paris at Lemoine College, he removed to Meaux, the subsequent bishop of which, William Briçonnet, was his friend and patron. By him he was installed in a quiet retreat, favourable to study and meditation, in the Benedictine Abbey of St. Germain des Prés, near Paris. The library of the abbey furnished all needful aids to the study of the classics and Holy Scripture. Faber was already one of those who were endeavouring to emancipate the interpretation of Scripture from the fetters of ecclesiastical tradition, and to establish a correct grammatico-historical understanding of it. In this effort he, of course, came in conflict with the prevailing doctrines of the Church, but he did not court opposition by an intentional exposure of polemical points. Notwithstanding his prudence, however, he was drawn into a controversy with the priests, in the year 1517, on the occasion of his publishing a critical research on

Die Aschen will nicht lassen ab,
Sie staubt in allen Landen.
Hie hilft kein Bach, Loch, Grub' noch Grab,
Sie macht den Feind zu Schanden :
Die er im Leben durch den Mord
Zu schweigen hat gedrungen,
Die muss er todt an allem Ort
Mit aller Stimm' und Lungen
Gar fröhlich lassen singen.

Noch lassen sie ihr Lügen nicht,
Den grossen Mord zu schmücken,
Sie geben für ein falsch Gedicht ;
Ihr G'wissen thut sie drücken :

Die Heil'gen Gott's auch nach dem Tod
Von ihn'n gelästert werden,
Sie sagen : in der letzten Noth
Die Knaben noch auf Erden
Sie sollen ha'n umkehret.

Diess lass man lügen immerhin,
Sie haben's doch kein Frommen,
Wir sollen danken Gott darin ;
Sein Wort ist wieder kommen :
Der Sommer is hart vor der Thür,
Der Winter ist vergangen,
Die zarten Blumlein gehn herfür,
Der das hat angefangen,
Der wird es wohl vollenden.

the subject of Mary Magdalene, in which he declared his disagreement with the traditional opinion concerning that saint. The syndic of the theological faculty of Paris, Natalis Beda, caused his opinion to be formally condemned by a decree of the Sorbonne under date of 9th November 1521. He was secured from personal assault by the king, Francis I., and his sister Margaret. When Briçonnet became Bishop of Meaux, he constituted Faber his vicar-general (May 1523), hoping that he would exert a reviving influence over ecclesiastical affairs. In this hope a reformation (in the sense of Luther) was not contemplated,—it had reference merely to a reform, in the sense of so many of the better magnates of the Church in that age. Under the auspices of the bishop, Faber translated the New Testament into French. In thus doing he followed the Vulgate, it is true, but he had already declared the word of Scripture to be the only admissible rule of faith. Even this appeared heretical. His commentary on the Gospels (1523) was placed by the Sorbonne upon the catalogue of prohibited books.

Beside Faber, Gerard Roussel (Rufus) and William Farel appear among the promoters of a more liberal tendency. Just about this time Luther's ideas had become known in France, where the name of *Lutheran*, therefore, began to be heard.[1] Faber and Roussel fled from the persecutions of the priesthood to Strassburg, and there found an asylum in the house of Capito. How, in France, the little troop of believers then flocked together under the protection of the Queen of Navarre, sister to Francis I., and were able to escape the persecutions of the Inquisition only by flight, we shall see at some future time.

In Italy the writings of the Reformers were introduced under strange-sounding names.[2] Luther's writings were dis-

---

[1] The University of Paris had, as we are aware, condemned the doctrines of Luther. Amongst those who took part in this step was the above-mentioned Beda, concerning whom Glarean of Paris wrote that he was no Beda venerabilis, but that he should rather be called *bellua* (wild beast).

[2] Philip Melanchthon was called Ippofilo da terra negra.

seminated by Calvi, a bookseller of Pavia, as early as 1519. The Augustinians of Turin were, for the most part, familiar with, and friendly to, the ideas of their brother Martin. That which Margaret of Navarre was to the Protestants of France, the Duchess Renata of Ferrara became to the confessors of the gospel in Italy.

Even in Spain, Luther's works became known at about this time. Frobenius succeeded in smuggling books from Basel across the Pyrenees. In the year 1525, we see Juan de Avila, the apostle of Andalusia, before the court of the Inquisition. We must, however, reserve our account of the religious movements on both peninsulas for a subsequent period.[1]

In conclusion, we have yet to direct our attention to the press, which, in conjunction with the living word of preaching, even at that time constituted a power which contributed more than can be computed to the diffusion of the new ideas. I am thinking at this moment not so much of the spread of the Bible and theological works; but I would call your attention to a field which, from its nature, appertains to the history of civilisation rather than to that of the Church, and presents to us a view of the popular sentiment of the age—in its ruder manifestations at times—rather than of the religious and ecclesiastical sentiment with which we have hitherto been occupied.[2]

It will be remembered that the Reuchlinian controversy called forth, in its day, a peculiar class of literature, of which Hutten was pre-eminently the leader. Now, it actually rained polemical pamphlets on both sides. Immediately after the discussion of Leipsic (1519), Eck became the target of

[1] In the meantime we will refer our readers to *Gerdesii Specimina Italiæ Reformatæ*, Lugd. Bat. 1765, iv.; and to M'Crie's *History of the Reformation in Italy in the Sixteenth Century* (German translation by Friedreich, Leipsic, 1819); and to the *History of the Extension and Suppression of the Reformation in Spain* (German translation by Plieninger, Tubingen, 1835).

[2] Comp. Karl Hagen, *Deutschlands litterarische und religiöse Verhältnisse im Reformations-Zeitalter*, vol. ii. (also *Der Geist der Reformation und seine Gegensätze*, vol. i.), Erlangen, 1843.

public ridicule. *Der gehobelte Eck* ["The Planed Eck (Corner)"],—*Eccius dedolatus,*—conjectured to be the production of Wilibald Pirckheimer, made short work with the famed polemic and theologian. According to it, all his "angles" [*Ecken*] were to be planed away in a violent surgical operation, which the poor doctor must needs unwillingly submit to. The bull of excommunication of 1520 also called forth satirical woodcuts and poems. The favourite form for such effusions was the dialogue, in the composition of which it was the custom to introduce both real and imaginary personages, and sometimes even mythological and allegorical characters.[1] The book of this sort that attained the greatest celebrity was the *Karsthans*, which underwent several revisions.[2] Karsthans was primarily a historical personage, a peasant who preached in the neighbourhood of Strassburg and Basel,[3] just as another peasant, named Wöhrd, held forth in the vicinity of Ulm and Augsburg;[4] the name of the former, however, became a collective appellation for that popular wit which appeared in the frock of the peasant, and which struck the decisive blow whilst the learned were bespattering paper with ink.[5]

To these productions may be added *Die fünfzehn Bundes-*

---

[1] Thus: *Kuntz und Fritz* (HAGEN, vol. ii. pp. 127 sqq.); *Ein schön Dialogus und Gespräch zwischen einem Pfarrer und einem Schultheissen, betreffend allen übeln Stand der Geistlichen und böse Handlung der Weltlichen* (pp. 186 sqq.); *Dialogus zwischen einem Mönch und einem Edelmann* (pp. 196 sqq.); *Zwischen einem Papisten und evangelischen Laien* (p. 210); *Gesprächbüchlein zwischen einem Pfarrer und einem Weber* (p. 217); *Gespräch eines Mönchs mit St. Peter, vor der Himmelsthüre* (pp. 179 sqq.).

[2] We may mention as pendants to the original *Karsthans* (HAGEN, vol. ii. pp. 183 sqq.), *Der Karsthans und der Kegelhans*, and *Der neue Kegelhans* of HUTTEN.

[3] RÖHRICH, *l.c.*, vol. i. p. 136.

[4] In the case of the latter, however, it appeared that he was not a real peasant, but a priest in disguise. He was recognised in Nuremberg by a woman who came from the same place from which he was. See HAGEN, p. 175.

[5] In the *Karsthans* appear Murner (who, together with Eck, was one of the chief butts of the day, but was also himself a pasquiler of the first order), Karsthans, a student, Luther, and Mercury. Murner (in the character of a cat) cries, "*Murman, murman,*" and Karsthans seizes a flail, but discovers the cat to be a parson and doctor of the Holy Scriptures, etc.

genossen (" The Fifteen Allies "), by one whose acquaintance we have already made—Eberlin of Günzburg (fifteen treatises on the principal questions of the age). It may readily be imagined that all these writings were not invariably pervaded by the finest tone in the world. There is in them much that is in the highest degree obscene—much that, notwithstanding some happy thoughts, is tiresome and stiff. Other passages are somewhat unintelligible to the reader of the present day, and therefore less enjoyable than they otherwise might be. The general impression which we receive from this literature is, that it had its origin in stirring times, and that the conflict was not confined to the learned, nor of a purely religious and ecclesiastical nature; but that it was an all-sided struggle, extending to all domains—a struggle between the old and the new, authority and emancipation. Never, however, must that deeper religious key-note be forgotten, by which the conflict of minds, with all its dissonances, seems to be upborne, and which is always perceptible enough for those who will hear it.

CHAPTER X.

THE REFORMATION IN SWITZERLAND—ULRICH ZWINGLE—HISTORY OF HIS YOUTH—HIS LIFE AT GLARUS AND EINSIEDELN—CALL TO ZURICH—HIS MODE OF PREACHING—HIS RELATION TO LUTHER.

WE have hitherto passed by Switzerland and its Reformation, and begin now to speak of them only after completing our survey of the other countries of Europe. This subject, by reason of its nature, demands a separate treatment; and as we formerly placed Luther in the foreground, we shall now accord a like station to the Swiss Reformer, although the connection of the latter with the history of Switzerland's Reformation differs from the relation sustained by Luther towards the history of the German Reformation. The personal fortunes of the Switzer are not so closely interwoven with the march of events as were those of Luther; yet, notwithstanding this, the character of Zwingle is sufficiently prominent and significant for us to commence our history of the Swiss Reformation with a brief biography of him.

Ulrich (or, as he liked to call himself, Huldrich) Zwingle [1] was the third of the eight sons of the amman of Wildhaus, an

---

[1] Besides the writings of Myconius and older works (by Nüscheler, Hess, Schuler, Tichler), comp. CHRISTOFFEL, *Huldreich Zwingli Leben und ausgewählte Schriften*, Elberfeld, 1857 (*Leben und ausgewählte Schriften der Begründer der reformirten Kirche*, vol. i.); J. C. MÖRIKOFER, *Ulrich Zwingli nach den urkundlichen Quellen*, 2 vols., Leipsic, 1867–1869; also CH. SIGWART, *Ulrich Zwingli, der Charakter seiner Theologie mit besonderer Rücksicht auf Picus von Mirandola*, Stuttgart, 1865; H. SPÖRRI, *Zwinglistudien*, Leipsic, 1866 (*Zwingli's Werke*, edited by Schuler and Schulthess); S. VÖGELIN, in the *Zeitstimmen*, Zurich, 1868.

elevated parish in Toggenburg. He was born on the 1st of January 1484, and was therefore only a few months younger than Luther. His mother's name was Margaret Meilin. She was related to John Meilin, Abbot of Fischingen, who treated young Ulrich with special favour, and loved him as his own child. His father's brother, also, was a clergyman, occupying the position of dean at Wesen. This man is deserving of great credit for the part which he took in the education of the talented boy. The clearer his perception of the extraordinary abilities of his nephew became, the more strenuously did he insist upon educating him for the Church. Accordingly, before Zwingle was ten years old, he was sent to Basel, which was at that time celebrated far and wide for its schools. At this place Zwingle attended the school of George Bunzli. That faithful preceptor, however, speedily remarked that his instructions, calculated simply for elementary scholars, were insufficient for the needs of the rapidly developing boy, and himself advised him to seek a higher institution. Zwingle therefore repaired to Bern, where, under the direction of the famous canon Henry Wölflin (Lupulus), he familiarized himself with the ancient classics. He early developed a poetic and, in a still greater degree, a musical talent. By means of the latter he became a great favourite, and the Dominicans, who at that time possessed much influence in Bern, endeavoured to persuade Zwingle to enter their order. His father and uncle, however, having no liking for the doings of the mendicant monks, withheld the youth from taking a step which he might afterwards have repented as heartily as Luther did. Partly in order to put an end to the dangerous relations subsisting between Zwingle and the monks, whose toils were set for him, and partly in order to furnish him with better opportunities for completing his studies, his relatives sent him to Vienna, there to pursue the study of philosophy, *i.e.* the Scholastic philosophy of the Church. Zwingle, with a mind already awakened and a taste already formed by the models of antiquity, could with difficulty accustom himself to the mazes of the schools; yet, in spite of this disinclination, he made himself thoroughly familiar with those systems which, at a later period, he was called to combat with all his force. At Vienna he made the acquaintance of Vadian, subsequently a reformer of St. Gall, with whom he always maintained a friendly connection. After a stay of two years in Vienna, he returned for a short time to his father's house, but, impelled by a thirst for learning, he soon repaired for the second time to Basel, where he obtained the situation of schoolmaster at St. Martin's. Whilst discharging the duties of this post, he had time and opportunity to pursue his own studies. He perfected himself in the languages, continued his application to philosophy, and employed the greater part of his leisure hours in music, in which his proficiency was so great that he was able to play on almost any instrument.[1] In this love for music he agreed perfectly with Luther, who assigned to it a higher place than aught except theology. Nor did Zwingle neglect theology, for a thorough study of which Basel afforded the finest opportunity.

Thomas Wyttenbach, a native of Biel, gave instruction in this sacred science at Basel. He was one of the first pioneers of the pure gospel in Switzerland. He reduced theology to a thorough study of the Bible, and, before the name of Luther was known, declared against many abuses of the Church, on whose power of the keys he placed less dependence than on the ransom paid by Christ. The latter, said he, is the key which unlocks for the human heart the shrine of the forgiveness of sins.[2]

[1] Comp. the extract from BERNHARD WEISS, *Geschichte der Reformat. zu Zürich*, in Füsslin's *Beiträgen*, vol. iv. p. 35; and J. G. MÜLLER, *Reliquien*, vol. iv. p. 123: "He was learned in the Greek, Hebrew, and Latin tongues, and his German was excellent, well conceived, and well expressed. He was finely instructed in these four languages. Nor did I ever hear of any one who was so proficient in the art of music—that is to say, in singing and in playing upon all musical instruments, such as the lute, the harp, the violin, the flute, the fife, the *Schwäglen* (on which he performed like a true Switzer), the drum, the dulcimer, the cornet, and the hunting-horn; anything of the sort he was able to manage as soon as he took it in his hands."

[2] Comp. KUHN, *Die Reformatoren Berns*, p. 47; and HALLER in Herzog's *Realenc.* vol. xviii.

At the feet of this teacher Zwingle met with a young man who was from that time his most intimate friend, and who subsequently became to him what Melanchthon was to Luther—we refer to Leo Juda of Rapperswyl.[1] The two youths listened eagerly to the lectures of their preceptor, and together received the degree of Master of Arts in the year 1512. Shortly after this event, however, their paths diverged. Leo became pastor of St. Pilt in Alsace, and Zwingle settled in Glarus, after being consecrated to the priesthood at Constance.

At Glarus, to whose pastorate he was summoned by the confidence of the community even before he had received clerical consecration, Zwingle pursued the study of the Bible with indefatigable diligence, without, however, neglecting the writings of the ancients, who offered vigorous nourishment to his intellectual mind. We shall be enabled to form some conception of the industry of the learned men of that age by the fact that Zwingle almost verbally committed to memory several Latin and Greek authors (Valerius Maximus, for instance), as well as the New Testament. In order that he might gain a proper apprehension of the latter, he with his own hand transcribed the Pauline Epistles, introducing on the margin the best glosses of the Church fathers and Erasmus. And all this was done during the discharge of an office whose burdens were by no means avoided. Zwingle already appeared as a reformer of morals and politics, although he had not yet entered the field as a religious and ecclesiastical reformer. He zealously opposed the moral corruption of the age, and the vices and abuses which prevailed among the people, although by this course creating many enemies. Especially

---

[1] He was born in 1482, and was the natural son of an Alsatian priest, who caused him to study under Crato at Schlettstatt. In 1505 he repaired to Basel. He is described as "an amiable, kind, gentle, and merciful man." He also was a lover of music. "He could play on the dulcimer and a little on the lute. He had a glorious voice, and sang treble so clearly that none excelled him." Comp. J. G. MÜLLER, *l.c.*, p. 126, after the *Miscell. Tigur.* vol. iii.; WIRZ, p. 108; Herzog's *Realenc.* vol. vii. pp. 123 sqq.; C. PESTALOZZI, *Leo Judä*, Elberfeld, 1860.

did he attack the system by which free Switzers drew pensions from foreign princes, and the enlistment of troops for the support of foreign powers. He justly classed patriotism among the Christian virtues, and was to that extent a political preacher, —a character which all must bear who would exert an influence over their contemporaries, particularly if they are members of a free state and if they live in extraordinary times. Hence Joh. von Müller[1] rightly observes with regard to Zwingle: "He had a patriotic and republican soul, of which he gave evidence in civil no less than in religious labours. He was not satisfied with leading his church into the way of truth, without laying down for his country all those moral precepts and principles which he conceived to be conducive to liberty. His zeal for civil order and household virtue, and for the innocent policy of a perpetual peace, was as great as that which he displayed in religious controversies. His discourses forcibly impressed his hearers with the necessity for a reform.[2]

Such a man was, on the one hand, entirely fitted for a chaplaincy in the army, a position whose duties he was called to fulfil amongst the troops of Glarus in the Italian wars, in 1512 and 1515; but, on the other hand, the discharge of those duties convinced him more and more thoroughly of the prejudicial effects of foreign mercenary service, and gave him opportunity to behold the increasing corruption of his countrymen in various respects.

It was during the period of Zwingle's residence at Glarus (about the year 1514) that the young Humanist made the acquaintance (at Basel) of the head of the enlightened tendency, Erasmus, whom, in youthful enthusiasm, he hailed as the "greatest of philosophers and theologians," whilst Erasmus called him his "fraternally beloved friend." It may be remarked in passing, that in subsequent years there was never

---

[1] *Allg. Geschichte*, vol. iii. p. 13.
[2] It is to this time that we must assign those writings of his which pertain more especially to politics,—his *Labyrinth*, and the *Fabelgedicht vom Ochsen und etlichen Thieren, den Lauf der Dinge begreifend*. See MÖRIKOFER, vol. i. pp. 13 sqq.

so violent a rupture between Erasmus and Zwingle as that which took place between Erasmus and Luther. Among the friends of Zwingle may also be numbered the sprightly Henry Loriti (Glareanus) of Mollis, who was four years his junior. He also was an adherent of Erasmus, and continued in connection with the old Church amid the struggles of the Reformation.

Shortly after Zwingle's return from the excellent school of the Milanese campaigns, in the summer of 1516, before Luther had given the first impulse to the German Reformation, Zwingle was called by the administrator of the princely foundation of Einsiedeln, Baron Theobald (Diebold) von Geroldseck, to the post of local pastor at that celebrated resort of pilgrims.[1] This also was a school for the subject of our sketch. Here there opened before him a wide field whereon to combat superstition, which found abundant nourishment in the history and appointments of the place.

[1] Some of the opponents of Zwingle still maintain that he was forced to leave Glarus because his moral reputation was damaged. Historic truth demands the candid admission of the fact that the young man was not free from every spot of sin (*ab omni peccati nœvo*). This his intimate friend and first biographer, O. Myconius, confesses. Similarly we read in Bullinger that some prominent individuals "were hostile to him because his conduct with regard to several women had come under suspicion; for at that time" (adds Bullinger, by way of explanation and apology), "the Papacy not permitting the priests to marry, the priesthood fell under sore suspicion and also into fornication and adultery. Added to this, Zwingle's musical taste and innate kindliness *made him suspected of more than he was really guilty of*." Of the highest value in this connection is the testimony of Zwingle himself, who never desired to pass as a saint in matters where he was conscious of the sinful propensities of his natural man. He says later: "Dear brethren, if they tell you that I commit sins of pride, gluttony, impurity, believe that it may be so; for I am, alas! subject to those and other vices. But if any one should say that *I teach wrong doctrines for the sake of money, believe it not, though they should swear to it most solemnly*" (epistle on the "Predigt von der reinen Gottesgebärerin Maria," *Deutsche Schriften*, vol. i. 1, p. 86). Here we touch upon the inmost kernel of Zwingle's moral character—a kernel which was indestructible. As early as his entrance upon his pastorate at Glarus, he maintained that *hypocrisy* and *lying* were worse than stealing. To be true and upright toward God and man under all circumstances was his inviolable vow (see CHRISTOFFEL, *l.c.*, p. 8). Finally, the best evidence that the people of Glarus were not tired of him, is to be found in the fact that they kept his place open for him for two years in case he should desire to return to it. It is true that there was a party adverse to him even in Glarus — not, however, on account of his morals, but on account of his politics: we refer to the French party.

To this lonely region, encircled by mountains, St. Meinrad, of the house of Hohenzollern, retired in the ninth century, and of him many marvellous stories are related. After his violent death by the hands of robbers, the cell of the saint was for a time deserted, but towards the end of the tenth century a cloister was erected on the spot through the exertions of Eberhard, provost of the cathedral of Strassburg. The wondrous consecration of the cloister, as narrated by tradition, contributed much to its celebrity. The legend runs as follows. St. Konrad, Bishop of Constance, was to perform the rite of dedication. On the eve of the solemnity, however, an invisible choir was heard singing within the chapel, and the next day, when the ceremonies were about to commence, a voice was heard to say three times in succession, "Stop; it has been consecrated by God!" The truth of this circumstance was avouched by a papal bull (of Leo VIII.); all further consecration by man was forbidden, and a special festival was instituted, the *Feast of the Angelic Dedication*, to celebrate which numbers come from all the district round about, and even from remote parts. The cloister soon received rich donations, and many noblemen of Germany and Switzerland were admitted within its walls. The donations ceasing at last, however, there was nothing better for the convent to do than to turn to advantage the lauded miraculous power of an image of the Virgin, which was said to have been presented to the pious Meinrad by St. Hildegard, abbess of the nunnery at Zurich. This image and the power to confer plenary indulgence, added to the privileges of the cloister by several papal bulls, attracted to the place, subsequent to the fourteenth century especially, a numerous throng of pilgrims of all ranks, who left behind them greater or smaller presents or fees.

That, as has hitherto been generally assumed, Zwingle opposed the abuses connected with the place as early as that period of his life of which we speak, cannot be longer maintained in the light of recent investigations;[1] for the sermon

[1] See MÖRIKOFER, vol. i. pp. 30 sqq.

which he is said to have preached about the time of his settlement at Einsiedeln, at the Feast of the Angelic Consecration, and in which he openly declared that the forgiveness of sins should be sought for not from the Virgin Mary, but from Christ alone, and wherein he also depreciated the worth of indulgences, pilgrimages, and cloistral vows generally, was preached at a later period, in the year 1523, when he was merely visiting Einsiedeln. Notwithstanding this, however, Zwingle's stay at this place was greatly blessed to him, though in an entirely different manner from that in which the convent cell at Erfurt was profitable to Luther. The Abbot of Einsiedeln, Konrad von Rechberg, who is described as a man of clear intellect, had placed the management of the establishment in the hands of the administrator Diebold von Geroldseck, who, though possessing no great learning himself, was an ardent friend to science and its devotees. A proof of his honesty of sentiment is visible in the fact that he caused the destruction of the boastful inscription over the entrance of the abbey, promissory of plenary absolution for all sins. In the nunnery of Fahr, also under his supervision, he introduced the reading of the Bible instead of matin-song. The amount of Zwingle's obligation to this excellent man may be gathered from a letter that he afterwards wrote to him, in which he calls himself his debtor, and speaks of the fatherly way in which Geroldseck watched over and protected him.

That was a noble circle of men into which Zwingle now entered. Among them we may mention the chaplain, Francis Zuigg, who, it appears, was instrumental in promoting the friendship which existed between Diebold and Zwingle; the assistant chaplain, John Oechslin, and the Italian Bombasius, who was particularly helpful to Zwingle in the study of Greek. Leo Judä did not yet make one of this circle, but was added to it later.

Though we are unable to affirm that Zwingle had already taken aggressive measures against the Romish Church, none the less true is his own testimony that in the year 1516, before he had heard anything of Luther, he began to preach the gospel of Christ—and he preached it most impressively.[1] Zwingle desired to *establish* something before he proceeded to abolish and destroy. The greatest injustice, therefore, is done him by those who assign him a place among the negationists simply, and place his whole work as a Reformer in the abrogation of abuses. Who can blame him for setting his hopes at first upon the high dignitaries of the Church, such as a Cardinal Schinner, with whom he was acquainted, and expecting help from them? Did not Luther, in the beginning of his career, credit the Archbishop of Mentz and even the Pope of Rome himself with the best intentions! Now, indeed, a change was about to take place. Among the friends whom Zwingle possessed outside of Einsiedeln was Oswald Geisshäusler (Myconius) of Lucern, who was at that time teaching the ancient languages at Zurich. This extremely active and zealous man was desirous of settling Zwingle in his own vicinity; when, therefore, towards the close of the year 1518, the office of parish priest became vacant in the great cathedral of Zurich, Myconius succeeded in procuring his friend's election to the place by a large majority of votes (on the 10th of December 1518). Zwingle could not, indeed, promise himself that his welcome would be universal. Though the majority were for him, the adverse party was by no means utterly insignificant. His enemies had been busy in spreading injurious reports as to his character, and his cheerful, joyous temperament, together with his love for music, gave great offence to those who held the essence of piety to consist in a gloomy and downcast deportment. They

[1] "To stand amidst the throngs of pious pilgrims and preach the gospel to them, and especially to influence many a man of the higher classes through the power of the word of God, was the task of Zwingle in Einsiedeln—a labour which brought its own reward. On Whitsunday of 1518 he preached on the man with the palsy (Luke v.). Amongst his auditors on this occasion was Caspar Hedio, at that time vicar of St. Theodore's in Basel. Upon him the sermon made a great impression. In a beautiful, thorough, earnest, impressive, and wholly evangelical manner, it brought home to him the spirit and power of the old theology." See MÖRIKOFER, vol. i. p. 39.

dubbed him the "lute-player and evangelical piper;" but, as Bullinger tells us, not a whit did he care for this. His liberal-minded religious principles were also known and offensive to many; the obscurants apprehended the downfall of their kingdom in case the doctrines of Zwingle should gain the upper hand, and they therefore tried every means in their power to render his position burdensome and distasteful to him.

With the first day of the year 1519, on the thirty-fifth anniversary of his birth, Zwingle commenced his ministry in Zurich, supported by the greater part of the burgher population, at whose head was the liberal-minded burgomaster Röust. The city was not unfamiliar to Zwingle. He had frequently visited it, and had received no very favourable impression with regard to it in a moral respect. So shameful was the life which he had found there (according to his own later testimony from the public pulpit), that he had inwardly hoped and had prayed to God that he might be kept from ever becoming a pastor there.[1] God, however, had ordered differently, and Zwingle accepted the proffered position with a trustful spirit. Here, again, it was the preaching of God's word on which he expended his whole power. He immediately discarded the method of preaching which had universally prevailed since the time of Charlemagne,—and which confined the speaker to prescribed sections of the Bible (*pericopes*),—and began to explain the Scriptures in a connected series of lectures, commencing with the Gospel of Matthew and passing then to the Acts of the Apostles, and the Pauline and other Epistles. He thus completed an entire cycle of sermons on the New Testament during the first four years of his ministry at Zurich. Many regarded this mode of procedure as a novelty. Zwingle, however, showed that, on the contrary, such was the primitive usage of the Christian Church, and appealed, for confirmation of his

---

[1] See MÖRIKOFER, *l.c.*, p. 42, where there may also be found a description of the moral condition of Zurich in the beginning of the sixteenth century.

statement, to the homilies of Chrysostom and Augustine. We here encounter a point of difference between the Zwinglian and the Lutheran Reformation. Luther, while grounding his whole Reformation upon the Bible and placing that book in the midst of the ecclesiastical system as the eternal candlestick upon the altar of God, did not feel himself called upon to depart from the usage of the Church in the matter of the pericopes, which stood in closest connection with the church year. And there is certainly something attractive in the idea of every Sunday and every feast day being stamped with its own distinctive mark by a given section of Scripture. A true evangelical order of worship should so combine the two methods as to ensure the satisfaction both of the liturgical and the homiletical needs of the congregation,—a result which might be effected by an all-sided use of the Bible, without binding oneself to the pericopes and yet freely profiting by them,—in such a manner that the riches of the divine word should in no wise be bound up, but yet should be distributed as significantly as possible throughout the seasons of the ecclesiastical year. The homiletical method introduced by Zwingle was observed by other Swiss and Upper German theologians. Thus, for instance, Œcolampadius at Basel, and Capito at Strassburg, adopted it; yet the Reformed Church has not held herself as entirely aloof from the pericopes as is generally supposed. The week-day sermons, customary at this time, were especially calculated to be turned to account as genuine Bible lessons. The institution of these did far more in the way of forwarding the evangelical spirit than is generally acknowledged; and in this direction also Zwingle manifested his activity. Whilst he explained the New Testament in his Sunday sermons, he expounded the Psalms in his week-day discourses, which, on the market days, were attended by numbers of the country people, who exhibited much eagerness to learn the way of salvation. He prepared these discourses with great care, and conscientiously consulted the original text. With new zeal he applied himself to the

VOL. I. Q

study of Hebrew, in which he was assisted by John Böschenstein, a pupil of Reuchlin's, who had repaired to Zurich from Wittenberg. It is this harmonious inter-working of a taste for the scientific and the practical that is so pleasing to behold in the life and labours of the Reformers, and especially of Zwingle.

Zwingle's sermons were particularly distinguished for a sobriety of intellect and a manly solidity, which, with all his flights of pious feeling, ever retained a firm footing on the earthly soil of existent time and circumstances, never losing themselves in misty and uncertain fancies.[1] If Zwingle were to reappear amongst us at the present day, certain persons might, perchance, consider his sermons deficient in evangelism, and too full of morals or politics, and charge them with possessing less mystical depth than those of Luther. But it should never be forgotten that the *Christian* life is not bound to one form; and having already compared Luther with the Apostle Paul, and Melanchthon with John, the ministry of Zwingle may remind us of that of honest James, or at times of earnest, fiery Peter, although he was destitute neither of Pauline clearness nor of the Johannean fervour of love. If we are to judge a tree by its fruits, we must necessarily conclude that the preaching of Zwingle was excellent in its way; for men of all ranks, the cultured and the uncultured, derived edification therefrom. Many thinking men, who had been driven from the churches by the spiritless babblings of the monks, returned to them again and strengthened their faith in

---

[1] "He disliked," says BULLINGER, "the irrelevant and affected babble of pulpit intricacies and the ostentation of useless words." And BERNARD WEISS testifies concerning him as follows:—"He said nothing for which he had not the warrant of the divine word. All his consolation he joyfully derived from God; and hence he admonished the whole city of Zurich to trust in God alone." It is evident from the reports of eye-witnesses that Zwingle's personal appearance was imposing: "He possessed a fine figure, a florid complexion, and was of more than medium height. His voice was not very powerful, but it went straight to the heart" (MÖRIKOFER, p. 55, after Bullinger and Kessler). It is pleasant to read that, amongst others, the deaf councillor, Hans Füssli, who had avoided going to church because he hated all priests, became one of Zwingle's most attentive hearers, and procured a seat close beside his pulpit.

the word of God, made clear to them by a judicious discourse. Thus, in Switzerland also, it was the *Bible*, and instruction drawn therefrom, that served for a foundation to the work of reformation; only with this distinction, that in *Germany* the Reformation was preceded by a decisive conflict in which the personality of Luther was mightily prominent, whilst in *Switzerland* there were more gradual and many-sided preparations for the work, so that the conflict which broke out there also was not so much a struggle of an individual with an opposing power towering high against him, as a struggle of previously-formed parties—a struggle in which individuals, such as Zwingle and Œcolampadius, are indeed prominent, yet without attracting attention so exclusively to themselves as was the case with Luther. Such will be seen to have been the facts throughout the subsequent course of the history of the Reformation. In Switzerland the struggle assumed a republican form; in Germany its form was more or less monarchical. Luther rules the German Reformation with his spirit to a far greater extent, and affects it far more decisively, than was the case with Zwingle in relation to the Swiss Reformation. No second person could have taken an equal rank with Luther; and even those who worked at his side, such as Melanchthon, Karlstadt, Bugenhagen, Justus Jonas, and Amsdorf, involuntarily and unsolicited entered into a subordinate relation to him—a relation resembling that which ministers sustain toward their sovereigns. Zwingle, on the other hand, was *succeeded* by a Calvin, who contests the supremacy with him in the opinion of many, and *accompanied* by a number of men, such as Œcolampadius, Berthold Haller, Osw. Myconius, Seb. Hofmeister, and Vadian, who were not his inferiors by so many degrees as were the rest of the German Reformers (with the exception, perhaps, of Melanchthon) the inferiors of Luther.

As the Swiss Reformation cannot be traced back to any *one person* with that definiteness which is possible in treating of the German Reformation and Luther, neither can it be referred to *one fact* so decisive as the indulgence traffic of Tetzel in Wittenberg. The indulgences proclaimed by Samson form, as we shall see hereafter, but a fleeting and subordinate item in the history of the Swiss Reformation, so many abuses of different kinds claim the attention at the same moment. And moreover, in Switzerland, the tendency of reform was from several diverse sides to one point; whilst in Germany it was from one point that subsequent changes were gradually developed in a certain systematic succession.

Independent of Luther, Zwingle had begun his work, and independent of Luther the work was to be maintained. True, Luther's writings speedily became known in Switzerland, for many of them were printed at Basel. Zwingle himself saw the first of them soon after his settlement at Zurich, in the year 1519. He, however, purposely abstained from perusing them with attention, and contented himself with recommending them from the pulpit after a cursory examination of them. He preferred to form his views independently through the study of the Bible and the Church fathers. Notwithstanding this, he did not in the sequel escape the charge of being an adherent of Luther. On the occasion of this charge, he thus expresses himself in regard to his relation to the German Reformer and his writings: " In the year 1516, before a man in our neighbourhood knew of Luther's name, I began to preach the gospel of Christ. Who called me a Lutheran then? . . . I was ignorant of Luther's name for two years after I had made the Bible my sole treasury. But it is, as I have said before, only the cunning of the Papists that causes them to load myself and others with such names. If they say, ' You must be a Lutheran, for you preach as Luther writes,' my answer is, ' I preach also as Paul writes.' Why not rather call me a Paulist? Nay, I preach the word of Christ; why not call me a Christian? . . . In my opinion, Luther is an excellent soldier of God, and one who has searched the Scriptures as earnestly as any man who has lived on this earth for the last thousand years. There has never been his equal as long as the Papacy has endured, in the manly and unshaken spirit in which he attacked the Pope of Rome. But whose deed was that? God's or Luther's? If you ask Luther himself, he will certainly tell you, 'God's.' Why, then, do you ascribe the doctrine of other men to Luther, when he himself ascribes his doctrine to God, and himself brings forth nothing new but what is contained in the eternal, unchangeable word of God? Pious Christians, do not suffer the glorious name of Christ to be changed into the name of Luther; for Luther did not die for us, but teaches us to know Him from whom alone we have all salvation. If Luther preaches Christ, he does it exactly as I do; though, thanks be to God, there have been led to God through him an innumerable multitude more than through me and others to whom God gives their measure, whether it be greater or less. I will bear no name other than that of my captain, Jesus Christ, whose soldier I am. . . . No man can esteem Luther more highly than I. Nevertheless I testify before God and all mankind that I never in all my days wrote a syllable to him, nor he to me, nor have I caused any other to write for me. I have avoided doing so not because I was afraid, but because I desired to show to all men the uniformity of the Spirit of God, as manifested in the fact that we who are so far apart are in unison one with the other, yet without collusion and without my deriving what I preach from him, *for every man does according as he has received from God.*"[1]

[1] *Uslegen und Gründ der Schlussreden oder Artikel*, in Zwingle's works (*Deutsche Schriften*, vol. i. 1, pp. 253 sqq).

CHAPTER XI.

GENERAL GLANCE AT THE CONDITION OF SWITZERLAND—CARDINAL SCHINNER—BERNARDIN SAMSON—FIRST BEGINNINGS OF THE REFORMATION IN OTHER PARTS OF SWITZERLAND—BERN—JOHN HALLER—RELIGIOUS CONDITION OF THE CITY OF BERN—THE JETZER AFFAIR—FRANCIS KOLB, BERTHOLD HALLER, AND SEBASTIAN MEYER—NICHOLAS MANUEL—BASEL—ITS POLITICAL CONDITION—BISHOP CHRISTOPHER VON UTENHEIM—FIRST REFORMERS: WOLFGANG CAPITO, WILLIAM RÖUBLIN, WOLFGANG WYSSENBURGER.

HAVING placed the figure of Zwingle in the foreground, let us now take a further survey of Switzerland in regard to its political and ecclesiastical constitution.

It will be remembered, from the general political survey of the second chapter, that, as early as the period of the Burgundian wars, Switzerland had lost its former independence, instead of which an increased political importance in the system of European states had gradually accrued to it. From that time on, the Confederates might be found in the service of foreign potentates, under the orders sometimes of the pope, sometimes of individual Italian grandees,—especially the Duke of Milan,—and sometimes, again, of France. With the latter they entered into an alliance a few years subsequent to the battle of Marignano (1516), after which Francis I. had concluded a perpetual peace with the Switzers. It was no rare thing for brother to fight against brother for the sake of filthy lucre; and before there was any ecclesiastical separation, the unity of sentiment was broken by political factions, and the passionate feelings which the different cantons afterwards cherished against each other on the ground of religious difference were sadly enough introduced by the diversity of political opinion. But few truly patriotic men were there who had the courage to hold themselves *above* the parties, and to defend the independence of Switzerland on every side. Such as there were, were also friendly to the ecclesiastical Reformation; at their head was Zwingle himself. Let us listen for a while to his warning voice.[1]

"It was through none other than divine power that our forefathers vanquished their enemies and obtained their freedom; this they acknowledged with thanksgiving to God, like the children of Israel, who, after their passage through the Red Sea, sang the praise of God. Therefore they never killed Christian people for the sake of reward, but fought for freedom alone, to the end that they, with their bodies and lives, their wives and children, might no longer be subject to the pleasure of the arrogant nobility. Therefore did God always give them victory, and increased their glory and their substance. Thus it was at the battles of Morgarten, Sempach, Näfels. Now, however, that we have begun to please ourselves, we have drawn down on us the wrath of God. And now the devil, the enemy of all the righteous, has raised up unto us in our day foreign potentates saying to us: 'You, strong heroes that you are, are fools to remain in your rude mountains; serve *us*, and you shall receive great possessions therefor.' What have we received? We have gotten ourselves, in the opinion of men, greater damage in the service of these potentates, at Naples, Novara, and Milan, than we ever sustained before, so long as the Confederation has existed. In our own wars we were, moreover, always victorious; in foreign wars we have

---

[1] "*Eine göttliche Vermahnung an die ehrsamen, weisen, ehrenvesten, ältesten Eidgenossen zu Schwyz, dass sie sich vor fremden Herrn hüten und entladen,*" printed in the edition of *Zwingli's Werke* issued by Schuler and Schulthess, *Deutsche Schriften*, part iii. pp. 287 sqq. We reprint it, approximating it to the modern style of discourse and writing. Comp. also HOLTINGER (in continuation of JOHN VON MÜLLER, vol. vi. p. 30).

always been defeated. Therefore let every one who takes up such inconsiderate feuds think first of his own welfare. What wouldst thou say of the stranger who should violently break into the land, spoil thy meadows, fields, and vineyards, drive off thy cattle, slay thy sons who protected thee, ravish thy daughters, spurn from his feet thy suppliant wife, miserably stab thee in thine old age before her very face, and at last burn down thy house? Thou wouldst think if the heavens did not part asunder and vomit forth fire, if the earth did not open her mouth and swallow such a wretch, that there was no God. If, however, *thou* do the like to others, thou thinkest it is the law of war. But that expression, 'the law of war,' what is it but violence? Use it as you will, it is and ever will be violence. Therefore woe unto them that call good evil and evil good (Isa. v. 20). With the evil money, evil customs are brought home; for foreign service is a school for all vices. This base practice of mercenary warfare is often excused with the words, 'We have need of wealthy masters; we are a poor people and have a rugged land.' How is it that, whilst for hundreds of years it was fertile enough to nourish our forefathers, it no longer suffices for us? It is because no one now is willing to work for his living as our forefathers did, because we are desirous of living in more splendour and ease than they were acquainted with.[1] Envy and selfishness have come in upon us; and this the foreign lords have remarked. They have scattered broadcast yet further lusts and desires,[2] and discord is the result. If their counsel were to

---

[1] *Ist war, so man sich nit vergnügen will zimmlicher narung und bekleidung, muss es etwann her kummen. Wenn aber dheiner (keiner) sich wyder strockte, denn er Decke hat, dörft es der Worten nit.* ["It is true that if a man will not be satisfied with the food and clothing that he can afford, the luxuries that he craves must be procured by some other means. But if no one stretched himself beyond his covering, there would be no provocative to extravagance or occasion for rebuke."] How applicable are these words to our own time and to the reasons offered in apology for revolutions!

[2] The speaker particularly laments departed simplicity, modesty, and chastity: "For our people have never come home from foreign wars without bringing with them some novelty in the way of clothing for themselves or their wives, or food or extravagant drink, or new oaths; and whatever sinful practice they

be completely fulfilled, the Confederation would even now be destroyed. Ay, they are on the watch; and if they are able to harm you, they will not fail to do so. Hence love constrains me to warn you whilst there is yet time, or they who cannot conquer you with iron and halberds will vanquish you with soft gold."

The religious relations of the confederations were as follows. All Switzerland was divided into six bishoprics—viz., Lausanne, Sitten, Como, Basel, Chur, and Constance, of which the last was the largest and most important. It embraced the whole of Eastern Switzerland to the Aar, with the exception of the Grisons, which were included in the bishopric of Chur. These bishoprics were formerly themselves in metropolitan connection with German, French, and Italian archbishoprics. Thus Chur and Constance were connected with the arch-

witness, they acquire with alacrity, so that it is to be feared that if they do not abandon these foreign lords, they will in time acquire still more injurious vices. All female chastity is likewise becoming weakened." The above exactly accords with the picture which GLUTZ-BLOZHEIM (continuation of J. VON MÜLLER, p. 504) gives of the morals of the time as described by contemporaneous authors: "The rage for splendour and the imitation of foreign customs was most visible in dwelling-houses and articles of food and clothing. The houses became more spacious, the window panes larger, and the window sashes more numerous. Finer wood was chosen for wainscotings, tables, chairs, beds, and wardrobes, which were ornamented with carvings. There must be a greater number and variety of dishes; it was not sufficient that these pleased the palate, they must also be distinguished for their rarity. Different sorts of spices were used in abundance, and everywhere sugar was employed. It was accounted a disgrace to quench one's thirst with wine of home manufacture; wines of various kinds must be drunk, foreign and compounded. Of most pernicious effect was the incessant change in dress. Grey cloth and drilling, the materials formerly used almost exclusively, were now seldom to be seen; silk became common in kitchen and stable, and was worn even by farmers. Every one strove to obtain fine cloths, velvet, costly furs, embroideries of silver and gold, and jewels, desiring thus to show off his wealth. Men ornamented their sides with daggers and swords of splendid workmanship, the points of their shoes with tips of gold and silver, and, frequently, their toes with rings; their coats and mantles were made with numerous folds, and their pantaloons were decked with a diversity of colours and numberless ribbons. The long train dresses of the women suddenly became so short that it was found necessary to make laws against the violation of propriety in this manner; folds next took the place of the trains; the finest Lombardy work was used in the decoration of the person. At the time of the everlasting peace with France, it was customary to dress according to the Spanish fashion."

bishopric of Mentz, Basel and Lausanne with Besançon, Como and Sitten with Milan. But, as we have previously seen, the papal policy directed its efforts toward the dissolution of the connection between the bishoprics and archbishoprics, and endeavoured to attach the former immediately to Rome, for the accomplishment of which purpose the nunciatures were especially serviceable. This institution of nunciatures always exercised a mighty influence over the political and ecclesiastical condition of Switzerland; and the papal legates, of whom there were often several in the country at the same time, played an important part in the history of the Reformation. It was they who, in direct opposition to the peaceful pastoral office of servants of Christ, made application for troops in behalf of the Roman See, competing with the ambassadors of powerful France; it was they to whose hands the direction of the indulgence traffic was committed; and it was they who were charged with the strangling of heresies at their birth. While the legates Ennius, Pucci, and William de Falconibus were for the most part entrusted with transitory commissions only, we, on the contrary, find in the cardinal-bishop of Sitten, Matthew Schinner, one who was constantly active in carrying out the designs of the pope, being an ardent representative of the papal interests, and also the person through whom the mind of the people could be most securely influenced.

Schinner was indeed a man of unusual talents. Born in Valais, of poor parentage, he had early consecrated himself to the Church, and by his learning attracted the notice of Jost von Silenen, at that time Bishop of Sitten, whose successor he afterwards became. The warlike Pope Julius II., needing his aid in recruiting troops, made him his legate in Switzerland, and presented him with the cardinal's scarlet hat, which gave occasion to witty remarks on the *bloody* business of spiritual potentates;[1] for he it was who enticed the Swiss

---

[1] "They rightly wear," says Zwingle, "red hats and mantles; for if you shake them, ducats and crowns fall out. But if you wring them out, the blood

into the fields of Novara and Marignano, and who conducted the recruitings generally in the most shameless manner.

With all this, Schinner, so far as scientific culture was concerned, belonged to that liberal party in the Church which found its representative in Erasmus. At the outset, therefore, he might well endure the scientific and clear-headed Zwingle; and he even loaded him with evidences of his favour. Zwingle himself had hoped for his assistance in the work of reformation, but was deceived in him as well as in the like-minded Bishop of Constance, Hugo von Landenberg. Zwingle, while still a resident of Einsiedeln, had made application to both these dignitaries, and had requested them to use their influence to check the growing abuses. From both, however, he had received nothing but promises; nor did they manifest any more zeal in the fulfilment of those promises than the German bishops evidenced in the cause of Luther.

Such was the condition of affairs when, in the month of August 1518, the Franciscan monk, Bernardin Samson, crossed Mount St. Gothard and entered Switzerland as apostolic general commissioner and indulgence seller. With an effrontery equal to that of Tetzel, he praised the pontifical indulgences and disposed of them for money. Zwingle was still at Einsiedeln whilst Samson was attending to his business in the small cantons; and even at that time he warned the people against the indulgence seller in his sermons, and spoiled his trade in Schwytz.[1] Samson did better at Zug. One of the revolting features of his conduct at this place was the harshness with which he drove the poor away as they thronged to the supposed fount of consolation. "Good people," his assistants would say, "do not crowd so; let those come first who have money: those who have nothing will be attended

of your son, your father, your brother, or your friend will run out." From BULLINGER's chronicle in Schulthess and Schuler (*Zwingli's Deutsche Schriften*, Part iii. p. 350).

[1] Thus BULLINGER, vol. i. p. 15. MÖRIKOFER, *Zwingli*, vol. i. p. 64, protests against the statement, because there is no further proof of it. Is not the testimony of Bullinger sufficient?

to afterwards." From Zug he proceeded to Bern, by the way of Lucern, canton Unterwalden, and the Oberland. At Bern the authorities at first refused him entrance into the city; but from Burgdorf, where he had stopped, he was able, by the aid of his friends, to prevail upon the council of the city to give him permission to display his wares in solemn state in the cathedral of St. Vincent. He, like Tetzel, offered plenary indulgences not for past sins alone, but also for those as yet uncommitted. The tickets of indulgence for the rich were written on parchment and sold for a crown and upwards; those for the poor were made of paper, and cost two batzes apiece.[1] The knight, " little James von Stein," drove a remarkable bargain with Samson. For a dapple-grey horse he bought plenary indulgences for himself and his little troop of five hundred mercenaries, for the inhabitants of his whole manor of Belp, and for all his ancestors.[2] Samson, on the last day of his presence at Bern, once more summoned the community to the cathedral by the sound of a bell, and from the steps of the high altar announced through his interpreter, Henry Wölflin, that the souls of all who would kneel for a brief prayer should be as pure as they were immediately after baptism; and when all the people sank upon their knees in prayer, he finally pronounced the souls of all the deceased inhabitants of Bern, whenever and however they might have departed this life, free from the torments of hell and purgatory.

Whilst the common people and even a few men of culture (amongst them Wölflin, of whom we have just spoken) acquiesced in this child's play, better and clearer thinkers were justly indignant at the outrage. Thus Wyler, who wrathfully exclaimed: "If the popes really have such power, they are the greatest scoundrels to suffer souls to languish so long in purgatory."

From Bern, Samson passed through the Aargau and Baden

---

[1] According to ANSHELM, vol. v. p. 334.
[2] *Um einen kuttgrowen (quittengrauen) Hengst*, ANSHELM, vol. v. p. 335.

to Zurich. When he had the audacity to affirm in the churchyard at Baden that he saw the souls of those who were released from purgatory flying up to heaven, a wag attempted a parody on him by shaking the feathers out of a pillow from the top of the church tower, and uttering the same words that were used by Samson, "Behold how they fly!" At this there was a general burst of laughter; Samson flew into a rage, and nothing but the assurance that the author of the joke was sometimes out of his mind saved him from maltreatment. Covered with opprobrium, Samson took his departure from Baden. At Bremgarten he fared no better. At Lenzburg, entrance had been refused him by the pastor of Staufberg; in fact, the Bishop of Constance himself had, through his vicar-general, John von Faber, forbidden the clergy of his diocese to have any dealings with Samson, because the latter had neglected to seek the episcopal permission to carry on his trade. Bullinger, the grey-headed dean of Bremgarten and father of the chronicler, had therefore stedfastly opposed him. He was to be intimidated neither by the threats and vulgar abuse of the monk, nor by the excommunication which he hurled against him;[1] but, proceeding to Zurich before Samson reached that place, he laid his complaints before the Diet there assembled. This body resolved to refuse the indulgence seller an entrance into the city. Samson, however, caused himself to be admitted by pretending that he had something to communicate to the Diet in the name of his master the

---

[1] Amongst other things, Samson said to him, burning with rage: "Since thou, beast that thou art, so insolently opposest thyself to the Holy See of Rome and revoltest against thy superiors, I pronounce upon thee the highest sentence of excommunication. Nor shalt thou be discharged of it until thou hast paid down three hundred ducats in ready money, as a penance for thy unheard-of insolence." And when the dean turned his back upon him, with the declaration that he would not be afraid to stand his examination at the proper place, Samson furiously continued: "I tell thee, audacious beast, that I am about to go to Zurich, and there I will accuse thee before the assembled Confederates; for never in all Switzerland or elsewhere have I met with grosser insult and contempt than from thee." The Diet, however, obliged Samson to release the dean from the sentence of excommunication without any compensation whatever (see C. PESTALOZZI, *Heinrich Bullinger*, p. 7).

pope. Still, the sale of his wares was denied him, and he was obliged to leave the city without having accomplished anything, and to make the best of his way across the Alps again " with his heavy money waggon drawn by three horses."

It will readily be imagined that Zwingle's sermons had contributed much to the creation of such a decided feeling, and even the vicar-general of Constance, Faber, his subsequent opponent, expressed to the Reformer his delight at the issue of affairs. The pope found himself constrained to take measures of conciliation toward the Confederates; and although he confirmed the statement that Samson had acted under his commission, he promised to investigate as to whether he had not exceeded his instructions, and to punish him if such had been the case.[1]

As has already been observed, the immediate consequences of Samson's sale of indulgences were not the same as those which attended the traffic of Tetzel in Germany. In the former we behold only a co-operative, and not a primary cause of the Reformation, whose beginnings in the different cities and villages vary considerably in character. Let us take a somewhat closer and more special view of these beginnings.

In Zurich a more liberal tendency had developed, even in earlier ages, side by side with the dark monkish spirit of ignorance and superstition. Although the exact extent of the influence which Arnold of Brescia's stay in Zurich had wielded upon the reformatory sentiments of the inhabitants of that city is uncertain, it is a fact that Felix Hemmerlin (Malleolus) waged war against the ignorance of the monks about the middle of the fifteenth century, and thereby gained for himself lifelong imprisonment in a cloister.[2] After him the voice of reproof was silent for a considerable time, until, with the beginning of the sixteenth century, the longing for a purer

---

[1] On the clever policy of Rome in regard to the indulgence traffic in Switzerland, comp. especially the section in MÖRIKOFER, vol. i. pp. 63 sqq.
[2] See REBER (Balth.), *Felix Hemmerlin von Zürich*, Zurich, 1846.

light became more and more intense. The reception which Zwingle met with at this place, and the method which he pursued with his sermons, have already been mentioned. In the midst of his labours, however, Providence saw fit to impose a sore trial upon him and his friends by visiting him with the plague in the year 1519. This dreaded scourge swept away 2500 men in Zurich in the course of a few months. Zwingle, who had gone to Pfäfers for the restoration of his health, impaired by his exertions, had scarcely heard of the actual outbreak of the long-feared pestilence at Zurich when all peace of mind deserted him, and the faithful shepherd returned to his flock, among whom he had not long remained when he himself was felled by the disease. During the reign of the pestilence and after its departure, he lifted up his soul to God in prayer—a fact to which the hymns that have come down to us from this period beautifully testify.[1] The report of Zwingle's death had spread through Germany and Switzerland when he recovered, though slowly and not without painful effects, which made themselves felt as he resumed his ministerial labours; for at the end of November he complained to his friend Myconius that his memory had suffered so severely from the pestilence as to cause him frequently to lose the connection of his sermons, and added that he still experienced a lassitude in all his limbs. Hardly was his recovery complete when new conflicts began for him; for the more influence he gained on one side, the more vigorously did his adversaries oppose him on the other. The canons of the cathedral, who would gladly have kept to the old practices, viewed with dissatisfaction the week-day sermons which Zwingle delivered, and the concourse of people whom he attracted. They drew up a paper, in which they brought a variety of charges against Zwingle, accusing him, amongst other things, of suppressing the rites instituted for the glory of God and the saints, in that he affixed too little value to the chanting of the hours, although

---

[1] See *Zwingli's Werke*, vol. iii. p. 369; MÖRIKOFER, vol. i. pp. 72–75; and the supplement to this chapter.

it was for that very purpose that the prebends had been established; of paying too little attention to the profit of the establishment, in that he was not sufficiently zealous in the collection of tithes; and of setting too low an estimation upon the administration of the holy sacraments, in that he had declared that five priests were sufficient for it. In general he sided, it was affirmed, more with the laity, of whose favour he was desirous, than with the priesthood, which he made contemptible in the eyes of the secular. He likewise brought contempt upon the inhabitants of the cloisters by representing them as ignorant people; and furthermore, it was asserted, he held the saints, the feast days, the mass, and the pope in low estimation. Even his personal character was attacked. He was charged with having violated the secrecy of the confessional, and with having proclaimed in the pulpit that which had been confided to him in the former place, etc. But neither these nor other artifices of his enemies prevented the issuing of a mandate by the Council of Zurich in the year 1520, to the effect that *all pastors should uniformly preach on the New Testament, and prove their doctrine from the Bible alone, discarding all innovations and human inventions.*

Luther had not in as short a time brought matters to as advanced a stage as Zwingle. One of the important points of distinction between the Swiss and the German Reformation, however, consists in the fact that the Swiss Reformers had, from the outset, more support from their respective governments, and acted more in unison with them, than was the case with the Reformers of Germany.

But everything was not gained when this mandate was procured. The spiritual authorities would not recognise the validity of this provision of the civil government, and from this time we find the Bishop of Constance, as well as his vicar Faber, both of whom had formerly shown favour to Zwingle, appearing, in connection with other malcontents, as antagonists of the Reformation. The course and consequences of this conflict will be related hereafter.

In Bern also and its vicinity the first traces of the Reformation may, despite many opposing elements, be found at this time.[1]

John Haller, a native of Wyl in Turgovia, at first curate in Schwytz, and afterwards prior of the convent of Interlaken, was a zealous opponent of the corrupt morality of the monks; and after his withdrawal from the cloister he continued his sermons against the errors of the papal doctrine at Zweisimmen, Thun, and Scherzlingen. Sebastian de Montfaucon Bishop of Lausanne, thought that he could best close the mouth of this troublesome censor by appointing him to the lucrative priorship of Amsoldingen, in the year 1520. Haller, however, was not diverted from his course by this gift, but, to the vexation of the bishop and the Bernese chapter, continued teaching in the same spirit as before, and even took a step that brought great odium upon him. After his sisters, who had kept house for him, had, one after the other, married, he himself finally abandoned celibacy and took for his wife the daughter of a burgher of Zurich. He was one of the first of the clergy who, after a long period of enforced abstinence from marriage, took upon himself its vows. The wedding took place in the house of the burgomaster Röust. When Haller's first son was born, Simon Lüthard, an aged priest, who was one of the sponsors of the child, exclaimed in the words of Simeon, in a parody that was certainly somewhat extravagant, "Lord, now lettest Thou Thy servant depart in peace!" (There is but a step from the sublime to the ridiculous!) George Brunner of Landsberg was another who was active in the reform of morals. The gloomy cloud of superstition had long brooded over the city of Bern, having assumed pro-

---

[1] On the Bernese Reformation, comp. G. J. KUHN, *Die Reformatoren Berns im 16 Jahrhundert, nach dem Bernischen Mausoleum umgearbeitet*, Bern, 1828 ; S. FISCHER, *Geschichte der Reformation in Bern*, Bern, 1827 ; STIERLIN, *Kurze Geschichte der Kirchenverbesserung zu Bern*, Bern, 1827 ; also a number of writings which appeared on the occasion of the celebration of the jubilee of the Reformation. The principal sources in earlier times are ANSHELM's *Chronicle* (ed. of Stierlin and Wyss, 6 vols., Bern, 1833), and the hereafter-to-be-cited representations of MANUEL.

portions that may be called truly fearful, if we think of the proceedings that gave rise to the Jetzer affair; and though a few of the noble families, such as the Mais, the Wattenwyles, the Manuels, and the Stürlers, favoured the dawning light, a great part of the nobility and the men of culture were, as the story of Samson evidences, still entangled in the same prejudices that had fastened their roots in the hearts of the people.

The Jetzer affair to which we have alluded was as follows[1]:—

The two orders of Franciscans and Dominicans had long been involved in a quarrel, in which the principal point of dispute was, whether the Virgin Mary was born with or without original sin. The Franciscans maintained that the latter was the case, whilst the Dominicans contended for the truth of the former hypothesis. The passion with which the contest was carried on was heightened into hatred by the mutual jealousy of the orders. The Dominicans, as the history of Zwingle's youth has already apprised us, were held in high esteem at Bern. In order, if possible, to increase this veneration and to cast their rivals, the Franciscans, into the shade, they devised a piece of shameful rascality that is without its equal in the annals of monkish corruption. They endeavoured to gain a simple fellow by the name of Jetzer, formerly a tailor of Zurzach, and at this time residing as a novice in their cloister, as a witness to the truth of their cause. The prior and a few of the brethren commenced by getting up apparitions in his room. They appeared to him disguised as spirits, and gave him feigned revelations from the holy Virgin, in which the Dominicans were declared to be the true adherents of the mother of our Lord, while the Franciscans were designated as her most dangerous adversaries. Emboldened by the success

---

[1] There is a diffuse but most original account of the affair, such as might be expected from an eye-witness, in ANSHELM's *Chronicle*, vols. iii. and iv. Our abstract of it is taken principally from STIERLIN's little book on the Reformation. Other incidents which we have noted may be found in HALLER's *Bibliothek der Schweizergeschichte*, Part iii. pp. 17–32.

of their deception, they caused St. Barbara, Mary, and the angels to appear to the man and hand him letters from heaven. Finally, they burned a mark in his hand with a hot iron—a mark which they declared to be of heavenly origin, and to represent one of the five stigmata of Christ. Jetzer screamed fearfully during the operation, but, in his pious vanity, felt not a little flattered at the idea of passing henceforth as a favourite of the Virgin. He submitted patiently to the binding up of his wound, upon which a salve was spread in order that it might not close, and told all who visited him of the visions of which he had been accounted worthy. The monks also boasted loudly of the affair before all the people. Upon one occasion, however, the deception came near being discovered, for the infatuated Jetzer recognised one of the monks under his disguise, caught him by the garment as he fled, and held him fast. The person whom he had apprehended escaped from him, however, with admirable dexterity by telling him that he had but wished to test him, to see whether he knew how to try the spirits and to distinguish between a genuine and a spurious visitation. The good-natured blockhead allowed himself to be silenced in this way, and gave himself anew to the mummery, encouraged by the praise awarded him for his sharp-sightedness in the matter of ghosts. An opiate having been administered to him, four other wounds were inflicted upon him,—one on his left hand, two on his feet, and one in his side, all of which were carefully kept open with ointments. The monks now bruited it everywhere that Jetzer bore in his mortal body the wounds of the Saviour. This report attracted a crowd of wonder-seeking visitors to the convent, and brought the Dominicans, as contrasted with the Franciscans, into high repute among the people. Jetzer went into convulsions when visited, and comported himself in such a manner as to excite universal horror. And the wild and disgusting ravings of this man were affirmed to represent Christ's passion in Gethsemane! But all these disgraceful proceedings, which tended to dishonour religion in the eyes of every sensible person, were not enough for the ambitious monks. Suddenly it was reported in the city that the image of the Virgin in the church of the Dominicans was weeping tears of blood. The people immediately ran in throngs to the church. The credulous, amongst whom there were learned men to be found,—such as H. Wölflin, for instance,[1]—were terrified at the wonder, and began to talk of the sore judgments that God must be about to send upon the city; more knowing ones, however, could not, after all that had previously occurred, avoid suspecting some deceit. It may readily be imagined, also, that the Franciscans were busy in characterising the doings of the Dominicans as trickery, even though, in a similar case, the Franciscans themselves would not have hesitated to employ a like weapon against their adversaries. Whilst the sentiments of the assembled populace were thus divided, Täschenmacher, the chaplain, leaped upon the steps of the altar, and, touching the figure, exclaimed in a voice that could be heard through the church, "It is all a cheat; it is nothing but red paint." The doubters were delighted at this discovery, but the deceivers and those who wished to be deceived raised a loud cry against the sacrilege committed by the chaplain. The dissentient opinions in relation to this occurrence gave rise to a general uproar among the burghers, and the city council found itself compelled to undertake a serious investigation of the matter. The Dominicans now tried to get rid of their burdensome tool before he could be used against them. They endeavoured to put poor Jetzer out of the way by a dose of poison. The fellow, however, conjectured their intention as they placed his soup before him.[2] He accordingly gave the mess to some young wolves that were brought up in the convent, and the animals immediately dropped down dead. But again the monks succeeded in cajoling him into silence, and we should

---

[1] A painter, who had been summoned to the city from Freiburg as an expert in his art, was also befooled.

[2] On another occasion they made use of a poisoned wafer for a similar purpose.

be tempted to believe that the simpleton was no mere instrument, but an accomplice in their guilt, were it not that the issue of the affair speaks favourably for him. Imagine, if you can, the audacity of the monks. Already half betrayed, they resumed the old game at the beginning. The nightly apparitions returned. The provisor of the monastery, attired as St. Catherine, and one of the monks, in the guise of the Virgin Mary, once more approached the couch of Jetzer. The latter, however, recognising the voice of the provisor, drew his knife from under the pillow and stabbed the false St. Catherine in the thigh, so that she let fall the vessel of holy water that she was carrying. A scuffle ensued, in which every one defended himself as well as he was able. Jetzer seized a hammer and gave the provisor a blow on the head with it; the other monk threw a tin can at Jetzer's head, but the can flew out of the window, dashing several panes of glass to pieces on its way. The tailor escaped, locking the door after him, and brought the prior and another of the guilty monks to the scene of action, in order that he might there convict them of their falsehood. "There, good fathers," said he; "fine doings are these! When will you have done with your knavery?"

The day of judgment and punishment for the hypocritical rascals came at last. True, the Bishop of Lausanne, who had called the government together, was not at first inclined to treat the matter very seriously, and Jetzer, from whom the monks had exacted a fearful oath, declined making any confession; but, being pressed more earnestly, he confessed sufficient to remove all further doubt as to the deception. The affair was now submitted to the pope, before whom the Dominicans had ere this triumphantly boasted of their miracles. The pope sent on his legate, Achilles de Grassis, who, in conjunction with the Bishop of Lausanne and Sitten, instituted a spiritual court, which was charged with the thorough investigation of every circumstance, even the most minute. The prior and his three confederates (Uelschli, Bolshorst, and Steinecker) were sentenced to pay the penalty of their crime by a disgraceful death. On the 24th of May 1509, on a scaffold erected on the street, they were stripped of their priestly vestments before the eyes of the whole populace, and expelled from the ranks of the clergy; on the 31st day of the same month they were burnt alive. Jetzer was sentenced merely to public exposure and banishment from the Confederation.

That this affair, which took place only ten years before the Reformation, must have contributed to excite the suspicion of all sensible men against the doings of monkish darkness, may readily be imagined. And yet the Bernese not only suffered themselves to be again fooled by the indulgences of a Samson, but almost at the same time at which the latter arrived in Switzerland, there occurred another piece of trickery relating to the skull of St. Anna.[1] A considerable number of devout persons at Bern had united in erecting an altar to this saint, and it was necessary, according to the belief of the age, that some sacred particle (some portion of her body) should be buried beneath this altar. Accordingly, the knight Albert von Stein[2] was despatched to the King of France with orders to solicit from him permission to remove a portion of St. Anna's body, which was contained in a convent at Lyons, to Bern. Albert, however, in order to avoid the solemn audience with the king and the possibility of a denial of his suit, bribed the sexton of the monastery to procure him the divine relic of the saint in consideration of a large reward. To this the sexton agreed, and delivered to the knight a skull that was carefully wrapped in a silken cloth, declaring it to be that of St. Anna. The knight, rejoiced at having so easily attained his purpose, took his journey homewards. In Lausanne he received the congratulations and blessing of the venerable bishop, and on reaching the gate of his native city he was met by all the clergy, the town council, and a large portion of the burghers, and escorted in solemn procession to

---

[1] Comp. ANSHELM, vol. v. p. 337.
[2] Comp. HOTTINGER (continuation of JOHN MÜLLER), vol. vi. pp. 26 sqq.

the church of the Dominicans. The skull was deposited in the altar amid imposing ceremonies, and the Bishop of Lausanne endowed the new sanctuary with power of absolution. But with what shame were all overwhelmed when, after a brief period, a letter was received from the abbot of the cloister at Lyons, containing a conclusive assurance that the body of St. Anna remained complete and undisturbed in its old place, and that the sexton had stolen a common skull from the charnel-house and sold it as that of the saint, for which offence he had already been brought to punishment. From the facts that we have related, it is evident that there was any quantity of work for the Bernese Reformers. We shall not until later be able to do justice to all their labours, but let us say a few words as to the beginning of them.

Francis Kolb, a native of Lörrach, had studied at Basel, and had been preaching at Bern since 1512. He belonged to the order of the Carthusians. Like Zwingle in Zurich, he appeared as a political reformer at Bern, and preached against foreign service. At a subsequent time, however, on his becoming associated with Berthold Haller and Sebastian Meyer, he also laboured for the purification of the faith.

Berthold Haller,[1] the principal Reformer of Bern (not to be confounded with the previously-mentioned John Haller), was born in the large Swabian village of Aldingen, in the year 1492. In the adjacent imperial city of Rottwyl, he attended the Latin school that there flourished under the directorship of the Humanist Michael Rubellus (Röttlin). At Pforzheim, where Haller was under the instruction of George Simler of Wimpfen, he sat on the same bench with Simon Grynæus and Philip Melanchthon. With the latter he contracted an intimate friendship, which continued through life. When he was eighteen he repaired to the University of Cologne, and became acquainted with Scholastic philosophy,

[1] M. Kirchofer, *Berthold Haller oder die Reformation von Bern*, Zurich, 1828; C. Pestalozzi, *Bertold Haller, nach handschriftlichen und gleichzeitigen Quellen*, Elberfeld, 1860 (in vol. ix. of the *Väter und Begründer*, etc.).

but afterwards regretted the time that he had spent upon this unfruitful study. After changing the place of his abode several times, he went, in 1518, to Bern as a teacher, and there speedily received a canonship, and soon afterwards, in 1521, the office of priest in the cathedral. A pleasing exterior, talent, application, great eloquence, and an unconstrained affability toward every one, made him generally beloved. His enemies, however, called him a pot-bellied heretic.

In common with Haller, Sebastian Meyer, of Neuburg on the Rhine, laboured for the diffusion of purified religion. Born in 1465, he was twenty-seven years the senior of Haller. Notwithstanding this circumstance, however, he was the constant friend of the younger man, and shared with him the joys and sorrows of the conflict. He had studied at Basel, and at several other celebrated Universities, and had then entered the order of the Franciscans. Since about 1511 he had taught in Bern as professor (*Lesemeister*) of theology. At an early period he went back to the Bible in his lectures; he explained the Pauline Epistles to the brethren of his order, and preached to the people, in a fruitful and impressive manner, on the apostolic creed, instead of narrating legends to them from the pulpit.

Haller and Meyer were, however, on account of their liberal-minded lectures, soon reported to teach erroneous doctrines; and at about the same time that the Bishop of Constance was taking the first steps against Zwingle, Sebastian de Montfaucon, Bishop of Lausanne, commenced proceedings against the Bernese Reformers, who were in close connection with Zwingle. In 1522 they were accused of heresy before the Council of Bern, and the surrender of them was demanded.

Whilst Kolb, Haller, and Meyer were labouring earnestly in the pulpit, the poet and painter, Nicholas Manuel,[1] was endeavouring to prepare the way for truth through the instrumentality of ridicule and derision. He had previously sung

---

[1] GRÜNEISEN, *N. Manuel's Leben und Wirken*, Stuttgart, 1837.

the Jetzer affair in a more serious than comic manner.[1] Now, however, on Shrove Tuesday of 1522, he caused a comedy of his own composition, entitled, *The Eaters of the Dead* (because the clergy fed upon the dead by means of the masses for departed souls), to be performed on the Kreuzgasse [street of the cross] by some students. The very names of the *dramatis personæ* indicate the tendency of the poem. There appears Pope Entchristilo [Antichrist], Cardinal Anshelm Hochmuth [Pride], Bishop Chrysostom Wolfsmagen [Wolf's-belly], Prior Frederick Geizsack [Miser], Dean Sebastian Schinddebauern [Flay-the-peasants], Abbot Nimmergnug [Never-satisfied], Purveyor Ohneboden [Bottomless], etc. Pastor Wetterleich addresses the holy father as " God at Rome in lieu of Christ," in the following words[2] :—

> " Die Laien merken unser List,
> Wo du nit unser Helfer bist.
> So gehts' uns ab in allen Dingen ;
> Denn sie wend (wollen) selbst der Schrift zudringen
> Der Teufel nehm' die Druckerg' sellen,
> Die alle Ding' in Deutsch nun stellen,
> Das alt' und neue Testament,—
> Ach, wären sie doch bald verbrennt ;
> Ein jeder Bau'r, der lesen kann,
> Der g'winnt's eim schlechten Pfaffen an."[3]

---

[2] *Ein schon bewertes Lied von der reinen, unbefleckten Entpfengknuss Marie, und darbey die war Histori von den vier ketzern prediger Ordens der Observantz, zu Bern in Eydgenossen verbrennt,* etc. See HALLER's *Bibl.* vol. iii. p. 24 ; KUHN, *l.c.* p. 279. The song, " however, breathes much of a Roman Catholic spirit." There is a reprint of it in GRÜNEISEN (in the supplement).

[2] [" The layman soon our wiles must see,
   If thou wilt not our helper be.
   In everything we'll sure be lacking,
   For all are to the Scriptures packing.
   The printers—whom may Satan seize on !—
   Are Germanizing all that's reason,
   The Testaments, both Old and New,—
   Would the knaves had their fiery due !
   E'en every reading peasant lout
   Can put an honest priest to rout."—TR.]

[3] Comp. KUHN, *l.c.* pp. 285 sqq.; WIRZ (Hottinger's edition), vol. iv. chap. i. pp. 383 sqq. GRÜNEISEN, p. 393 : " Ein fastnachtspyl, so zu Bern uff der hern fastnacht, inn dem MDXXII. jare, von burgerssöhnen offentlich gemacht ist, darinn die warheit in schimpffs wyss vom Pabst vnd einer Priesterschaft gemeldet

Let us turn now to Basel. This city, having arisen from the ruins to which the earthquake of 1356 reduced it, had raised itself, during the second half of the fourteenth, and especially during the fifteenth century, to the rank of the more important free cities of the German Empire. The great Council held at Basel, the University soon after founded there by Pope Pius II., the association within its walls of some of the greatest men of letters, and the residence of Erasmus there, as well as the excellent printing establishment of the city, contributed much to the increase of its fame. Since 1501 it had been a member of the Helvetic league. Important changes had taken place in its constitution, the burgher trades guilds having assumed a more independent posture in relation to the nobility of the High Chamber, and obtained important privileges in regard to the election of councillors and burgomasters.[1]

The nobility, though somewhat restricted in its preroga-

würt. Item ein ander spyl, daselbs vff der alten fastnecht darnach gemacht, anzeigend grossen vnderscheid zwischen dem Pabst vnd Christum unserm seligmacher" (the well-known parody in which Christ enters upon an ass and the pope upon a tall war-horse). The assertion that Manuel also wrote the so-called *Bohnenlied* [Bean song] against the indulgences, is founded upon a misunderstanding. Anshelm says only that the Shrovetide comedy on indulgences was "carried, together with the *Bohnenlied*, through all the streets" (v. p. 338), without determining whether the latter also was the work of Manuel or not. Haller, vol. iii. p. 71, notes it as the production of Manuel without ever having seen it himself. He says merely: "It must be of a vehement character, for the proverb is still current at Bern (and elsewhere also), when something exaggerated is to be described, 'That surpasses the *Bohnenlied*;' just as the story of Jetzer has given rise to the expression *jetzern*, to indicate the incessant tormenting of any person." The proverb concerning the *Bohnenlied* originated, more probably, in the Bean feast [*Bohnengastmahl*, held on Twelfth Night] and the Bean king [*Bohnenkönig*—the one to whose share fell the *bean* baked in the cake handed round at the festivity]; at this festival the *Bohnenlied* was sung as an ancient popular song. See GRIMM's *Wörterbuch*, under 'Bohnenlied.' [SANDERS (*Wörterbuch*, vol. ii. p. 133) seems to think that the proverb owes its origin to the *length* of the *Bohnenlied*, of which, he says, 999 verses are still extant.—TR.]

[1] Comp. OCHS, *Geschichte von Basel*, vols. iv. and v. On the Reformation in Basel, besides Ochs and the chronicles of Ryff, Wurstisen, etc., comp. (on the opposite side) the *Reformations-chronik* of the Carthusian monk GEORGE (published by Buxtorf, Basel, 1849); also the biographies of Œcolampadius which we shall mention farther on. A brief review of the subject is to be found in the *Basel'sche Neujahrsblatt* for 1868. For special particulars see HALLER, *Bibl. der Schweizergeschichte*, vol. iii. p. 45.

tives, still possessed an abundance of power in the government, and now strove to ensure its own welfare in ecclesiastical as well as temporal matters by preserving a conservative course; the common people hoped, as usual, to gain by the overthrow of the existing order of things; but the better portion of the burghers, who fortunately composed the kernel of the city, by their vigorous measures, on the one hand, decided the dilatory government to take action, and, on the other, calmed the violence of the multitude. At the head of this higher burgher class, and acting as its representative in the government, may be seen the burgomaster Adelberg Meyer, whilst his colleague Henry Meltinger (of the High Chamber) favoured the opposite party.

Basel continued to be distinguished in an ecclesiastical point of view by being the residence of the *bishop*, although the relation of the burghers to that dignitary had sustained considerable alteration through the accession of the city to the Swiss Confederacy, to the detriment of the episcopal interests. The bishop disapproved, as tending to the general curtailment of the power of the nobility, the political changes that had taken place.

As a man and as a Christian, apart from his episcopal dignity, Christopher von Uttenheim was possessed of clement and liberal sentiments, sincere piety, and irreproachable morals. A friend of Erasmus, he was himself a lover of letters, though disinclined to hasty innovations. He was, moreover, advanced in age when the Reformation began, and he may almost be said to have avoided it more than to have used violent endeavours to check it. His motto, "*My hope is the cross of Christ; I seek grace, and not works*,"[1] is indicative at least of an affinity in his view of faith to that of the Reformers. Similar to him in sentiment was his coadjutor, Nicholas von Diessbach, and

[1] *Spes mea crux Christi; gratiam, non opera quæro,* inscribed upon a pane of painted glass which has come down to us from the bishop, and which is still to be found in the so-called *Antistitium*. Further particulars concerning him and his reformatory efforts are given by HERZOG in his *Beiträge zur Geschichte Basels*, vol. i. (1839), pp. 33 sqq.

so also were a few more of the better disposed members of the chapter of the cathedral.

The University was less active in the cause of the Reformation than we should, at the first glance, suppose would have been the case. As a creation of the pontifical throne, its very foundation necessarily appeared to admonish it to revere the rights of its sovereign, although, to take a higher view of the matter, science should never lend itself to the protection of interests foreign to itself. It was, therefore, all things considered, a vain and fruitless undertaking on the part of the man who was at that time rector of the University —Romanus Wonnecker, professor of medicine—to pledge himself to put all Lutheranism to shame in a public disputation.[1]

Notwithstanding what we have just said, the University of Basel was indirectly efficacious in promoting the spread of the Reformation not only in Basel itself, but also outside of the city and in the remaining portions of Switzerland. We have already remarked the stirring effect which the lectures of a Thomas Wyttenbach had upon Zwingle and Leo Juda. Thus also the learned native of Glarus, Henry Loriti (Glareanus), diffused a clearer knowledge from his philosophical chair, even though he himself, like his friend Erasmus, remained in the communion of the Romish Church.[2]

Erasmus assumed toward the Reformation of Basel an attitude similar to that which he maintained toward the Reformation in general. In his whole personality he was averse to the popular strivings. It was always against his will that he was compelled to co-operate in the diffusion of light, even in his own immediate vicinity.

Amongst the men who gave the first impulse to the Reformation in Basel we will mention first Wolfgang Fabricius

---

[1] The principal burden of his complaints was the *tempestuosam dicacitatem Lutheri* [the tempestuous raillery of Luther].

[2] He does not seem to have borne a very desirable character. In the judgment of Œcolampadius, he was *homo ad maledicentiam et inepta scommata natus*. Comp., however, HENRY SCHREIBER, *Loriti Glareanus*, Freiburg, 1837, p. 4.

Capito (Köpfli), an Alsatian,[1] who, from the year 1512, occupied the position of preacher in the cathedral, and at the same time discharged the duties of professor in the University, and who was on terms of friendly intercourse with Erasmus. He lectured to the students on the Gospel of Matthew, and in the pulpit expounded the Epistle to the Romans. By means of his independent biblical investigations, his eyes were speedily opened to several errors of the Romish Church, and in the year 1517, before he could have known anything of Luther's action in Germany, he is said to have no longer been able conscientiously to read mass. He even, as he himself writes to Bullinger,[2] sketched with Zwingle, at Einsiedeln (?), the fall of the pope before the same idea entered the brain of the Reformer of Wittenberg. It is certainly the more surprising, in view of all this, that this same man should subsequently have reproached Luther for his bold reformatory zeal, and have sought, after the manner of Erasmus, to persuade him to greater moderation.[3] We have reference here to the letter which Capito, who (after fostering the brightest hopes in regard to the Reformation in Basel[4]), was called, in the year 1520, to the court of the Elector of Mentz, and wrote thence to Luther at the Wartburg, warning him against an excess of haste and violence.

It was with unwillingness that the people of Basel beheld the departure of their teacher. In his footsteps trod Caspar Heid (Hedio), a native of Ettlingen in the margravate of Baden, who, as vicar of St. Theodore's[5] and afterwards as

---

[1] He was born in 1478, at Hagenau, where his father was blacksmith (hence the name of Fabricius) and councillor. He at first studied medicine, but afterwards applied himself to theology. He pursued his studies at Freiburg. Comp. RÖHRICH, vol. i. p. 149; JUNG, *Geschichte der Reformation in Strassburg*, vol. i. pp. 86 sqq.; BAUM, *Capito und Butzer*, Elberfeld, 1860.

[2] In a letter of the year 1536. Comp. JUNG, *l.c.* p. 91.

[3] See chap. vii.   [4] Comp. SCULTET, *ad ann.* 1520, p. 35.

[5] See WIRZ, vol. iv. chap. i. p. 103; JUNG, *l.c.* p. 81. On the death of Lutenwang, priest of St. Theodore's, Hedio was not, as he and the congregation had hoped, chosen to be his successor—a circumstance which excited the displeasure of the inhabitants of Little Basel. He received, in compensation for his disappointment, the chaplaincy of St. Martin's.

chaplain at St. Martin's, continued to explain the biblical books in the spirit of Capito,[1] thus exciting, like his predecessor, the hatred of the monks.[2] "I desire," he wrote, in 1520, to Zwingle, "to go on with the gospel where Capito left off; so captivated am I with sound doctrine. There are, however, a few monks and stupid babblers here who, in their sermons, do not scruple to turn the people away from those who hold that it is upon the gospel that Christianity is mainly built." Hedio was also in correspondence with Luther, whose doctrine he acknowledged to be of God.[3] This preacher himself soon received and accepted a call to Mentz. The Franciscan monk, Konrad Kürssner (Pellican), a native of Ruffach in Alsace, and, since 1519, a lecturer at the University of Basel, was also enthusiastic in favour of Luther's opinions, and even prepared a reprint of his writings. At about the same time we see, finally, another combatant appear, in the person of William Röublin, pastor of St. Alban's. He was born at Rothenberg on the Neckar, and is described as a learned and zealous man. He preached against the sacrifice of the mass, purgatory, and the invocation of saints, and attracted crowds of auditors, so that upwards of 4000 persons were frequently present at his sermons. When, in 1521, relics were carried about in the great procession on Corpus Christi day, Röublin bore through the city, instead of relics, a beautifully bound Bible, upon which was inscribed in large letters: "*Biblia*,—that is the true relic; all others are but dead men's bones."

This striking procedure excited great displeasure among the priesthood. Röublin was accused before the bishop, and by the latter complained of to the civic council. The burghers, however, espoused his cause, and when it was rumoured in the city that the clergy were desirous of imprisoning him, a tumult

---

[1] He lectured on Matthew, and wrote letters about that Gospel to Zwingle.

[2] The monks declared, in reference to the Hebrew and Greek characters, which were unintelligible to them, "Everything that goes crinkle-crankle is Lutheran."

[3] See Jung, p. 81.

ensued on the square of the Franciscans. The burghers sent a committee to the council, entreating that they would spare them their preacher, who taught nothing save what was founded on Holy Writ, and that they would protect him against the persecutions of the chapter. In order to preclude further mischief, the council despatched the recently-elected burgomaster, Adelberg Meyer, with a few other members of their body, to the square where the burghers were assembled, "with a view to obtaining more precise information as to their demands, and also, in particular, as to their numbers." Every effort was made to appease the excited mob. The clergy, however, did not rest until they had removed the hated pastor from the city. They urged their suit before the council until the latter finally sent for Röublin, and, as the story runs, banished him, unheard, from Basel. This gave rise to fresh murmurs among the burghers, although they did not again make any popular demonstrations. On the other hand, fifty honourable women of St. Alban's Church, belonging to different ranks in society, endeavoured to present, through a burgher of repute, a plea for their pastor before the council, but an audience was refused them.

We may at first regard this course of action on the part of the Government as harsh, and feel inclined to take up the cudgels on behalf of Röublin as one who was unjustly persecuted. But when we learn that this same man eventually went over to the Anabaptists, that, as pastor of Wytikon in the canton of Zurich, he promised the peasants to release them from tithes and taxes, and that, for the purpose of irritating his opponents, he made an ostentatious display on the occasion of the marriage which he soon afterward contracted, we can readily conjecture that there was an admixture of impure elements in his earliest zeal for reformation,—though his efforts therefor were doubtless well intended,—and consequently that the council may have had good reasons for dismissing him as a disturber of the peace. There is something strikingly ostentatious in the very act which led to his dismissal. The work of a true evangelist and reformer is to study and explain the Bible, but not pompously to parade it. Consolation for his departure was also the more speedily found from the fact that another soon took his place in the free promulgation of Bible doctrines. This was Wolfgang Wyssenburger, preacher at the hospital. Of him the chronicle of Fridolin Ryff speaks as follows : " This learned young man also began to preach the truth as contained in the divine word. He gained the adherence of his congregation in a much greater degree than that accorded to his predecessor (Röublin). He inaugurated the reading of the mass in German instead of Latin, in order that the people might understand what they heard. With this the priests were not particularly well pleased: they did not, however, succeed in ousting him as they had ousted Röublin ; *for as he was a burgher, and his father a member of the council and high in favour with his fellow-citizens, they were forced to let him remain.*"

The fact that Wyssenburger was a burgher, and that his father was an esteemed member of the council, may certainly have had some weight with the people of Basel, and the confession is amusing in its simplicity and artlessness. But that was not the sole consideration that guided our fathers[1] in the recognition of merit, for their joyful enthusiasm in the cause of the Reformation grew still stronger after the *foreigner* John Œcolampadius was called into their midst.

[1] [It will be remembered that this was written at Basel.—Tr.]

SUPPLEMENT TO CHAPTER XI.

ZWINGLI'S PESTGEDICHTE.

1. *Im Anfang der Krankheit.*

Hilf, Herr Gott, hilf
In dieser Noth,
Ich mein', der Tod
Syg an der Thür.
Stand, Christe, für ;
Denn du ihn überwunden hast.
Zu dir ich gilf [gelle, schreie] :
Ist est din Will,
Züch us den Pfyl ;
Der mich verwundt,
Nit lass ein Stund
Mich haben weder Ruh noch Rast !
Willt du dann glych

Todt haben mich
Inmitts der Tagen min,
So soll es willig syn.
Thu wie du willt,
Mich nüt bevilt [beschwert],
Din Haf [Gefäss] bin ich,
Mach ganz ald [oder] birch.
Denn nimmst du hin
Den Geiste min
Von dieser Erd,
Thust du's, dass er nit böser werd,
Ald [oder] andern nit
Befleck ihr Leben fromm und Sitt.

2. *Mitten in der Krankheit.*

Tröst, Herr Gott, tröst !
Die Krankheit wahst [wächst],
Weh und Angst fasst
Min Seel und Lib.
Darum dich schyb [wende]
Gen mir, einiger Trost, mit Gnad,
Die gwüss erlöst
Ein jeden, der
Sin herzlich B'ger
Und Hoffnung setzt
In dich, verschätzt
Darzu diss Zyt all Nutz und Schad.
Nun ist es um ;
Min Zung ist stumm,

Mag sprechen nit ein Wort ;
Min Sinn' sind all verdorrt,
Darum ist Zyt,
Dass du min Stryt
Führist fürhin ;
So ich nit bin
So stark, dass ich
Mög tapferlich
Thun Widerstand
Des Tüfels Facht [Anfechtung] und
    frefner Hand.
Doch wird min Gmüth
Stät bliben dir, wie er auch wüth.

3. *Zur Genesung.*

G'sund, Herr Gott, g'sund !
Ich mein', ich kehr
Schon wiedrum her.
Ja, wenn dich dunkt,
Der Sünden Funk'
Werd nit mehr bherrschen mich uf
    Erd,
So muss min Mund
Din Lob und Lehr
Ussprechen mehr
Denn vormals je,
Wie es auch geh'
Einfältiglich ohn' alle G'fährd.

Wiewohl ich muss
Des Todes Buss
Erliden zwar einmal,
Villicht mit gröss'rer Qual,
Denn jezund wär'
Geschehen, Herr !
Nach [beinahe] gfahren hin,
So will ich doch
Den Trutz und Poch [Ungestüm]
In dieser Welt
Tragen fröhlich um Widergelt,
Mit Hülfe din,
Ohn' den nüt mag voll kommen syn.

[The following translation of Zwingle's Plague Hymns, taken from the translation of D'Aubigné's *History of the Reformation*, published by Robert Carter, in New York, 1844, is by John Alexander Messenger. The translator has preserved much of the spirit and rhythm of the original.—Tr.

"1. *At the Beginning of the Malady.*

"Lo! at my door
Gaunt Death I spy!
Hear, Lord of life,
Thy creature's cry!

"The arm that hung
Upon the tree,
Jesus, uplift—
And rescue me.

"Yet, if to quench
My sun at noon
Be Thy behest,
Thy will be done!

"In faith and hope
Earth I resign,
Secure of heaven,—
For I am Thine!

"2. *In the Midst of the Malady.*

"Fierce grow my pains:
Help, Lord, in haste!
For flesh and heart
Are failing fast.

"Clouds wrap my sight,
My tongue is dumb;
Lord, tarry not,
The hour is come!

"In Satan's grasp
On hell's dark brink
My spirit reels,—
Ah, must I sink?

"No, Jesus, no!
Him I defy
While here beneath
Thy cross I lie.

"3. *On Recovery.*

"My Father God,
Behold me whole!
Again on earth
A living soul!

"Let sin no more
My heart annoy,
But fill it, Lord,
With holy joy.

"Though now delayed,
My hour must come,
Involved, perchance,
In deeper gloom.

"It matters not;
Rejoicing yet
I'll bear my yoke
To heaven's bright gate."]

CHAPTER XII.

JOHN ŒCOLAMPADIUS—RELATION OF ERASMUS TO THE REFORMATION AND TO LUTHER—ULRICH VON HUTTEN AT BASEL AND MÜHLHAUSEN—HIS QUARREL WITH ERASMUS—HIS DEATH—RELATION OF ERASMUS TO ZWINGLE—HISTORY OF THE SWISS REFORMATION CONTINUED—OCCURRENCES AT ZURICH—FIRST RELIGIOUS CONFERENCE AND ITS RESULTS—ICONOCLASM — SECOND DISPUTATION (KONRAD SCHMID, COMMANDER OF KÜSSNACHT).

JOHN HAUSSCHEIN (Œcolampadius[1]) was born at Weinsberg[2] in Franconia, in 1482, and was consequently but a year older than Luther and Zwingle. His parents were in comfortable circumstances. His father was at first desirous of devoting him to a commercial life, but his mother (who was a Pfister of Basel) preferred that her son should become a man of learning, and the inclinations of the boy harmonized with her wishes. Œcolampadius at first attended school at Heilbronn, and afterwards went to Bologna, the most celebrated law school of the day, intending there to fit him-

---

[1] Comp. his life by S. HESS, Zurich, 1793; BURCKHARDT's *Reformationsgeschichte von Basel*, Basel, 1818; the *Reformationsalmanach* for 1819; J. J. HERZOG, *Leben Johann Oekolampads und die Reformation der Kirche von Basel*, 1843, 2 vols.; K. R. HAGENBACH, *Johann Oekolampad und Oswald Myconius, die Reformatoren Basels*, Elberfeld, 1859.

[2] Weinsberg, famed for "the fidelity of its women," had not been untouched by heretical influences. The Saxon John Dräudorf, who was burnt at Worms in the year 1425 as a Hussite heretic, had, previous to his death, addressed three letters to the burgomaster and council of the town of Weinsberg; in one of these he comforts them in view of the excommunication pronounced upon them by the pope. See KRUMMEL, JOHAN DRÄUDORF (*Theol. Stud. und Krit.* 1869, i.).

self for the career of a statesman and jurisconsult. But neither the Italian climate nor the study of law suited him, and he therefore exchanged the skies of Italy for those of Germany, and law for theology. After a brief sojourn in his native town, he repaired to Heidelberg,[1] and applied himself with all possible diligence to the study of the ancient languages. Frederick, Count Palatine of the Rhine, hearing of the many admirable gifts of the young man, appointed him instructor to his children. This position, however, did not seem particularly to please Œcolampadius; and he soon gave it up and again repaired to a University, although his parents had already procured a benefice for him in his native place. At this time it was to the University of Tubingen that he went, where John Reuchlin was teaching, and where he also contracted an intimate friendship with Capito. Not until after his stay at Tubingen, and after another period of study at the University of Heidelberg, did he accept the pastorate which had been offered him at Weinsberg, and which was still kept open for him. In this conduct we behold a proof of the conscientiousness of the man; he refused to enter the Lord's vineyard as a labourer therein until he had thoroughly prepared himself for the work. He did not, however, long retain the pastorate in his native town, for his friend Capito, who was at this time in Basel, exerted himself to procure the settlement of Œcolampadius there also. The latter accordingly received, in 1515, a call from the Bishop of Utenheim to the position of preacher at the cathedral. His stay there was not long at this time.[2] Whilst it continued, Œcolampadius came into literary contact with Erasmus, whom he assisted in the preparation of that edition of his New Testament which was issued in 1516.

[1] According to Capito, whom most biographers have followed hitherto, (Ecolampadius went to Heidelberg earlier than this, when he was in his twelfth year. But the University register of that city points to the year 1499 as that of his matriculation. See the author's *Œcolampad*, p. 5.

[2] His residence at Basel was further interrupted by a visit to Weinsberg. See HERZOG, vol. i. pp. 117 sqq.

We have but scanty knowledge of the public labours of Œcolampadius at Basel. Shortly after this he was appointed preacher at the cathedral at Augsburg. He was induced to resign this latter office by two considerations: on the one hand, he drew upon himself the hatred of the other clergy of the place by his free-spoken sermons; and on the other hand, the cathedral where he preached was too large for his feeble voice. He now retired to Altenmünster, a monastery of St. Bridget, situated in the vicinity of Augsburg—entering it, however, upon condition that he should be obliged to do nothing contrary to the word of God, and that he should be able to leave it whenever he wished. In this cloistral retirement, which was at first soothing to him, but which subsequently had an oppressing effect upon him, he composed several works, and also made himself acquainted with the writings of Luther. Even here, however, he speedily attracted suspicion, and Glapio, the Franciscan monk and confessor of Charles v., was his particular opponent. By him he was accused at the Diet of Worms of being an adherent of Luther. If this had been proved against him, he, as well as Luther, would have been put under the ban of the empire. He therefore quitted the cloister, after a two years' residence in it, confessing that he had "lost the monk, but found the Christian" (*amisi monachum inveni Christianum*). He next found protection at Mentz with his friends Capito and Hedio, through whose mediation he was received by Francis von Sickingen, the active friend of the Reformation, at his castle of Ebernburg. Here, as chaplain of the castle, he at once applied himself to the task of a more profitable arrangement of the services of the sanctuary, introducing, instead of the daily masses, edifying lectures on the Bible and explanations of the Pauline Epistles. He, however, went cautiously to work in his reformations, "conceding some things for the sake of custom and others for the sake of love." Before Sickingen lost his life in his feud with the Elector of Treves, Œcolampadius, in November 1522, accepted an invitation from his friend Andrew Cratander, the printer, at whose house in Basel he found a friendly shelter.[1] For a time he lived, like Erasmus, in literary seclusion, occupying himself principally with the preparation of an edition of the homilies of Chrysostom, a work which he had commenced during his residence with Francis von Sickingen. It was not long, however, before this distinguished man, whom Basel sought to retain as an ornament to the city, received an appointment, though not a particularly brilliant one at the time. Zanker, the aged and gouty pastor of St. Martin's, being no longer able to discharge the duties of his office, Œcolampadius was assigned him as an assistant.[2] Insignificant as this position of a simple vicar was, it was exceedingly important in its relation to the reformation of Basel, for from this time forth Œcolampadius wielded a steady influence as a preacher. With his practical labours he early conjoined an academical activity, explaining the prophet Isaiah at the University even previous to his formal appointment as professor of theology at that institution. Erasmus seems to have been ill pleased at the growing usefulness of his learned friend. But Luther was heartily rejoiced at the work that he had undertaken, and, in a letter of June 1523, wishes him success in his prosecution of it as follows [3]:—

"May the Lord strengthen thee in the exposition of Isaiah which thou hast undertaken, though Erasmus, as I have heard, is not pleased with the task that thou hast set thyself. But let not his displeasure lead thee astray. . . . He has done that for which he was ordained: he has introduced the languages and drawn men away from profitless studies. He

---

[1] Comp. HERZOG, vol. i. p. 202, note (in opposition to the general assumption accepted by us in the first edition of this work, that Œcolampadius went to Basel in consequence of Sickingen's death). The Carthusian monk George places the arrival of Œcolampadius in December; he says that the latter "went to Basel under cover of a divine call, as a deserter from the faith, and set himself in opposition to the truth."

[2] "Who knows," says Ocns, "whether, if Zanker had not had pains in his limbs, we should have been reformed?" (vol. v. p. 449). But that is carrying pragmatism too far.

[3] DE WETTE, vol. ii. No. 505.

will probably die, like Moses, in the land of Moab, for he is no guide to the better studies that lead to piety. There is nothing that would please me more than his total abstinence from explaining and paraphrasing the Scriptures, for his spiritual growth is not sufficient for this work. . . . He has done enough in uncovering evil. But to point out the good and lead to the land of promise is not, as it seems to me, his portion. But why do I speak so much of Erasmus? It is enough that thou art not led astray by his name and fame, and that thou rejoicest the more when something displeases him in matters that concern the Scriptures, since all the world knows that he either does not or *will* not understand anything about such matters."

This severe criticism of Luther upon one who in his time passed for the most learned man in Europe, gives us occasion to recur to that portraiture of Erasmus which we abandoned at the threshold of the actual history of the Reformation, and induces me, in continuation of the present chapter, to insert a few remarks on Erasmus' relation to Luther, as well as to the Reformation in general and its friends.

It will be remembered that Luther, in his conversation with the two Swiss students whom he met at Jena, inquired, amongst other things, after Erasmus, but learned only that he "*kept himself very quiet and secret.*" And thus, from the very beginning of the conflict, Erasmus conducted himself as a prudent observer, who desired to ascertain in what direction the wind was blowing before he committed himself to any party.

It shall be our care to refrain from too severe a judgment of this waiting attitude on the part of a man who was advancing in years and timid by nature. Men are, in accordance with the wise provision of God, differently constituted. It is not every one who is born to be a hero or a martyr. It is true that a want of courage assumes the aspect of a moral defect in decisive moments; and thus it was with Erasmus. But from a want of courage to an absolute want of principle is a long step. That Erasmus was far behind Luther in character and fidelity to principle, none can fail to perceive. But we have no right to stamp him, on that account, as a cowardly hypocrite, a cold and frivolous scoffer, perfectly indifferent to religion, and acting solely from egotism. Erasmus undoubtedly walked in the slippery path of worldly wisdom, —a course which, as contrasted with the thorny but honourable way that Luther and Zwingle had the courage to tread, necessarily and deservedly redounded in many instances to his discredit. It is certainly impossible to justify the conduct of Erasmus, or to recommend it for imitation; and in contemplating his ambiguous posture toward the Reformation, we are unavoidably reminded of much that the Founder of Christianity has said concerning those who, having put their hand to the plough, turn back from it. To endeavour to gain some just conception of this conduct by examining the whole course and position of the man, and to institute a natural connection between it and the ideas which he himself had formed in regard to the Reformation, are the duties of an honest historian. Erasmus had formed, on the subject of reformation, opinions one-sidedly rooted in his peculiar intellectual and æsthetic tendencies, and in them alone—opinions which it was now impossible for him to shake off. The liberal sciences he held to be the *only* means by which the darkness of the monks could be put to flight, the abuses of superstition remedied, and a brighter and fairer age be inaugurated. He at first believed Luther to be a Reformer after his own heart, a man of liberal and enlightened brain, an author full of wit and taste; and the circumstance that this same man excited the enmity of the monks by his attack upon Tetzel must necessarily have prejudiced Erasmus in his favour. And, indeed, the only ground which Erasmus and Luther can be said to occupy in common, is to be found in the fact that they both drew upon themselves the most implacable hatred of the monks, by whom they were always classed together; for try as Erasmus might, in the sequel, to wash his hands of all connection with the cause of the Reformers, the *monks* could not be persuaded that he was not in league with the Augustinian of Wittenberg. It soon, however, became only too manifest to Erasmus that he had been mistaken in Luther. As his acquaintance with that Reformer progressed, he regarded Luther himself as a coarse monk of contracted intellect and pious prejudices—one who, in view of his mystical mode of thought, would be most likely to prove injurious to the interests of æsthetics, and to · be a hindrance to enlightenment in the *Erasmian* sense of that term. In like manner Luther, for his part, speedily saw that he would have no support in Erasmus, and went so far as to doubt the Christianity of his principles. He gave expression to these doubts in the year 1516,—before the conflict, therefore,—in letters to his friends Spalatin[1] and John Lange, the latter of whom was prior at Erfurt. To Lange he wrote[2]: "I read our Erasmus, but daily lose confidence in him. One thing, indeed, pleases me in him, and that is that he rebukes, with equal constancy and learning, not only the regular clergy, but all priests, accusing them of inrooted and drowsy ignorance. *But I fear he does not sufficiently spread forth Christ and the grace of God, of which he knows but little. Human things stand higher in his estimation than divine things.*"

Notwithstanding all this, these two men may be seen approaching each other in the year 1519; nor can it be denied that Luther, by his conduct on this occasion, laid himself open to the charge of inconsistency. He who in 1516 passed so unfavourable a judgment upon Erasmus, was induced by the persuasions of the pliant Capito, three years later, to write a flattering letter to Erasmus,[3] speaking of the harmony that subsisted between them, and excusing himself in an almost servile manner for venturing to draw near so distinguished a man "with unwashen hands" (*illotis manibus*). He calls him *his* Erasmus, his ornament and hope, the amiable

[1] DE WETTE, vol. i. No. 22. [2] *Ibid.* No. 29. [3] *Ibid.* No. 129.

one, and speaks of himself as his *humble* brother in Christ. What explanation shall we give of this procedure of Luther's? Had he changed his opinion of Erasmus in the three years that had elapsed? This is scarcely possible; for in the year 1518 he gave expression to similar sentiments in regard to him in a letter to Spalatin, confessing, only, that he esteemed him highly as a man of letters, and that he took his part against those who, because of their slothfulness, despised learning.[1] Or did he hope, by this frank acknowledgment of the man's worth, and by the cordial manner of his approach to him, to win him for those things which, in the writer's view, he as yet lacked? Did he hope to convert him? or was it really a momentary weakness, and did he, who in every other case relied exclusively upon the protection of God, refusing the proffered services of tried friends, believe, in an hour of frailty, that Erasmus was necessary to him, and that he must by all means gain him? Be this as it may, Luther attained none of these ends. Erasmus answered him in a manner whose subtilty was at least highly creditable to his prudence, but in which he undisguisedly expressed his sentiments in regard to reformation.[2] He courteously returned the compliments which Luther had paid him, praised the liberal-mindedness of the latter, but gave him plainly to understand that he would prefer that the Reformer should act upon his own responsibility, in order that people might not think that there was an understanding between them. He then endeavoured to prove to him the necessity of proceeding with mildness rather than with violence; the Apostle Paul, he declared, did away with the law by interpreting it *allegorically*, and thus the people should be *gradually* led to the truth, their prejudices being accommodated as much as possible. He warned him against violence, and invoked the divine blessing upon his labours.

In the same year Erasmus was presented with a gold cup by the archbishop Albert of Mentz. The letter of thanks

[1] *Epp.*, ed. Basel, 1540, vol. iii. p. 244.   [2] DE WETTE, vol. i. No. 53.

which this called for he sent to his friend Ulrich von Hutten, who was at that time in the service of the archbishop, requesting him to deliver it to the prelate. He took occasion in this letter to express his opinion of Luther,—the more designedly because the dispute about indulgences nearly concerned the Archbishop of Mentz as their administrator. He defended Luther in great part,—to his honour be it said,—censuring only his too great vehemence in certain instances. Hutten, however, instead of handing the epistle to the archbishop, published it in print, without consulting Erasmus, and even went so far as to alter the text, substituting "our Luther" where Erasmus had simply written "Luther." By his indiscretion he made Erasmus appear, against his will, as an open adherent of Luther. It was probably the intention of Hutten, in performing this not very praiseworthy act of friendship, to constrain Erasmus to a more open declaration in favour of the Reformer. But its effect was exactly the contrary. Erasmus, inspired with distrust for the Lutheran party, now made constant efforts to free himself from all connection with either Luther or Hutten, and exerted all his skill in the endeavour to clear himself, in the eyes of the pope and other magnates,—for whose favour he certainly cared more than he should have done,—of all suspicion of participation in the ecclesiastical Reformation, or connection with its movements.

There is on record a noteworthy and highly-characteristic conversation which the elector, Frederick the Wise, had with Erasmus at Cologne, previous to the Diet of Worms; it was on the subject of Luther and his cause, and may be introduced here.

Let Spalatin, who was an eye-witness of the meeting, be our informant on this occasion.[1] "His electoral grace sent for Erasmus to come to him at his inn of The Three Holy Kings, and there in the parlour, in front of the fireplace, in the presence of me, George Spalatin, led him into discourse,

[1] See MARHEINEKE, vol. i. pp. 225 sqq., and others.

and asked him all manners of questions. And though Duke Frederick of Saxony, my most gracious lord the elector, would have been very glad if Rotterdam had spoken the Netherlandish German with his electoral grace, that might not be; Rotterdam stuck to his Latin, which, as a master in it above thousands of others, he spoke in such a manner that it was good Latin and yet plain and intelligible, so that the august Elector of Saxony understood him so well as to tell me all that I should say in reply to him. His electoral grace asked Rotterdam through me, Spalatin, whether he thought that Dr. Martin Luther had erred hitherto in his doctrine, sermons, and writings. Rotterdam smacked his lips before he gave answer. At this my most gracious master, Duke Frederick of Saxony, opened his eyes very wide, as his way was when he talked with people from whom he desired a reliable answer. Then Erasmus of Rotterdam went on and roundly said these words in Latin: *Lutherus peccavit in duobus, nempe quod tetigit coronam pontificis et ventres monachorum*—that is to say, 'Luther has sinned in two things: first, in that he has laid violent hands upon the pope's crown, and secondly, in that he has assailed the bellies of the monks.'" Thus did Erasmus seek to parry the elector's question by a witticism. Soon after this conversation Erasmus wrote down some thoughts on Luther, the tenor of which was highly advantageous to the latter (there was no danger in praising Luther to the Elector of Saxony), and handed the paper to Spalatin. Scarcely, however, had it left his hands when he recalled it, fearing that it might be attended with disagreeable results to himself. "So timid," adds Spalatin, "was Rotterdam in his confession of the truth."

Several of the friends of Luther and the Reformation were not a little scandalized at Erasmus' increasing coldness toward the work. With none, however, did the disposition which he manifested involve him in more bitter dissensions than those which arose between the knight Ulrich von Hutten and himself, in which personal considerations were also mingled. If

Luther and Erasmus differed much in character, in a certain point of view the personalities of *Hutten* and Erasmus present still greater extremes. True, as contrasted with Luther, they resemble each other in one particular—viz., that they both strove to bring about a reformation from the quarter of enlightenment, learning, and wit, rather than upon any deep foundation of faith; for even in the case of Hutten, it seemed to be a deep-rooted hatred of the stupidity and impudence of the monks, and in part also a political indignation at the ignominy which had been inflicted upon the German nation, that called him into the battle, more than any independent Christian and dogmatical conviction. As Strauss has correctly shown, it was not until Hutten came under the influence of Luther that his rage against Rome assumed a more theological colouring. But so far as personal character is concerned, Hutten undoubtedly presents the greatest contrast to Erasmus. Erasmus was refined in manner: Hutten was unpolished and "horseman-like" [*reitermässig*].[1] Erasmus, if not an epicurean, was at least a sensitive eclectic: Hutten, on the other hand, was almost a cynic. Erasmus was timid and prone to keep back the truth: Hutten was always ready for a fight, and defiant in words as well as in deeds. Both were ambitious, irritable, and passionate, but each was so in his own peculiar way; how could these two men long walk together without mutual provocation? In the affair of Reuchlin, Erasmus had been too timid and retiring to suit Hutten; and now that he was playing the same ambiguous role in Luther's cause, Hutten wrote him a letter censuring his conduct, and showing him that, by his shuffling behaviour, he was injuring both sides, instead of doing any good to either.[2] This step Erasmus seemed to resent. And when, shortly after this, upon the death of Francis von Sickingen, Hutten arrived, a fugitive,

[1] According to PLANCK's expression. On the other hand, it may be remembered (as STOCKMEYER suggests) that a *knight* [*Ritter*] was also a *horseman* [*Reiter*].
[2] Comp. the letter which the author published in *Theol. Stud. und Krit.* for 1832, p. 631.

at Basel (1522), there ensued between the two men an open outbreak of hostility, which has left upon the fame of Erasmus a stain that cannot be entirely effaced. The affair happened on this wise. Hutten came, poor, sick, and a fugitive, to Basel. Here he thought that he should find in Erasmus an old friend, who would receive him hospitably and help him farther on his way; at the same time he purposed administering a reproof to him on the score of his behaviour. Erasmus, however, wished to avoid a meeting that would prove so disagreeable to himself. Nor can we blame him very severely —as he was in delicate health, and habituated to a quiet and orderly house — for not regarding it as a pleasure to share his table and room with one who was accustomed to put not the slightest constraint upon himself; who was likely to bring a throng of other guests with him, and to borrow from his host as much money as he wanted; and who, moreover (why conceal it?), was suffering from a disgusting malady, which, as his foes were wont to assert, he had brought upon himself by his dissolute manner of life.[1]

It cannot, therefore, greatly surprise us to learn that the nervous and peevish Erasmus sent word to the wandering knight, that, unless he had something of particular importance to communicate, he need not trouble himself to pay him a visit, as he (Erasmus) feared that an interview might be attended with disagreeable results; and if this were all, we should find no difficulty in excusing Erasmus for pursuing such a course, in his peculiar situation, since he gave evidence of his readiness to render Hutten every other assistance in his power.

But far more offensive than the pardonable reserve of Erasmus is the duplicity of which he was guilty in relating the circumstance to others. Thus he wrote to Melanchthon

---

[1] See, however, HERDER, *Gallerie grosser und weiser Männer* (*Werke zur Phil. u. Gesch.* vol. xiii. p. 79). A capital sketch of Hutten's character may be found in STOCKMEYER's essay in *Beiträge zur vaterländischen Geschichte*, vol. ii. (Basel, 1843), pp. 55 sqq. For particulars see STRAUSS, *l.c.*

that he had declined Hutten's visit not simply for fear of the hatred of the Papal party, but *principally* because that needy knight, who had been stripped of every necessary, was but seeking a nest where he might die; and he would not only, he continued, have been obliged to harbour the knightly braggart himself, but also with him a whole troop of pretended friends of the gospel. In another letter, however, which was addressed to a certain Laurinus, and was made public shortly after the occurrence, he endeavours to excuse himself for his neglect of hospitality, and writes as follows:—" Hutten was here for *a few days* (and yet the knight stayed eight weeks in Basel); he did not visit me, nor did I call upon him; yet I should not have denied myself to him if he had come to me,[1] for I still retain an affection for him as an old friend, and as a man of a happy and merry disposition. His other affairs do not concern me. But on account of his illness, he was unable to leave his heated rooms, which I cannot endure; and thus it was that we did not meet."

Hutten, having received from the magistrates of Basel a friendly recommendation to leave the city, repaired to Mühlhausen in Alsace, where he published a violent polemic against Erasmus, designing in this production so to show off the man's deficiency of character as to leave him not a single good quality—ay, morally to annihilate him. Erasmus failed not to reply to the knight. He defended himself with wit, and gave Hutten many a sharp blow on account of his roughness and brusqueness, and the disorderliness of his conduct.[2] The fugitive knight, finding no place of abode in Mühlhausen, next went to Zurich, where he found a faithful protector and maintainer in Zwingle. The latter recommended the sick

---

[1] This was but an excuse, for Hutten appeared publicly in the street, and frequently passed Erasmus' house.

[2] On this unedifying dispute (*Expostulatio Hutteni-Erasmi Spongia*), comp. HERDER, *l.c.*; MÜNCH, *Hutteni Opp.* vol. iv.; BÖCKING, vol. ii.; WAGENSEIL, *U. v. Hutten nach seinem Leben*, etc., Nuremberg, 1823; MEINERS, *Ueber das Leben und die Verdienste U. v. Huttens*, in the *Lebensbeschreibungen berühmter Männer*, vol. iii. pp. 322 sqq.; and (in apology for Erasmus) STOLZ, *Ulr. v. Hutten gegen Des. Erasmus*, etc., Aarau, 1813. See STOCKMEYER, *l.c.*

man to his friend Abbot Russinger, at the baths of Pfäfers. Hutten returned thence to Zurich uncured. The quiet island of Ufuan, in the lake of Zurich, now presented itself as his last retreat. Its pastor, Hans Schnegg, a capitulary of Einsiedeln, and a man of some experience in the healing art, tried his skill upon him, but in vain. In the last days of August this man, who had been so tossed about by the waves of destiny, yielded to his last illness at the age of thirty-five years and four months. His pen and his knightly sword were almost the only things that he left behind him. His grave is unknown, for the cloister of Einsiedeln, to which Ufuan belonged, would not suffer the stone to remain which a Franconian knight had placed upon the last resting-place of the wanderer within a few years after his death.

Let us now return to Erasmus. In his writing against Hutten he had spared no opportunity to assure the world that he did not share the opinions of Luther and his party, and the time speedily arrived when he was to be seen in open combat against the latter. To this step Luther's previously-mentioned controversy with Henry VIII. of England gave occasion. That monarch, having discovered that it was impossible to effect anything against the Reformer, persuaded Erasmus to espouse his cause. The latter, already irritated by the polemical writings which had passed between the two opponents, and incited by the Papal party, at last took up his pen with the intention of writing against Luther. He wisely chose a subject the treatment of which would in no wise derogate from his dignity in the eyes of the enlightened and cultured—one which, on the contrary, afforded him an opportunity to exhibit a liberal mode of thought, which yet was in harmony with the Church and in contrast to that which he regarded as the dull, monkish theology of Luther.

Luther's creed in relation to the doctrine of grace and free-will was, as we already are aware, strictly Augustinian. He, together with the patron saint of his order, maintained that original sin has destroyed every particle of good in man, and entirely taken away his freedom of will. To Erasmus, with his style of philosophizing, this doctrine necessarily appeared irrational and dangerous, and he believed that in it he had found the weak spot of Lutheranism, where he might the most readily give the system its death-stroke. In the year 1524, therefore, he wrote his treatise on *Free-Will*, to which Luther replied by his tractate on the *Bound Will*, and which called forth a still further exchange of writings, evidencing plainly that the two men took their departures from entirely different points of view, and hence necessarily apprehended the weighty question in entirely different ways. Erasmus apprehended it as a question of the schools; to Luther it had become a vital question of the highest import. Erasmus answered it from abstract Scholastic notions; Luther replied to it from the experience of his heart. Of this experience Erasmus had no conception; it was therefore impossible for him to follow his opponent into the depths of a mystery which must needs be understood from within. The controversy accordingly led to no result. Erasmus abode by his rationalistic, and Luther by his supernaturalistic conception of the matter. The latter was firmly convinced that Erasmus understood nothing of grace, because he had not passed through the school of temptation and of the Cross; and it was on the basis of this view that he explained his entire reformatory system, of which worldly wisdom seemed to be the guide.

A better understanding existed between Erasmus and *Zwingle*—the Swiss Reformer, by his predominantly humanistic tendency, offering to Erasmus more points of contact than were presented by Luther. Henry Loriti (Glareanus), who had been on friendly terms with Zwingle from his youth, specially contributed, as the "shadow of Erasmus" (thus a modern historian entitles him), to the maintenance of a good feeling between the two. He defended his aged friend against the suspicions which severe judges raised against his character, and endeavoured to restore the balance of friendship whenever it threatened to be disturbed by intermeddlers. We therefore believe that we shall best conclude our examination of Erasmus by introducing a passage from a letter written by Glareanus to Zwingle on the 20th of January 1523 :[1] "Erasmus is an old man, and longs for repose. Each party would fain win him for its own, but he is unwilling to belong to any party. And which could prevail upon him to join it ? *He sees plainly whom he should avoid, but whom he should join he knows not.*" Glareanus, furthermore, testifies that Erasmus constantly confessed Christ in his writings, and declares that he never heard anything pass his lips that was inconsistent with Christianity.

Let us now resume the thread of our history of the Reformation of Zurich.

As in Wittenberg, so in Zurich, the impurer elements of the Reformation might be seen associated with its purer qualities, and a false external zeal of liberty mingled in the work of wholesome correction—only with this distinction, that in Zurich there was need not only to ward off, by decided measures, something that had pressed in from without, but also prudently to prevent the development of the evil germ within. If the German Reformation at first exhibited itself in its purity—we might almost say in its ideal form—in the personality of Luther, becoming spotted with a coarser earthly admixture only after it had become the property of the community, the task of the Swiss Reformers, on the other hand, was to guide and restrain that which had proceeded immediately from the people, and to conduct the tumultuous torrent into a safe channel.

A misapprehension of Christian liberty was evidenced in Zurich by a few burghers, who not only themselves opposed the ecclesiastical fasts, but also endeavoured to force their dependents to eat flesh on the appointed fast-days.[2] The municipal authorities, desiring to quell these disorders, com-

---

[1] *Opp.* vii. p. 263. Comp. Mörikofer, *Zwingli*, vol. i. pp. 181, 182.
[2] Wirz, vol. iv. p. 217. Röublin, who had been exiled from Basel, took a prominent part in these disorders.

missioned Zwingle and his colleagues to instruct the people in their sermons in regard to the disputed point. Zwingle not only complied with this requisition in his discourses, but also issued a printed treatise,[1] wherein he, in accordance with the example of the Apostle Paul, who had to contend against similar misunderstandings, showed that true Christian liberty consists not in external things,—in eating and drinking,—but in the renewal of the inner man. In spite of this discreet procedure on the part of Zwingle and the Government, the Bishop of Constance made a great noise over what had occurred, and sent a spiritual deputation to Zurich, consisting of Melchior Vattli, the suffragan bishop, John Wanner, the cathedral preacher, and Dr. Brendli, in company with whom Zwingle appeared before the assembled council. He appealed to his manner of preaching, which was well known to the members of the council, they being for the most part eager listeners to his discourses, and himself proposed to the Government to allow the continuance of the fasts as an external ecclesiastical ordinance until such time as there should be a general agreement in regard to them, based upon free Christian conviction. The Bishop of Constance, however, was not satisfied with this arrangement, but issued a pastoral letter to all the priests and laymen of his diocese, greatly lamenting that such disorders should arise just at this particular time, when the Turks were assailing Christendom; he complained exceedingly that in every place the learned and the unlearned were disputing with each other about divine things,—about the mysteries and ceremonies of the Church,—and he prescribed a special form of prayer, to be used at each celebration of the mass, in deprecation of the evils threatening from the new doctrine. He also sent a separate letter on the same subject to the prior and chapter of Zurich. The bishop was supported in his efforts by the Diet, which was assembled at Lucerne, and which issued a mandate interdicting preaching to all those

---

[1] *Von Untersehied der Spysen, von Aergerniss und Verböserung*, Schuler and Schulthess, i. 1.

preachers who, according to *its* opinion, disturbed the peace and created dissensions. Zwingle and his friends, meanwhile, endeavoured to adjust all differences through the medium of friendly instruction. They wrote letters of admonition to the bishop and to the whole Confederacy, in which they essayed to demonstrate the necessity of a reformation.[1] But this procedure excited their opponents to still more violent measures. Several of the adherents of Zwingle were accused and deposed from their offices. His own life was several times attempted, and he owed the frustration of the plots of his enemies to nothing save the kind guidance of Providence and the vigilance of his friends.[2] The number of these true friends and admirers of Zwingle was visibly increasing. Leo Juda had arrived at Zurich during the period of which we speak, and was preaching at St. Peter's the same doctrines that Zwingle proclaimed in the minster; Caspar Grossmann was holding forth in the hospital; Simon Stumpf at Höngg, Ulrich Pfister at Uster, and many others besides were publishing the truths of the gospel. Controversies were carried on not in writing only, but also in the pulpit, and it even happened at times that the preacher was interrupted and taken to task by his hearers in the midst of his discourse. Thus Leo Juda once interrupted an Augustinian monk who had been abusing the new doctrine. It must be confessed that the house of God was not the place for such discussions, and it was therefore deemed advisable to call for a special disputation at a proper time and place. This step Zwingle prevailed upon the Government to take. The latter accordingly summoned all the clergy of its jurisdiction to appear at the council-house of Zurich on the 29th of January 1523, when efforts would be made to arrive at the truth through the medium of learned discussions between the two parties. The Bishop of Constance and the deputies of the states assembled at Baden, as well as a number

---

[1] See the writing entitled, *Ein fründlich Bitt und Ermanung etlicher Priester der Eidgenossenschaft*, etc., Schuler and Schulthess, vol. i. p. 30.

[2] See WIRZ, vol. iv. pp. 234 sqq.

of learned men belonging to the neighbouring cantons, were likewise invited to this "*disputation*," which was to be carried on in German. From Bern came Sebastian Meyer, and from Schaffhausen, Dr. Sebastian Wagner (Hofmeister). Œcolampadius, on the other hand, declined the invitation to attend. He had become convinced of the fact, the truth of which experience afterwards confirmed, that, as a rule, little results from such public religious conversations; although these Zurich disputations, particularly the second of them, might be regarded as an honourable exception to the generality. "What," exclaims the peace-loving Œcolampadius, "does a disputation produce except contention? What is the fruit of contention but open quarrels? What result have these other than hatred? And where hatred is, how can truth find entrance?"[1]

Early on the morning of the 29th of January 1525, about six hundred foreigners and natives assembled at the council hall of Zurich. There were present among the number several doctors and prelates from foreign Universities. Burgomaster Röust opened the proceedings with a speech, inviting any who desired to enter the lists against Master Zwingle. Faber, the vicar of the Bishop of Constance, then endeavoured to show that this was not the place for a dispute on matters of faith. If Zwingle, as a private individual, would visit him at Constance, he would receive him hospitably and treat him with all possible kindness, but he had no mind to dispute. The Catholic doctrine had been as it now was for ages, and should therefore not be changed. Furthermore, they should wait, he said, for the immanent action of the Diet of Nuremberg and for a general council, or, if they were disposed to dispute, they should carry on their debates at the Universities of Cologne, Paris, or Louvaine.

Zwingle, however, in reply to these words of the vicar,

---

[1] *Quid parit disputatio quam disceptationem? quid disceptatio? lites; quid lites? odium. Ubi odium, quomodo veritati salvus est locus?*—The words appear in a letter of 21st January to Hedio. Comp. above, Melanchthon's views on the discussion of Leipsic.

reminded the assembly that it was no question of antiquity and custom that engaged their attention on the present occasion, but one of truth itself, thus answering as Luther answered the pope's letter to the Diet of Nuremberg. As for the councils for which Faber proposed to wait, the synod of pastors there assembled was as valid a council, he affirmed, as any council of bishops, for in the ancient Church a bishop signified nothing more than an overseer, watchman, or pastor; and Christ had declared, "Where two or three are gathered together in my name, there am I in the midst of them." The opinion of Universities might, he said, be dispensed with, as there were as many learned men at Zurich as could be found in any of the above-mentioned schools. The Holy Scriptures constituted their standard of judgment. These were to be obtained at Zurich in the Latin, Greek, and Hebrew tongues; the grand requisites, therefore, were an accurate knowledge of the languages and a just interpretation. Faber, on the other hand, claimed that it might not be required that every pastor should understand the original languages of the Bible. The apostle himself declared that there were many gifts, and the *gift of languages* is a special one—a grace or gift of which he could not boast, "as he was inexperienced in the Hebrew tongue, ill instructed in the Greek, but tolerably proficient in the Latin."[1]

When Zwingle had finished his speech, the burgomaster once more invited any in the assembly who might have objections to urge against the new doctrine to present them now. Zwingle himself seconded this invitation. For a long time, however, no one would venture upon the assault. At last the voice of a spectator on the threshold was heard saying: "Where are the great men who boast so valiantly in the streets? Let them come forward; here is the man whom they abuse. Ye can all talk over your wine, but there is none who will dare bestir himself here." There ensued a

[1] Comp. the acts of the disputation, as given by Hegewald, in Schuler and Schulthess, i. pp. 105 sqq., and additions therein cited.

general peal of laughter, and Faber, to save his honour, must needs, willingly or unwillingly, engage in a discussion. The principal subjects of dispute were the intercession of saints and the mass. Besides Zwingle and Faber, Meyer of Bern, Hofmeister of Schaffhausen, and Dr. Blansch of Tubingen took part in the discussion. It would lead us too far from our immediate path to follow the course of this disputation. The same thing was observable here as at the Leipsic disputation, and as at all subsequent discussions, viz. that the disputants entertained different opinions in regard to the very premises from which they were to start. Thus some appealed to the Holy Scriptures as the one ground of belief, whilst others referred to the traditions of the Church, the authority of ecclesiastical assemblies, etc. The Council of Zurich, which had ere this, in the year 1520, issued an order to the effect that all preaching should be in accordance with the Scriptures, now published the following decree:—" Since no one has been able from the Holy Scriptures to convict Master Ulrich Zwingle of heresy, he shall continue, as heretofore, to proclaim the holy gospel and the genuine divine Scriptures in accordance with the Spirit of God, and to the best of his belief and ability. Furthermore, all other priests, pastors, and preachers in the city and in the country shall neither undertake nor preach anything save what they can prove from the holy gospel and the true divine writings, and shall, moreover, refrain from all abusive language." Upon the issue of this decree of the council, Zwingle exclaimed, " Praise and thanksgiving be unto God, who will cause His holy word to have the mastery in heaven and on earth! God Almighty will doubtless give unto you, my lords of Zurich, strength and might on still other occasions to maintain the truth of God, the holy gospel, in your portion of our land, and to further its preaching. Of this entertain no doubt, the almighty and eternal God will reward you. Amen."[1]

[1] Descriptions of the discussion appeared on both sides (see Schuler and Schulthess, *l.c.*). Nor was there any lack of fugitive pieces of satire on the

There is one notable feature of this discussion to which we must call attention, and which will give us some idea of the paucity of theological studies during that time. When Zwingle was insisting upon the duty of every pastor to read the Holy Scriptures, or at least the New Testament, in the original, one of the clergy present asked, "How shall a pastor who has but a small living raise enough money to purchase a New Testament?" To which Zwingle replied, "There is no priest so poor as to be unable to buy a New Testament if he has a desire to learn. Or it may be that he will find a pious burgher or some other person who will buy him a Bible, or else lend him money that he may get one for himself."

Soon after the discussion, several steps were taken at Zurich in order to the realization of the Reformation. A beginning was made by the nuns in the cloister of Œtenbach. Zwingle had for some time been preaching to them, and several entertained a desire to leave the cloister, which desire was granted. The monks in the cloister of Kappel at first undertook to bring about a reformation amongst themselves, after which several of them quitted the monastery and entered into the estate of matrimony; those who were learned became pastors, and the unlearned adopted some useful trade.

A better spirit also commenced to manifest itself in the chapter of canons, which had previously been adverse to Zwingle. The majority of the canons expressed to the Government their desire to make some better disposition of their time than they had done heretofore. Instead of the hour chants and the performance of lifeless ceremonies, it was proposed that edifying studies and scientific pursuits should henceforth be the object of this association, in conformity to the original design of its founder, Charlemagne. The foundation was accordingly turned into an academic institution, calculated especially for the preparation of future theologians.

subject. To the latter class pertains the *Gyrenrupfen* ["Plucking the Vulture"], which several burghers of Zurich composed against Faber. Comp. HALLER'S *Bibliothek*, iii. pp. 74 sqq.

It received a constitution fully adequate to the exigencies of the time, and which lasted until the first decades of the present century.

It was, however, not the intention of the Reformers to stop at the reformation of individual institutions. The public service of God was subjected to manifold and increasing changes. In the place of the Latin services, German singing and a German liturgy were introduced. In the administration of the sacrament of baptism, superfluous and superstitious rites were omitted. In this particular the Reformed Church outstripped the Lutheran, which for a long time retained the ceremony of exorcism, for instance. But even these were but isolated steps toward reformation. The attention of the church-going community was now claimed by two subjects of prime importance, which had hitherto, more than anything else, captivated the senses—we refer to the *mass* and *images*. In reference to the former, it was Zwingle's desire first to prepare the minds of the people by written treatises. In regard to the images, he was anticipated by a man who subsequently exhibited a mental tendency similar to that of Karlstadt and the Zwickau prophets: his name was Ludwig Hetzer. He issued a pamphlet with the following title: *Urtheil Gottes, wie man sich mit den Bildern halten solle* ["The judgment of God in regard to the treatment of images"]. This violent production created a great uproar among the people, and led to steps similar to those whose occurrence at Wittenberg we have deplored. An iconoclastic storm burst forth, in which a cobbler called Nicholas Hottinger took a leading part, expressing himself in a truly Vandal-like spirit. He would gladly, he declared, present a cask of wine to the hospital if he might be permitted to destroy all the paintings and votive tablets in the Wasserkirche.[1] This man and his

---

[1] He seems, according to Bullinger, to have been possessed of some education. But it was just that half-culture that led, in those days as well as in these, to radicalism. Comp. HOTTINGER (JOHN VON MÜLLER's continuation), vol. vi. p. 450.

band rushed through the city. A large crucifix in the Stadelhof, near the upper gate of the city, was overturned, and others would have shared its fate if a check had not been put upon these proceedings. Hottinger's associate, Laurence Hochrütiner, had previously been guilty of similar conduct. With a few of his associates he had broken into the minster of Our Lady, dashed the ever-burning lamp to pieces, poured out the oil, and, with mocking gestures, sprinkled his companions with it. The Government could not permit such outrages to pass unpunished. The perpetrators of them were arrested and committed to prison; their sentence was suspended, however, until a clear opinion, in accordance with the word of God, should be arrived at concerning the sanctity of images. Accordingly a second discussion was appointed for October, to which the bishop and the cantons of the Confederacy were again invited. Several declinatures and excuses were sent in on this occasion, as on the former one; yet at this time, as before, men of importance appeared, such as Joachim von Watt (Vadianus), of St. Gall, upon whom, in connection with Christopher von Memmingen (a native of St. Gall) and Sebastian Hofmeister, the presidency devolved. There were present about nine hundred persons, about three hundred and fifty of whom were clergymen.

The course of this discussion is remarkable in the extreme. In it a variety of opinions were expressed, even amongst the *friends* of the gospel, relative to images and their use in the Church, and also in regard to fasting and other things. Forasmuch as voices were heard—such, for instance, as those of Simon Stumpf and Conrad Grebel—inclining, in every respect, to a fanatical radicalism, and which, whilst they appealed to pretended inspirations of the Spirit, exhibited mindfulness of no external commands, it is doubly refreshing to listen to the voice of moderation from the lips of another man, who, with evangelical wisdom and clemency, undertook to allay the storm, and, even at the risk of being misunderstood by Zwingle and his friends, steered towards the true mean. This was

Conrad Schmid of Küssnacht, commander of the Knights of St. John.[1] He was a man after God's own heart, pious and sedate, moved by no passion, of a tranquil mind and dignified exterior, temperate in speech and action. He was the son of a farmer of Küssnacht. Although a few years the senior of Zwingle, he was united to him by ties of the closest friendship, and through him had become acquainted with the writings of Luther. This individual delivered a discourse, in which he undertook to demonstrate that all our actions should be founded upon God's word and the pure gospel. These teach us to know Christ as the one Mediator, to whom alone honour is due. If, then, we have recourse to the saints, and honour them instead of the living Christ, we are certainly guilty of idolatry. And it is this false belief in the saints which must first of all be removed, if possible, through the preaching of the divine word. The removal of this belief must precede the abrogation of visible images, which are of less consequence. "We should not," remarked this judicious speaker, "snatch from the grasp of the weak the staff upon which he is leaning without giving him a substitute for it, otherwise we should fell him to the earth. Granting that it is a wavering reed upon which he is reposing, suffer him to retain it in his hand, and show him at the same time a strong staff; he will then of his own accord let the reed drop, and will stretch out his hand for the strong staff. Thus let the timorous and the weak keep the images to which they cling, and *inform* them that there is no life, holiness, or grace in them. Then let a strong staff be exhibited,—Christ Jesus, the one Comforter and Helper of all troubled ones,—and they will themselves find that they no longer need the images, and will gladly let them go and lay hold on Christ. He who has Christ's true image in his heart cannot be harmed by an external image, even if he be still dependent upon it. The Apostle Paul himself let the images of the Athenians alone, and taught simply that

---

[1] Comp. the canons' New Year's book for the youth of Zurich, which is furnished with a portrait of the man, 1825.

there was no grace or divinity in them." Schmid expressed similar sentiments in regard to the custom of fasting. This was also a case in which we should refrain from giving offence to a weak brother. Here, also, he appealed to the example of the apostle, who said that he would rather eat no flesh all his life than offend a brother. Only in matters essential to faith should we dread no offence.

Excellent and well meant as these exhortations were, they did not meet with universal approval, and Zwingle himself was dissatisfied with them. And, indeed, it is always difficult to decide, at epochs of importance, how far the system of moderation is advisable, and to what extent that which commends itself to the unprejudiced intellect in times of tranquillity may be employed when minds are heated and already distracted in the direction of one or the other extreme. The post of a mediator—even one who is endued with the fullest privileges—is always in such a case difficult to fill, and the peaceful doctrinist finds the ear of the multitude closed, whilst the eyes of all are fastened upon the mouth of the enthusiastic party orator, who, with decisive energy, steers right or left towards his goal. The intentions of the commander were certainly the best and sincerest in the world. His yieldingness was not the timid and calculating compliance of an Erasmus, but resembled that which was afterwards shown by Melanchthon,—the yieldingness of the Christian sage, who, from love to Christ and His peace, not from the fear of man and the love of the world's peace, avoids harshness and violence. And yet we cannot think hardly of Zwingle and Sebastian Hofmeister for their inability completely to concur in the milder sentiments of their friend, especially at this decisive moment. Hofmeister interrupted the commander by remarking that he confined himself too much to generalities, and thus evaded the matter that at present claimed their attention; and Zwingle made the following observation: "The assertion of my lord and brother the commander, to the effect that every one should first receive instruction through the divine word, has my entire approval, and I hope that Leo and I have not been negligent in imparting such instruction; but God forbid that we should call images, staves or sticks for the timid and feeble. Had the useless priests and bishops preached the word of God commended to them as earnestly as they have run after useless things, matters would never have come to such a pass that the poor layman must learn to know Christ from the wall and from pictures."

Zwingle would not allow that the example of Paul among the Athenians (cited also by Luther against the prophets of Zwickau) was applicable here. The Athenians, he affirmed, were heathen who knew no better, but it was a different thing in the case of Christians. It was the duty of such to know better, and abuses among them were therefore the less tolerable. Moreover, if the abolition of unprofitable customs were to be deferred until offences should cease, such customs would never be abolished. Nor do we ever, continued he, attain to such internal goodness that victory over all external evil follows thence as a matter of course. We should therefore give ear to the clear declaration of Scripture, which tolerates no images—least of all those of gold and silver, whose value puts them beyond the reach of the poor.

The commander professed himself satisfied with this reasoning.

In the afternoon a similar discussion was carried on with regard to the mass. Zwingle called the disputation relative to images a "childish affair" in comparison with that relating to the mass, which he regarded as a "dispute of prime importance." In the latter discussion, as well as in the former, various modifications appeared in the views of the Reformed party. Commander Schmid could not rest satisfied with that view which regards the Lord's Supper as a mere memorial feast. He looked upon the consecrated elements not as simple memorial signs, but as seals and tokens of the grace of God, and held that in partaking of those elements we receive something from God rather than render aught to Him. On this very account he could not regard the mass as a *sacrifice*. He claimed, however, that care should be taken not to enter upon too general a subversion of established usages before the people had been instructed. Some had spoken too harshly in declaring that the mass was *of the devil.* "We who dwell in the country," he continued, "must frequently hear grosser expressions than come to the ears of you who reside in the city." Zwingle himself confessed that some rather harsh utterances of his own might have led to gross exaggerations, which he much regretted. There were many, he said, who caught up only the severe expressions in his sermons. In this respect his experience was like that of Luther, for numbers, he declared, "learn nothing from the books of that well-instructed man save the sharpness (*Räsi*) of his words; few make account of his pious, faithful heart, with its love for the truth and for God's word." Nevertheless, error must be combated. And thus upon this point also a dispute arose between the parties. Pastor Steinlin of Schaffhausen defended the doctrine of the sacrificial nature of the Lord's Supper, appealing to the Old Testament in support of his opinion. He beheld in the action of the priestly king Melchizedek, who "brought forth bread and wine" at the return of Abraham from the slaughter of the kings (Gen. xiv. 18–20), a type of the sacrifice of the mass. Zwingle, however, discovered nothing in this presentation of food to Abraham and his train other than would be implied "if our faithful brethren of this Confederation were to come hither, and we were to set wine and bread before them in token of our friendship."[1] Here also the violent party were for pressing impetuously forward. Grebel wished for the immediate abolition of the mass; Zwingle was in favour of devolving the further prosecution of the matter upon the magistracy.

[1] Steinlin also objected to Zwingle's explanation of the words of institution, in which explanation he gave *is* the signification of *imports*. He pointed to a portrait of the mayor which hung in the saloon, remarking that, although it was a picture, no one would say, "That *imports* the mayor;" they would say, "That *is* the mayor." A picture or figure is more than a sign.

Subordinate questions of greater or less importance were also discussed. Balthasar Hubmeier demanded that, instead of the Latin reading of the mass, the vernacular should be employed in the celebration of the Lord's Supper, since Christ certainly did not converse with His disciples in Hindostanee [*Calicuttisch*] at the institution of the sacrament. In this demand Zwingle concurred. On the other hand, the latter regarded some things as of little consequence, upon which Grebel and his sympathizers laid too great stress. Some, for instance, were desirous of substituting ordinary (leavened) bread for the unleavened wafer. The unleavened bread was retained. Furthermore, Grebel declared that it was an abomination to mingle the sacramental wine with water, after the Romish custom. He also objected to the custom of placing the bread in the mouth of the communicant, and desired that it should be put in the hand of each one, for "we (the laity) are as much entitled to touch the body of Christ as are the priests." The self-communion of the priests was also discussed.

Touching the principal subject of the day, it was agreed that a stop should be put to that head and front of abuses, the traffic in masses.

In conclusion, the excellent commander, Schmid, addressed the assembly. After having moved that nothing should be done too hastily, he turned to those members of the Government who were present, with the following words:—"You, gentlemen, have heretofore helped many a worldly prince to the possession of his domain for the sake of money. Now, for God's sake, help Christ, our Lord, to regain possession of *His* dominions, that He alone may be worshipped, honoured, and invoked throughout your jurisdictions, that He alone may rule in us Christians, and that He may be esteemed by your people as the one true Mediator, Redeemer, and Saviour, to fulfil which offices His Father gave Him. Charge yourselves with this cause as brave and Christian men. If Christ were suffered to be the only Lord and Master over all things, and quietly to complete His work in us, we should enjoy brotherly tranquillity, Christian peace, and the divine favour and grace here in time, and in the world to come everlasting life. May God give the same to you and all Christians! Amen."

And the same Sebastian Hofmeister, who had previously interrupted him as an opponent, joined in the amen of the godly speaker with the words: "Blessed are the utterances of thy mouth!"

Vadianus having inquired whether any one else in the assembly was desirous of speaking, Zwingle again rose and said: "Gracious lords, and all of you, dear brethren, I beseech you earnestly to hold fast to the word of God. The Lord will not forsake him who thus acts. I have heard with pain that it was reported here and there last evening that we were proposing to put the body and blood of Christ into sleeping cups. Surely no one would entertain such a thought as this!" The idea of being thus misunderstood was so painful to him that he could not refrain from tears, and his friend Leo was obliged to go to his relief. The latter made the following remarks: "If God will, we will all of us abide by the gospel, and gladly will I lay down my life for it if there be need. They may kill the body, but they cannot kill the soul. But let us never use the Scriptures for strife or vainglory, but for the amendment of our lives. And if I have spoken harshly to any one in the course of this discussion, I beg that I may be pardoned for so doing." Zwingle also begged once more that his "clumsy words" might be forgiven.

The presidents then resigned their office, and Vadianus expressed the hope that the Government would find ways and means to maintain the word of God without giving offence to the weak. Röust, the aged burgomaster, who had stood at the head of affairs for eighteen years, promised that this should be done. "I myself," he modestly declared, "pass sentence upon spiritual things as a blind man judges of colours. Such being the case, however, we must seek for counsel in the word of God. Do all of you pray with me that His grace may be with us."

Under the influence of this exalted state of feeling, the men who had been arrested for the commission of the above-mentioned excesses were recommended to the mercy of the council, the disputants cordially shook hands, and separated in peace.[1] Few discussions have had so edifying and satisfactory an issue as this second disputation of Zurich in October 1523.

[1] Comp. on this second disputation, Schuler and Schulthess' edition of *Zwingle's Works*, vol. i. pp. 459 sqq.

CHAPTER XIII.

IMMEDIATE CONSEQUENCES OF THE SECOND DISPUTATION OF ZURICH—BANISHMENT AND MARTYRDOM OF HOTTINGER—HIS LAST STRUGGLES—THIRD DISPUTATION—ABOLISHMENT OF THE MASS AND OF IMAGES—A EUCHARISTIC CONTROVERSY PREVIOUS TO LUTHER'S (JOACHIM AM GRÜT)—ZWINGLE'S CELEBRATION OF THE SACRAMENT; AND HIS LITURGY—ZWINGLE'S SERMONS (ON THE CLEARNESS AND CERTAINTY OF THE DIVINE WORD; AND THE SHEPHERD).

THIS second conference at Zurich (October 1523) was attended with blessed results for the work of the Reformation. It was necessary to inflict some punishment upon the persons who had occasioned a disturbance in the matter of the images, but their sentence was of a mild character. Hottinger, the cobbler, who had been the most culpable of those who were engaged in the affair, was banished for two years. Unfortunately, however, he fell into the hands of the Confederates in Baden, and was put to death by them in spite of Zurich's intercession in his favour. His request that he might speak once more to the people from the scaffold was rudely rejected. "We are not here to be preached to," said the amman of Uri, Jacob Troger; "we will have no prating. Away with him!" The syndic of Lucerne said: "His head must come off once; but if it grows on again, we will adopt his faith." To this Hottinger replied: "Be it unto me according to the will of God; may He forgive all who are against me and who are instrumental in my death. To the Lord upon the cross it was said, 'Come down, and we will believe on Thee.'" The crucifix that was held before his eyes he rejected with contempt, and pointed from the wooden cross to the true cross through which we obtain salvation—namely, Christ's sufferings and death. To the bystanders he said: "Weep not for me, but for yourselves." He repeated the Lord's Prayer and the Creed with great earnestness, and commended his spirit into the hands of his God and Redeemer.

The authorities of Zurich now proceeded without delay to the accomplishment of a reformation in accordance with law and order. Zwingle was commissioned to draw up instructions for the proclamation of the divine word, which were henceforth to be followed by all preachers.[1] These instructions, together with the proceedings of the disputation, were sent to the Bishop and University of Basel, the Bishops of Chur and Constance, and to the twelve cantons of the Confederacy. As may be imagined, they did not everywhere meet with a favourable reception. A considerable number of assistants and chaplains refusing to perform mass, and the prior and chapter entering a complaint against them before the council, the three pastors of the city of Zurich were commissioned to hand in an opinion as to the proper mode of procedure in regard to the mass and images. It was accordingly proposed[2] that, for the sake of the weak and timid, certain usages of the mass, in reference to liturgical chants and lessons, should be allowed to continue, but that no one should be compelled to retain them; but, above all things, the pure word of God should be earnestly preached, and therefore everything should be removed from the order of the services of the mass which did not, in accordance with the Holy Scriptures, have for its object the promotion of the glory of God and Christ. The images should be abolished, but with all forbearance and tranquillity. This admonition

---

[1] See Schuler and Schulthess, vol. i. p. 541.

[2] Advice concerning images and the mass, Schuler and Schulthess, vol. i. pp. 566 sqq.

was the more necessary in view of the fact that in some of the churches iconoclasm was threatening. (In Zollingen, images and altars had been dashed to pieces at Whitsuntide.) In other churches, on the contrary, there was a disposition to retain the images. These also were to be dealt with in a forbearing manner. If particular churches should agree within themselves to retain their images and tablets for a while, they should be permitted so to do, but upon the condition that there should be no burning of candles in honour of the persons thus commemorated.[1]

But in order to go still farther, and to present to the opponents of the Reformation a final opportunity to make good their cause, a third disputation was appointed for the 13th and 14th of January, which, however, led to no alteration of the resolutions adopted. The adherents of the old religion should be left to their faith, it was decided; but should they set themselves in opposition to the commands of the magistracy, "the way out of their benefices should be shown them." At Whitsuntide of 1524, the Government of Zurich issued a reformation mandate, declaring the abolition of the abuses of the mass, and providing for the preaching of a sermon early in the forenoon of each day, "as the human soul can best be fed from the living word of God." On the feast days the sacrament was to be administered in both kinds, in accordance with the form indicated in the Scriptures, and in the German language. The images were to be abolished. But in order that all might be done in an orderly manner, the magistracy appointed particular persons to whom the business was committed. The sums that had hitherto been expended in the decoration of images were henceforth to be appropriated to the poor, who are created in the image of God. "It is not our intention," the Government affirmed in its mandate, "forcibly to constrain any in matters of faith

---

[1] "Söllend sy doch davor keine Kerzen brennen oder einich Zünselwerk da haben, und sölichen Bildern mit Zünseln noch sunst kein eer anthun" (Schuler and Schulthess, vol. i. p. 582).

teachers, however, must preach nothing but the divine word. To watch that such shall be the case befits our function as magistrates. Finally, there must be a cessation of all abusive and opprobrious language, for it is to peace that we are called. If any man have the true faith, let him thank God for it and teach his brother by a good example with love. Love suffereth long; love uniteth and edifieth all things. If, then, the work be begun in God's name and in hope, He will Himself guide the ship with His own hand."[1]

To the city of Zurich, therefore, incontestably belongs the merit of having, with her powerful example, taken the lead of the other states of the Confederacy in promoting the cause of the Reformation. To this state of affairs the personal presence of Zwingle doubtless contributed; in no greater degree, however, than the courageous spirit of a Government and burgher population conscious of strength adequate to the resistance of attacks from without. A less favourable feeling toward the innovations was manifested in the country than that which obtained in the city; this was owing partly to the unwillingness of some to disturb the old neighbourly relations with Zug and Schwytz, and partly to the circumstance that others, especially those whose territories bordered on the contiguous canton of Baden, were most exposed to the attacks of their opponents. A few districts even petitioned the Government not to be too hasty in its proceedings.[2] "Willingly would we," thus ran the message from Altstätten and Albisrieden, "risk our lives and our property for the sake of the worshipful city of Zurich; but having done this, could we be sure that she would not shut her gates upon us, careless of us forsaken ones?" And the people of Thalweil expressed themselves as follows: "We beseech you, gracious sirs, that you will not, for the sake of one or two persons, be they clerics or laics, begin a war,

---

[1] See HOTTINGER (continuation by JOHN VON MÜLLER), vol. vi. p. 471.
[2] HOTTINGER, l.c. p. 478.

though we are excellently well pleased with all that you have done hitherto."

Not only the country people of Zurich, however, but all the other states of the Confederacy, with the exception of Schaffhausen, looked upon the step that Zurich had taken either as a downright sacrilege, or at least as too precipitate a measure. Notwithstanding that the purer light of Christian knowledge had already, in Basel and Bern, begun to chase the darkness away, the strength requisite for an unconditional decision in favour of the new order of things, and for joining Zurich in the vigorous progress of the latter, was still absent. The forest towns and Freiburg were strongest in their declaration against the action of Zurich; this, however, they were from principle, because of their preference for the old. But Bern, Basel, Soleure, Glarus, and Appenzell assumed a neutral and mediate position. They represented to their sister city in a friendly manner, but still with censure, that it allowed too much influence and too swift progress to the new doctrine. Zurich, however, would not depart from the track which it had commenced to tread, and it speedily had the satisfaction of seeing most of the above-named states, whose sentiments in regard to its course were of a more lenient character, themselves sooner or later brought over to the Reformation.

The Bishop of Constance tried once more to exercise his authority over the renegade city. On the Wednesday before Corpus Christi day, he sent a letter to the Council of Zurich in vindication of the images and the mass. Zwingle was commissioned to reply to this communication, which he accordingly did in the "Christian answer of the burgomaster and Council of Zurich to the most reverend Lord Hugo (Hugo von Landenberg), Bishop of Constance."[1] On the same day on which this reply was sent (it was St. Vitus' Day, June 15), the magistratic measures for the abolition of the images were carried into effect. Everything went on in the most orderly

[1] *Werke*, vol. i. pp. 584 sqq.

manner. The shrines containing relics were opened, and the bones taken out and buried. The bones of even the patron saints of the city, Felix and Regula, were thus interred. Processions also ceased from this time forth. The great procession which on every Whit-Monday had wended its way to Einsiedeln, with cross and banners, went thither no more. The organs were banished from the churches. The voice of singing was silent for a considerable time; though here we have reference not to congregational singing, for that had never been practised, but to the singing of the priests as they celebrated the mass.

The principal change still in anticipation was the transformation of the mass into a simple celebration of the Lord's Supper, in accordance with the design of its institution. At the second disputation, the significance of the sacrament had been discussed in its doctrinal bearings. But even now, at the eleventh hour, as it were, a combatant was announced who undertook to dispute Zwingle's view of the Supper and his apprehension of the words of institution. This individual was the town-clerk (under-secretary), Joachim Am-Grüt by name. The different letters that had been exchanged with the Episcopal See at Constance, etc., had passed through his hands. He had been silent hitherto, but he now felt constrained to speak, fearing that the innovations in matters of faith would bring disaster upon the city of Zurich. He assailed (as Steinlin had already done at the religious discussion) that interpretation of the sacramental words in conformity to which *is* must be regarded as equivalent to *signifies*. So ably did he conduct his cause, that at a further discussion of the subject which took place on the 10th of April, and in which the city pastors and some of the members of the council participated, there was but a feeble majority in favour of Zwingle. This circumstance occasioned the latter so much anxiety that the controverted question followed him even into his dreams, and disturbed his night's repose. While he slept, some one (he was unable more particularly to describe the person[1]) showed him the passage in Ex. xii. 11, where it is declared, "It *is* the Lord's passover." He awoke, sprang out of bed, found the passage, and convinced himself anew of the correctness of his interpretation. On the following Maundy Thursday he preached with joyous confidence on the Eucharist, and regained to his opinion those who had begun to doubt its correctness.

The last doctrinal objection having thus been set aside, measures were taken for the celebration of the Lord's Supper on the Zwinglian platform.

For the altar was substituted the "table of the Lord," which was covered with a simple cloth. A basket containing cakes of bread,[2] which could be broken, was placed upon this table, together with wooden goblets, in which wine was handed about. A most simple ceremony, certainly, when compared with the magnificent ritual of the mass! And yet Zwingle was far from breaking entirely with history and tradition, as he has been ordinarily accused of doing. Such things as seemed to him inconsistent with God's word were mercilessly done away with. But, on the other hand, he manifested his conservativeness in retaining the old lessons, the Apostles' Creed, etc.—ay, he even preserved the old responsories. This ancient Zwinglian liturgy has come down to us, and we take the more pleasure in presenting it in this chapter from the fact that an aversion from everything liturgical is censured by some and lauded by others as a genuine feature of the Reformed Church.[3]

The celebration of the Supper is simply but solemnly and worthily introduced by the following prayer on the part of

---

[1] *Ater an albus fuerit nil memini,* was the expression subsequently used by Zwingle in regard to this occurrence. Nothing but a misunderstanding of this proverbial saying, or malice, could so construe the words as to make them expressive of uncertainty on his part as to whether it was the suggestion of a good or an evil spirit.

[2] "Unraised" (unleavened) bread was employed.

[3] See *Action oder bruch des Nachtmals, gedüchtnuss oder danksagung Christi, wi sy uf Ostern zu Zürich angehebt wird im jar als Zal* MDXXV. (*Werke,* vol. iii. p. 233).

the "watchman" [*Wächter*][1] or pastor:—"O almighty and eternal God, whom all creatures justly honour, adore, and magnify as their Master, Creator, and Father, grant unto us poor sinners that we may with true fidelity and faith render unto Thee that praise and thanksgiving which Thine only-begotten Son, our Lord and Redeemer Jesus Christ, hath commanded us believers in memory of His death; through the same our Lord Jesus Christ, Thy Son, who liveth and reigneth (*rychsnet*) with Thee, in the unity of the Holy Ghost, to all eternity God. Amen."

After the reading of 1 Cor. xi. 20 sqq., the ministers, together with the whole congregation, say, "God be praised." And now follows the responsive service:—

"*The pastor:* Glory be to God on high. *The men:* And on earth peace. *The women:* Good-will towards men (*ein recht gmüt*). *Men:* We praise Thee, we bless Thee. *Women:* We worship Thee, we glorify Thee. *Men:* We give thanks to Thee on account of Thy great glory and goodness, O Lord God, heavenly King, Father almighty! *Women:* O Lord, Thou only-begotten Son Jesus Christ, and Holy Ghost! *Men:* O Lord God, Lamb of God, Son of the Father, that takest away the sins of the world, receive our prayer. *Men:* Thou that sittest at the right hand of the Father, have mercy upon us. *Women:* For Thou only art holy. *Men:* Thou only art the Lord. *Women:* Thou only art the Highest, O Jesus Christ, with the Holy Ghost, to the glory of God the Father. *Men and women* (together): Amen!"

In agreement with the old rubric of the mass, the deacon now utters the peace greeting: "The Lord be with you;" to which the people respond: "And with thy spirit." Then is read the discourse of the Lord contained in John vi. 17 sqq., in which Christ calls Himself the Bread of Life. After the reading of this passage, the deacon kisses the book (this also was retained in accordance with the old custom) and says:

---

[1] It is thus that Zwingle translates the word ἐπίσκοπος (*overseer*). We approximate the words of the prayer to the written language of to-day.

"For this be praise and thanks unto God;" to which the people reply: "Amen." Then follows the Creed, responsively repeated by the men and women, and the Lord's Prayer [*das Vater unser*].[1] The minister then again recites a short prayer and reads the words of institution. After the Lord's Supper has been partaken of, a thanksgiving, taken from Ps. cxiii., follows, it also being read responsively; after which the congregation is dismissed with the words, "Depart in peace."

It may undoubtedly be said that Zwingle, from motives of prudence which dissuaded him from a universal overthrow of ancient customs, here retained more of the old ritual than he would have done had he in this order of divine service been intending to furnish a form for subsequent ages. This liturgy exhibits disconnected remnants and fragments of an old and partly worn-out structure rather than a remodelled form of evangelical worship, drawn up in accordance with a unitous liturgical principle. But it would be injustice to reproach Zwingle for this. The remodelling and revivifying of divine worship, considered in its more artistic phase, must of necessity be left to a later period. The great gain wherein the days of the Reformation rejoiced, and which it is impossible highly enough to appreciate, was the uncurtailed enjoyment of the word of God freely preached. It was, undeniably and with right, upon this *preaching* that greatest stress was laid; nor is it Zwingle the *liturgist*, but Zwingle the *preacher*, who lays paramount claim to our admiration.

Let us take our station for a few moments under Zwingle's pulpit, and hear from his own mouth the testimony of his evangelical sentiments. There are two sermons in particular which call for our attention. One was delivered before the Augustinian nuns of Oetenbach, previous to the first disputation of Zurich, and treats " of the clearness and certainty of the word of God;" the other, whose theme is

---

[1] Thus it is styled in this liturgy, and not (as became the custom in the Reformed Church at a later period) *Unser Vater*.

"The Shepherd," was preached immediately after the second disputation.[1]

In the first of these sermons, Zwingle's posture toward the word of God, in which word his entire reformatory work was rooted, is most clearly presented to our eyes. In face of all who strove violently to suppress God's word, or cunningly to adulterate it, he maintains the idea—the guiding thought of his life and ministry—that the absolute certainty of salvation may be found in the word of God, and found in such a manner as to be intelligible to all who will understand it. Until the time of which we speak, none but monks had been permitted to preach in the nunneries. Now, however, Zwingle preached before the inmates of one of them as a secular ecclesiastic. He vindicated his conduct, in respect of this innovation, in his letter to the prioress and convent of Oetenbach, on sending them the printed sermon. The leading thoughts of the sermon are as follows :—Man was created after the image of God, and for this reason bears within him a yearning after God. Man's looking up to God is a proof that there exists in us some little friendship (kinship), likeness, and resemblance to Him. Plants do not look up to man; they are not of his race. But the lower animals look up to man, with whom they have a certain kinship. Man does fully look up to God, of whose race we are, as Paul teaches us. Besides this yearning of the human soul after God, it has a longing for eternal blessedness. Though history tells of some who did not concern themselves about God and their eternal happiness (as, for instance, the Neros, Sardanapaluses, etc.), such are but melancholy exceptions to the general rule; and even they bore within them the fear of damnation. The "brutish" [*vichisch*[2]] man does not, indeed, perceive the things of the Spirit of God. Man must be renewed after the Spirit of God,

---

[1] To be found in the first volume of Zwingle's German writings. With these may also be compared the sermon on the pure Virgin Mary (1522) and that on divine and human righteousness (St. John's Day, 1523), in the same volume.

[2] Thus Zwingle translates the term ψυχικός, which Luther renders the 'natural" man. [So also the E. V.]

as a man created after God in righteousness and holiness. The outer man must be broken in order to the growth and fashioning of the inner man. This process takes place by means of God's word. He who loves God must also love His word, the word of the heavenly Father. By it the spiritual man is nourished far more vigorously than is the physical man by physical bread. God's word is so sure and strong that everything that He says is done from that very hour in which He utters His word.

We see that Zwingle, in his conception of the "word of God," does not take his departure immediately from the *written* word, as first; to him the word is the living creative word of God, through which all things are made (an idea which he shares with the more noble of the Mystics). He next, however, shows, by pointing to the sacred history of the Bible as contained in the Old and New Testaments, how God's word (revelation) came to man in that form. He regards Christ as the sum of all revelations, and excellently does he present His world-historical import. "Who," he asks, "ever became greater in this world than Christ? Alexander and Julius Cæsar were great, and yet they had scarce half the circuit of the world beneath them. But from the rising and the setting of the sun, there have come to Christ such as have believed on Him. Ay, the whole wide world has believed on Him, and recognised and magnified Him as the Son of the Highest, and His kingdom is without end."

It is true, however, that the word of God must be received with *faith*—*i.e.*, with trust, in a suitable frame of mind.

It is always this unconditional trust in the promises of God—this surrender of the heart, of the whole inner man, to God—upon which Zwingle insists as often as he speaks of faith. It is in the same manner that he regards the miracles. "The whole of the teachings of the gospel," he says, "are nothing but the certain assurance that whatever God has promised He will assuredly perform." Not all, however, have true faith, *i.e.* a true disposition and taste for the divine word: "A good strong wine is relished only by a healthy person; such a one is cheered and strengthened by it—it warms all his blood; but one who lies sick with a wasting disease or a fever dare not taste it, let alone drink it: he wonders, rather, that those who are in health can like it. Now this is not the fault of the wine, but of the disease." The greatest punishment that God can inflict upon man is to deprive him of His word (for a time), just as a father most sensibly punishes his child by refusing to speak to him. None but a filial temper is susceptible to the teachings of the divine word. This assertion proves itself. When did any council need to decree that men must hold God's word to be true? Let the wise and the contentious consider this. God's word commends itself to the honest and truthful mind by reason of the clearness which it has; for "whatsoever is clear must derive its clearness from Him who is clearness itself." Man can receive nothing except it be given him from above. No man comes to Christ save him who has learned to know Him through the Father. Neither doctors, nor church fathers, nor the pope and the Papal See, nor councils, but the Father of Jesus Christ is the true Teacher to whose school we must go. God has hidden things from the wise of this world and revealed them unto babes. To the little and lowly the Lord turns: "He loves not to send up His voice to those that are seated on lofty chargers; and moreover they might not hear Him, by reason of the magnificence of their horses, servants, music, and triumphal shouts." The gospel contains nothing about a throne of Peter. In vain do we seek to support it and keep it firm by means of the gospel. It is not to the men that wear mitres and are clothed in purple (bishops and cardinals) that Christ, who calls Himself the Bread of Life, directs us. The man who is satisfied by *Him* has no more need of the food that those offer him. "Come unto *me*," says Christ (in the text of the sermon), "all ye that labour and are heavy-laden, and I will give you rest." And again Zwingle admonishes: "Put all thy trust in the Lord Jesus; that is, be sure that He who suffered for us is the reconciliation for us before God to all eternity."

Zwingle's apprehension of the gospel was ample, and in conformity to the spirit, not the letter. "Not that alone that was written by Matthew, Mark, Luke, and John, but all that God has ever revealed to men, thereby assuring them of His will," is by Zwingle comprehended in this word "gospel." He declares himself most decidedly against the wresting of isolated passages as proofs for this or that doctrine, and against all those bungling exegetes who "would wantonly force words to suit their own purposes." He says well: "We must not pluck a single floweret from its stalk and plant it rootless in a flower garden; we must dig up its roots, and plant them, together with the earth that adheres to them, in our garden. We must suffer the word of God to retain its own peculiar nature, for only thus can it plant a right sense in thee and in me. Many, however, are 'sewed so tightly into their ass' skin,' that when the natural meaning of a passage is declared to them, and they can make no objection to it, they say that they cannot understand it thus; for it must needs be that many should have a juster understanding of a thing than one or a few (referring to the consent of the fathers, councils, etc.). If this were so, then must Christ be untrue; for the multitude of the priesthood were of a different opinion from Him. Nor can the apostles have been in the right, for whole cities and countries were opposed to them. And even at the present day, unbelievers are ten times more numerous than believers. Is their opinion therefore correct, and ours incorrect? And have not the papal councils erred oft and grievously? Can they not now again be in error? Since, therefore, all men are liars, we find at last none but God who can with perfect security inform us of the truth, in such a manner that we can no longer entertain any doubt thereof. Sayest thou, 'Where shall I find Him?' Seek Him in thy closet, and pray unto Him there in secret—for He seeth thee—that He will give thee understanding of

His truth... Devoutly invoke God's grace upon thyself; pray that He will give thee His spirit and mind, to the end that thou mayest be filled not with thine own thoughts, but with His, and rest assured that He will instruct thee in the true understanding (of the Scriptures), for all wisdom is of God the Lord."

In conclusion, Zwingle beautifully testifies of the method in which he himself arrived at an insight into the word of God.

"I know assuredly that God teaches me; for I have had consciousness of His presence. Do not, I entreat you, misinterpret (*ufrupfen*) this saying of mine. I suppose that in my young days I gained as much from human teachings as my contemporaries, and when I began, seven or eight years ago, to rely wholly upon the Holy Scriptures, the philosophy and theology of the contentious would fain have won many a concession from me. I finally came to the pass of thinking (under the guidance of the Scriptures and the word of God), 'Thou must let all those things alone, and learn God's meaning from nothing but His own simple word.' I then began to supplicate God for His light, when the Scriptures became more intelligible to me (although I read simply them) than if I had read never so many commentaries and expositions. Now that is a sure sign that God is at the helm; for I should never have arrived at such a point through my own slender capacities. You may now see that it was not through any arrogance of mine that I attained to my present convictions, but that it was by making a complete surrender of myself (to God). And so let all art drawn from the philosophers (the Scholastics) meet with its downfall. What philosopher taught the disciples? God chose them as simple and foolish ones to proclaim Himself and His word, that He might shame the wise of this world. The very God who enlightens us gives us to understand that His speech is of God. If thou feel not this, regard thyself as belonging to those who have ears and hear not. And we believe, and ever shall believe, that God's word should be held by us in highest honour (that only is the word of God that comes from the Spirit of God), and that no other word is deserving of such faith as this; for it is certain that it is self-teaching, self-unrolling, that it enlightens human souls with salvation and grace, and causes them to be of good courage in God. Ay, this blessedness begins even in time—if not in its substantial form, yet in the certainty of a comfortable hope. That hope may God increase in us and not suffer to expire. Amen."

Zwingle's apprehension of the office of a preacher and curate of souls is exhibited in his treatise entitled, *The Shepherd*. This work grew out of a sermon which he preached shortly after the second disputation, and sent, in the year 1524, to his friend James Schurtanner (Ceraunolateus), pastor at Teufen. In accordance with the parable of the Lord recorded in the tenth chapter of John, he represents Christ as the Good Shepherd whom we should follow. Avoiding all speculative questions (*heimlichen Verständen*) concerning the incarnation and birth of Christ, he plants himself directly on historical ground, beginning with the things that Christ did and taught after He had manifested Himself to this world (*in diese Welt geöffnet*), from the moment when Simeon took Him in his arms and said to His mother, "Behold, this *child* is set for a fall and rising again of many in Israel, and for a sign which shall be spoken against." For such a destiny as this every shepherd must still hold himself in readiness. He must not allow himself to be withheld from performing his work by the representations of others, even if those others should be his own parents. Even Christ would not suffer the interference of His mother. He says, "Whoso loveth son or daughter more than me is not worthy of me." Like Christ, the pastor must take up his cross and deny himself. It is only when he shall have "emptied" himself that he can be filled with God, putting all his confidence and trust in God. He must proclaim repentance and forgiveness of sins to the world. But he himself, as a good shepherd, must go before the sheep by a good example. He must practise in works what he teaches in words. He must not put on a hypocritical dress, "decking himself outwardly with a cowl, while within he is full of avarice; he must not make low external prostrations and be inwardly of a haughty mind; he must not wear a white frock and be inwardly unchaster than a wild boar; he must not murmur many psalms and forsake the clear word of God," etc. He must, on the contrary, preach nothing but the word of God in accordance with the Holy Scriptures. But the mere learning of the letter of the word will not enable him to do this, unless God incline his heart to put faith in the word and "not to warp it to suit his own views," but to let it work freely as God shall suggest. There is no vice that Christ rebuked with more severity than the dissimulation and hypocrisy of the Pharisees. This vice is still in vogue in the world. The shepherd must take up arms against hypocrisy, and that fearlessly; he must, like Christ, be willing to lay down his life for the sheep. He must not be afraid to face the high and mighty ones of earth and tell them the truth, even as did the prophets of the Old Testament and John the Baptist. Faith and love are the weapons with which he must fight. Where true faith and godlike love are, man knows that to die for God's sake is gain. As a shepherd treats his sheep differently, dealing with each according to its peculiar disposition (striking some, pushing others, piping to others and alluring them to him—ay, taking the weak up in his arms and carrying them), so the spiritual shepherd must do with his sheep, and love will teach him always to resort to the right expedient. True love, however, can be found only with Christ. We cannot attain to it by our own ability and reason. "Therefore let him who would have the love of God, beseech God to give him a true knowledge of His Son, and true trust in Him; for when he has those he has love." And what reward has the shepherd for all this? None other than that which Christ promised to Peter (Matt. xix. 29). But the shepherd's first care must not be his reward. That is the manner of servants, not of sons. Sons work faithfully in their father's service, leaving that father to give them what he pleases.

Zwingle next contrasts the true shepherd with the false. "False shepherds are false prophets—wolves in sheep's clothing. Thus false shepherds even now strive with all pious words to prejudice the powers that be against the faithful, accusing the latter of preaching sedition and the like. They appeal to the Church. But they are not the true Church, any more than Belial is God. They care not for the sheep but for the fleece. They ought to know that God's Church—*i.e.* His flock—should be fed from no other pasture than the word of God. Since that is everywhere abundantly preached, they ought not to lament that there is confusion, but rejoice that the pasture of the divine word is everywhere growing so finely."

Zwingle, after still further developing the figure of the false shepherd, makes the following classification:—To false shepherds belong—1. Bishops who teach nothing at all (and how many such are there!); 2. Those who, though they teach, teach not the word of God, but their own dreams; 3. Those who teach the word of God, yet not to the glory of God, but with a reference of all things to their head, the pope; 4. Those who, whilst they teach the word of God, are careful not to touch heads that are high, from whom offence comes: these are flattering wolves and deceivers of the people; 5. Those who do not practise what they preach; 6. Those who do not take up the cause of the poor, but who suffer them to be oppressed; 7. Those who bear the name of shepherds, but rule after a secular manner: these are the worst of werewolves; 8. Those who gather riches, filling their purse and their pockets, their granaries and their cellars; and lastly, and 9thly, he includes in the category of false shepherds all who look away from the Creator to the creature. This last is a constantly-recurring idea of Zwingle's—that, namely, the base-lying corruption of the Church consists in the deification of the creature. He regards as true idolatry the having recourse to other than God. Papists he looks upon as worse idolaters than the heathen. The latter have but worshipped their gods in images, and have never set up a living man as a god. The Papists, however, have called the pope their God.[1] The reward of false shepherds is indicated in the Scriptures. Though it is not our place to strike them dead without ceremony, they should at least be deprived of their offices. Moreover, if they are not peaceably banished from the land, God can raise up an Elijah who shall in one day slay 450 priests of Baal and 400 priests of the high places [E. V. and G. V., *groves*].

In conclusion, the speaker addresses himself first to the good and then to the bad shepherds. The former he admonishes to perseverance, to patience, to earnest prayer that God will confirm the "mighty" work that He has begun and bring it to perfection. The latter he adjures as follows: "If there is left in you a spark of faith in God and humanity toward men, for God's sake, and for the sake of the human race, spare the poor people whom you have so long caused to suffer hunger and loaded with insupportable burdens. Do not plunge the whole world into confusion to gratify your avarice and love of magnificence. Lean not for support on the reed out of Egypt, that is, on the princes and mighty men of this world. That staff will break in your hand, and wound you sorely. Where does the strength of a king reside except in his people? If the king is not helped to protect you by the people, who are now everywhere in crowds hanging upon the word of God, where is your safety? where the king's strength? God has had patience with you long enough; He will come at last with a rod, and there will be as little prospect of your arising from your fall as there is of Lucifer's return to that heaven from which he was precipitated. Therefore set your hope elsewhere, even on God, the 'Quieter of all hearts.' May He lead you to a knowledge of Him, to the end that you may humble yourselves under the mighty hand and the cross of Christ, and be saved with all the faithful! Amen."

---

[1] That some flatterers, at least, did this, we have already seen. Zwingle admits that the like was done in the old Roman world in relation to the emperors.

CHAPTER XIV.

REVIEW OF THE REFORMATION OF ZURICH — ZWINGLE'S CO-LABOURERS, LEO JUDA, OSWALD MYCONIUS, AND MEGANDER — SYNOPTICAL VIEW OF THE BEGINNING OF THE REFORMATION IN OTHER PORTIONS OF SWITZERLAND : BERN, BASEL, MÜHLHAUSEN, BIEL, SOLEURE, SCHAFFHAUSEN, THURGAU, ST. GALL, APPENZELL, AND THE GRISONS—INTERIOR SWITZERLAND.

THE last chapter showed us that the Reformation of Zurich reached its conclusion by the introduction of an order of divine service of which preaching formed the central point. The Lord's Supper still constituted the acme of this service, though it was no longer, like the old sacrifice of the mass, celebrated every day, but, on account of its high import, was almost exclusively confined to the solemn festivals of the Church, of which it formed, as it were, the crown. Four times a year—at Easter and Whitsuntide, in the autumn and at Christmas—the Lord's Supper was ordered to be celebrated as of old. In this celebration the whole congregation took part, and, as we are informed, in gratifying numbers, whilst the ancient service of the mass could boast of but few adherents. These few supporters of the former system desired that a church of their own might be furnished them for the celebration of the mass, and proposed to take the one that was attached to the cloister; but their request was denied.

We also, in conclusion, made acquaintance with Zwingle's mode of preaching. The utterances of his own mouth must put to silence the oft-repeated charge that the Reformer of

Zurich lacked the religious depth and earnestness that impress us so strongly in Luther. The modes of preaching of the two men are undoubtedly different, and there is a particular charm to cultivated minds in comparing the manner of the one with that of the other. But is not this diversity of gifts in the *one* Spirit something for which we ought specially to give God thanks? *In the one Spirit*—I use the expression intentionally, in view of the accusation that the Zwinglians had a spirit other than that of Luther. At the very foundation of their personalities the two men are in sympathy, although in the method of bringing the internal treasures of their hearts to the consciousness of themselves and of others they may in many respects diverge, in conformity to the variable constitution of their characters, of God's providential dealings with them, and of the stations in life which He assigned them.

Zwingle no more occupied a solitary position in Zurich than did Luther in Wittenberg. We have already precursarily mentioned Leo Juda of Rapperswyl, who was the companion of Zwingle in his studies at Basel (chap. x.). At Whitsuntide 1522, this man, who was settled at Einsiedeln, received a call to the pastorate of St. Peter's at Zurich, whither, in the year 1523, he removed, and was thenceforth the inseparable companion and co-labourer of Zwingle. He was known in Zurich solely by the name of "Master Lion" [*der Meister Leu*]. The powerful voice and heroic courage of the man must, as appears from a letter from Zwingle to Myconius, have corresponded with his name.[1] This very Oswald Myconius, having been driven from Lucerne on account of his evangelical sentiments, assisted, by his acceptance of the post of school teacher at the Frauenmünster, in increasing the number of Zwingle's co-workers. We shall recur to him at some subsequent period. Kaspar Megander (Grossmann), priest at the church of the Dominicans, and James Ceporinus (Wiesendanger), who, as professor of Hebrew, represented the biblico-philological element in the work, also lent a hand to

[1] *Leo iste in Heremo rugiens* (*Epp.* i. No. 19).

seasonable reforms whenever occasion offered. It would require a special history to tell of all the directions in which the spirit of reform manifested itself—of what, for instance, was done in the way of caring for the poor and the sick. Let us dwell for a moment, however, on the so-called branch of "*prophecy*." Under this strange-sounding title, which had reference to the apostle's injunction to the Church at Corinth (1 Cor. xiv.), a series of Bible lessons was introduced and conducted in the following manner. After the offering of a short prayer, sections of the Bible were read aloud in a certain order, and at first explained, after the original text, by the professors [*Lesemeister*], in the narrow circle of the clergy, in the "assembly room of the chapter," being afterwards applied in church to the edification of the whole congregation and the needs of everyday life. These Bible lessons took the place of the canonical hours of the foundation. They were commenced 25th June 1525, under the direction of Zwingle.[1]

We shall now leave the metropolis of Zurich, and examine the further progress of the Reformation in the remaining districts of Switzerland.

At Bern opinions were still divided in regard to Haller and Meyer. Both had been stigmatized as heretics by the Bishop of Lausanne. The Government, however, in order to avoid all disturbances, issued, on the 15th of June 1523, an order similar to that which Zurich had promulgated three years before—to the effect, namely, that nothing but the gospel should be preached. Each party, however, interpreted this decree in its own favour, and there was needed nothing but some outward inducement to call forth fresh disputes. A watch was kept upon the utterances of Meyer and Haller, and anything of a suspicious nature was turned into a pretext for complaint. Thus especially their adversaries seized upon a conversation which, upon the occasion of a visit to the female cloisters on the island, Haller, in presence of Sebastian Meyer

[1] For particulars see GÜDER's article in Herzog's *Realenc.* vol. xii. pp. 232 sqq.

and the theologian Wyttenbach of Biel, had had with the nun Clara May. This conversation related to cloistral life, the merit of which was called in question. Haller was misrepresented as saying that all nuns followed the calling of the devil, and that they therefore belonged to the devil. Such an accusation was sufficient to constitute a capital charge, it being a municipal statute that any one who should seduce a nun from the island was liable to the penalty of death. The enemies of the gospel were not able to accomplish their designs in this instance, however. They did not even effect the banishment of the evangelical teachers—a mode of punishment which was proposed by some as an act of special favour; and the authorities were satisfied with forbidding them to visit the cloisters, and directing them to their *sermons* as the sphere of operation appointed them.

Less forbearance was shown, soon after this, toward the wife of a scholar of considerable note, who had permitted herself to express some doubts concerning the sanctity of the Virgin Mary. This lady was the wife of the celebrated town physician and historiographer, Valerius Anshelm. During a visit to a watering-place, she had asserted, in opposition to a friend of the Papacy with whom she had unwisely entered into a theological discussion, that "Our Lady was nothing but a woman like herself, and that the grace of her Son Jesus Christ was as necessary to her as to the rest of the faithful; therefore *she* could not bestow salvation upon any one." She also defended the marriage of priests, on the ground that the priests in the Old Testament married. As her husband was already hated as a foreigner (he was from Rottweil in Swabia) and an advocate of new doctrines, this unwise utterance of his wife was bruited everywhere, related with additions, maliciously misrepresented, and finally carried before the council. Some were desirous of drowning the poor woman, others proposed to put her in the pillory, and others still were of opinion that she should be banished. She was finally sentenced to pay a fine of twenty florins and to make an apology before the bishop. Her husband refusing to allow her to comply with the latter requisition, his enemies caused him to be deprived of half his salary, and he finally quitted the city in indignation. He subsequently (1525), however, returned to Bern, where he met with an honourable reception, and was appointed town historian. It is from him that we derive the circumstantial and valuable Bernese chronicle which has been republished in modern times.[1]

Though expressions adverse to cloistral life did not meet with the approbation of friends of the ancient customs, and though any who were guilty of such expressions thereby exposed themselves to danger, these facts did not hinder further progress toward a better state of things. That such was the case is shown by the conduct of the nuns of Königsfelden, who, like those in the convent of Oetenbach at Zurich, petitioned the council to absolve them from their vows. The Government believed at first that they were desirous merely of a more comfortable and luxurious life, and granted them many liberties and alleviations, hitherto unenjoyed by them in their convent. To this action, however, they replied that "they craved no favours to the body, but desired that aid should be given to their *spirits* and ease to their consciences; and they petitioned that they might be mercifully remembered and released as innocent prisoners." Their request was granted. An order issued in 1523 left it to the option of every nun either to remain in the convent or to leave it. Several availed themselves of the liberty accorded them, and entered into the state of matrimony.

But new disputes were now about to hinder the work of the Reformation at Bern. The opponents of this work had succeeded in attracting to the city a vigorous champion of the old system, hoping thus to counterbalance the innovations that were daily gaining ground. The Dominican monk John Heim, hitherto a resident of Mentz, was called to the office of

[1] The already-cited edition of STIERLIN and WYSS, in the preface to the first volume of which may be found the information relating to Anshelm.

preacher at the convent of his order in Bern. When the old jealousy of the Dominicans and Franciscans is recollected, it will be readily understood that this measure could not fail to be provocative of quarrels in those excited times, as the Reformer Sebastian Meyer belonged to the order of the Franciscans. Pulpit controversies were speedily introduced; and here, as at Zurich, it happened that listeners took their stand at the foot of the pulpit and contradicted the preacher. When Heim, on one Sunday, affirmed that Christ did not, as the evangelicals taught, make satisfaction for sins once for all, but that, on the contrary, the heavenly Father must daily be reconciled to men by the sacrifice of the mass and by good works, two burghers interrupted him by remarking that "*that was not true.*" Thereupon a great tumult ensued. Heim's adherents encouraged him to go on; he, however, declared that he would prefer to give up preaching if every one was to be allowed to make objections to what he said. The matter was brought before the council, and after a lengthy discussion, in which some took the part of the preacher, while others espoused the cause of his opponents, no agreement could be arrived at, save that both of the controversial preachers, Heim as well as Meyer, should be banished from the city and its jurisdiction—an order which, however, was accompanied by the declaration that this procedure was intended in no wise to derogate from the honour of the preachers. Thus, with Heim, the deserving Sebastian Meyer was also sent away. The latter proceeded to Basel, abandoned his order, married, and soon after went to Augsburg, where for a considerable time he preached the gospel with success, returning to Bern after the Reformation of that city was achieved. Haller was now left alone, and the difficulties of his position increased with the increasing attempts of his enemies to get him also out of the way. He was exposed to plots such as surrounded Zwingle at Zurich, but, like the latter, happily escaped them.[1]

[1] KIRCHHOFER, *Berthold Haller*, p. 49 (after ANSHELM).

Since the establishment of Œcolampadius as assistant at St. Martin's, the pure gospel had continued to put forth its roots in Basel. A circle of evangelical teachers soon gathered about Œcolampadius, actively supporting him by their lectures and other ministries.[1]

The year 1523 passed away amidst the quiet labours of these men, without being marked by any important events— a state of affairs which was due especially to the stringent order of the council, forbidding all remarks of an abusive character from the pulpits of both sides. During this time, a few of the regular clergy quitted their cloisters and former manner of life; among others who thus acted was the learned Conrad Pellican, who took leave of the Franciscan order, and was appointed professor of theology. The year 1524 was one of more marked importance than its predecessor, by reason of the presence at Basel of a man distinguished in history, and the occurrence of two nearly synchronous and weighty disputations.

William Farel,[2] who is justly regarded as a forerunner of Calvin, his reformatory labours having been performed chiefly in France, Geneva, and French Switzerland (Neuenburg), came in this year to Basel. He was born in 1489 at Gap in Dauphiny, and was of noble descent and tolerable fortune; he had been brought up in the strictest principles of the Papacy, yet had with difficulty obtained from his parents, who were involved in the prejudices of the nobility, permission to devote himself to study. Through the influence of his celebrated instructor, James Faber Stapulensis, who had embraced the

---

[1] Pre-eminent among these, besides Wyssenburger, were Marx Berschy of Rorschach, priest at St. Leonard's; Hans Sündli of Lucerne (Lüthard), preacher of the Franciscans; and Thomas Geierfalk from St. Gregory's Valley, preacher of the Augustinians. These were joined somewhat later by Balthasar Vögeli, assistant at St. Leonard's, and Œcolampadius' assistants at St. Martin's, Boniface Wolfhard and Jerome Botanus.

[2] KIRCHHOFER, *Das Leben Wilhelm Farels, aus den Quellen bearbeitet*, 2 vols., Zurich, 1831; C. SCHMIDT, *Etudes sur Farel*, Strassburg, 1834, and *W. Farel und Peter Viret* (in vol. ix. of the *Väter und Begründer*), Elberfeld, 1860; C. JUNOD, *Farel, Réformateur de la Suisse romande et Réformateur de l'Eglise de Neuchatel*, Neuchatel and Paris, 1865.

pure doctrines of the gospel after attaining an advanced age, the ardent youth had himself been won over to these doctrines, and had become strengthened in his convictions by much original thought. At Paris and Meaux he had associated with others like-minded with himself, and had already begun to translate the Scriptures into French. Persecutions breaking out against the adherents of the new doctrine, obliged him, however, to leave France. He sought refuge in Switzerland, whose soil he first touched at Basel, where he encountered his friend Anemund and other refugees. Farel met with a cordial reception at the house of Œcolampadius, at whose instance the Government granted him permission to hold a public disputation, a privilege which had been denied him by the University. Upon this, however, the members of the University had recourse to the episcopal vicar, Henry von Schönau, and obtained from him a prohibition forbidding all priests, students, and any who were connected with the University to take part in the discussion, on pain of excommunication and expulsion. This prohibition had the effect of exasperating the Government, which, instead of *allowing* the discussion as heretofore, now, in defiance of the bishop and the University, actually *commanded* that it should take place, and enjoined it upon all, as a duty, to attend it. The mandates of the Government relating to this subject give evidence of the favour with which it already regarded the Reformation. The mandate of 24th February speaks of Farel's project as originating, " it is to be supposed, in the suggestion of the Holy Spirit," and the propositions submitted by him were found by the council to be " not unseemly, but in accordance with the gospel, and calculated to do good rather than harm to men." The order to appear at the disputation runs as follows : " The council ordains that one and all, and especially pastors, preachers, priests, students, and every one connected with the University, should take part in this disputation. To any person opposing the same, all grinding, baking, buying, and selling privileges, either for himself or his household, shall hereafter be denied; in like manner all beneficiaries or feoffees of the council, setting themselves in opposition to the disputation, shall be deprived of their benefices."

Thirteen propositions were drawn up by Farel, directed chiefly against work-holiness, ceremonies, fasting, and the invocation of saints, and, on the other hand, insisting strongly on faith in Jesus Christ as the only ground of our salvation.[1] "Christ" (it is declared in the first of these theses) "has given us the most perfect rules of life, to which we may not add anything, and from which we may take nothing away." "The vocation of a Christian teacher demands," it is claimed in the fifth thesis, "that such a one should apply himself to the study of the word of God, and pursue it with such zeal as to account nothing higher." "He who doubts the gospel," the seventh asserts, "suppresses it; and he who does not honestly love his brother and fear God more than man, is ashamed of the Lord." "He who hopes for eternal blessedness and justification through his own strength and merits," the eighth thesis teaches, "and not through faith, exalts himself, and, blinded by unbelief, makes himself, by his assumed free-will, a god." "Our guiding-star," says the thirteenth thesis, in conclusion, "should be Jesus Christ, who through His power rules all things, and not any natural star or other element. We hope that this may be the case in the future, when all things shall be regulated in accordance with the rules of the gospel, and all strife, which every Christian must abhor, shall be done away with, to the end that the peace of God, which passeth all understanding, may dwell in our hearts."

"Run," his invitation to the combatants concludes,—" run hither, as the Lord admonishes us, with Christian hearts, and strive that the word of God alone may be victorious. This I

---

[1] These theses may be found in manuscript in RYFF's *Chronik*. Printed copies of the same are to be found in KIRCHHOFER, vol. i. p. 21; in BURCKHARDT's *Reformationsgeschichte von Basel*, pp. 39–41, and *Neujahrsblatt*, 1868, pp. 22, 23, and elsewhere.

admonish and entreat you to do for the sake of our Redeemer, Jesus Christ, who has so earnestly commanded us to care for our neighbour."

The disputation took place in the hall of the University. No record of the proceedings is extant. The issue, however, is announced by a contemporary in the following words:— " Much good came of it. The word of God grew and prevailed greatly. Many Christian teachers arose in consequence thereof."[1] Farel remained several months longer in Basel, where he formed with other congenial minds ties of friendship destined to endure beyond the grave. He subsequently became pastor at Aigle in French Bern. We shall meet him again on Romanic soil.

A few days previous to this disputation, another of a somewhat different character had taken place. The priest of Liestal, Stephen Stör of Diessenhofen, had married, and was desirous of vindicating this step publicly, in a German disputation. A large audience made their appearance on this occasion, and not one of Stör's opponents dared make any objection to his course. On the contrary, several of those who were present supported him in his opinion. Boniface Wolfhard, assistant at St. Martin's, finally took upon himself the rôle of antagonist, simply for the purpose of at least ventilating the arguments usually urged *in favour* of the celibacy of the priests; but Stör refuted his objections, to the perfect satisfaction of Œcolampadius and the rest. This same Stephen Stör, however, like Röublin, subsequently joined the Anabaptists, and, playing the demagogue, excited the Liestalers against Basel during the Peasant War. It is a remarkable fact, and one of general interest, that several of those men, whose sentiments were of a violent cast, laid a preponderant and one-sided emphasis upon the marriage of the priests, as if it were on that alone that salvation depended. This was the case with Karlstadt, Röublin, Stör, and many others. Here, as in other matters, they attached too much importance

[1] Ochs, vol. v. p. 460 ; Kirchhofer, *l.c.* vol. i. p. 24.

to externals, things of sense, which, as natural consequences of an increased liberality of principle, were perfectly right and in order, but which, considered by themselves outside of their connection with the life of faith, might readily assume a self-seeking character, and give occasion to bitter remarks on the part of the opponents of the Reformation. It is matter for regret in our own time that a so-called liberal party in the Catholic Church should pretend to anticipate all good results from the abolishment of celibacy *in itself alone*. While marriage does not *unhallow* the priest of God, neither is it able, *in and by itself*, to *hallow* him, without the presence of something higher, which hallows wedded life itself, and gives to it its Christian consecration. Accordingly, we see that true Reformers—such as a Luther, a Zwingle, an Œcolampadius—did not enter into the estate of matrimony until they had established the work of reformation in its deeper foundations, thus causing the accusation of their antagonists, to the effect that they had reformed for the sake of marrying, to refute itself.

Œcolampadius, who had hitherto discharged his duties at St. Martin's as simple vicar, was in this same year (1524) appointed pastor of the parish, and was soon after created professor of theology: these appointments he received upon condition that he should introduce no innovation in religious matters without the knowledge of the council. The Government, however, showed itself inclined to accede to reasonable changes. It was with its permission that Œcolampadius caused the German language to be employed by his assistant in the administration of the sacrament of baptism, and that, aided by the same assistant, he dispensed the Lord's Supper in both kinds. By his lectures he disengaged the attention of the people from mere external matters, and pointed them to the living Christ; and thus the ostentatious rites of the mass, the processions with crosses, and other vain ceremonies ceased of themselves. On the other hand, there was more diligent attendance upon the week-day sermons, of which the monks affirmed that they smelt of Lutheranism. As regards Œcolampadius' mode of preaching, we have to say that at Christmas of 1523 he began, in pursuance of Zwingle's example, to explain the Holy Scriptures in their connection. Of this practice his "Public Lectures" (Demagories) on the Epistles of John furnish a gratifying evidence.[1]

At about this time the Government (in imitation of the preceding action of Zurich and Bern) issued an order, granting to all monks and nuns permission to quit their cloisters and choose for themselves some honourable employment as burghers. The first who availed themselves of this permission were the regular clergy of St. Leonard's,[2] who, on the 2d of February 1525, solemnly laid aside the robes of their order, and, in consideration of a life annuity (of 62 gold florins) ceded their cloister, with all its immunities, to the Government. Their example was speedily followed by the other convents, including the nunneries.

Hitherto we have considered only Zurich, Bern, and Basel in the condition of ecclesiastical and religious ferment. Let us now turn to the districts and towns in the neighbourhood of these cities, that we may see how attempts to reform the Church were there made and received. Our attention is first engaged by the neighbouring city of Mühlhausen, at that time connected with Basel by a defensive alliance. We know that it was to this place that Ulrich von Hutten repaired after having in vain sought for shelter at the hand of Erasmus. Here he found a few individuals who were already friendly to the new doctrines—namely, James Augsburger, Otto Binder, and Bernard Römer. In the year 1523 these three men submitted to the authorities a written opinion, recommending

[1] *Œcolampads Bibelstunden, volksfassliche Vorträge über den 1 Brief Joh. Aus dem Latein von Christoffel*, Basel, 1850.

[2] The Carthusian monk George contemptuously calls them *religiosuli* (monklings), and regards as a punishment of apostasy the fact that few of them long survived the abandonment of their vows. The sentiment is such as might be expected from one who can never find words sufficient to deplore the desolations occasioned by the "Lutherans."

the substitution of prayers for the daily early masses, the singing of the Psalms in German, the abolition of processions and useless feast days, and the introduction of better morals and discipline among the clergy and laity.[1] This opinion met with much approbation, particularly as the town-clerk, Gamsharst, was favourably inclined toward the gospel, and was soon followed by a corresponding religious mandate; so that the Reformation of Mühlhausen may be regarded as accomplished as early as the year 1524, proof of its achievement being furnished by the fact that from that time the town refused obedience to the Bishop of Basel. It will readily be understood, however, that the people of Mühlhausen could take this step at an earlier period than those of Basel, who lived under the immediate guardianship of the bishop, and were in closer connection with the Helvetic Confederation.

In Biel, another city connected with the Confederation, Thomas Wyttenbach, the former teacher of Zwingle, preached against many abuses of the Church, and married, in 1524, at an advanced age. His example was followed by seven other priests. This circumstance drew upon him the persecutions of the Papal party. He was ousted from his situation, but repaired to a convent, where he preached to crowds of listeners. The number of his adherents was increased by the hostile measures resorted to against him, and the reformatory tendency soon prevailed in Biel to such an extent that it

---

[1] In reference to divine worship this opinion exhibits a strictly *reformed* type of doctrine. The sacraments are regarded *simply* as signs. There is no reference to a *baptismal grace*, the existence of which was maintained by the Lutheran Church; but it is taught that the "baptism of water" is not necessary, that the service of God is purely internal, and to be evidenced by faith and love: "In short, the real and true service of God consists in no external things, either in water baptism, or the Lord's Supper, or in the singing of psalms, or in any ceremonial work. But in faith and trust in God through Christ, God is truly glorified and worshipped in spirit and in truth and rightly served." Comp. PETRI, *Der Stadt Mühlhausen Geschichten* (written in the beginning of the seventeenth century), Mühlhausen, 1838; GRAF, *Geschichten der Kirchenverbesserung zu Mühlhausen in Elsass*, Strassburg, 1818; RÖHRICH, *l.c.* vols. i., ii., iii., and the author's article in Herzog's *Realenc.* vol. xx. p. 187.

was called in the adjacent district the *heretic town* [*Ketzer-städtchen*].[1]

In Solothurn, the schoolmaster Dürr (Macrinus) was looked upon as an adherent of Zwingle, and was persecuted by the Franciscans. He regained his position, from which he had been dismissed, only upon pledging himself to silence in regard to the points at issue. Among the cantons of Western Switzerland, Freiburg entertained the most violent prejudice against Zwingle and his doctrines. This city was in general but little distinguished for scientific pursuits. Agrippa von Nettesheim, a scholar of the fifteenth century, who resided at Freiburg for some time, characterises it as "entirely destitute of all intellectual life,"[2]—a description which continued, on the whole, to apply to it in the age of the Reformation, although its mayor, Peter Falk, a friend and patron of Zwingle, formed an honourable exception to the general ignorance and superstition of its inhabitants. Hans Kuno, chaplain at the church of St. Nicholas, was banished from the place for exclaiming,—prompted by the official burning, through the public executioner, of proscribed writings,—"Father, forgive them; they know not what they do." John Holland, dean of the cathedral, a man who enjoyed the esteem of all, was also banished for no other cause than that he carried on a correspondence with the Bernese Reformers.[3]

More progress was made by the Reformation in Eastern Switzerland, where the evangelical doctrines possessed a strong point of support in Zurich and its Zwingle. Vadian, burgomaster of St. Gall, and Hofmeister of Schaffhausen, were two of Zwingle's most intimate friends, having also presided at the second disputation of Zurich, and taken the liveliest interest in all the proceedings thereof.

Sebastian Hofmeister,[4] whose real name was Wagner (Car-

---

[1] KUHN, *Bern's Reformatoren*, pp. 59–70.
[2] *Ex Friburgo Helvetiorum, omnium scientiarum cultu deserto et destituto.*
[3] HOTTINGER (JOH. V. MÜLLER), vol. vi. pp. 410–412.
[4] See his biography by KIRCHHOFER, and the Schaffhausen *Jahrbücher*.

pentarius), was born at Schaffhausen in 1476. He belonged to the order of the Franciscans, had been educated in Paris, and for a time discharged the duties of a professor at Zurich. He was subsequently called to his native city, where he ministered as a preacher at various churches. By his opposition to the mass and other abuses, he gained the approbation of some and excited the passionate hostility of others. His opponents could devise no means of improving their cause other than the calling of Erasmus Ritter, a celebrated champion of Rome, to the city. In consequence of the second disputation of Zurich, however, this personage was so powerfully won over to the views which he had undertaken to combat as to give the glory to truth, and himself join the ranks of the labourers at the work of reformation. Michael von Eggenstorf, abbot of All Saints' cloister, a pious man and a lover of learning, who had become acquainted with Luther's writings, also worked in a reformatory spirit upon the monks who were under his supervision, and finally surrendered his convent into the hands of the Government. The latter soon afterwards abolished the mass and images.

On the shores of the lake of Constance, in the environs of the city of the same name, a sentiment favourable to the Reformation speedily manifested itself among the population of Thurgau. From Stein on the Rhine, and from Burg, Zwingle's friends, Erasmus Schmid and John Oechslin, laboured for the diffusion of the gospel in the adjacent communities of Thurgau. Nor was there any lack of opposition, especially on the part of the nobility and the Thurgovian governor. Whilst a portion of the Carthusians in the cloister of Ittingen became favourably inclined toward the Reformation, the prior and even the cultured and enlightened provisor, Jodocus Hesch, opposed the incoming of the Zwinglian doctrines. This difference finally led to bitter and bloody quarrels, in one of which the prior and provisor were maltreated by a mob that stormed the cloister, while the building itself was given to the flames,—

a melancholy mistake on the part of reformatory zeal, which had yet other bloody consequences.[1]

In St. Gall, Vadian or Joachim von Watt[2] laboured with blessed results. He was born at the same place, on the 30th of December 1484, of illustrious and prosperous parents. He studied at Vienna, and entered into a lasting bond of friendship with his contemporary Zwingle. After leading a somewhat dissolute life, he was brought back to the right way by the earnest admonition of a merchant, the friend of his parents. From this time forth his life was devoted to diligent study— primarily to that of the classics. Virgil served him for a pillow. Numerous journeyings gained him an acquaintance with remoter countries (Poland, Hungary, Carinthia). He had distinguished himself as a poet and author, and had been crowned with the poet's laurel by the Emperor Maximilian I. He had everywhere formed connections with learned men, and in 1518 had returned to his native city at precisely the right time to render it important services during the plague as town physician. Subsequently, in 1526, he was summoned by the confidence of his fellow-citizens to the highest place in the magistracy, the post of burgomaster. He was therefore not a theologian by profession. His learning, however, was so many-sided, his zeal for the pure word of God so great, his connection with Zwingle so firm, and his acquaintance with the church luminaries of that period so extensive, that he deserves the name of a Reformer. As burgomaster of his native city, he laboured in the interests of reformation by gathering a circle of evangelical preachers about him and discussing the Scriptures with them—ay, this layman explained the Acts of the Apostles to his brethren of the clerical

---

[1] On the Reformation in Thurgau and the Ittingen affair, which latter forms a lamentable episode in the history of the Swiss Reformation, comp. MÖRIKOFER, *Zwingli*, vol. i. pp. 234 sqq.

[2] See FELS, *Denkmal schweiz. Reformat.*, St. Gall, 1819; PRESSEL, *Joachim Vadian, nach handschriftlichen und gleichzeitigen Quellen*, Elberfeld, 1861 (in vol. ix. of the *Väter und Begründer*); and the author's article in Herzog's *Realenc.* vol. xvii. p. 564.

profession. Among the latter, Burgauer, the town pastor, and Wolfgang Wetter were those who first preached in the spirit of the Reformation. Soon afterwards Balthaser Hubmeier of Waldshut repaired to St. Gall, and preached there to large concourses of people in the open fields. In the sequel, however, this man adopted the errors of the Anabaptists. A purer evangelical ministry was developed, in 1524, by John Kessler[1] (Ahenarius), whose acquaintance we have already made. Kessler had studied first in Basel, and then in Wittenberg under Luther and Melanchthon, at the same time pursuing the trade of a saddler. In this respect he resembled the learned Colin and his pupil, Thomas Plater, who were ropemakers. He delivered lectures (*Lesenen*) on the Scriptures, at first in the houses of burghers and then in guild rooms, and attracted large numbers of people, who listened to him with hearty approbation. The Diet, assembled at Baden in August, complained to the Government of St. Gall that "unconsecrated and mean persons were permitted to preach." The name "Kessler," indeed, gave rise to a misunderstanding, causing its owner to be regarded by some as an actual tinker, "going about through the country and living upon what he made by mending pots, pans, and kettles." Kessler suffered himself to be persuaded to abandon the lectures for a while. A short time after this, however, from 2d February 1525, he gave instruction in the Bible in the parish church of St. Lawrence, in conjunction with Wolfgang Schorant (Ulimann) and the schoolmaster Dominic Zili.

Franz Geisberger, abbot of St. Gall, looked with disgust upon the heresy that was growing and becoming prevalent in the very environs of his ancient monastery; and disagreements accordingly ensued, here as elsewhere, between the inmates of the convent and the friends of the Reformation. Notwithstanding this, however, the latter went joyfully on its way, and, almost at the same time as at Zurich and Schaffhausen, the churches of St. Gall were purified of images and pictures,

---

[1] See BERNET's *Biography*, quoted above.

and the people contented themselves with hearing the word of God instead of the mass. The Diet of Appenzell likewise resolved, in 1524, that all the priests and clerics in the canton should preach nothing but what they could prove from the gospel. Here also, however, opinions were divided; James Schurtanner in Teufen, Walter Klarer in Hundwyl, and others being in favour of the Reformation, while Theobald Huter, pastor of the capital of the canton, was most decided in his opposition to it. We have already seen how the seed of purer doctrine was scattered in Glarus through the medium of Zwingle's earlier residence there. His labours were carried on in the town of Glarus itself by Valentine Tschudi, by Fridolin Brunner in Mollis, John Schindler at Schwanden, and Gregory Bünzli at Wesen (the latter was possibly the former teacher of Zwingle at Basel). Zwingle himself kept up his connection with the people of Glarus. On the 14th of July 1523 he dedicated the exposition and rationale of his *Schlussreden* "to the honourable, prudent, and wise Amman, Council, and Assembly of the Canton of Glarus," as "formerly his sheep," but now "his gracious friends and dear brethren in Christ."[1]

The Rhætian Leagues [the Grisons] probably received their first reformatory impulse from Zurich. Zwingle was in correspondence with several members of the allied states, among whom was Martin Säger, town provost of Maienfeld, and an admirer of Luther and his writings. The preacher Bolt (Bürgli), who proclaimed the gospel with great earnestness and impressiveness in Fläsch, a parish adjacent to and dependent on Maienfeld, was also from the lake of Zurich. In Malans, John Blasius preached. A large portion of the Zehngerichtenbund[2] favoured the Reformation. In the rugged St. Antonierthal [Valley of St. Anthony], Henry Spreiter preached.

---

[1] *Werke*, vol. i. pp. 170 sqq.
[2] [The last formed of the three leagues of which the canton of the Grisons was composed, the first being the *Gotteshausbund* and the second the *Oberbund*. See Zschokke's *Geschichte des Schweizerlandes*, pp. 96 sqq.—Tr.]

In the Prättigau also and Davos, the district "back of it," where Pastor Conradi preached, the newly-risen light was greeted with joy. At Chur, James Salzmann (Salandronius, called also Alexander), a school teacher, ventured to declare himself in favour of the Reformation under the very eyes of the bishop. A man of greater importance than he was John Dorfmann (Comander), a friend of Zwingle, who was chosen pastor of St. Martin's at Chur in the year 1524. His name is usually among the first mentioned when the Reformers of the Grisons are spoken of. Deserving of a place by his side was Philip Saluz (Gallitius) from the Münsterthal. The latter, when a young chaplain of but twenty summers, preached in the mountain village of Camogask in Oberengadin, concerning the perfect and sufficient merits of Christ, and the trust which the sinner should repose therein alone. He was opposed by Bursella, dean of Engadin. Besides Saluz, James Biveroni preached the gospel in a similar spirit in Oberengadin. With a view to checking the increasing innovations, the Leagues published, on Quasimodo Sunday 1524, during a session of the Diet at Ilanz, an edict forbidding any clergyman to leave his benefice on pain of deprivation. Nor did the prince-bishop of Chur, Paul Ziegler of the Ziegenberg, rest until he had accomplished the banishment of the preachers of Fläsch and Malans, notwithstanding Zwingle's earnest intercession with the three Leagues on their behalf.[1]

Valais manifested little inclination toward the Reformation, its general intellectual status being as yet too low for it to favour any liberal movement, although it did produce a few talented men, such as the celebrated Cardinal Schinner and the original Thomas Plater, at this very time. The last-mentioned individual has handed down to us some remarkable anecdotes illustrative of the ignorance of his countrymen and

---

[1] A. PORTA, *Historia Reformationis Ecclesiarum Rhæticarum*, 1771–1774; CHR. KIND, *Die Reformation in den Bisthümern Chur und Como*, Chur, 1858; LEONHARDI, *Philipp Gallicius, Reformator Bündens*, Bern, 1865; C. PESTALOZZI, art. "Komander" in Herzog's *Realencyc.* vol. xix. pp. 723 sqq.

of the priests of the canton.[1] Plater was accustomed to make an excursion once in a while from Zurich, where he was pursuing his studies, to his native place, upon which occasions it readily happened that the fiery and impetuous youth became involved in theological disputes with the priests. Once, while discussing the question as to whether the Apostle Peter was ever at Rome, he drew forth his Greek Testament in support of his assertions. The priest who was his antagonist at the time disclaimed, however, all knowledge of that book, but declared that he derived his information from his grandmother. "So," said Plater, "your grandmother is your Bible?" The same ecclesiastic was endeavouring to vindicate the invocation of saints by the citation of that passage in the Psalms where it is said that "God is wonderful in His works." Upon this Plater stooped down to the earth, and, breaking off a blade of grass, remarked, "If all the world were to conspire together, it would be unable to make the like of this little weed," thus intimating that a consistent carrying out of his opponent's sentiments would involve the adoration of the grass as well as of the saints. The priest withdrew, silent and abashed. The effect which the sermons of a certain Lucius Steger produced upon the inhabitants of Valais is involved in obscurity. He is said to have attacked the system of oral confession and to have recommended the writings of Zwingle.

It was in the interior of Switzerland that the reformatory ideas found the greatest difficulty of entrance. Lucerne occupied nearly the same platform in point of culture with Freiburg. The nobles, fettered by the pensions which they received from foreign countries, manifested a disinclination toward the efforts for reform; the people were rude, and the clergy ignorant. Under these circumstances, Oswald Myconius (Geisshäusler), a native of Lucerne, who had held the office of school teacher in that city since the year 1520,

---

[1] See Plater's *Life* by FRANZ (St. Gall, 1812), pp. 90 sqq., and his *Autobiography*, published by FECHTER, Basel, 1840; G. FREYTAG, *Bilder aus der deutschen Vergangenheit*, vol. i. pp. 95 sqq.

had a difficult position to maintain. Notwithstanding his careful avoidance, during his hours of instruction, of all mention of Luther's name,—although he professed his principles,—he fell under suspicion of being an adherent of that Reformer, a "Lutheran schoolmaster," was frequently brought before the council, and was finally, together with his friends Zimmerman (Xylotectus), Jost Kilchmeier, and Colin, banished from the city. He repaired to Zurich, where he remained until, at the death of Œcolampadius, he was appointed antistes at Basel.[1] Dean Bodler had the chief share in effecting the banishment of the evangelically minded from Lucerne. Even at that time, however, there were not wanting voices that declared that "the lamp [Lucerna] of the Confederacy had suffered its light to go out, and that there remained but a little end of wick, that was afraid to burn because of its own fatness."

On turning at last to the primitive cantons of Switzerland, we are struck by the remark of a modern historian (Hottinger),[2] who says, and not wrongfully, that in passing judgment upon the inhabitants of the mountain districts of the Confederacy, a different standard is required from that which may be employed in relation to the more level portions of the country. He calls our attention to the great historical and patriotic reminiscences which had grown into the most intimate connection with the faith that the people had hitherto professed. "An indignation that we can easily comprehend," says he, "must have taken possession of the inhabitants of Uri or of Schwytz upon learning of the contemplated abolition of pilgrimages and the whitewashing of the walls of the churches. Did they not yearly repair to the consecrated battle-field of Morgarten and to the chapel of William Tell, where simple memorials invited them to combine a grateful remembrance of

---

[1] M. KIRCHHOFER, *Oswald Myconius*, Zurich, 1813; HAGENBACH, *Œcolampad und Myconius*.

[2] In his continuation of JOHN V. MÜLLER (vol. vi. pp. 413 sqq.), a work which we have frequently cited, and of which we have gratefully availed ourselves.

the heroes of the fatherland with the adoration of those heavenly helpers to whom the pious faith of the actors in the mighty scenes of old thankfully ascribed the strength that was requisite for the accomplishment of their work? Could the abrogation of fasts and the introduction of priestly marriage fail to excite the ire of the man of Unterwalden, who was accustomed to revere in the self-denial of his far-famed Brother Claus the highest degree of earthly holiness?" The disputes over dogmas must have seemed to these simple men to be something that stretched far beyond their horizon, since they valued their priests not according to their standing as men of learning and acute theologians, but in proportion to their honourable walk and simple, good-hearted piety. Hence the reply of the Obwaldners to the invitation which the citizens of Zurich extended to them on the occasion of the second disputation of Zurich: "We are always ready to serve you, but we have no men of particular learning, but only pious, honourable priests, who expound to us the holy gospels and other sacred writings as our forefathers were accustomed to explain them, and as the holy popes and the council (*sic*) have commanded."

We do not, of course, mean to assert that the pure preaching of the word of God might not have taken root even in these cantons had the requisite conditions been present, or that the people were destitute of power to appreciate such preaching. We have already beheld the rays of the new light streaming forth from Einsiedeln whilst Zwingle and, subsequently, Leo Juda preached there under the protection of a noble abbot. Conrad Schmid, commander of the Knights of St. John, whom we meet with in the preceding chapter, won over to his way of thinking one Wernherr Steiner, governor of Zug, by a discourse that he delivered in Lucern. Steiner subsequently became a particular patron of the Reformation. Much inclination for the pure gospel was at first manifested in the canton of Schwytz. After Zwingle had exchanged his quiet ministry there for the greater one that devolved upon him at Zurich, his assistant, George Stähelin, laboured for some time as pastor of Freienbach, on the lake of Zurich. He relates the following:—" So I took it in hand and found a right willing people. The gentry of Schwytz, when they wished to ride out, arranged it so as to come to church on Sundays, and thus I had a table full of guests every Sunday. There came even a few from the March to hear the preaching." Can we, however, be astonished that these people, unable, as they were, to exercise a proper discrimination, were prejudiced against the Reformation itself by such extreme proceedings, in the spirit of Anabaptism, as Balthaser Traxel, pastor of Art, was guilty of?

We have now brought our consideration of both the German and Swiss Reformations down to the close of the year 1524. We have viewed each in its peculiar connection and on its own soil, and, amid much that is homogeneous in principle, have found many varieties in application and execution. The German Reformation presents itself to us, as we have already remarked, more as a connected whole, wherein Luther is to a greater or less degree the head; while the Swiss Reformation appears to be rather a co-agency of different powers. In the case of the former, we behold, at first, *one man*, who, opposed to the mighty colossus of the German Empire, clears the way for reform by a prodigious act of courage; and not until he has alone withstood the chief violence of the storm that threatened destruction to himself and his undertaking, do the elements which opposed him sunder, thus preparing the way for an ecclesiastico-political separation. In Switzerland, on the other hand, teachers of the gospel and Governments work hand in hand, and the people take a livelier and more decided interest in the struggle. But that very democratic principle that was here predominant, and that asserted its authority from the outset, increased the difficulty of avoiding certain errors and excesses. Such excesses did not invariably proceed from positive fanatics, or from men who were connected with the riotous Anabaptists; but in the first paroxysm of reformatory zeal, *others* were misled into momentary precipitancies. It was, manifestly, nothing but youthful bravado that led young Thomas Plater, to whom we have already alluded, when acting in the capacity of amanuensis to Myconius at Zurich, to abstract an image of St. John from the church in order that he might heat the stove with it,—in accomplishing which theft he addressed the image as follows:—" Come down, Jackey; you must go into the stove though they do call you John." Neither Myconius nor Zwingle knew of this affair at the time, and they certainly would not have approved it. But they were unable to hinder every act of the kind. When they were endeavouring to prevent a false zeal from doing violence to things that had hitherto been accounted sacred, they were obliged to take issue upon precisely those subjects that appeared most important to the people; hence the strenuous disputation concerning the *images* and the *mass*, because the people were familiar with these and had them constantly before their eyes. Not that Zwingle did not know full well that the abolition of such external abuses was not the only thing to be accomplished, and that it was necessary to achieve something *positive;* that the prime desiderata were *faith*, and that fundamental conviction which expresses itself in *confession* and assumes a further and more definite form in dogma. But that which, considered from a purely theoretical point of view, appears to be *first*, viz. an understanding relative to the principles of conduct, is in reality the *last*, the concluding point, action instinctively taking the precedence of perfected knowledge. Circumstances pressed for action before an agreement as to principle and theory had been arrived at in all things. It was high time for the more judicious and intelligent portion of the nation—the Governments, supported by their preachers—to take the matter in hand, and suppress such customs as were offensive before they were attacked by the brutality of the mob. In these considerations we may read an explanation of the fact that the Swiss Reformers, in order to provide against a worse disaster than simplicity, went farther than the Lutheran Church of Germany in the abolition of all that addressed itself to the senses in the service of the sanctuary, stripping the churches of their decorations until they assumed a deplorably naked aspect. Shall we reproach the fathers of the Reformed Church for thus doing? Assuredly not; no more than we should reproach the physician who resorts to energetic measures to counteract an acute malady. Those measures may be painful, but they are for our healing. There is another question, however. The crisis being long since over, would it be a sin against the reformed principle to begin to permit religious art to exercise its influence again upon the worship of God even in the Reformed Church? We cannot see that it would. Since the Lutheran Church of Germany was allowed to retain much of what the Swiss Reformation abolished, why should not its liturgical treasures be made use of (with intelligence and discrimination, of course) by the Reformed Church of to-day, for the elaboration of the cult of the latter? We go still farther, however. Not only do we not regard the difference between the two churches in cult as invincible, but we refuse to concede that character to those far deeper differences in dogma with which we shall occupy ourselves in the next chapter; although, on the other hand, we are equally removed from ignoring the difficulties which spring up now and again to meet those who honestly seek after the truth. Here also we have no business to reproach either one person or another, to cast blame upon Luther or upon Zwingle, or to assume that it was in their power to overleap the conflict which was a sacred affair of conscience to them both. It is rather the task of Protestant theology to apprehend this antithesis psychologically and historically, as springing from the different personality and nationality of the German and the Swiss Reformer; but it is in a still greater degree the task of Protestant theology, or rather of the whole Protestant Church, to pass beyond the original antithesis by deepening, not superficializing it, and thus to arrive at a possible understanding. Though in the very days of the Reformation its opponents had the triumph of seeing dissensions arise among the authors of the " new faith" relative to precisely those subjects in which the Catholic Church had hitherto found the mystical bond of her unity, *we* should not accord to the modern enemies of the Reformation the pleasure of beholding in such discord the beginning of a necessary " self-dissolution " of Protestantism; but should rather trust that the spirit of evangelical truth will, after the confessors of the latter have been long enough divided into two camps, of which each held fast a *moiety* of the truth, lead all into the *whole* truth.

CHAPTER XV.

THE EUCHARISTIC CONTROVERSY—IMPORT OF THE LORD'S SUPPER—PARALLEL BETWEEN LUTHER AND ZWINGLE—KARLSTADT—ZWINGLE—ŒCOLAMPADIUS—ERASMUS—BRENZ AND THE SWABIAN SYNGRAMMA—WORDS OF PEACE FROM ŒCOLAMPADIUS.

IN the night in which the Lord Jesus was betrayed, He took bread, gave thanks, brake it, and said: "Take, eat, *this is my body*, which is broken for you; this do in remembrance of me." In like manner, also, He took the cup after supper, and said: "This cup is the new covenant in my blood; this do, as oft as ye drink, in remembrance of me."

When we consider the simple narrative of the apostle,[1] comparing it with the similar records of the evangelists, and fix our eyes upon the fact as it is related, letting it work upon us purely as it is, without troubling ourselves as to what subsequent expositions have attached to it, a feeling must come over us which it is difficult to put into words, and still more difficult to reduce to any system of words and ideas.

We behold the Redeemer for the last time within the circle of His disciples. Sadness takes possession of His great soul when He looks upon His loved ones, from whom He is to be parted, whom He must leave in the world as sheep without a shepherd in the midst of ravening wolves. But no; He will

[1] 1 Cor. xi. 23-25. Comp. Matt. xxvi. 26-29; Mark xiv. 22-25; Luke xxii. 19, 20.

not leave them orphans: *He*, the Lord, will continue to live in them, forming *one* body with them, whereof He is the Head! *His* blood, His heart's blood, shall flow in their veins; He will *live* in them and they in Him. He is the true food and the true drink; He is the true vine, whence the branch draws its sap, and without which it can do nothing. The grain of wheat, truly, must fall into the earth and die; but after having died, it shall spring up and bear fruit a thousand-fold. For those beloved ones He suffers His body to be broken; for them He sheds His blood, and for all who shall confess themselves to be His. Oh, that touching parting! Heartily, says He, has He desired to eat this meal with them once more. Henceforth, however, He would drink no more of the fruit of the vine until He should drink the cup of joy with them in the heavenly kingdom.

The deeper and simpler a *symbolical action* is—and where is there one deeper and simpler than this?—the more manifold are the constructions of which it is susceptible. This manifoldness of significance, however, is no disadvantage; one construction does not contradict another; they are but so many refractions of the one ray of light that penetrates into the innermost recesses of the soul, until it reaches the point where distinct consciousness vanishes. Though some may pre-eminently discover in the solemn act the sentiment of sadness produced by approaching separation, others that of self-communicative and self-sacrificing love, and others still that of the joyful hope of reunion; though some may, in the Lord's Supper, celebrate pre-eminently a memorial feast of Jesus' sufferings, and others an act of internal union with the Redeemer; though the *symbolical* nature of the act may appear to the consciousness of some more clearly than to that of others, so that the intellect of the one class distinguishes more acutely between the symbol and the thing symbolized, while to the more profoundly affected feeling of the other class, all is resolved into one great mystery,—notwithstanding all these differences, the Supper of the Lord continues to be a sacred feast of brotherly love, a *communion*, a bond that unites all the confessors of Jesus into one great family of God, since they are all partakers of *one* bread and all drink of *one* cup. And, regarded only from this point of view, what a grand solemnity it is! The physical need that man has in common with the beast, the necessity for *eating* and *drinking*, how is it ennobled by such a feast of religious fellowship? In partaking of that feast, we tear our eyes and hearts from earth, and lift them up to heaven (*sursum corda!*), and become mindful of our heavenly destination, which is that of children of God. Here every barrier is levelled that sunders man from man. Poor and rich, young and old, all assemble about one gracious table. Bread and wine, the daily elements of nourishment that hold our earthly bodies together, are converted into the bread of heaven, into a drink of deep significance — a serious, sacred thing, a *sacrament*, that leads to everlasting life. Who could have believed that the very thing that was designed by its Divine Author to be the medium of the most intimate *union* of Christians, would become, not once, but *often*, a subject of division — ay, of bitterest and bloody conflict, of most cruel persecution! Yet, long ago, the insignificant circumstance of the use of unleavened bread by the Romish Church, and of leavened bread by the Greek Church, aided in consummating the separation of these two great ecclesiastical bodies. Again, it was the Church's denial of the cup to the laity, and the demand for its extension to them on the part of the Bohemians, that brought the bloody Hussite war upon a large portion of Europe. It was, furthermore, the *mass*, into which the original celebration of the Supper had been transformed, that gave occasion to those offences which it was the aim of the Reformation to abolish. Not to mention all the other abuses that superstition attached to the mass—all the abominations, *e.g.*, of poisoned wafers, with which hypocritical wickedness profaned the most holy. It is saddening to see how human error can pervert that which is fairest, and can change the most precious treasures into an atrocious mockery, the most healing medicines into poison! And again, it is this holy sacrament of the Lord's Supper (the Eucharist), which contained the germ of that dissension that broke forth between those great men of the sixteenth century, Luther and Zwingle.

Hitherto we have seen these two men pursuing the work of the Reformation independently—one in Saxony, the other in Switzerland. In their personalities they have much in common with each other. Vigour, earnestness, courage, sterling worth and decision of character, sincere and hearty piety, challenge our admiration in both. Both are men of their people, loved and honoured by those who approach them without prejudice, hated by the adversaries of light and by time-servers; in both we discern an equal readiness to lay down property and life for the cause of God, the cause of Jesus Christ, in which they perceive the wellbeing of humanity to be involved. The necessity for the individual *I* of the natural man to perish, in order that it may attain to true life as a new man in Christ, may be gathered from Luther's preaching as well as from Zwingle's; it is proclaimed as by *one* mouth by both these witnesses for the truth. If we examine the religious basis of these similarly-attuned minds, so far as a glimpse of it is allowed us, we shall say that we could conceive of the existence of a cordial bond of friendship between these two men, whilst it seemed to be perfectly natural that Luther and Erasmus were mutually repellent. At the same time, there is a certain unmistakeable difference between the two Reformers, which, though it did not *necessitate* a conflict between them, yet renders such a conflict in some degree intelligible. Without taking upon us to decide which of the two is the greater, let us contemplate them impartially, side by side, each in his *own* greatness, according to the measure that God has given him, thanking God for the success which He has permitted to attend upon them both. If we feel particularly attracted toward a life that develops only by battling its way with infinite labour through opposing forces, that passes through the purifying fires of temptation in a more striking manner than any other, —a life that must needs undergo wondrous conflicts, and borne, as it were, by a higher power, lifted out of and above itself, enters into combat with all the devils of hell, in this case our enthusiasm will be aroused by Luther rather than by Zwingle. Or, in other words, if we were about to choose a material for poetic treatment,—a character capable of being dramatically worked up, of being handled in such a manner as continually to reflect the conflict and strength of human nature, a character in which should be portrayed the whole inner world of the affections, with all the manifold phases and involutions of the latter, from the tragic to the humorous, the childlike and naive,—we should unhesitatingly select Luther; for Luther's nature is more poetic than that of Zwingle, and I appeal to the reader's own experience to say whether the little that he has hitherto learned of Luther's life has not made a livelier, richer, and, I might say, more highly-coloured impression upon him than what has been narrated of Zwingle. For Switzers, it would be a ridiculous national pride or confessional narrow-mindedness to refuse to allow this; for without the reflection of Luther's greatness, our own Reformed Church, even that of Switzerland, would not be that which it now is in its connection with the great whole.

But the more unprejudiced our admission of the facts above stated, the less possible will it be to accuse us of partiality, if, on the other hand, we recognise those points in which Zwingle is *superior* to the Saxon Reformer. Although *understanding* [*Verstand*][1] may not be the sole faculty that constitutes and determines the intellectual life, it is, nevertheless, an important condition of that life, without which we should

[1] [" I use the term *understanding* not for the noetic faculty, intellect proper, or place of principles, but for the dianoetic or discursive faculty in its widest signification, for the faculty of relations or comparisons, and thus in the meaning in which *Verstand* is now employed by the Germans."—SIR W. HAMILTON. From WEBSTER's *Dictionary*, ed. of 1877.—TR.]

grope in darkness and lose ourselves in mist, though we possessed the greatest abundance of sensibility [*Gemüth*]. Now it is this very faculty of calm and deliberate understanding which Zwingle possesses in a more developed form than Luther. Luther had not *more sensibility* (for understanding and sensibility maintained the most perfect equipoise in Zwingle), but more *imagination*, more *buoyancy* of mind, than the latter. Zwingle, on the other hand, excelled Luther in firmness and security of judgment in individual cases. He was more sober and judicious, and, manifestly, more free from prejudices; and while Luther not seldom *bordered* on fanaticism, so that there was but a step between his enthusiasm and downright exaggeration, Zwingle always abides within the bounds of moderation. It is, therefore, almost laughable when Luther, in the midst of his fanatical fury of passion, calls honest Zwingle a fanatic,—a man who was so far removed from all fanaticism! It must be that by this name it was intended to designate the idealistic feature of his character (and that, indeed, was obnoxious to the blunt realism of Luther). For the rest, let us look at his portrait. That energetic, firm, full head; that striking physiognomy, hewn, as it were, in stone; that broad forehead; that full, clear eye; that well-closed mouth, with its rounded lips—but enough! I leave the task of perfectly interpreting this picture to a Lavater, who discovers in it "earnestness, reflection, manly decision, the power of concentration and action, a clear-sighted, penetrating intellect,"[1] and appeal to history alone for a living commentary on the likeness. If we consider further the difference in the external circumstances, the surroundings and the fortunes of these two men, we shall find it still easier to comprehend how it was that each one, in his own circle, thought and acted differently from the other. Luther's was a thoroughly *Germanic* nature; he was a son of Thuringia. Zwingle was a genuine *Switzer*, a son of the Alps. In this respect, also, points of contact between the two present them-

[1] See LAVATER's *Physiognomik*.

selves to our view. Both may be regarded as representatives of their respective nations; they issued from the people, and they had perfect command of the language of the people, being never at a loss for the right expression, blunt though that may have been, and bordering on the plebeian. The prevalent quality of the one was a mystical intuition; that of the other, strong practical sense. Luther was a *monk* in the deeper meaning of the term, the sense in which we understand it to denote a man of a predominantly contemplative turn of mind; Zwingle was a *secular cleric*, also in the better sense of the word, a man who had early learned to grasp the earthly relations of life by their natural, practical side, and to turn his own experience to practical account. *Luther's* surroundings were monarchical; Zwingle was the son of a republic. The former was thrown upon himself from the beginning of the struggle, and only gradually received the protection of his prince against the mighty Empire; Zwingle was protected by a high-minded Government, though exposed to many personal dangers. The course of study pursued by these two men was also different. Luther, in his cloister, amidst a thousand temptations, had recourse to the melancholy Augustine, the profound Tauler, and the Mystics; Zwingle had, to a greater degree, formed his mind on the genial classics, the vigorous models of the ancient world. (In this respect he occupies an intermediate position between Luther and Erasmus, the latter of whom seems to have thought more highly of him than of the Saxon Reformer.) Applying these premises to the theology of the two men, and to their method of explaining the Scriptures, we find in Luther more of the profound investigator, whose attention is directed chiefly to the inner world and its mysteries; in Zwingle, more of the sober thinker, who scans all things with the utmost consideration, and applies all things to practical life and morals in the civil and domestic community. We have noted elsewhere the deep insights into the spirit of the Bible which Luther obtained, and his translation of its language into the language of the German heart—a translation characterised by a fluency and melody to which Zwingle, with his harsher speech and style, could scarcely have attained. It is possible that, in relation to the spiritual import of the Bible, Luther possessed a more prophetic mind than Zwingle, if by such prophetic mind we understand that faculty of divination which, without being conscious of the detailed series of reasons for a conclusion, is able to strike the very place in which the finer threads of the entire subject meet. Luther's whole mode of viewing the world and worldly relations was, to use a modern term, Semitic, and immediately connected with the biblical sphere of view; Zwingle's was more a Japhetic mode of view, whose effort it was to translate the ideas couched in the figurative style of the Orientals into the more abstract mode of thought connected with European culture. He viewed the Bible as he viewed the classics, objectively. Therefore, when it was requisite that the letter of the Bible should be scrutinized with exegetical acuteness, that neither more nor less should be discovered in particular passages than they actually contain; when a grammatico-historical explanation of Scripture was called for; when some one was needed who should apprehend the figures and expressions thereof by means of a just appreciation of the genius of the language, and by natural relations of life, and who should be able to furnish a *learned* response to any questions that might be raised, Zwingle was incontestably the better exegete of the two. He was less apt to be carried away by his feelings, and to be beguiled from the straight road by mystical fancies, although he was by no means insensible to the eternal beauties and unfathomable depths of the divine word. The difference in the religious views of the two Reformers is strikingly illustrated by their different conceptions of the dark power of evil. It was as far from Zwingle's mind as from Luther's to deny the existence of the devil, or to attempt to explain him away from the Scriptures. Zwingle, as well as Luther, beholds in him the adversary of Christ and of His Church; and when he has an exegetical encounter with him, he does not evade him.

He, however, is not nearly as much employed with him as is Luther; and he knows nothing of any personal conflict with him, or, still less, of diabolical apparitions and tricks. This difference of view is further manifested in their variant modes of apprehending the person of Christ. Luther beholds in Him not the God-man simply, but frequently the pure divinity,—humanized and incarnate, it is true, but born *as God*, lying *as God* upon His mother's breast, dying *as God*, etc.; whilst Zwingle puts a far sharper distinction between the divine and human natures in Christ, separating them at times so widely that the personal unity of the Redeemer appears to be lost in the process. Luther's habits of thought were more concrete, Zwingle's more abstract; hence in Luther a spirituo-sensuous contemplation predominated, in Zwingle reflection and criticism prevailed;[1] in Zwingle, the understanding and the sensibilities appear in general to be more distinct from each other, whilst in Luther they run into one another. The predominant faculty of Zwingle's mind was reflection; the predominant faculty of Luther's, intuition.

I have travelled far from the direct track of my narrative in order that I might finally arrive at my theme, the conflicting interpretations of the sacramental words of institution. And yet such an explanation was necessary to prevent that superficial view of the case which would regard these two men as quarrelling—from the mere love of dispute, or from caprice—about one little word upon which, certainly, everything is not dependent. The visible attachment of the dispute was undoubtedly to the word *is* or *signifies*. That, however, is but the external handle by which we can grasp the two different theological modes of thought of the disputants—the extreme point in which those modes of thought terminate. If these men, who were both too deeply involved in the storms of the time to engage in any such undertaking as that of which we are about to speak, had each had leisure to work out a theological system, it is certain that their labours would

---

[1] Comp. SCHENKEL, *Das Wesen des Protestantismus*, vol. i. pp. 331 sqq.

have resulted in the production of two different systems,—systems not contradictory of each other in their fundamental opinions, but varying considerably in their modes of contemplation and expression; for, even in the sacramental controversy, the accurate observer will have occasion to remark, in the Lutheran and Zwinglian dogmatics, several variations not immediately touching the words of institution, but bearing upon other points whose connection with the subject of controversy is apparently but remote.

To come now to the matter in question, I may, without doubt, take it for granted that we are all agreed as to the fact that both Reformers were equally in earnest in the affair; that neither of them regarded the Lord's Supper in the light of a mere useful ordinance of the Church, but that they assuredly partook of it with the most serious devotion, and in that worthy, well-tried frame of mind which the apostle so earnestly enjoins. Both, likewise, were agreed that this simple transaction which Jesus instituted must be reduced once more to its *biblical* foundation and *historic* origin. Both rejected the abuses of the mass, the idea of a repeated sacrifice, etc. Even the *transubstantiation of the bread*, in the sense in which this is taught by the Romish Church, was repudiated by Luther as well as Zwingle. (It was for his doctrine in regard to this point that Luther was so severely censured by Henry VIII. of England.) Zwingle, however, went farther in this respect than Luther. Though Luther did not, with the Papists, assume that the bread, after it had been consecrated by the priest, was wholly changed into the Lord's body, he did assume a substantial (real) presence of that body, a presence which we cannot understand, but which we must *believe*. He assumed, as the view was subsequently expressed, that the body of the Lord was contained *in*, *with*, and *under* the bread, and that every one, even an unbelieving person, partook of this body *really* and substantially. He held the same opinions in regard to the wine of the blessed cup and the thereunder contained blood of Jesus. In support of his view, he appealed to the omnipotence of God, to whom all miracles are possible, and consequently this miracle of the sacrament also,—an argument which would open the door to all sorts of superstition, for in what circumstances could we not appeal to God's almighty power? Not that the thing was *possible*, but that it *actually occurred*, was what demanded proof; and it was requisite that Luther, in conformity to his own theory of belief, should here adduce *scriptural proof* if he hoped to attach suitable weight to his tenet. It was just here, however, that the difficulty lay. Christ had nowhere expressed Himself more fully on the subject than in the words of institution; He had furnished no commentary thereupon, and every man possesses the right to make such a commentary himself, provided he exercise that right conscientiously. Accordingly, there remained for Luther nothing but to take the word *is*, in the terms of institution, in a perfectly literal sense, to lay a disproportionate stress upon it, and to attach his whole proof to it; whilst Zwingle and his adherents most clearly showed that the word *could* not have this literal meaning. It was, indeed, easy for them to prove their assertion, the Bible being full of pictorial expressions, rhetorical figures, similes, and metaphors, and we must needs almost have our eyes intentionally closed if we would not see clearly *here*. Thus, when Christ says, "I am the vine" (I cite Zwingle's illustrations), He certainly does not mean that He is a vine in the natural sense of the word; when He called Peter a rock, He did not mean that the apostle, instead of being a man, consisting of flesh and bone, was a mere stone, etc. Every child, we should think, might understand this. But how does it happen that *Luther* did not understand it, that he *would* not understand it, that he *could* not understand it, situated as he was? Assuredly, it was not mere obstinacy on his part. Luther appears to me too great, too venerable, for me to venture to accuse him of this. Precisely because the matter seems so simple that every child must comprehend it, we cannot deem Luther so narrow-minded as not to have apprehended the A B C of the commonest rhetoric, or to have been unable to distinguish between a simile and a literal saying. People are often far too ready to pass judgment upon great men; they apply the ordinary measuring rule of so-called common sense to their colossal forms, and consign all that will not accommodate itself to this to the region of foolish conceits. In this method of measuring, that golden mean is lost in the employment of which the fewest inequalities are to be found, because it has neither height nor depth.

Manifestly, therefore, if we would not judge Luther unjustly, we must seek another and worthier reason for the remarkable pertinacity of his assertion than a deficiency in insight and goodwill. And this reason is to be found in history itself. In the first place, it is to be noted that the controversy was started neither by Luther nor by Zwingle, but by that very Karlstadt who had already, by his violent proceedings at Wittenberg, his iconoclasm and his connection with the Anabaptists, exhibited the character of a dangerous enthusiast. Upon leaving Wittenberg, he had repaired to Orlamünde. There also he had removed all the images from the churches and abolished infant baptism. He had also declared against the use of the confessional previous to the participation in the Lord's Supper, etc. In the month of August 1524, Luther, in pursuance of a commission of the elector, visited Jena. He there preached against the iconoclasts. Karlstadt himself was present upon this occasion. In a conversation with Luther, he repudiated the charges of being a disturber of the peace and of making common cause with Münzer. At the same time he accused Luther of heresy in regard to the Lord's Supper. Luther was ready and willing to fight out the matter with him in a disputation. He therefore invited him to Wittenberg, promising to procure him a free conduct thither. He also, in presence of witnesses of this conversation, put a gold florin into Karlstadt's hand, as a sign that the latter was authorized to write against him. Karlstadt triumphantly held up the florin, saying, "This is *arrabo* (a pledge), a sign that I am empowered to write against Dr. Luther, and I beg that you will all be witnesses hereof."[1] No oral disputation ensued. Karlstadt was soon obliged to leave Orlamünde, and led thenceforth a restless and wandering life. He repaired to Strassburg, and afterwards to Basel. At the latter place he preached his tractate, *On the Antichristian Abuse of the Lord's Bread and Cup.* The Council of Basel were far from manifesting any approbation of this production, but, on the contrary, imprisoned the printer of it. Karlstadt next came forward with a new explanation of the words of institution, an explanation so *forced* that we cannot marvel at its failure to win the approval of Luther. Karlstadt asserted that it was not concerning the bread that Jesus said, "This is my body," but that, in breaking the bread, He pointed to His own body, saying of that, "This is my body which is broken for you." The breaking of the bread appeared, according to this view of the case, as a mere accompaniment to the speech; the symbolical action lost its significance, and sank into an empty and prosaic ceremony. Let us try now to put ourselves in Luther's place. He had earnestly assailed the abuses of the Church, and called forth a struggle which occasionally filled the Reformer himself with anxious fears. His design had never been to unhinge Christ's Church itself, and to overthrow the structure of centuries. He wished merely to restore all things to the true foundation; his desire was to *reform*, not to revolutionize. This Karlstadt now comes in his way, turning everything topsy-turvy, abolishing all connection with the ancient Church, putting everything out of joint, and kindling a fire difficult to extinguish. Baptism, *one* of the sacraments, had already been assailed by fanatics. Must the other sacrament now be abandoned to their will? Whither would that lead? The word and the sacraments were, according to

---

[1] Comp. Luther's *Letters*, DE WETTE, vol. ii. Nos. 618, 620; also the account of Preacher Reinhard of Jena, *Wess sich Dr. Karlstadt mit Dr. Luther beredt zu Jena* (WALCH, vol. xv.).

Luther, the foundation-pillars of the Church; they could not be shaken without threatening the downfall of the whole building. They must mediate the connection of the Reformation with the old Church. If this bond *should* be severed, the Protestants' Church would stand in air; it would lack all historical ground; it would, indeed, be a sect, a shoot cut off from the vine, a member cast off from the great body. Luther neither did nor could desire such a state of things as this. It was not the *Catholic* Church,—the *universal, i.e.* the *Apostolic* Church,—which holds fast to doctrine, to baptism, and to breaking of bread, from which he wished to separate himself, but only the *Roman* Catholic, the papistic, the degenerate, the disfigured Church. It was with these thoughts working in his breast that (in the beginning of the year 1525) he wrote, in the utmost indignation, his treatise, *Against the Heavenly Prophets of the Images and Sacrament*. The language of which he made use in this tractate was certainly not the most refined. He called Karlstadt an ass, who pretended to a mastery of the Greek whilst he really understood neither German nor Latin. He compares him to a stork pleased with its own chattering. The Holy Ghost, he declares, speaks clearly, orderly, and distinctly; but Satan, he affirms, mumbles his words, and talks without order, confounding all things. With a true instinct, he remarks that none would more heartily rejoice over the dissension that had broken out than the Papists. In this fact also he beheld a stratagem of the devil. He was glad, however, that the devil was now coming forth into the light of day; he had been whispering about in the dark long enough, but he [Luther] had now tempted him out with a florin, which, by the grace of God, had been well expended, and which he did not regret. He would not be persuaded that there was not an empty over-refinement of reasoning at the bottom of an exposition of Scripture which strove to bring the mysterious within the grasp of the ordinary human understanding. He declared that the most contracted of minds would prefer to believe that there was nothing but bread and wine present in the sacrament, rather than that Christ's body and blood were concealed therein. No great wit was necessary for that. If one was but bold enough to maintain such an opinion, he would find plenty of followers. But if we should once begin to explain the Scriptures to suit the ordinary comprehension of men, there would soon be not an article of faith left, for not one was there that did not exceed man's reason. With equal right might it be affirmed that it was impossible that God's Son should have become a man, and that the Divine Majesty, whom heaven and earth cannot contain, should have been enclosed in the narrow womb of a woman, and have permitted Himself to be crucified. Thus Luther.

And now, what posture did Zwingle assume toward this affair? The contested point was by no means a new one to him. We have seen how he defended the figurative apprehension of the sacramental words against Am-Grüt, the under-secretary of Zurich. He also regarded the controverted question as one of great importance, and looked, with the same confidence as Luther, up to God as Him who must needs open to us the right understanding of His word.[1] So far as Karlstadt's book was concerned, he openly confessed that some things in it had pleased him, while others had displeased him. The artificial construction which Karlstadt put upon the words of institution was as far from recommending itself to the sound exegetical sense of Zwingle as to the believing soul of Luther. He admirably compared Karlstadt to a man who was provided with good weapons, but did not know how to use them, and so buckled his helmet on his breast and his shield on his head. He agreed with Karlstadt, however, in thinking that the eating of the body and drinking of the blood of Christ must be performed only after a *spiritual* fashion, such as that of

[1] Comp. Zwingle's letter to Matthew Alber, preacher at Reutlingen, March 1525 (*Opp.* iii.; *Latin*, i. p. 589). This letter was published somewhat later. At the same time Zwingle developed his views in his work, *On True and False Religion* (*Commentarius de religione vera et falsa*), which he dedicated to Francis I., and in the thereto-appended *Subsidium de Eucharistia*.

which the Lord Himself speaks in the Gospel of John (chap. vi.). A *spirituo-corporeal* eating seemed to him as great a contradiction in terms as "wooden iron" (*hölzig Schüriseli*). The fact that the word *is* is employed in the Scriptures numberless times when it has the sense of *signifies*, he sought to substantiate by some striking instances, such as, The seven kine in Pharaoh's dream *are*, *i.e. signify*, seven fruitful and unfruitful years; the *seed* in the parable of the sower *is*, *i.e. signifies*, the word of God, etc. (comp. above).

I refrain from giving a circumstantial description of this controversy, which was carried on in writing for several years. To the professed man of letters it is, indeed, highly interesting; to others, however, it would be productive of little edification, and many things connected with it are better concealed than laid open to the light of day. In addition to what has already been said, I will remark simply that even peace-loving Œcolampadius became involved in the dispute. In the main he agreed perfectly with Zwingle. His treatise on the meaning of the sacramental words[1] is in every respect deserving of commendation, both for exegetical thoroughness and doctrinal sobriety.

In the very beginning of his treatise, Œcolampadius takes occasion to vindicate himself from the charge which Luther was always ready to make against the opponents of the doctrine of the bodily presence of Christ in the Lord's Supper. He declares that it is not the intention of persons who oppose this doctrine to rid Christianity of all that is wonderful and mysterious, *i.e.* to rationalize it. There certainly are mysteries, he affirms, which pass our reason. Such a mystery is the incarnation of the Son of God. But it is one thing to recognise these mysteries in the Scriptures and another to put in mysteries that were not originally there. The Lord's Supper, it is true, may in a certain sense be called a mystery (*mysterium ecclesiasticum*). This it is, however, from the fact that

[1] *De genuina verborum Domini: Hoc est corpus meum, etc., juxta vetustissimos auctores expositione liber*, Basel, 1525.

it conserves a religious idea under a sensuous covering (symbol and mystery are cognate terms). The Lord's Supper is designed to lead us from the visible to the invisible. But from this very fact it cannot itself be something secret and not understood. That which is intended for our edification must not be an unknown thing (*non ignota sint oportet, quæ ædificare debent*). The apostles do not speak of the first celebration of the Supper in such wise as to convey to us the impression that it was something hidden and secret. The disciples do not manifest the slightest astonishment when the Lord offers them the bread and the cup; they partake of the repast simply as a passover. If Peter objected to the Master's washing of His feet, how much more strongly would he have objected if the Lord had really proposed to him to eat His flesh! Œcolampadius next has recourse to the history of doctrinal theology. He finds that his views were entertained by the fathers of the Church, especially Tertullian, Chrysostom, and Augustine. It was reserved for the Middle Ages, as he demonstrates, to make this simple transaction a subject of superstitious veneration. His zeal is next directed, not so much against Luther's doctrine as against the adoration of the sacrament, as practised in the Romish Church and especially prominent at the feast of Corpus Christi. On that occasion may be seen "women in bold attire, priests meretriciously decked in princely splendour, armed soldiers with a defiant air. All that was once contemned by the apostles, and that vanishes into nought when compared with the glory of the cross, is here represented as of the highest account. Here we see nothing but gold and silver, precious stones, pictures, images, plays, cymbals, canopies ornamented with pictures of beasts, coverings of purple, flowers, weapons, banquets, but little sober-mindedness, and still less—ay, nothing at all—of religion." After this digression, which certainly did not touch the point at issue, but which shows us how anxiously Œcolampadius was striving to avoid every conception of the Lord's Supper which might again lead to any deification of the creature, he proceeds to a more particular explanation of the sacramental words. Of the fact that they contain a trope, every unprejudiced person must be convinced.[1] It was not difficult to cite instances in point from the Scriptures, such as, "That rock was Christ;" "John was Elijah;" "Woman, behold thy son." That, moreover, the figure was a suitable one to denote the thing intended is further manifested. As the bread that serves to nourish man's body is broken, so Christ's body is broken in order to the feeding of the soul with heavenly food. Had Christ meant that we should eat His body *in* the bread, He would have expressed Himself more clearly to that effect, saying, "*In* this bread is my body;" whilst, as it is, He simply says, "This *is* my body." Thus Œcolampadius saw in Luther's apprehension of the passage a departure from the simple meaning of the sacramental words. The passage in which Jesus speaks of eating His body and drinking His blood (John vi.) bars the way to every material conception of the terms of institution, like the cherub with the flaming sword at the gates of Eden. Of a *bodily* presence of Christ since His exaltation to heaven, the Scriptures say nothing; in fact, the contrary is affirmed. Not until the last day will the Lord truly appear again in the body. Till then we must think of Him as in heaven. Our faith is thus directed to Christ and His reconciling passion, and not to a participation in His body in the Lord's Supper. He is Himself the true bread of our souls, feeding us now with faith and hereafter with eternal glory.

The Council of Basel at first declined to permit this treatise to be published. The friends of the Papacy had not failed to assail it, even before it was given to the press, as perilous to Christianity. The council therefore petitioned Erasmus for his opinion on the subject. That clever man returned an

---

[1] Œcolampadius varies from Zwingle in his apprehension of the trope grammatically only; he retains the *is* without changing it into *signifies*, but holds that the trope is contained in the predicate, the word *body*: "This is (figuratively speaking) my body."

evasive answer to their application. The treatise of Œcolampadius, he said, was, in his opinion, learned, eloquent, and well written; he would even add that it was pious, if that epithet could properly be applied to anything that conflicted with the universal sentiment of the Church, from which, in his view, it was dangerous to swerve. In consequence of these expressions of Erasmus, the council refused its consent to the printing of the treatise, and it was subsequently issued at Strassburg. Be it observed in passing, that Erasmus retired more and more completely behind this barricade of the Church's infallibility. He remarked, for instance, that if the Church were to command him to hold the tenets of Arianism, he would straightway become an Arian. He thus stopped the mouths of his opponents, whilst he apparently surrendered his liberty, and yet made free use of it in his own person.[1]

Œcolampadius had sent his treatise to his friends in

[1] That Erasmus' personal sentiments in regard to the transubstantiation of the bread in the Lord's Supper were very liberal, and sometimes even trifling, is shown by an anecdote concerning him which dates from an earlier period. He was once conversing on the subject with his friend Chancellor More. The latter maintained the following proposition: "Only *believe* in the presence of the body and you really *have* it." Erasmus was silent. Some time after this he borrowed a very fine horse of More to assist him on his journey homeward. This horse pleased him so well that he kept it and took it over the sea to Holland with him. When More demanded the return of his property, Erasmus replied, "Only believe that you have your horse and you certainly *have* it (in Latin distichs in G. MÜLLER, *Reliquien*, vol. iv. p. 410). [See also D'AUBIGNÉ's *History of the Reformation*, vol. iii. p. 223:—

" Quod mihi dixisti nuper de corpore Christi :
    Crede quod habes et habes ;
Hoc tibi rescribo tantum de tuo caballo :
    Crede quod habes et habes."—TR.]

Erasmus here manifested that he did not comprehend the nature of faith, confounding, as he did, super-sensuous and sensuous belief. And yet it is the case with many that their faith is nothing but persuasion and imagination. Such as these, Zwingle says, "remind one of the story of that painter who tried to persuade certain noblemen that he had decorated their church with beautiful paintings, which, however, were visible to none but persons of noble birth. The noblemen, not wishing to compromise themselves, declared that they saw the pictures. Thus when those great teachers (Luther, etc.) cry out that whoever does not believe in the real presence of Christ's body is not a Christian, everybody desires to be considered a Christian, and so professes a belief in the real presence, even if he truly does not believe in it at all " (MÜSCHELER, *l.c.* p. 165).

Swabia, John Brenz at Schwäbisch Hall, and Erhard Schnepf at Wimpfen, hoping for their assent to his doctrines. He was, however, mistaken in this hope. His friends were already prejudiced against the teachings of Zwingle, and consequently against those of Œcolampadius also. With twelve other Swabians they published the so-called *Syngramma*, of which Brenz was the author.[1] This tractate was not entirely destitute of passion. It is true that the former friends of Œcolampadius expressed their regret at being obliged to write against him, but declared that the cause of truth demanded that they should do so. In their eyes, the attacks upon the doctrine of Christ's bodily presence in the Lord's Supper lost all weight, from the mere fact that Karlstadt, Zwingle, and Œcolampadius were themselves at variance in their explanation of the sacramental words. As misers hate each other, and yet are animated by the self-same passion for wrongfully appropriating the property of others, so the opponents of the real presence disagree amongst themselves, being united only by the common outrage which they perpetrate upon the sacrament. Brenz could not deny the frequent use of tropes in the Holy Scriptures; he thought, however, that Œcolampadius was guilty of gross error in thence concluding that *all* passages of Sacred Writ, and so, by consequence, the controverted passage relating to the Lord's Supper, must be understood figuratively. Though the raven is black, the swan is not black also; though Absalom is handsome, Thersites is not. The words, "This is my body," must be taken in just as literal a sense as those that Christ addressed to the man with the palsy, "Thy sins are forgiven thee;" or these, "Peace be with this house;" or, "I am the resurrection and the life." With Christ, saying and doing are one. When the Lord uttered the sacramental words

---

[1] *Syngramma clarissimorum, qui Halæ Suerorum convenerunt, virorum super verbis cœnæ Dominicæ pium et eruditum, ad Jo. Œcolampadion, ecclesiasten.* Comp. HARTMANN and JÄGER, *Joh. Brenz*, Hamburg, 1840, ii.; and HARTMANN, *Johannes Brenz Leben und ausgewählte Schriften*, Elberfeld, 1862, pp. 42 sqq.

over the bread on the memorable night, by those very *words* He instituted a real connection between Himself and the bread. He enclosed His body in the words, so that whoever receives the bread, receives His body *with* the bread. It is then remarked, not without a certain delicacy of perception, that even in human relationships a host shows true hospitality to his guests only when he not merely sets before them meat and drink, but also gives *himself* up for their enjoyment. This observation, however, did not precisely hit the mark, for Œcolampadius himself had taught the self-same thing, namely, that Christ is the true meat and the true drink; but as a host does not permit himself to be corporeally discussed by his guests, but offers them a spiritual feast by affectionately devoting himself to their entertainment, this illustration proved nothing that was intended to be proved by it. That, in general, good Brenz and his co-labourers, with all their unmistakeable warmth of feeling and endeavour after profundity of doctrine, were lacking in clearness and definiteness of thought, must be confessed even by their defenders.[1] Œcolampadius answered the *Syngramma* by his *Antisyngramma*. Other theological magnates of the time—for instance, at a somewhat earlier period, Bugenhagen, and afterwards Bilibald Pirckheimer, at Nuremberg; Theobald Billican, pastor of Nördlingen; and Urbanus Regius, at Ulm—also took part in this controversy, the details of which we do not design to pursue farther. We will only mention that in the year 1526 Luther issued a violent treatise,[2] in which he unceremoniously designated the teachings of Zwingle and Œcolampadius as doctrines of the devil. Zwingle and Œcolampadius failed not to reply to this imputation. The former wrote his *Clear Instructions concerning the Supper of Christ; designed for the simple, that they may not be deceived*

---

[1] See HARTMANN, *l.c.* How the Swabian apology penetrated still farther into the mazes of Scholasticism, discussing with great particularity, but not to the edification of the reader, the old story of the mouse that nibbled a consecrated wafer, may also be seen in the work to which we have referred.

[2] In the preface to AGRICOLA's German translation of the *Syngramma*.

by the subtilties of any. After repeating his former utterances and giving grounds for them, he concluded with this " question of a simple lay-Christian " :—

> " Sag mir an, ob du's weisst,
> Dass Vater, Sun, und Geist,
> Fleish und Blut, Brot und Wyn,
> Allesammt *ein* Gott mög syn ? " [1]

In this writing, as elsewhere, Zwingle treated Luther with all possible respect: " It was his desire to refrain from all hostile contact with that most learned man, and in no wise to attack him." Œcolampadius, however, felt himself inly called upon to point out to the Reformer of Wittenberg, for whom he also cherished a high esteem, the wrong which he had committed; this he did in all sincerity of love. We think that we cannot close this unedifying section of the history of the Reformation better than by the presentation of the following passage, which affords a beautiful instance of the peace-loving sentiments of the Reformer of Basel, who would so gladly have poured a soothing balm into the ever widening wound of controversy. In his *Reasonable Answer to Dr. Martin Luther's Instructions on the Sacrament,* he justly reproaches the latter for the passionateness of his attack upon Zwingle and himself, and then goes on to make the following remarks:—" Passion has thrust its spurs so deep into your mettlesome spirit that it prances and rears, and can see in us nothing praiseworthy, be it rough or soft; and if one discover its error to it, it complains piteously that the faith is being overturned. . . . The Christian reader will, however, perceive that these are the words of an angry man who can speak no otherwise; such an one, having broken his bounds, thinks there is no greater sin and injustice in the world than for any one to touch him. It is a grievous thing, and enough to plunge heaven and earth in ruins, for one to

---

[1] [" Tell me, prithee, if thou know'st,
How Father, Son, and Holy Ghost,
Flesh and blood, bread and wine,
Can in one God all combine ?"—Tr.]

tell him that, as a man, he may be mistaken, and that those who rely upon him may also be in error. Ah! this is not right, my brother. We should not think that the Holy Spirit is confined to Jerusalem, Rome, Wittenberg, or Basel, to your person, or to the person of another man. In Christ alone is fulness of grace and truth, and from Him is communicated of the same now to one and now to another, as you yourself know full well. . . . I wish from my heart that the princely, gentle, and joyful spirit of Christ may return to you. And if you have aught that is good and that will glorify God and be of service to your neighbour, teach it in all meekness, after the precept of the apostle. May God grant to you and to me that we may advance in the knowledge of His Son. Amen."

CHAPTER XVI.

IMPORTANCE OF THE EUCHARISTIC CONTROVERSY—THE PEASANT WAR—MÜNZER AND THE TWELVE ARTICLES—VIEWS OF THE REFORMERS (BRENZ, MELANCHTHON, LUTHER) IN REGARD TO THE SAME—INSURRECTIONS OF THE PEASANTS IN SWITZERLAND (ZURICH AND BASEL)—MARRIAGE OF ZWINGLE AND LUTHER—DOMESTIC LIFE OF THE REFORMERS, AND LUTHER'S CIRCLE OF FRIENDS.

WE have called the sacramental controversy, which engaged our attention in the last chapter, an unedifying and unrefreshing transaction; and such it certainly was. It cannot but affect us painfully to see the most noble of men, individuals who were distinguished at once for their liberality and their piety, at variance upon so sacred a subject; and that subject one which, from its very nature, should have been the thing of all others to reunite them in the bond of peace, supposing that bond to have been by any means ruptured. Thus in the ancient Church, the Roman bishop Anicetus, and Polycarp of Asia Minor, forgot, in the common breaking of bread, their point of difference in regard to the time of the celebration of Easter.[1] But with all our regret for the extent to which the controversy proceeded, we cannot, without laying ourselves open to the charge of superficiality, term the dispute an insignificant combat of words, or hold that the disputants on both sides were governed either by a censurable obstinacy or by prejudice. I have already shown

[1] [See Bower's *History of the Popes*, vol. i. p. 13.—Tr.].

that Luther and Zwingle, notwithstanding all the gifts of divine grace that they possessed in common, differed greatly from each other in natural disposition, education, course of life, and position. We will not reconsider those differences, but will proceed to a closer examination of their posture toward the Lord's Supper and its celebration. That this feast is, in the first place, a memorial feast, at which we thankfully remember the death of Jesus, is a fact which Luther was himself obliged to admit. This view of the matter, however, did not suffice for him. To him, Christ was not merely the founder of a religion, who, like the human founder of a human work, retired from His work at death and surrendered the conduct of it to others. To him, Christ was the Lord and Head of the Church, who, though in heaven, is still linked, by the bond of faith and love, to that Church, which still sojourns, struggling, on earth; and according to his way of thinking, this bond is confirmed afresh to the Church at the sacred feast of which we speak,—the vital communion, whereof the Lord had spoken in language so significant (John vi.), being there effectuated. He could not conceive of the Lord's Supper as a feast at which the guests assembled to celebrate the memory of an absent host, but held that Christ must there be present among His disciples. He and his followers, however, certainly misunderstood the meaning of the Swiss Reformers in supposing that the latter celebrated the Lord's Supper *without* Christ, and aimed at partaking of nothing but bread and wine.[1] Yet we are unavoidably impressed with the thought that in the reformed view (as we shall call it for the sake of brevity) the *historical* element of the celebration has a more prominent place than the idea of a vital connection with the Lord, the desire for a renewal of which is visibly and presently exhibited by

[1] Another combatant from the Lutheran camp, one JACON STRAUSS, preacher at Eisenach (originally of Basel), had plumply accused the Zurichers of partaking of nothing but "dry bread and sour wine." See his pamphlet (1526), *Wider den unmilden Irrthum Meister Ulrich Zwingli's;* also Zwingle's answer: *Ueber Doctor Strussen Büchlin* (*Werke*, vol. iii. p. 469).

participation in that celebration as a means to such renewal. This latter consideration was not wholly absent in Zwingle's case, as may be proved; it, however, remained in the background, until, as we shall see farther on, it was brought into full recognition by Calvin.[1] As the antithesis of opinions presents itself to our eyes in the first stage of the controversy, we have to say that, according to Zwingle's view, the Lord's Supper predominantly exhibits *our* confession of Christ as having died for us; while according to Luther, the communicant should, above all things, rejoice in view of the fact that Christ confesses *him*, condescends to *him*, suffers him to partake of Himself. The difference may likewise be thus expressed. According to Zwingle, the Church publicly testifies its gratitude to the Lord, its relation toward Him in the sacrament being thus essentially an *active* one; according to Luther, on the other hand, each individual member of the Church *receives* salvation from above, *receives* that bread of life which is Christ Himself, thus maintaining a more *passive* relation to the Lord. The testification of thanks might readily be regarded as a *performance of something, a work;* while Luther, here as elsewhere, in accordance with his entire system of faith, makes a perfect surrender of himself to grace, and to the mysterious working thereof in the sacrament. Might not this self-surrender, however, supposing the earnestness of a Luther to be lacking, itself become an external, dead work (*opus operatum*), in which a man might give himself up to an obscure impression without being sensible of any religious motives? It was against such an event as this, against a dead mechanicalness in the observance of the sacrament, such as had long enough ruled the Romish mass, against a relapse into this mechanicalness, that Zwingle desired securely to guard himself and his followers. Though some may accuse him of prosaicism in his mode of viewing the

---

[1] Even *before* Calvin, however, it appeared in Swiss confessions; in the First Confession of Basel, of the year 1534, and the Second (First Helvetic) Confession of 1536, for instance.

sacraments, this very prosaicism has its own great value, when contrasted with the stupidity and slothfulness of spirit into which the masses so readily sink, when they gaze wonderingly upon the mystery from without, instead of making inward experience and appropriation of it. This same prosaicism, again, is justified, when compared with a subjectivism which gives a too imaginative colouring to conceptions that accompany a lively sensibility, and thereby repels calmer, more reflective, and less excitable natures.

The principal stone of stumbling and rock of offence which the Reformed Church, even in its later development, has never been able to get over, and which really lay in the way of a mutual understanding between the two parties from the very beginning, was to be found in the fact that Luther could not content himself with a *spiritual* presence of Christ, but maintained the actual presence of the Lord's *body* in the bread, *the taking, eating, and receiving of that*, in accordance with the literal explanation of the words of institution. And in regard even to this view, the fact cannot be ignored that it was assuredly not without some design that Christ accompanied the giving of the bread to His disciples with the words, "Take, eat: this is my body." Zwingle had no right to change the words *"this is"* into a downright "this *signifies.*" Œcolampadius came nearer to the mark in placing the figurative element of the speech (the trope), not in the copula, but in the predicate. An *image* and a *sign* are two different things. If an artist, desirous of giving us pleasure, were to unveil before us a picture which he had prepared of a loved departed one, we should thank him poorly if we were to say, "Ah, that *signifies* my father, or my friend," as the case might be. We would cry out with rapture, "That *is* my father!"[1] The image does not cease to be an image, but we enter into a livelier connection with it than with the mere sign, or emblem, or however it is called. The Reformed

[1] Reference has already been made to this difference in our account of the second disputation of Zurich. See p. 302.

Church, however, passed beyond the mere sign; in its later confessions it even plainly declared that in the bread and wine it beheld not bare and naked signs, but seals and pledges of divine grace, although it has continually protested against an identification of the image and the thing figured, and against a *bodily* reception of the Lord. Luther's persistent retention of his own standpoint is the less censurable from the fact that in the first stage of the conflict, Zwingle's prosaic exposition must have struck him as somewhat chilling. Luther was, in his whole manner of thought, a downright *realist*. It was not his vocation to spiritualize religious ideas by the rarefying process of reflection; in such a course he saw a vain super-refinement of reasoning, if not an absolute temptation of Satan. With his solid and substantial nature, he loved, in all his religious conceptions, the massive, the firm, and palpable, as is evidenced, also, by his battles with a corporeal devil.

If we were to deprive Luther's character of this attribute, which forms, as it were, the outside husk or shell thereof, it would no longer be that vigorous and sturdy Luther nature from the contemplation of which we derive a peculiar pleasure, even though it is coupled with some coarseness, for which we must make allowances. The longer our eyes are fastened upon this mighty man of faith, the farther our glance penetrates through the thick shell to the wholesome kernel of a heart blessed in God and filled with divine joy and courage—a heart, the sight of which deprives us of all desire to quarrel with its possessor. By the conflict between Luther and Zwingle we are involuntarily reminded of a contrast between the religious qualities of mind and heart which showed itself in the ancient Church and has continued to the present time. As Tertullian was to Origen, so, in a certain degree, was Luther to Zwingle. Men who are under the more direct sway of the sensibilities, who are impressed by the incomprehensible and inscrutable as by a higher power, to which unconditional submission is due, will feel themselves more attracted toward Luther; men who are more given to reflection, and in whom the understanding is the predominant faculty, though their possession of feeling cannot, for that reason, be disputed (only they like to take account of their feelings, head and heart performing their different functions more independently), will incline more to Zwingle's way of thinking. But what we have already remarked, we would here repeat; we will not attach ourselves to one of these men, and reject the other, but will rejoice in both of them, even when they exhibit qualities or actions that cannot claim our admiration.

Above all, Luther's resentment against the "sacramentarians and enthusiasts" will appear in a milder light, if we consider in what a peculiar conglomerate of repulsive elements the controversial point relative to the sacrament presented itself to him. After all the confusion that Karlstadt had excited at Wittenberg, can we blame Luther for regarding that individual's attack upon the sacrament as a new outrage, in the perpetration of which the man who, in his judgment, laid unclean hands upon all that was holy, made a fresh assault upon the Church? And we must pardon him for imagining that Zwingle was a second Karlstadt, when we consider how prone every one is, in times of excitement, to group different parties from his own standpoint, and to regard a casual agreement in individual particulars as a certain sign of party sympathy. And further, when we see the Peasants' War bursting out at precisely the same time with the sacramental controversy, and behold that raging madman, Münzer, playing a principal part in the former, Luther's change of front, in face of that spirit of opposition which was pressing resistlessly forward, and his energetic command to halt, must become doubly explicable to us.

We will now turn from the theological conflict of divines, which has perhaps already detained us too long, to the field of politics, and to the conflict of which that was the scene,— a conflict touching not upon notional and verbal definitions, not even upon the relation of souls, thirsting for salvation, to God and the Redeemer, but upon very real things (in a worldly sense), upon rights of the soil, the forest, and the pasture, or, taking a higher apprehension of the matter, not indeed upon "the general rights of mankind" (for that is too modern an idea), but (to use the language of our fathers) upon the relation of subjects to their superiors, of superiors to their subjects,— hence, upon a social, ethico-political question.

Parallel with the sacramental controversy runs the history of the German *Peasant War.*

Long before the Reformation, there had been revolts of the countrypeople against their lords, and such disturbances had broken out *immediately previous* to that event, a proof that revolution is not the offspring of reformation. In the then prevailing condition of things, when the peasant was (in point of fact, though no longer according to the letter of the law) a serf, and often most shamefully oppressed by spiritual and secular lords,[1] such revolts were easily intelligible. As early as towards the end of the fifteenth century, in 1491, an insurrection had taken place among the peasants of the Netherlands, of Swabia, and of Alsace; on account of the *shoe* which the insurgents bore aloft on a pole as a military ensign, or had painted on their banners, the alliance then formed was called The League Shoe [*Der Bundschuh*], and it diffused itself steadily through Upper Germany. In 1503 we meet with similar disturbances in the bishopric of Speier, and in 1514 we encounter the like in the bishopric of Würzburg. That the conflict in ecclesiastical matters, excited by Luther, exerted a reactionary influence upon political affairs, cannot, we admit, be denied. The logic of the peasants did not distinguish with theological acuteness between the State

---

[1] "The peasants had no rights in the Diet, were without representatives, and destitute of money with which to institute proceedings in the imperial courts; they were too far removed from the emperor, and were a prey to every caprice of their superiors."—RAUMER, *Geschichte Europas seit den* 15 *Jahrhundert,* vol. i. p. 374. Comp. SOUCHAY, *Deutschland während der Reformation,* pp. 71 sqq., 162 sqq.; HAÜSSER, *l.c.*

and the Church, nor can we think it strange that this should have been the case. "The precipitate attacks," says Raumer,[1] "upon age-hallowed opinions and customs in the Church, the appeals to the sense and judgment of the individual, speedily found their counterpart in secular circles. When people were rejecting all the demands of the pope, was it to be expected that the claims of the parson and the nobleman would retain their sanctity? When the Reformers were treating crowned heads with an utter want of decency" (and here Luther comes in for a share of the blame by reason of his conduct toward Henry VIII.), "could the sacrilegious echo of the rabble fail to make itself heard? If the peasant was permitted to pass judgment on heavenly things, might he not presume to have an opinion upon the rights of the chase and the pasture?" etc. This logic was, nevertheless, incorrect and precipitate. It does not do to confound religious and secular matters, and there is a world-wide difference between liberty of thought and belief, and independence of action in civil life. Even in the ecclesiastical domain, the Reformers desired nothing less than absolute independence. God's word, and not the subjective sentiment of the individual, was the arbiter upon which they depended in all cases; and that word distinctly inculcates submission to superiors, and condemns all rebellion. But let us first examine the course of events themselves, before taking a more particular view of the sentiments of Luther and the other Reformers in regard to those events, and of the position which they assumed at this important crisis.

Thomas Münzer, who had been banished from the electorate of Saxony on account of his excesses, and had for a time succeeded in gathering adherents in Switzerland, especially in Klettgau and the district about Basel, had finally retired to Mühlhausen in Thuringia, where a large portion of the people lent him an approving ear. Nor would it have been strange if he had met with the same approbation everywhere, for he

[1] *Geschichte Europas seit den 15 Jahrhundert*, vol. i. p. 374.

flattered the people in every possible way, and, having thus excited the vanity of the populace, depicted Luther as a haughty fool, arch knave, and flattering rogue. If he previously lauded him as "the lamp of the friends of God," he now called him the Wittenberg pope, and accused him of preaching "a fabulous and honey-sweet gospel." And, in truth, his ways and those of Luther diverged widely. "Münzer," says Von Raumer, "desired a political revolution of affairs which should be brought about by the people and accomplished by violence. This was a sentiment that completely separated him from Luther." We are touched by a feeling of pity for this man, who, judging from what we know of him, must have originally exhibited noble capabilities. He, like Luther, had been powerfully affected by Tauler; but while Luther progressed from mystical obscurity to true scriptural knowledge, Münzer abandoned himself more and more to a false spiritualism, which leaped over every historical medium of religion, and thus, by consequence, over the written word, regarding such media as the letter that killeth. "It would not profit a man," he declared with brutish coarseness, " if he devoured a hundred thousand Bibles."

Münzer was soon joined by an eloped monk, whose name was Pfeifer. This man surpassed Münzer in wildness, and carried his violence so far as to threaten to drive his colleague himself from the city if he continued to set his face against the employment of vigorous measures in support of their cause. Whilst Münzer and Pfeifer were thus engaged in Saxony, Upper Germany was visited by a regular insurrection of the peasants.[1] Twelve articles expressing the demands of the

---

[1] SARTORIUS, Geschichte des Bauernkrieges, Berlin, 1795; OECHSLE, Beiträge zur Geschichte des Bauernkrieges in den schwäbischfränkischen Grenzlanden, Heilbronn, 1830; MENZEL, Neuere Geschichte der Deutschen, vol. i. pp. 167 sqq.; JÄGER, Schwäbischfränkische Reformationsgeschichte, Appendix; ZIMMERMANN, Geschichte des grossen Bauernkriegs, Stuttgart, 1856; H. SCHREIBER, Der deutsche Bauernkrieg, Jahr 1825 (Freiburger Urkundenbuch), 1864; ALF. STERN, Ueber die zwölf Artikel der Bauern und einige andere Aktenstücke aus der Bewegung von 1825, ein Beitrag zur Geschichte des grossen deutschen Bauernkrieges, Leipsic, 1860; HÄUSSER, Ref. Geschichte, pp. 103 sqq.

countrypeople were riotously proclaimed as the fundamental principles of a new order of things about to be introduced. The contents of these articles remind us only too forcibly of similar demands in more modern times. It was required that the tithes should be abolished, and that other imposts should be diminished; that the forests of the different parishes should be parcelled out; that parishes should be endowed with the right of choosing their own pastors;[1] and that the privilege of hunting and fishing should be accorded to them. Nor did they rest satisfied with publishing these demands: they followed them by threats;[2] and finding that even threats failed to meet with a hearing, they lent them emphasis by acts of violence. Fire and sword became the order of the day.[3] Cloisters and religious foundations were treated with especial severity, and barbarous cruelties were practised on the persons of the nobles, their wives, and their children. Two hundred cloisters and castles were destroyed in Franconia alone. Objects of ecclesiastical veneration were devoted to ridicule and turned to profane uses. Of the robes used in celebrating the mass, Münzer had a gown of state prepared for his wife. Similar indecencies were perpetrated by the Black Forest peasants in the convent of St. Blasius. The wafers were taken out of their repository and swallowed in numbers, with the words, "Now we can eat a multitude of Lord-Gods at one time."

The most shameful scenes were enacted at the storming of Weinsberg, the birthplace of Œcolampadius. The peasants, who had come to an understanding with the burghers of that

[1] They wished, it is true, to choose such "as would preach the pure gospel," "since it is only by true faith that we can come to God, as it is by His mercy alone that we are saved." They also demanded the right to remove a pastor "in case of his unbecoming behaviour."

[2] "Some of the peasants told their pastors that if they would not make common cause with them, they would deduct from their livings and benefices," JÄGER, p. 297 (from the manuscript chronicle of Weissenhorn).

[3] It was a common saying that "he who did not die [of sickness, it is to be supposed] in the year 1523, who was not drowned in 1524, or slain in 1525, could tell of wonders" [*Wer im Jahr* 1523 *nicht stirbt,* 1524 *nicht im Wassen verdirbt, und* 1525 *nicht wird erschlagen, der may wohl von Wundern sagen*].

town, put all the nobles to death, accompanying their cruelty with the rudest mockery. The most revolting example of their barbarity is to be found in their treatment of Count Ludwig von Helfenstein. He was driven upon the outstretched spears of the peasants, whilst a lad, who had formerly eaten of his bread, played on the fife before him with mocking gestures. The countess besought the mercy of these savages on her knees, but besought in vain. The child that she held in her arms was wounded; she herself was maltreated and taken to Heilbronn on a dung waggon. But fearful was the reckoning to which the fifer was brought. He was fastened by a chain to a post and surrounded with flames. A crowd of knights meantime feasted their eyes on the horrible contortions of the despairing youth.

As a general thing, the lords seemed desirous of excelling the peasants in barbarity. As an instance of more than Turkish atrocity, we may cite the action of the Margrave Cassimir of Anspach, who had the eyes of eighty-five rebellious peasants put out for saying that they no longer wanted him in their sight, and then sent them, a throng of blind beggars, into exile. The cutting off of fingers and similar mutilations were accounted acts of mercy. And who does not shudder at the *spiritual* severity of the Bishop of Würzburg, who travelled through the land with the executioner, and, together with the blood of the insurgents, shed that of the evangelicals in streams! About 50,000 men, at the smallest computation, lost their lives in this unholy war.[1] There was less bloodshed in the Saxon provinces, where the insurrection was not general, but was principally confined to the crew of Münzer, which, though indeed several thousand strong, carried on its own independent operations. There war could also be made upon the insurgents more systematically. Duke George of Saxony, Elector John the Stedfast, successor to his brother Frederick the Wise, who had died about this time, Landgrave Philip of Hesse, and Duke Henry of

[1] RAUMER, *l.c.*

Brunswick, equipped their armies against the insurgents, whom they encountered near Frankenhausen.[1] Their proceedings against the rebels were marked at first with all possible clemency. A herald, bearing equitable proposals of peace, was despatched to them; but, in defiance of all the laws of war, Münzer caused this envoy, who was the son of an aged noble, to be killed and hewn in pieces. Münzer, who, in his proclamations, always signed himself "Münzer with the sword of Gideon," applied all the eloquence of religious and political fanaticism to the inspiring of his people with courage. He admonished them to wait upon the help of God, who never forsakes His own; and a rainbow appearing at that instant in the sky, he declared it to be a favourable token, as they had a rainbow painted on their banner. He boastingly asseverated that he would fain catch all the enemy's bullets in his mantle, that none of them might injure those who were under his command. Passages in the Bible and hymns were misemployed in the endeavour to sustain the excited spirits of the band. Then, with apparent resolution, they moved into the field, singing, "Come, Holy Spirit, God the Lord!" But when the artillery began to play upon their ranks and their fortification of waggons was broken through, their courage failed and they took to flight. Several were taken and executed—a fate which Münzer shared. He is said to have repented of his error, and to have awaited the death-stroke with fear and trembling.[2]

If we next inquire as to the connection which the peasant uprising sustained toward the ecclesiastical Reformation, it may be replied, as we have already intimated, that the con-

---

[1] ROMMEL, *Geschichte Philipps des Grossmüthigen.*

[2] His anguish of mind rendered him incapable of repeating the Creed, and Duke Henry of Brunswick was obliged to say it for him. Comp. on this remarkable man, SEIDEMANN, *Thomas Münzer*, Dresden and Leipsic, 1842. In regard to the results of the whole movement, we can say with HÄUSSER, *l.c.* (p. 117): "Not only did the Peasant War fail to afford any relief to the class with whom it originated, but it also was the occasion of a deep rent in the nation; it injured the great reform movement, and paralyzed political life for a long period."

nection was for the most part an external one. The demands of the peasants did not at first assume a theological colouring, but the twelve articles closed with the statement that if any one could refute them from Scripture, they [the peasants] were ready to obey the word of God. But we should be in error were we to suppose that *only* adherents of *Lutheranism* took part in the insurrection. Very many upholders of the old faith participated in the movement. Thus earlier peasant alliances of previous years had declared the intention of the leaguers to recognise only "the most holy father the pope" as their rightful lord; and even at this time some most distinctly affirmed that they had nothing whatever to do with the newly risen evangelical doctrine.[1] The relation of the parochial clergy to the movement likewise varied with circumstances. Some few ministers suffered themselves to be carried into extremes; of the number of such were Pastor Strauss at Eisenach and the two Pastors Walz and Kirschbeisser in Swabia. The last two were put to death in consequence of their action in the matter. The better minded and judicious evangelical preachers endeavoured, on the other hand, to avert the storm, although they gave no sanction to the system of oppression pursued by the masters. They beheld in this movement a judgment of God. When God will punish men, said one whom we have already encountered in the sacramental controversy, John Brenz of Schwäbisch Hall, He sets wolf on wolf, wicked superiors on wicked subjects, wearying one with the other. It wounded this man to the soul when a field, "laughing with corn," was "wantonly wasted" by the huntsman; and he held that the mighty Nimrods were responsible in the sight of God for the havoc that they committed. Self-help, however, appeared to him inadmissible. He claimed that evangelical liberty was not to be confounded with political liberty. "Christ will be the Captain not of those who draw the sword, but of those who bear the cross. The sword belongs only to the magistrate; subjects must study peace." To suffer, he

[1] Stern, *l.c.* pp. 6 and 100.

taught, is the Christian's privilege whereof he can boast—suffering is the throne which befits him.[1]

If we now examine the views entertained by the Saxon Reformers relative to this movement in their own country and at a distance, we shall find that here also there was a difference between Melanchthon and Luther. Melanchthon, as a closet student, and one who was unacquainted with the material wants of the common people, exhibits from the outset more *aristocracy* of sentiment than Luther. Somewhat one-sidedly entangled in the bare theological view of liberty, and placing himself too little in the position of a people that was at that time, without a doubt, sorely oppressed, he maintained that a Christian might be free and joyful in his God even while subjected to outward oppression. He held that the unwillingness of the peasants to be bondmen manifested an outrageous and violent spirit.[2] Prejudiced by the long-established political notions and customs of his time, he thought that bond-service was as holy a work as raising men from the dead at the command of God. Hunting and fishing *were* privileges which were seemly only for the great lords, and not for the peasants.[3] Nay, he even thought that the peasants had too easy a time: "The Germans are such an unmannerly, wilful, bloodthirsty people, that they really ought to be treated with far greater severity than they now experience." At the same time, however, he admonished the princes to act judiciously towards the peasants, and to give free course to the gospel, and in general to be friendly and affectionate to their subjects.

Melanchthon, like all the other Reformers, maintained the *divine right* of princes. Obedience to the powers that be, even though they were twice as rigorous as was actually the

---

[1] HARTMANN, *Johann Brenz*, pp. 14 sqq.

[2] See the thoughts which he sent to the elector palatine in the spring of 1525; *Luther's Werke*, vol. xvi. p. 32; MARHEINEKE, vol. ii. p. 119; PLANCK, vol. ii. p. 185.

[3] And yet the peasants demanded the right of the chase not for pleasure, but simply that they might protect their fields from the devastations of the game.

case, he held to be the sacred duty of every Christian, and all opposition to them he regarded as resistance against the decree of God. As a true Christian, he might and must find in that liberty which the Son of God brought to men, the only true liberty which more than makes up for the lack of any other. As an intellectually free man, a man of culture, and a sage, he could and must value the good things of life in accordance with another than earthly standard, and find his satisfaction in something different from that which the multitude of men regard as happiness. But perhaps he did not sufficiently consider what a lofty eminence of Christian life, what pure devotedness of faith, and at the same time what intellectual power and culture, are necessary to make these principles efficacious for a man's comfort under an oppressive government, and to enable him to bear even the chains of slavery with a noble pride. He had lived too little among the peasants and common people to *feel* the pressure under which many groaned. Himself belonging to the higher ranks of society, he was a stranger to the needs of the so-called third estate. As a man of learning he had had personal experience of nought save the indulgence of princes; especially of that of the wise and noble sovereign of his own land, who was but just deceased, whose memory he was at this very time cherishing with such lively gratitude, and who had really been a *father* to his people.[1]

Luther entertained in the main similar sentiments to those of Melanchthon. He, also, justly regarded the spiritual, the evangelical liberty for which he battled as the prime thing; and he, too, looked upon every revolt against the powers ordained of God as a sin meriting punishment. Even he held,

[1] On the political sentiments of this excellent prince, see the *Reformations-Almanach*, first series, p. xliv. note. From his deathbed he wrote to his brother John as follows: "Let them endeavour to make a clement settlement with the seditious peasants, for this rebellion is a serious affair, and it may well be that the poor people have had too much put upon them." "We princes oppress the people in all manner of ways, and this is not right." In his last will he commanded that his subjects should be dealt with as gently as possible in regard to taxes.

with a rather strong aristocratic leaning, that "the common man must needs be a bearer of burdens, else would he grow wanton." But as a man of the people he *knew* these burdens, and had a sympathizing sense of their pressure when that became excessive. Better than Melanchthon he, with all his spiritual mode of thought, could also appreciate the material necessities of the people; and though opposing most zealously any confounding of ideas which would make civil freedom *one* with Christian liberty, he still perceived the justice of introducing into earthly relationships timely reforms. He therefore at first regarded the revolt of the peasants with more indulgent eyes than did his learned colleague Philip. It is true, he could not approve of the affair, but he *was* able to trace it back to very intelligible causes, and he therefore would not condemn the insurgents to the nethermost hell. The princes, he alleged, were themselves much to blame for the rebellion; they had committed too many excesses in the way of taxes and extortions,—this was especially the case with the spiritual lords,—and it was the judgment of God that had now overtaken them. Let us hear his own words on the subject.

"The sword is upon your necks," he declares to the princes,[1] "and yet you think that you sit so firm in the saddle that you can never be thrown down. Such security and haughty audacity will be the means of breaking your necks, as you will see. Many times before this I have warned you to beware of that saying in Ps. cvii. 40: 'He poureth contempt upon princes.' You are striving after such a catastrophe; you *will* have your skulls broken; no warning or admonition is of any avail. . . . For know this, dear lords, God is so ordering things that men neither *can* nor *will* endure your fury long; nor *ought* they to submit to it; you *must* become other than you are and give place to God. If you will not do it peaceably and willingly, you must be made to do it by

---

[1] In the tract entitled, *Ermahnung über die zwölf Artikel der Bauerschaft in Schwaben; Luther's Werke*, vol. xvi. p. 58.

violence and destruction. If *these* peasants do not accomplish this, others must. And though you should rout them all, they would still be undefeated, for God would raise up others."

If *this* is not the language of a free man, a man far removed from all servility, I know not where such language may be found. Now, however, having shown to princes and lords that the spring of the evil is in themselves, he demonstrates with equal conclusiveness the fact that he has always held himself remote from every revolutionary movement, that he has confined himself to his teaching, and has ever fought against rebellion; but that, because men have not given heed to the voice of the word, the rude violence of the "prophets of murder" has now—after a sinful fashion, it is true—asserted itself. "If I had a mind to revenge myself on you," he continues, "I might now laugh in my sleeve at you and complacently look on at the doings of the peasants, or join myself to them and help to make things worse than they are. *But from that may my God preserve me, now as hitherto.*" "Fear *God* and regard *His* anger. If it be His will to punish you as you deserve, as I fear it is, He *will* punish you, and that though the peasants were a hundred times fewer than they are; He is able to turn stones into peasants. If you can still be advised, dear sirs, for God's sake give place a little to wrath. A drunken man thinks a waggon-load of hay must give way before him; how much more ought you to leave your raging and your headstrong tyranny, and act reasonably toward the peasants, as toward drunken and erring men. Do not begin a conflict with them, for you know not what will be the end thereof. Try gentle measures at first, because you know not what God will do, lest a spark go forth and kindle all Germany, so that none can quench it. Our sins are before God, therefore we have His anger to fear if but a leaf rustle, and much more when such a host bestirs itself." He next turns to the articles of the peasants, subjecting them to an examination, and adjudging several of them to be not unreasonable. He, however, speaks to the peasants with an earnestness equal to the sharpness which he had previously employed in his discourse to the princes, setting before the former the great sin of violent rebellion. After citing instances from the Old and New Testaments, he points them to his own example: "Pope and emperor set themselves furiously against me. Now, how did I bring it about, that the more the pope and the emperor raged, the more my gospel progressed? I drew no sword, nor did I demand vengeance; I collected no mob and made no disturbance; but I helped to defend the secular powers, even those that persecuted the gospel and me, to the extent of my ability." He then once more admonishes them to refrain from mingling *their* cause, be it as good and right as it might, with that of the gospel, thus making the Christian name a cover for their impatient, unpeaceable, unchristian undertaking.

The boundary lines of *revolution* and *reformation* could not well be drawn more clearly, more forcibly, and more sharply than in this truly classical production. It is pervaded by the kindest intentions and most perfect liberality of a genuine friend of the people—one who sympathizes with the lowliest among them, and is concerned for their spiritual and bodily interests; but it is also filled with the wisdom and moderation of a burgher who is a faithful adherent of law and order; and, finally, it is informed by the higher, prophetical moral energy of an evangelical teacher, penetrated by the holiest principles of the Christian life. In a word, in it prevails the language of a *Reformer*—language that keeps the beautiful and worthy mean between that of the cringing absolutist and that of the demagogic radical. But this did not suit the stormy passions of the rabble. What cared they for gospel and gospel liberty? what for culture and the higher life of the spirit? what concern of theirs were tranquillity and order? what, conformity to justice and law? The freedom-preaching sermons of Münzer and his apostles had long ago transported them beyond every scruple as to whether it was right to lift the sword against the ruling powers. "It is high time," it was declared in Münzer's proclamation; "it is high time—*on, on, on!* It is time: the scoundrels are like frightened curs. Show no mercy, though Esau give you good words. Regard not the misery of the wicked. Have no mercy, let not the blood grow cold on your swords; hammer away on your anvil at Nimrod," etc. Who could restrain these wild beasts after they had once been let loose? what could be employed to repel the violence of this raging rabble but violence? Thus Luther found himself in the position of all who, after they have warmly defended the rights of the people, perceive themselves to be misapprehended, and even derided and assailed, by the very ones whom they have befriended; and all this because they will not make common cause with the works of darkness. The peasants and their leaders despised Luther's book. He therefore issued another and more violent writing, which not only drew upon him at that time the hatred of all seditious persons, but which has, even to this very day, brought him into ill repute with many as a despotic aristocrat, a hater of the peasants, an enemy of the people. The language of this "little book against the robberly and murderous peasants,"[1] is incontrovertibly strong and offensive; but, like every effort of needful resistance against outrage, it is excusable. "In the foregoing little book," he says, "I did not permit myself to judge the peasants, because I hoped they might listen to justice and better instruction. But before I could turn about, they had rushed on, sword in hand, forgetful of their professions, and are robbing and raging, and acting like mad dogs." Hence he advises that they should be treated as such. It is his recommendation (one that certainly sounds severe in the mouth of a good man) that people should throttle them, stab them, dash them in pieces, wherever it was possible, secretly and publicly, just as we are obliged to kill a rabid dog: "If you do not attack *him*, he will attack *you*, and the whole land with you." He commands men to take the field

[1] *Luther's Werke*, vol. xvi. p. 91; MARHEINEKE, vol. ii. p. 127.

against this crew of robbers in the name of the rulers of the country, and characterises such a procedure as a holy work, and one that must be well-pleasing to God; "for whoever is slain upon the side of the lawful powers will be a true martyr in God's sight, if he fight with a good conscience, for he goes in obedience to the divine word." And after recommending the exercise of all possible clemency toward such of the peasants as might be taken prisoners, and toward those who had been led away by them against their will, he exclaims once more: "Therefore, my lads, release here, deliver here, help here; have compassion upon the poor people; stab, strike, strangle there, whoever can! If in so doing you lose your life, you could not have a more blessed death; for you will die in obedience to the divine word and commandment, and in the service of love, which ordains that you should rescue your neighbour from the bands of hell and the devil!"[1]

We can comprehend that these occurrences, combined, as they were, with the lamentable sacramental controversy, must necessarily have produced a frame of mind in consideration of which we should readily pardon many a harsh expression on Luther's part. Any one who is able thoroughly to transport himself into his position, the painfulness of which was aggravated by bodily sufferings, will refrain from passing sentence unjustly upon him, and will also descry the pure silver gleam of an honest and sterling character flashing forth from the fiery glow of an overflowing angry zeal. He will be satisfied with the candid confession of the man who declares himself: "If I am to have a fault, I would rather speak too harshly, and come out with the truth too vehemently, than play the hypocrite and conceal the truth." Let us therefore take to heart the

[1] Comp. Luther's letters to Dr. Rühel, DE WETTE, vol. ii. Nos. 696, 705, 707; and MENZEL, l.c. p. 216. The following words occur in one of the letters to John Rühel: "The wise man says, *Cibus, onus et virga asino*,—oat-straw to the peasant. They will not listen to reason, therefore they must listen to the rod [*virgam*], the guns,—and it serves them right. We should pray for them that they may become obedient; but if they do not so, there is scant mercy for them: let the guns whistle among them, or they will grow a thousand times worse than they are."

words of Matthesius, who depicted Luther's life in a series of sermons, and who expresses himself as follows in regard to his vehemence:—

"We who travel along on the high road or the common footpath cannot and should not pursue after those who leave the beaten track and take their way across water, woods, mountain, and valley. *Much less should we lightly pass sentence upon the earnestness, ardour, and zeal of great men; they have their singing-master in their own hearts;* he often comes down upon them and stirs them up, drives them on and leads them frequently to places whither they had no thought of going; and God, meantime, blesses and prospers their ways, and brings their journey to so marvellous an issue that every beholder is fain to cross and bless himself thereat."[1]

As might have been expected, Luther's book gave offence on all sides, and called forth disapproving voices from every quarter.[2] "What a hubbub I have raised," he writes, "with my little book against the peasants. All that God has done to the world through me is forgotten now. Lords, priests, peasants—all are against me, and threaten to take my life." He felt compelled to vindicate himself in another publication, entitled, *An Epistle from the Author of the Hard Book against the Peasants*. Even in our own day sentiments are much at variance in regard to Luther's conduct in the Peasant War. How often has he been accused, sometimes of inconsistency, sometimes of servility to princes, or at least reproached with his limited theological standpoint, which allowed him to recognise only what he called evangelical liberty,—the liberty of a Christian,—but rendered him indifferent, nay, rather inimical to those human ideas of freedom which have become the common property of subsequent centuries. Many delight to discover in this passage of Luther's life a remnant of monkish prejudice, and cease not to contrast the Augustinian monk of

---

[1] See MÜLLER's *Reliquien*, vol. iv. p. 59, note.
[2] Luther's letters of this period are full of expressions relative to this matter. Comp. Nos. 617, 660, 705, 707, 708, 714, 715.

Wittenberg with that free son of the mountains, the democratic Zwingle, with his enthusiastic championship of the rights of the people. Into the justice of this comparison we will not investigate further at present. Certain it is, however, that revolt against the legal powers, as embodied in the Peasant War, and as appearing in Switzerland also in alliance with Anabaptism, was as little sanctioned by Zwingle as by Luther; and there is no doubt that the former would have endorsed the opinion pronounced by Luther on sedition and rebellion.[1] "It is a bad thing to murder or banish tyrants; it is an example that soon gains ground, giving rise to a general wantonness, so that men call those tyrants who are not tyrants, and murder them just as the mob see fit. We must not pipe much to the mob; they are so easily enraged. . . . If wrong must be suffered, it is better that *we* should suffer from the *rulers* than that the *rulers* should suffer from the *subjects*. For the mob has and knows no moderation, and in every individual thereof there are more than five tyrants. Now it is better to suffer wrong from *one* tyrant—that is, the ruler—than from innumerable tyrants—that is, the mob."

The disturbance among the peasants of Germany communicated itself to Switzerland. The province of Zurich was the first affected. When, in March 1525, the governor of Eglisau was desirous of carrying the fishing laws into effect, the peasants opposed him, urging the trite plea that God had made water, woods, and fields, birds, four-footed game, and fishes, free. A messenger being despatched to them by the council, he was received with a shower of stones. In like

---

[1] From the treatise, entitled, *Ob Kriegsleute auch in einem seligen Stande sein können* (*Werke*, vol. x. p. 570; MARHEINEKE, ii. 265). Comp. RAUMER, p. 37. Comp. also the words of Philip the Magnanimous, Landgrave of Hesse: "Rulers stand in need of most honour when they are contemned, perhaps even when they have erred. Therefore subjects should help to bear such disgrace of their rulers and bring them to honour again, in order that men may live together in peace and honour. If rulers never erred, their honour would never be in danger; but because they are fallible, and because their honour is imperilled by that fallibility, God will protect them and has given command to honour them," RAUMER, *l.c.* p. 373.

manner, the peasants of the seigniory of Grüningen made a raid upon the cloister of Rüti, whose abbot had taken to flight after securing the valuables of the cloister, and treated themselves to whatever they found in kitchen and cellar. They also took possession of Bubicon, the house of the Knights of St. John. Finally, they resolved to make known their grievances to the magistracy in a series of twenty-seven articles, of about the same purport as the twelve articles of the peasantry of Swabia. Similar demands poured in from the county of Kyburg, the seigniories of Andelfingen, Eglisau, Greifensee, Regensberg, and Knonau. The magistracy in vain sought to instruct and appease the malcontents. The people assembled 4000 strong at Töss (near Winterthur), and assumed a menacing attitude. To the deputy sent them from the council they replied, that "they had now become the masters; *they* would ride and let the lords go on foot." Elderly and venerable men in the assembly in vain strove to calm the excited minds of the multitude. The only one who succeeded, by his firmness and wisdom, in allaying the storm in some measure was Rudolf Lavater, the revered governor of Kyburg. Even he was unable to prevent gross excesses on the part of the craving masses, whose gormandizing and potations cost the nunnery at Töss and the neighbouring town of Winterthur heavy sums. The telling and popular eloquence of Zwingle was requisite on this, as on many another occasion, to effect, in alliance with the Government, a treaty of peace, which in the course of the summer was concluded at Zurich.[1]

On the festival of the apostles Philip and James (1st May), 1525, a rumour spread through the city of Basel, to the effect that an association of burghers had conspired to make an attack upon the cloisters.[2] The conspirators, it was asserted, were in connection with the seditious countrypeople, with whom an agreement had been made to open the gates of the city as soon

---

[1] For details see Mörikofer, *Zwingli*, vol. i. pp. 294 sqq.

[2] See Ochs, v. pp. 492 sqq., and Falkeisen (ms.). Both have drawn their accounts chiefly from Ryff and the chronicle of the Carthusian monk George.

as they should approach it. The Council of Little Basel, to whom the Carthusians had applied in their consternation at the intelligence, immediately took measures to ensure safety. Watches were posted extending as far as to the bridge over the Rhine, and the Carthusians passed the night in terror. The next day the grand council assembled for the purpose of investigating more particularly into the rumour. It soon became evident that the story of a conspiracy within the city was without foundation, but that the rumour relative to a gathering among the countrypeople was correct. The messengers of the council immediately took horse, with the intention of repairing to the various districts and ascertaining the grounds of the existent dissatisfaction. Upon their arrival at Liestal, however, they found the peasants from the districts of Farnsburg, Waldenburg, and Homburg already assembled at the first-mentioned place. The insurgents had sent a general notice through the country summoning all to present themselves at Liestal on this day. Those who resisted this command were threatened with the burning of their houses, and to many the statement was made that the notice was in the name of the Government. Several cloisters—such as Schönthal and Olsberg—had already been attacked and plundered by them, while the inmates had been put to flight. The cellar of the chapter of Liestal was emptied.

On the following day the deputies of the council called before them commissioners from the assembled countrypeople, and reminded them how faithfully the Government had watched over their interests hitherto; how many benefits it had showered upon them in times of war, of dearth, of fire, etc.; and how it had provided the needy with money, corn, and all other necessaries. Having made this appeal, the deputies entreated the peasants to disband. They promised to ride themselves to the different places and make further inquiries concerning their grievances. The commissioners took their departure without giving any definite answer. They then had the drum beaten and summoned all to a meeting near the upper gate. Here the assembled peasants took an oath, and held a council in regard to the reply to be given. Upon re-entering the town, they sent word to the deputies that they would give them their answer in the afternoon. This answer was one of deeds. At noon another alarm was beaten, and all were commanded, in consideration of their oath, to meet at the lower gate, whence they were to march upon Basel.

Whilst these things were transpiring, the authorities of Basel had assured themselves of the loyal sentiments of the burghers of that city. The guilds were assembled and conversed with. The burghers were asked whether they were still willing to share the good and evil fortunes of their rulers, or if they had any grievances to complain of. As a result of these investigations, a unanimous good feeling and a disposition to abide by law and order were found to exist in the city. It was now noised through all the streets that the peasants were marching on the town. They had made their approach to the place in the late twilight. They had assembled near Mönchenstein and Muttenz, and had scoured the surrounding country. The cloister of Engenthal, in the vicinity of Muttenz, was set on fire, and the nuns were driven away. They also attacked the cloister of Scharenburg and the Red House, pillaged and ravaged whatever fell in their way, and spread terror before them. The gates of Basel were shut, an alarm was tolled, and every one repaired armed to the appointed squares of the city. The peasants had by this time advanced as far as the little chapel in front of the Eschenthor [Ash Gate]. The younger portion of the burghers requested permission to make a sortie upon them. The council, however, was unwilling to resort to violent measures before once more trying the effect of kindness upon the insurgents. Accordingly, the two chief men of the council, Henry Meltinger and Adelberg Meier, were, under cover of an escort of armed burghers, sent out to the peasants with instructions to ascertain the cause of their conduct. The answer which they received was very unsatisfactory. Soon after this, envoys from Zurich, Bern, and Solothurn made their appearance, with a view to bringing about a peace. At the persuasion of these mediators, the countrypeople withdrew, leaving only a committee, who were charged with the settlement of their affairs. An amnesty was demanded and granted, though not unconditionally. The ringleaders — and among them Stephen Stör in particular, the parish priest of Liestal—were to be brought to punishment; Stör, however, fled and escaped to Strassburg. All others who had written seditious letters were also to incur punishment. The points at issue, which were now read, related to the serfdom of the peasantry, taxes, the privilege of fishing and fowling, and the like.[1] During the discussions, and for several days afterwards, watches and tours of inspection were diligently maintained both in Basel and Liestal, and three gates only were left open in the former place. All bells, with the sole exception of the council-house bell, were silenced for three weeks. There was a constant fear lest a spark of insurrection might still be glimmering, concealed, in the city. Several suspicious personages were taken into custody, one of whom was imprisoned for a long time and put to the rack, but no certain information bearing upon any of the burghers was gained. At a later period (1532), the countrypeople are said to have become sensible of their wrong-doing, and themselves to have renounced all claims to the treaty.

Let us now turn from theological and politico-social disputes to a more peaceful picture—namely, that of the *family*. Luther's form here appears invested with an entirely new greatness. The quondam monk is revealed to view as a house father and house priest, as the founder of the German parsonage; and the picture is an attractive one, whether we contrast it with the serried phalanx of the Romish priesthood, destitute of all family ties, or with the Münzer's mischievous rabble, the underminers of the very foundations of the family.

[1] See the original report in the note in Ochs, v. p. 500.

Here Dr. Martin Luther stands on the same platform with his theological opponents, Zwingle and Œcolampadius, and we are therefore justified in uniting in one general picture the home life of both German and Swiss Reformers.

Of the men whose names we have mentioned, Zwingle was the first to marry. He wedded, on the 5th of April 1524, Anna Reinhart, the widow of John Meier von Knonau. This lady is said to have been very beautiful. She had a son and two daughters by her first marriage. Envious persons, among whom we may name the Anabaptists, accused Zwingle of marrying her for her wealth. And yet, besides the splendid dresses, rings, and valuables that she possessed, but of which, as the wife of a simple pastor, she would no longer make any use, she brought him but 400 florins in ready money. Zwingle, however, declared that he regarded her property as something which did not in the slightest degree concern him. What he prized more than riches was the treasure of a pious heart. Such a heart, filled with trust in God, he had learned to esteem in the widow, and he had also, some time previous to his marriage, taken a fatherly liking to his future stepson, the hopeful Gerold Meier von Knonau—a sentiment of which he gave proof by caring as a real father for the further development of the youth. Of the children by his own marriage, only his son Ulric and his daughter Regula arrived at maturity; the others died at a very early age. But Zwingle was not permitted long to enjoy the pleasures of domestic life.[1] When he gave up his spirit on the bloody field of Kappel (1531), his sorely-tried widow, who in the same battle lost the son of her first marriage, her daughter's husband, her brother-in-law, and her brother, was left dis-

---

[1] We are acquainted with far fewer features of the family life of Zwingle than of that of Luther ; but from expressions in various letters, and from a letter which still remains to us, written by Zwingle from Bern (11th January 1528) to his " dear housewife," in which, amongst other things, he begs her to send him his *Tolggenrock* [blotted gown] (his ink-stained wrapper), we can form a tolerably correct idea of "the pious simplicity and cheerful poverty" of the home of the Zurich pastor. Comp. MÖRIKOFER, vol. i. pp. 212 sqq.

consolate with her two remaining little ones. Years afterwards she experienced the joy of seeing her Regula united to the pious theologian Rudiger Gualter, who afterwards published the writings of Zwingle. It would be superfluous to attempt to describe the feelings of this afflicted woman. The poet Usteri has celebrated the grief of the widow in a beautiful piece, entitled, *Der armen Frouwen Zwingli Klag*.[1]

About a year after Zwingle's marriage, in June 1525, amid the storms of the sacramental controversy and the Peasant War, Luther was married to Katharine von Bora.[2] Katharine von Bora (Bore) belonged to the ancient and noble family of the Von Hugewitzes, and in early youth was placed in the noble Cistercian nunnery of Minptschen, not far from Grimma, in Saxony. On the night of Good Friday, 4th April 1523, Katharine, and eight other young ladies, to all of whom the veil had grown too burdensome, were, not without the knowledge of Luther, abducted from their convent by Leonard Koppe, a burgher of Torgau, assisted by a few of his friends. From Torgau the fugitives proceeded to Wittenberg, where Luther provided for their accommodation. Katharine was received into the house of Philip Reichenbach, the burgomaster. Luther had at first so little intention of marrying her as to take all possible pains to find her a worthy husband. A wooer soon announced himself in the person of Henry Baumgärtner, a patrician of Nuremberg. This individual, however, changed his mind in the sequel; and Luther, after having fruitlessly admonished him that he must make haste if he wished to marry Fräulein von Bora, as another suitor had

---

[1] This poem is given at length by CHRISTOFFEL (Appendix, p. 413).

[2] For an account of her, as well as of Regula, comp. the *Reformations-Almanach*. The prolix work of W. F. WALCH, *Wahrhaftige Geschichte der seligen Frau Katharine von Bora* (Halle, 1751-54, 2 vols.), contains a circumstantial denial of the suspicions raised against her. We search the book in vain for pleasing characteristic touches of portraiture. Among more modern biographers we may mention BESTE (1843) and HOFMANN (1845). On Luther's household see KEIL'S *Lebensumstände* and MÜLLER'S *Reliquien*, iv., but particularly Luther's *Table Talk* and *Letters*.

presented himself in the interval, proposed for her hand, through his friend Amsdorf, in behalf of one Glatz, a preacher of Orlamünde, who had signified his desire to make Katharine his wife. But the lady, with perfect frankness, declared that she could not make up her mind to bestow her heart and hand upon any save Nicholas Amsdorf or Luther himself. The latter, who a year previous to this, in 1524, had laid aside his monkish habit, thereby plainly declaring his absolution from the vow of celibacy, took the matter into consideration and prayed over it. Having, in his own conscience, become firmly convinced of the propriety of the step which he contemplated, he proceeded without delay to its execution. On the Tuesday after Trinity Sunday, 13th June 1525, accompanied by his friends, Dr. Bugenhagen, the painter Lucas Kranach, and a jurisconsult named Apelles, he repaired to Reichenbach's house and there solicited the hand of Katharine in marriage. She at first regarded his petition as a jest, but speedily betrayed the earnestness of her own desire. Friend Bugenhagen then joined the hands of the contracting parties, and thus accomplished the betrothal at once. A fortnight afterwards Luther gave a marriage entertainment, at which his parents were present. The town councillor of Wittenberg sent him a wedding gift of fourteen measures of different kinds of wine, among which were Malvoisie and Rhine wine. Katharine was twenty-six years of age at this time, and Luther forty-two. Judging from her portrait by Lucas Kranach (to be found, together with that of Luther, at the Museum of Basel), her face must have been not exactly handsome, but cheerful, prepossessing, and good-humoured.[1] She impresses one as a good German wife and housekeeper. Luther's enemies accused her of being proud, and many go so far as to affirm that she made the great man, whom neither emperor nor pope could subdue, feel the weight of her supremacy. But even though Luther, in his playful letters, sometimes calls her "Lord Kate," and occasionally in his *Table Talk*

[1] The Carthusian chronicle, however, calls her *speciosissimam, ut dicunt*.

utters some laments over his household cross,[1] this very good-humoured and open recognition of her sway proves that there was nothing so terrible about it. On the contrary, he bears her witness in his will that "she always treated him affectionately, respectfully, and considerately, as a pious, faithful spouse, and served him not simply as a wife, but as a servant." A learned woman Katharine was not, for her convent training did not give her even an ordinary knowledge of things that were transpiring in the world around her. Thus Luther relates that in the first year of their married life she often sat with him whilst he was studying; and that not knowing on one occasion what to talk about, she said to him, "Doctor, is the Grand Master in Prussia the brother of the Margrave?" Luther, however, seems to have acquainted her with many portions of his writings; upon reading her passages from his polemical treatises against Erasmus, she exclaimed, "That Erasmus must be a right venomous toad." That, notwithstanding her neglected education, she was no *ordinary* woman, is sufficiently demonstrated even by her distinct declaration that she would have none but Amsdorf or Luther for a husband; and if she did pride herself somewhat upon being the wife of Luther, surely the sentiment was an excusable one.

In 1526, a year after Luther's marriage, Œcolampadius married. The rapid succession of these marriages of the greatest of the Reformers drew from Erasmus the bitter remark that the Lutheran tragedy seemed to him to be becoming a comedy, since every complication finally resolved itself into a wedding.[2]

Vibrandis Rosenblatt was the choice of Œcolampadius. She was the daughter of John Rosenblatt, a knight and colonel of the Emperor Maximilian I. She, like the wife of

[1] He declares, for instance, that if he had to marry again, he would hew himself an obedient wife out of stone, for there were none such in reality.

[2] A few of the Reformers entered into wedlock after attaining quite a venerable age. William Farel, for instance, married when he was in his sixty-ninth year. After six years of wedded life he was blessed with a son.

Zwingle, was a widow when she married Œcolampadius, having previously been united to another man of learning, by name Ludwig Cellarius. It was the singular lot of this lady to marry four learned men in succession, a circumstance which Wurstisen pronounces "*a remarkable instance of good fortune;*"[1] for after the death of Œcolampadius she became the wife of Wolfgang Capito, and finally was married to Martin Bucer. She subsequently accompanied the latter to Cambridge. She died at Basel on the 1st of November 1564, and was buried there in the minster by the side of Œcolampadius. In regard to her personal character, we know little [2] besides what Œcolampadius himself writes concerning her in a letter to Farel: "She is a good Christian woman, without fortune, but of good ancestry, and a widow. She has also passed through a school of suffering. I should have preferred it if she had been a little older than she is; hitherto, however, I have failed to discover in her the slightest trace of youthful wilfulness or levity." Three children, a son and two daughters, were the fruit of this union, and to all of these Œcolampadius gave significant names in baptism. The son was called Eusebius, the daughters were Aletheia and Irene. *Piety*, *Truth*, and *Peace* were to wreathe the household altar, and accordingly, when dying, he said to the relatives whom he left behind him: "Take care that they become what they are called—pious, peaceable, and true."[3]

Though it would give us pleasure to dwell for a while longer on the marriage of the Reformers, and to catch some glimpses of the domestic life of all of them, we are compelled, in default of intelligence in regard to the Swiss Reformers, to limit ourselves principally to the presentment of a few features from the life of Luther, which, without binding ourselves to

[1] *Epitome*, p. 92; Ochs, vol. v. p. 54.
[2] Compare, in addition to the *Reformations-Almanach*, Von Brunn's short biography of Vibrandis.
[3] Eusebius died in Strassburg at Capito's house, in the year 1541. Aletheia was married to Christian Sorbius, a preacher in Strassburg, and Irene to J. L. Iselin, in Basel, in 1569.

the observance of chronological order, we will group together here as at a convenient resting-place.

It has already been remarked that the physical health of Luther was affected subsequent to his sojourn at the Wartburg, and that his mind was frequently filled with gloomy images. The sacramental controversy and the Peasant War contributed further to the embitterment of his life, and tears were often to be seen chasing each other down his cheeks. Two years after his marriage, in 1527, he was attacked with a violent illness, from which he did not think he should recover. During the course of it he spoke to his wife as follows: "My dearest Kate, if the dear Lord our God will take me to Himself at this time, submit, I beseech thee, to His gracious will. Thou art my lawful wife; be sure of this, and have no doubt whatever of it. Let the godless, blind world say what it will; order thy ways in accordance with God's word and hold firmly to it, and thou wilt have a sure and stedfast consolation against the devil and all calumniators." He then asked after his little son. "Where is my darling Hänschen?" The child, on being brought to him, smiled at his father, and Luther said: "O thou good, poor little baby! Now do I commend my darling Kate and thee, poor little orphan, to my dearest, good, and faithful God. Ye have nothing; but God, who is a Father to the orphan and the Judge of the widow, will doubtless nourish and support you." He then prayed for his beloved ones, saying: "My dearest God, I thank Thee from my heart that Thou hast willed that on earth I should be poor and a beggar; for this cause I can leave neither house, field, grounds, gold, nor goods to my wife and little son. As Thou didst give them to me, I re-commit them to Thee. Thou rich God, nourish them, teach them, preserve them, as Thou hast hitherto nourished me, O Father of the orphan and Judge of the widow!" He then spoke to his wife about some silver cups in which his whole wealth consisted. At this Katharine was for a moment somewhat cast down; she controlled herself, however, and said with quiet composure: "My dearest Doctor, if it be God's will, I would rather you should be with the dear Lord our God than with me. But I and my child are not the only ones to be considered at this time; there are many pious Christian people who still have need of you. Do not trouble yourself, my dearest husband, on my account; I commend you to His divine will; I hope and trust that God will graciously spare you to us."[1] Katharine's hope was not confounded. God spared the life of her beloved husband. After falling into a beneficial sweat, he recovered. He was, however, subject to frequent and alarming attacks. At the end of the same year in which he had been so ill, he suddenly fainted. Upon coming to himself he looked at his wife, with a gentle but significant smile, and said: "Kate, suppose that lightning stroke had made an end of me. Thy will be done, O Lord God! Death is not bitter to the Christian, for he has Christ for a mercy-seat, and in Him life." This lightning flash also passed, however, and left Luther almost a third of his life's pilgrimage to accomplish.

If we question what it was that filled, occupied, and cheered this man during all those moments which he spent otherwise than in public activity and on the field of combat, we shall find that in private as well as in public his life was a *rich* one,—that it was a life full of faith, of love, of cordial interest in all that was great, good, and beautiful.

Prayer occupied the place of honour amid his daily engagements. Although opposed to all mechanical habits of prayer, such as were customary in the Romish Church, he maintained the necessity for a certain order and regularity in the practice of this Christian duty; and it is touching to behold the pure, childlike simplicity with which this great man discharged a duty so sacred. "Every morning and evening, and often during his meals," we are told,[2] "he said his prayers, just as

---

[1] [The reverence of Katharine for her husband, the Reformer, is evidenced by her use of the plural pronoun in addressing him.—Tr.]

[2] Keil, after Matthesius.

he had been used to do in the cloister from his youth up. Besides this he repeated his Shorter Catechism like any little schoolboy, and constantly occupied himself in reading. His Psalter was his prayer-book, and the Catechism his manual of devotion. From these he derived comfort, instruction, and admonition. In all important business, prayer was to him the beginning, the middle, and the end." " I think," says Luther in one place, " that my prayers are stronger than the devil himself; and if this were not true, things would long since have gone very differently with Luther. . . . . If I remit prayer for a single day, I lose much of the fire of faith."[1] It would be impossible to cite here all of the many and glorious passages relating to the power of prayer which we find scattered through his writings, or to present all of his utterances in regard to the right mode of praying. Deserving of note are the written instructions which, in the year 1534, he gave to Master Peter, a barber, and which contain a complete exposition of the Lord's Prayer, the thoughtless "gabbling" [*Zerplappern und Zerklappern*] of which he could not strongly enough censure. The fact that our thoughts should always be in attendance on our prayers, he very clearly illustrates to the barber. " A good and diligent barber," he says, " must always have his thoughts, wits, and eyes fastened upon his razor and his customer's beard, and must not forget what he is about whilst he handles his implement ; but if he insist upon gossiping as he works, or if he be thinking of or staring at something else, he may readily cut a man's lips or nose off, or even cut his throat. Thus everything, to be done well, must have the whole of a man, all his wits and all his faculties. . . . . How much more does *prayer* need the heart, singly, entirely, and alone, if it shall be the right sort of prayer!" Luther himself confessed that he was still sucking the paternoster like a child, eating and drinking it like an old man, and that he could not get enough of it.

[1] W. Farel tells us "he could pray with such fervour that all who heard him were drawn heavenwards." KIRCHHOFER, *l.c.* vol. ii. p. 169.

But Luther did not confine himself to the ordinary prayers of the day. Often, when his heart impelled him, he would rise from his seat, walk to the window, lift up his eyes and his hands to heaven, and pray for half an hour. His confidence in prayer was manifested in an elevating manner, especially in important crises of his life. I will cite but two instances of this fact, of which one occurred on the occasion of his father's death, and the other during the illness of his friend Melanchthon. The former presents a touching example of submission to the will of God, whilst the other reveals the mighty power of faith.

While Luther was in Coburg, during the session of the Diet of Augsburg (1530), he received the sad intelligence of the death of his father. His wife manifested a tender tact upon this occasion, in the endeavour to alleviate his grief, by sending him a likeness of his beloved daughter Magdalen; this she caused to accompany the melancholy letter that a friend had been obliged to write. After Luther had read the letter, he said to his friend Dietrich, " Well, my father is dead too." He then seized his psalm-book, retired to his room, wept until he could weep no longer, prayed till his heart had recovered its composure, and then resumed his wonted bearing. What a vast contrast between such behaviour as this, beautiful in its manliness, and an artificial sentimentality![1] Magdalen, the dear child whose likeness was to console Luther, died a short time after the death of his father, and it was Luther then who must needs comfort his mourning wife. This he essayed to do as he grasped her hand and said, " Dear Kate, think how well it is with her where she has gone."

The other instance of Luther's earnestness in prayer, to

---

[1] Ochs (vol. v. p. 659) unjustly accuses Œcolampadius of *coldness* because he thus writes concerning his sick son Eusebius: "My Eusebius is not as strong as he is tall. His cough almost chokes him. Perhaps the Lord will yet call this boy to Himself." This, we admit, is the language of manly brevity, but it is also the expression of sadness and submission. Our age is over dainty in this respect; people attribute too great a virtue to mere words, and lamentation is made to supply the lack of faith.

which we have referred as connected with Melanchthon's illness, is familiar to all. In 1540 Melanchthon fell sick when on a journey, and retired to his bed at Weimar. The elector sent a carriage to bear Luther to his friend's side. Upon his arrival he found the sick man apparently at the point of death: his eyes were lustreless, his mind was gone, speech and hearing had departed, his countenance was changed, and his temples were sunken. He ate and drank nothing, but lay in a state of unconsciousness. Luther was much alarmed, and said to his friends: "May the Lord preserve us! How the devil has abused this organ of divine truth!" Then turning to the window and placing himself with his back to the company, he prayed fervently to God. "The Lord," says Luther himself, "was constrained at this time to grant me my desire; for I threatened to have nothing more to do with Him, and poured into His ears all the promises to importunate prayer that I could bring from the Holy Scriptures, so that He must needs hear me if I was ever again to trust His promises." He then confidently took Melanchthon by the hand, saying, "Be of good cheer, Philip; you will not die." He also spoke other words to him out of the fulness of his heart; and, behold! Melanchthon began to revive; his consciousness gradually returned to him, and in a few days he was on the road to recovery. I do not cite this passage in the Reformer's life with a view to encouraging a belief in miracles, or to justify the too familiar and well-nigh offensive tone of Luther's prayer. As has already been remarked, many actions of great men, which can be endured and understood when considered in connection with the age in which they lived, and the circumstances of their lives, would justly merit censure, and would sink to the level of impertinences if they were to be imitated by others. There are certain things that are beautiful but *once* and in their own place, and that are therefore inimitable. Nor would I think of elevating Luther's external mode of prayer, his *mannerism*, as I might say, to the position of a general rule. He himself would be the last to approve of such a course. Let every man here make use of his Christian liberty as a Protestant—*i.e.*, one whose Church prescribes neither times, nor forms, nor gestures of prayer. But this, at at least, is certain—to wit, that the true *spirit of prayer* that energized a Luther, is the only spirit whence true and wholesome reformatory fruits can proceed; and without doubt, a lack of steady progress in the betterment of State and Church, and a failure in right undertakings—such, even, as would be for the common profiting of all—to win an abundant measure of the divine blessing, are chargeable in great measure upon a deficiency of true unction in prayer.

Next to prayer, work, and especially the searching of the Scriptures, was Luther's daily food. He knew, indeed, the impropriety of excessive labour and the necessity of relaxation; and hence it was that upon one occasion, when his friend Melanchthon was labouring too zealously upon a treatise in confutation of his opponents, and even neglected his meals in consequence of his intense application, Luther took the pen from his hand, remarking, "We cannot all the time serve God by working, but we must also serve Him by resting; therefore is it that He gave us the fourth commandment and enjoined the hallowing of the Sabbath." And Luther really provided for his own relaxation and for the strengthening of his physical man in a manner that was well adapted to secure the ends in view. He had a turning-lathe, upon which, in his leisure hours, he made all sorts of articles, and he also took much interest in working in his garden. (Several of his letters relate, amongst other things, to such occupations, for they contain requests sometimes for tools and sometimes for different kinds of seeds.) Occasionally, however, he forgot the golden rule of moderation which he gave to others. Being at one time engaged in an exposition of the twenty-second Psalm, a portion of Scripture which, on account of the Messianic promises therein contained, seemed to him particularly weighty, he shut himself up in his study, with a little bread and salt, and there, for three days and three nights, remained at his desk. His family, meantime, vainly sought him through the house and in the adjacent garden. At last some one ventured to burst open the door of his study, which was locked. Not until then did Luther, whose abstraction from worldly matters had been complete, arouse from his dream. He was at first inclined to reprove those who had thus forced an entrance upon his retirement, but soon professed his satisfaction and returned to the bosom of his family.[1] Life in the family circle, the company of his children, and his cheerful intercourse with friends, sweetened many an hour for Luther. Let us listen to his own testimony in regard to the beauties and joys of domestic life. "If," says he, "you see a woman faithfully and diligently busied with her children, and you be an honest, good man, your heart is drawn out toward her, and yet you feel that you are not stirred by earthly thoughts, earthly joy, or earthly lust. It is God's work in her that you have an inward perception of, and it is the very power of His Holy Spirit that causes you to perceive this and that stirs your heart, and you cannot but be friendly to her, without claiming any return."

Children Luther regarded as the greatest blessing of marriage. "They cement and preserve the bond of love," he declared. Glorious and deep were the glimpses which he gained of the children's world and the nature of childhood; how, indeed, could it be otherwise with him, pure and child-like man that he was? He frequently expressed his admiration for the faith and the prayers of children. "They are much more learned in faith," he says, "than we old fools." He would often gaze with quiet, fatherly emotion at his children as they played, or sat at table, as they studied,

[1] See MÜLLER, *Reliquien*, vol. iv. p. 26 (from Moz, *Leben Luthers*), and (HIRSCHFELD) *Unterhaltendes Historienbuch*, Ulm, 1833. The rest of the Reformers also were diligent workers. Zwingle was particularly observant of *regularity* in the division of his day's work, differing in this respect from Luther, who was in a greater measure guided by impulse. On the division of Luther's time, see NÜSCHELER, p. 123, and MÖRIKOFER, vol. i. pp. 327 sqq. (after Bullinger). The intense application of Calvin is well known. For particulars [relative to Calvin's habits of work] see below (under Calvin).

prayed, or—quarrelled. From every circumstance he drew wise Christian instruction and food for his heart. Once, as he rode one of his little daughters upon his knee, he asked her, "Leuchen, what will the holy Christ bring you?" Upon her confiding to him her childish hopes, he said, "Little children have such sweet thoughts of God, as that He is in heaven and yet is their God and dear Father." Soon afterwards he expressed a wish that he had died when he was yet a child, and said that for this he would gladly have given up all the honour which had befallen him in the world and which he might still receive. On another occasion, when his children had been disputing and speedily became reconciled, he remarked, "Dear Lord God, how art Thou pleased with such children's life and sports—ay, all their sins are nothing but forgiveness of sins." At still another time, as his children's eyes were fixed with pleasure and patient desire upon a dish of beautiful fruit, he said, "He who would behold a picture of one who rejoices in hope, has here a true presentment of the same. Oh that we might look for the last day with such a cheerful hope!" As one more illustration of this portion of our subject, I will here insert a letter written by Luther from Coburg, in the year 1530, to his eldest son[1]:—

"1530.

"Grace and peace in Christ, my dear little son! I am glad to see that you study well and pray diligently. Continue thus to do, my little son. When I come I will bring you a beautiful fairing. I know a pretty, pleasant garden; there are many children walking there; they have on little golden jackets, and they gather beautiful apples under the trees, and pears, and cherries, and plums; they sing, they jump about, and are merry; they have also beautiful little horses with golden bridles and silver saddles. I asked the man who owns this garden whose these children were; he said, 'These are the children that like to pray and study, and that are good.'

[1] DE WETTE, vol. iv. No. 1228.

Then said I, 'Dear man, I, too, have a son, whose name is Hänschen Luther. May not he come into the garden and have some of these beautiful apples and pears, and ride on these splendid little horses, and play with these children?' Then the man said, 'If he likes to pray and to study, and to be good, he shall come into this garden, and Lippus and Jost [the sons of Melanchthon and Justus Jonas] may come too; and when they are all here together, they shall have fifes and drums and lutes and all sorts of stringed instruments, and they shall dance and shoot with little cross-bows.' And he showed me a fine meadow in the garden, made ready for dancing. On the bushes that bordered it there were hanging fifes and drums of pure gold, and silver cross-bows. But it was early, and the children had not yet had their breakfast, so that I could not wait for the dancing, but said to the man, 'Dear sir, I will go right away and write all about this to my dear little son Hänschen, that he may pray diligently and study well and be good, so that he too may come to this garden; but he has an Aunt Lena whom he must bring with him.' Then said the man, 'So it shall be; go and write to him thus.' So, dear little son Hänschen, study and pray cheerily, and tell all this to Lippus and Jost, that they too may study and pray; and then you shall all come together to the garden. I commend you now to Almighty God. Greet Aunt Lena, and give her a kiss for me.—Your dear father,

"MARTIN LUTHER."

Dearly as Luther loved children, he was a strict advocate of discipline; and much as he disapproved of an excess of severity, such as he had himself experienced, he also warmly condemned that weakness which suffers self-will and sin to flourish in children. We should punish, was his simple maxim, in such a manner as to keep the apple always by the side of the rod. One of his sons once committed a fault, and was for three days not allowed to approach him until he had begged his pardon. His wife and several of his friends petitioning him on the lad's account, he said, "I would rather have a dead son than an undisciplined one. It is no empty saying of St. Paul's that a bishop should be a man who ruleth well his own house, having obedient children, to the end that others, being thereby edified, may take example by him and not be offended. We preachers are placed so high, in order that we may set a good example to others. But our ill-mannered children are an offence to others; the urchins would sin by virtue of our privileges. And though mine were to sin often and to commit all manner of rascalities, I should not hear of it; people would not tell me of it, but would conceal it from me, and so it would be as the old proverb says, 'If anything goes wrong in our own houses, we are the last to know of it; not until it has been bruited through every street do we hear thereof.' Therefore we *must* punish the boy, and not cover our eyes with our hands and let him go unrebuked."

Like all pure-minded men, Luther possessed a lively feeling for the beauties of nature, in whose temple he loved to linger, and in which, as elsewhere, he gave scope to his theological thoughts. His *views* of nature were, indeed, not those of modern times, but were mediæval; the devil seemed to him to have a place everywhere, and especially to rule in water. To the sublime doctrine of the descent of man from the ape he had not risen. On the other hand, he regarded the devil as the great progenitor of the monkey race. He also put faith in the devil's foisting of changelings upon mothers, and in other extravagant stories. And yet none of these things obscured his joy in God's rich nature. He might sometimes be seen standing, absorbed in quiet admiration, before a fine fruit tree, or holding a rose in his hand[1] and praising the Creator for its wonderful structure; or he would gaze at a little bird building its nest, and from this "doctor of theology" gain a stronger faith in the Father who nourishes the birds of

---

[1] All this is in strict accordance with the *Table Talk*. Comp. especially the two sections relating to God's works and the creation.

heaven; or, again, he would lift his eyes to the starry sky and lose himself in reverie over the wondrous course of its bright orbs. And though he deeply deplored that fall whereby man became an exile from Paradise, his faith made itself a new paradise out of the fragments of the visible creation. " Ah," he once sighed amid the fragrant blossoms of a lovely spring, " ah, how would man, if Adam had not sinned, have recognised God in all His creatures; how he would have praised and loved Him in all, so that he would have considered and beheld God's omnipotence, wisdom, and goodness, even in the tiniest floweret! For of a truth, who can understand how God can, of the dry ground, make so many different sorts of flowers, of such fair colours, such delightful odours, the like of which neither painter nor apothecary could produce? God can bring green, yellow, red, blue, brown, and all manner of colours out of the earth. All this Adam and his children would have turned to the honour of God; they would have praised and magnified Him, and would have used all creatures with thanksgiving, such even as we now use with disgust and displeasure, or rather such as we ignorantly *mis*use, just as a cow, or other unreasoning animal, tramples the loveliest and sweetest flowers and lilies under its feet."[1] Luther's example affords a proof that a fine and delicate *appreciation of nature* may develop within poetic and religious minds even when *natural science* is far behindhand, just as, on the other hand, there may be a highly-developed *science* of nature where this appreciation is entirely lacking.

Luther also enjoyed the gifts of nature with gratitude and wise moderation, and rejoiced over them in the cheerful social circle. Ripe, luscious fruit he preferred to all other dainties, and he thought that Adam himself, before his taste was depraved, would rather have eaten it than partridges; he held also that the paradisaic fruit was far superior to any that we have now, our finest peaches being in comparison with it nothing but miserable crab-apples. Nor did Doctor Luther, as is well

[1] *Tischreden* (Frankfort edition), p. 41.

known, despise the gift of the vine, although in this respect his sanction has been much abused by many. On what authority the familiar couplet, "Who loves not wine, woman, and song," etc., is ascribed to Luther, I know not; I have at least no reliable documents to prove that he was the author of it. He used, however, to say, "We ought to give our guests a good drink, that they may be cheerful, for the Scripture says, ' Bread strengtheneth man's heart, but wine maketh him cheerful.'" Like his learned colleague Philip, he set a high value upon the different sorts of fine wines that were presented to him at weddings and other festivities. When, on some festive occasion, he sat, a generous host and grave father of a family, at the hospitable board garnished by the happy faces of his children, and spread, in honour of a few friends, Jonas, or Bugenhagen, or Amsdorf, or a stranger guest, with a Martinmas goose, or, it might be, venison sent him by the elector from the seigneurial kitchen, or some carp or trout caught by Luther in his own fish-pond,[1] in addition to the vegetables which he himself had raised, he was, if we may trust his own confession, happier than many a nobleman or prince; words of earnestness and pleasantry flowed, in gracious alternation, from his lips,[2] and diligently did his guests gather up the spiritual crumbs which fell from the table, that nothing might be lost. Thus originated the greater part of that collection of memorable speeches and actions (memoirs), prepared by Aurifaber and given to us under the name of

[1] See *Tischreden*, p. 41 (*b*).

[2] One anecdote more. A friendly strife once occurred between Luther, Melanchthon, and Bugenhagen, who were assembled at the house of Camerarius, as to who could compose the shortest blessing. Luther said, *Dominus Jesus sit potus et esus*; Bugenhagen repeated in Low German, *Dit und dat, trocken und nat, gesegn' uns Gott*; Melanchthon, briefly and well, *Benedictus benedicat*. Such and similar traits in the lives of the Reformers show us how men on whom the weightiest affairs were pressing still had room, in the midst of trusted friends, for the joyousness and the innocent jests of social life. ZIETZ, *Bugenhagen*, p. 218. The wholesome instruction which Luther gave the son of a merchant of Hamburg, who had taken the liberty of helping himself with his fingers to a goose that was served at the Reformer's table, see in KEIL, for the year 1545; and MELANDER, in his *Joco serio, de studioso quodam Hamburgensi*, vol. i. p. 522.

Table Talk [*Tischreden*], of which we must say, however, that not every particular can be strictly vouched for.[1]

Next to what Luther regarded as the highest and holiest, he loved *music*. This it was that gave a zest to the cheerful meal, and that banished the gloom of many a sad hour of the Reformer. At the table, and after rising from it, he frequently sang or played on the lute; and when he had worked until he was weary and was desirous of putting a check upon his thoughts, he instituted a little house concert, in which he was assisted by his friends. Seufl, the Bavarian composer, who at that time set several of the Psalms to music, was a special favourite of his. Luther himself played upon several instruments, and delighted not a little in the progress that music had made in his day. He declared that King David would have marvelled had he been a witness of this advance. He strongly recommended that all young persons should learn music, and especially desired that school teachers and preachers should be accomplished in this sacred art. He would not look at a preacher who could not sing. "I am not satisfied," he says, "with any man who despises music, and this all fanatics do. For music is a gift of God, not a gift of man. It also drives away the devil and makes people cheerful. Occupied with it, men forget all anger, unchastity, pride, and other vices. Next to theology I give music the nearest place and highest honour." And again: "The devil is a sad spirit and makes men sad, and he cannot abide cheerfulness; hence it is that he flees farthest from music and stays not when men sing, especially when they sing spiritual songs. Thus David alleviated the distress of Saul by playing on his harp

---

[1] The most recent edition of this work was prepared by FÖRSTEMANN and, after his death, by BINDSEIL, 1844-48. From this we obtain additional particulars of the history of the *Tischreden*. It was, primarily, from the reports of Luther's table companions, Anton Lauterbach, Veit Dietrich, Hieronymus Besold, Johann Schlag of Haufen, Johann Matthesius, Georg Rörer, and others, that JOHN AURIFABER, court preacher at Weimar, compiled the *Colloquia Lutheri*, which he first issued in 1566, and which passed through several editions. After him, others—Andreas Stangwald, Nik. Selnekker, J. G. Walch (vol. xxii. of his collected works)—have also issued editions of the *Tischreden* of Luther.

when the devil plagued the king." As we have already remarked, Luther stood on common ground with Zwingle in his love for music.

Luther also valued secular music in its proper place, and entertained a lenient opinion of the practice of dancing. "It is a question whether dancing, from which many evils are wont to arise, can be reckoned amongst sins. Whether dancing was customary among the Jews or not, I do not know. But because it is customary with us to invite guests, to array ourselves in our best, to eat and to be merry, and also to dance, I see not how the custom can be repudiated. It is the abuse of it only that must be avoided. That sin and wickedness are committed is not to be ascribed to the dance. When all things are honourably conducted, thou certainly mayst dance with the rest of the guests. Faith and love are not driven away by dancing, or children could not be permitted to dance."[1] Luther, as he says of himself, did not belong "to those long-visaged saints who judge and condemn others, who upbraid a maiden if she do but go to the dance or wear a red dress." He says: "God can endure (if people are but Christians) that every one should dress and adorn himself according to his own ideas, and that he should live comfortably in honour and seemly pleasure, providing only that moderation be observed in all this."

With so rich a mind and heart as those which our Luther possessed, he could well do without earthly goods. Nor did he ever strive to acquire them. "As a preacher," he wrote to the elector, who had presented him with some cloth for a gown, "it is not fitting that I should possess a superfluity, nor do I desire it." He, indeed, was not ashamed to accept such gifts of love when they seemed to flow from a kind heart; he preferred, however, to be independent, and accepted only such things as were absolutely necessary. The elector

[1] See KEIL, *Lebensumstände Luthers*, p. 46. Calvin's opinions on this subject were far stricter, as were also those of Knox and all his Puritan adherents.

once offered him a small share in a mine, for the benefit of his son; this he refused. On another occasion, his friend Bugenhagen brought him 100 florins as a present from some nobleman. Luther would not accept any of this money, but gave half of it to Melanchthon and the other half to Bugenhagen himself, whereupon a noble and magnanimous rivalry among the friends ensued. Luther, nevertheless, arrived at some degree of worldly prosperity. He not only owned gardens and real estate in and around Wittenberg, but he also at a later period of his life purchased the two small farms of Wachsdorf and Zeilsdorf, for the latter of which he paid 610 florins. Katharine directed the management of this farm, and was by Luther jestingly called the Frau Doctor Zeilsdorferin.

Notwithstanding Luther's small income he was exceedingly hospitable and beneficent. He kept a free table for poor students. His house was open to all who were oppressed, to every stranger as well as to every friend. He not only frequently recommended poor persons to the elector, or to other beneficent individuals, but he also himself set an example in affording them aid. Upon one occasion when a poor man sought his presence and complained of his destitution, Luther's ready money was exhausted, and his wife was confined to her bed. Not willing, however, to dismiss the man without relieving his wants, the Reformer procured him some money which had been presented to his children by their god-parents, and gave this to the poor fellow. To his wife, who looked somewhat grave when she discovered what her husband had done, he said, "Dear Kate, God is rich, He will give us some more." Wherever he could dry tears, cause joy, create happy faces around him, he did so, and did so for the most part in secret, without regard for reward or thanks. As he was driving once with Doctor Jonas and a few other friends, Luther gave an alms and Jonas did the same. "Who knows," said the latter, "when God will return me this!" But Luther laughed heartily at him, saying, "As if God did not give it to you at the first! We ought to give freely, simply, of pure love, willingly."

This anecdote leads us to Luther's circle of friends, concerning whom we must say a few words more. A few pleasant features of *their* domestic life are preserved to us.

Melanchthon was married before Luther, in November 1520. The name of *his* wife also was Katharine. She was a daughter of the burgomaster Jerome Krapp, and was born in the same year with her husband. His wedding day was the only day when the conscientious teacher permitted himself to intermit his lectures.[1] His wife is described as simple in her manners, pious, and charitable. Housekeeping cares were often a heavy burden to the professor, on account of his inadequate salary. The good couple frequently deprived themselves of the most necessary articles, in order that they might be able to help the poverty-stricken ones who daily applied to them. The happy father was warmly attached to his children, of whom he had four—two sons and two daughters. Upon one occasion, when a French savant visited the famous "teacher of Germany," he found him with a book in one hand, while he rocked the cradle with the other. In hours of spiritual conflict, he, like Luther, found comfort in his children. His little daughter, on going into her father's study one day, found him weeping, and climbed up on his knee and wiped the tears from his eyes with her apron. This little circumstance affected him deeply, and taught him the difference between a Christian sage and a frigid stoic. He was not exempt from family crosses. A hopeful boy was snatched from him by death, and his other son caused him much anxiety by his levity. One of his daughters was united in marriage to the learned Sabinus, but was not happy in this relation. The other became the wife of the physician Caspar Peucer, whom we shall meet hereafter on the field of theological controversy. Melanchthon's house afforded shelter to

---

[1] He acquainted the students with this intermission by a significant notification on the blackboard :—

" A studiis hodie facit otia grata Philippus,
  Nec verbis Pauli dogmata sacra leget."

many strangers, and among the number of these to many who were persecuted for their faith's sake. He frequently sold vessels of gold and silver in order that he might relieve the oppressed. He was a father to the students, and understood how to reprove their rude excesses, when these occurred, with friendliness and yet with severity. On the occasion of one nocturnal disturbance, this peaceable man went among the excited students with a hunter's spear in his hand, and even became engaged in a personal affray with a furious Pole. The student was expelled.[1] Melanchthon was an unusually hard worker. He rose soon after midnight. His best writings were the fruit of the early morning hours. The day was occupied with his official business, of which we shall frequently have occasion to speak hereafter.

Justus Jonas, who was called from Erfurt to Wittenberg in 1521, and was afterwards removed to Halle, was one of Luther's nearest and dearest friends. The great Reformer manifested a peculiar predilection for him. Jonas also married a Katharine, the daughter of an old Saxon warrior whose name was Henry Falke. This person, like the wife of Luther, was called "Kate," and the two Kates were the warmest of friends. This excellent woman, to whom Luther addressed one of his letters (after the removal of Jonas to Halle), calling her "his gracious friend and beloved gossip,"[2] died in giving birth to her seventh child, in December 1542. Her whole life, her husband declared in loving tribute to her memory, was made up of friendliness, grace, and sweet modesty. It was a sore grief to him when the children asked him, as they sat at table or gathered round him at night, when their dear mother would come back to them. They comforted themselves with the idea that she had gone in a carriage to Dr. Martin's (at Wittenberg), until little Joachim was convinced by a dream, in which he had a vision of her, that she was with the Lord Christ in heaven. Jonas also lost his

---

[1] Schelhorn, *Ergötzlichkeiten*, ii. p. 57 (for the year 1555).
[2] De Wette (Seidemann), vi. No. 2546.

eldest daughter and his first-born son, and the other son who was left to him occasioned him much concern. The later life of this man (he married twice after the death of his first wife) was altogether a sad and trying one. And thus in his house there was no lack of tests of faith, though the testimonies of divine assistance were also present.[1]

John Bugenhagen (Pomeranus) was the actual pastor of Wittenberg. Luther, who represented him when he was absent, called himself only his "sub-pastor" (vicar). On the other hand, Bugenhagen, who, it will be remembered, had married Luther, was the father-confessor of the Lutheran household—an office which he exercised with great freedom. On more than one occasion he comforted his friend in temptation, and once said to him: "God is utterly provoked with you; He thinks, 'What shall I do with this man? I have given him so many great and glorious gifts, and yet he despairs of my grace.'" Luther received all such admonitions in humility, as an obedient penitent. For the rest, he imparted to his Dr. Pommer everything that stirred him either to seriousness or to mirth. Bugenhagen's own domestic life offers little of a striking character. In October 1522 he married a sister of Master George Rörer, his co-labourer in the translation of the Bible. The name of this lady was Eva. The fact of his having, in his treatise on the marriage of priests (*De conjugio episcoporum*, 1525), encouraged other clergymen to marry, at least shows that he did not regret having taken this step himself. But to his mind, also, nothing surpassed the knowledge of Christ, in whom he knew all the treasures of wisdom to be hidden.[2]

We cannot turn away from Luther's friends without mentioning the most trusted amongst them all—Nicholas von Amsdorf, who accompanied him to Leipsic and Worms,

---

[1] Pressel, *Justus Jonas*, *l.c.* pp. 117 sqq.
[2] His motto was :

"Si Jesum bene scis, satis est si cetera nescis;
Si Jesum nescis, nil est quod cetera discis."

who helped him to allay the storm of fanaticism in Wittenberg, and who also aided him in the translation of the Bible. Amsdorf was but a few weeks younger than Luther, having been born on a knightly manor near the village of Grossen-Zschopa, not far from Wurzen, on the 3d of December 1483. On his mother's side he was related to the noble-hearted Staupitz. He discharged the office of dean in the foundation church of Wittenberg for a short time only, and was removed as early as 1524 to St. Ulrich's Church at Magdeburg. We shall have occasion hereafter to speak of his later fortunes, which were deeply interwoven with the history of the Reformation. His disposition was vehement and impetuous, and not altogether free from contentiousness. This latter quality was associated in his case, however, with an unshakeable fidelity of adherence to Luther, while he seemed to agree less well with Melanchthon. He was not made for the quiet joys of home. He remained unmarried, and took a certain pride in calling himself, in the storms which burst over him, an exile for the sake of Christ (*Exul Christi*); he, however, acted the part of a tender brother to his sister, who was married to Caspar Teutleben, and took also an affectionate interest in his nephews, whom he educated at his own expense. In the midst of his numerous theological controversies, it is remarkable that he cultivated a very pacific taste—that of gardening.[1]

Passing from this domestic still-life of the Reformers, we shall, in our next chapter, direct our eyes once more toward the field of conflict; abandoning our late exclusive scrutiny of persons, we shall again fix our attention on the cause with which they were occupied, and resume the general thread of our narrative where we suffered it to drop.

[1] Pressel, *N. von Amsdorf*, Elberfeld, 1862; and Schwarz in Herzog's *Realenc.* vol. i. p. 289.

END OF VOL. I.